THE WORKER IN ME

Tracey Maguire

Copyright

The Worker in Me
Copyright © Tracey Maguire, 2017
First published 2017

All rights reserved. Without limiting the rights under copyright reserved above, no part of this publication may be reproduced, stored in or introduced into a database and retrieval system or transmitted in any form or any means (electronic, mechanical, photocopying, recording or otherwise) without the prior written permission of both the owner of copyright and the above publishers.

Original illustrations/ Photographs by Tracey Maguire

www.traceymaguire.com

National Library of Australia Cataloguing-in-Publication entry(pbk)

Creator: Maguire, Tracey, author.

Title: The worker in me : can the truth be vengeance / Tracey Maguire.

ISBN: 9780992430504 (paperback)

Subjects: Maguire, Tracey.

Real property--Fiction.

Courts--Cases--Fiction.

Revenge--Fiction.

Betrayal--Fiction.

Change--Fiction.

Psychopaths--Fiction.

PREFACE

I've travelled far and wide to write this book, and yet I've been nowhere but the places I've already been. This time travel of mine has been somewhat enlightening, due to the fact, that on this trip I've had my eyes opened and my mind cleared.

In life, we find that it's impossible to travel the path of purity and goodness, until we know exactly what that path entails. It's a rather extreme path to travel, and one would be living by extremes to pursue it. What I mean is... I don't think any of us were meant to travel it, to compare to it, nor suffer in attempting it. Adam and Eve couldn't negotiate it either. It's not negotiable.

The error of their ways

We're all born into error. Our environment is filled with the errors of the ways that were travelled by others, before us. As we grow into adulthood, we develop our lives according to the truths fed to us by our authority figures. The flaccid self-justifications of the people we looked up to, have created the dynamics for our own self-justifications, and the lives we go on to lead. By about mid-life, some of us are a wakeup. We wonder about the ways people take, and we wonder about our own ways. Are there other ways to go? We can go back and question the so-called truths, cross them out, and change the answers, or we can continue down the same old paths.

We can always start again

It takes courage to know the truth, because knowing, does indeed cause upheaval. We become aware of the holes and weaknesses in the scripts passed on to us, and wonder at the roles we've played? Have we studied the right script? Has it been an authentic performance?

Foundations are destroyed in the exploration of where, and what, the true story is. Suddenly there's nothing holding us up, and everything holding us down. We take that fall and find grace.

Making the claim

Personal injury is hard to recover from, especially when you can't see where all your injuries are. It's been a painful journey for me. I now understand why errors are sometimes blessings, and why blessings can be the error of our ways. I now understand more about me, why I did what I did, and was what I was. I'd travelled all this way with my eyes shut, just to survive.

This book may only be my thoughts, on a voyage exploring what lies beneath, and on the surface. What lies?

The Voyage

It's not a voyage I'd recommend to everyone. Some people are already grounded, and on solid enough foundations already. I am not. I never was, and as I write this, I'm still all at sea. I'm due to move into an old garage with my unpublished books and my clothes.

The Garage

But I have my thoughts. These are all mine.

I'm inviting you to know my thoughts, but only on the proviso that they inspire your own thoughts. We won't all have the same thoughts. I don't want you to think the same things as me, because I may well find you boring. Think up something original. Stand behind your opinions, and keep them open to change. Voice them by all means, for one who voices, can inspire more thought in others.

THE WORKER IN ME

Are we being defined by our occupations? Are we pigeon-holed into certain personality types based on the jobs that we do? Do we just base this on previous experiences with people we've already had dealings with from those same occupations? Is it the occupations we remember, or the actual people themselves? Are we all being tarred with the same brush, or are there special brushes for different occupations?

Brushed off

Why do I feel like Carrie Bradshaw, just typing away with so many questions from a voice prattling away inside my head? I was reminded of her because of her style of writing. She asks a lot of questions. Once the questions have arrived into her psyche, she seems to stumble upon the answers. They just appear out of the blue, as she goes about her day-to-day life. She can now recognize the answers, because she became aware of the questions.

Do the questions find the answers, or do the answers find the questions?

My mind thought it appropriate to offer that short bit of entertainment. That's all it is really. It's just a TV show with a character named Carrie Bradshaw, but she's in my psyche as a modern writer, and a person with a fascination for human nature. I've made use of it just to give you an example of what I'm talking about, and to see if we're all conscious.

Example 1

Anyway, I got to thinking, that we must be moulding ourselves with the help of a stereotype. We get an impression of an occupation from people that we meet in our day-to-day lives. We may even mix the impression up with bits from many different people who happen to be in that same line of work.

I'm raising some serious questions in this book for our own good, but mainly for my own good. These are just two, so pertinent to my life right now.

1. Can we still be as original and authentic years down the track, or will our occupation have taken over?
2. Is there any scope for originality and authenticity, within our chosen occupations?

'The Looker in Me'

I remember being drawn to the 'look' of an occupation. I was drawn to a business-suit-wearing, flash-car-driving, mobile-carrying, fast-talking, confident-walking, wheeling-and-dealing, money-making, real estate agent. That was my visualization. That was how I visualized myself in the occupation I was pursuing.

When you want something badly, you dream about it, and you visualize and fantasize about being 'it'. This is how our dreams are made into a reality. They don't come to fruition overnight, but with hard work and small steps in the right direction, the goal is ours and we become 'it' eventually.

Or something along those lines

These are my lines. I've come to fruition, but not along the lines of my occupation. I've come to fruition, since crossing over the lines.

> **Fruition:-** n. [see FRUIT] 1. the bearing of fruit; 2. fulfillment; realization.

Reading between the lines is hard reading. It's reading deep into the meaning, and deep into the reasons, for all the lines. These are the first of my lines to see the light of day, and there's a reason why I've written them and put them before you.

These are the lines of reason. They're my lines.

Knowing me, knowing you

How are real estate agents perceived? Do some real estate agents bring the industry down? Do we find ourselves posted to lower pigeon-holes, because of people's bad experiences? Do we get a label attached to us at the very first meeting? Are we already up against it, and trying to rip off the falsely applied label, from the start? Is there already a hurdle to jump, before we've even shaken a hand? Are they waiting to see the similarities to the last experience they had? Are they looking for the same bad signs in us? Do they only remember the bad experiences? Do the good experiences make any sort of an impression?

Ten questions to get you used to my lines of questioning

If an industry has a bad reputation, does it mean that people working within the industry feel the same way about their colleagues? Do real estate agents dislike real estate agents? Are we suspicious of each other? Are we on guard? Are we wary? Do we have anything in common? Are we of a type? Are we seeing our own type reflected? Is a good reputation earned over time, and/or is a bad reputation earned over time? I believe that these questions need to be answered for. I'll be answering them for me.

I shouldn't have to answer for that

I believe we are stigmatized by this instant label, and spend the rest of our time either trying to measure up to it, or trying to measure down to it. If it's a bad label, do we try to separate ourselves from it? Is it the good label we want, or the bad? Is there a difference, and is it just another measurement? Which label is the more successful?

Be careful of the undercurrents

Have you ever been to a party where you've been introduced to strangers and one of them takes an instant dislike to you? You've sensed how they're repelled by you, and you can't ascertain why. There seems to be no reason you can think of, for the effect you're having on them, because they've only just met you. They behave rudely and ignore you. They try to make you aware of their utter dislike.

It's an undercurrent

It's confounding. It can make you feel unstable. You question yourself as to whether you've caused their rude behaviour. Have they heard something? Have you done something? You consider whether you've met them before somewhere. You're baffled as to why there's a stand-off.

Just to test this notion more fully, you increase your charm and draw them into a conversation. You want to be sure that their reaction is genuine, and that their coldness is indeed directed at you. It is! You've been towed under.

Getting caught in an undertow

I'm flawed! At this point I'm irritated and now feigning indifference. Fuck it! They can go jump! I haven't done anything wrong. I go on to ignore them, and try to enjoy my evening out, but some-thing's now stuck in my gullet, and I'm feeling somewhat pissed off. The evening's been spoiled. I'm caught in the rip.

You ask the host of the party, some days later – "What's up that bloke's arse? He was so rude to me, and I don't know why!"

"Oh, that's just Bob – he just hates real estate agents."

This is how we live folks! Ask any real estate agent.

This is a generalization. This is also a good demonstration of how minority groups get treated every day. This is what we call discrimination. You've done it, and I've done it. We're all quite discriminating sometimes.

Is a rescue an option?

Can you imagine a similar situation happening in your own office? Can you imagine how demoralizing this can be, when it happens at your business premises, with your name on the door stating your licensee status? It's disrespectful and downright insulting. It's hurtful, humiliating, and embarrassing. Over a long period of time, it can be soul destroying.

I wasn't imagining it

I've had to endure this behaviour from others on too many occasions to mention. This has taken place in front of my staff, my family, and others. 'Others' could include tradesman, tenants, landlords and friends. It happens in front of anyone, and everyone. It happens when you're innocent of a crime. People taking advantage of a real estate agent's situation, love an audience. Bullies love an audience.

There are no butts about it

Have you any idea of the strength you need, to remain joyful, welcoming, vivacious, witty, sincere, confident, enthusiastic, professional, knowledgeable, sympathetic, and of service to the public, every day? It's hard. It's a strain. It becomes a habit. It becomes such a habit, that you start doing it all the time. You do it at home, at sport, while shopping, at restaurants, at parties and every other place you ever find yourself in. You're always on guard for rips.

Watching out for dangerous rips becomes an obsession. When you're caught in a rip, you're all at sea, but you can't see your way to safety. The only thing you have for safety is your board. A board can be used for buoyancy. It can keep you afloat. (This is a defining moment right here. You'll know what this means, if you get to know me.)

> **Buoyancy:-** n. [< Sp. *boyar*, to float] 1. the ability to float in liquid or air; 2. the power to keep something afloat; 3. cheerfulness; 4. the ability to recover quickly after a setback – buoy'- ant adj.

Your buoyancy becomes your life. Your work becomes your life.

Keeping afloat

I learned through experience, that this was the key to becoming a successful real estate agent. I thought that integrating both my work life, and my home life, was the key to success. Be the same people in both roles. It was a serious mistake. It almost cost me my life, and it most certainly cost me my potential. It has, in fact, cost many real estate agents their lives. They just burn out. They lose their soul. They lose their person. They lose their sense of direction. They don't know if they're coming or going. They don't know up from down. They become a crab, and sidestep their way through life at the expense of themselves. They side step the opportunity to be authentic. They can go great distances by sidestepping, but they're only sidestepping the self. I know of real estate agents that have sold their souls. They're lost souls now.

Selling out is the name of the game

It had been described to me, early on in my career, what a real estate agent's job description was. The following is an apt description given to me by a mutual learned friend, who surprisingly remains in a similar line of work:

1. Prostitute;
2. Cab driver;
3. Counsellor;
4. Profiler;
5. Chess player.

I might have added a couple here, but he'll recognize the players.

It's worth explaining that I don't feel like explaining. It's an old profession, and it's about giving the customer what he or she wants. It's about free rides in the family car, and listening to other peoples' family problems. It's also about making sure you have the right people in your car so that it pays off down the track. You must be able to predict unforeseen happenings, with the foresight to see a hoax when it comes knocking. You must always have a getaway planned, or a 'get my way' planned.

These are the jobs of a real estate agent, only we tend to glorify them for you, and for ourselves. There's not as much glory as you think. Where is the glory?

Closing the deal

The best real estate agents are trained and experienced in winning people over. They must be good at winning the business over, and away from the competition. We must be able to win as many people as we can, in order to get paid. Our money comes from the ability to win people over. Don't, for one second, think that it's about how good we are at selling your home. It's not. It's about how good we are at selling ourselves to you. Any real estate agent will tell you that you can't talk somebody into buying a house, or can you?

(Any good real estate agent will never tell you that! An honest one will!)

A buyer will make his/her own decisions as to what house they like. A ten-year-old can sell a house. It's just showing a tangible item. There's not a lot to it really, unless the nature of the property is more complex. You probably need to know a little more, for a complex.

This is what I've always believed, but I realize now, that it may not be as true as I want it to be. Have I forced a sale?

Did I talk you into it?

I've never counted my chickens until they've hatched, because I've been disappointed in the past. You can achieve many sales through negotiation and an acceptance, but they can still fall through at the eleventh hour. We call this the 'Bom'. It's awful when you see it written down in the Day Book, or texted to your mobile phone. It can be a shock to the system. It stands for 'Back on Market'. It means you must start all over again, but this time around, it's worse.

You now have a disgruntled vendor, and you're the one that looks bad. You appear to the vendor as a trickster and a fake, and you're a big let-down. You've led the vendor on a merry dance, and now you've dropped him on his arse. The phone call to break the news is never easy. It must be made. The listing is now in the balance. You must do the balancing act like your life depends on it.

Stand-up Paddle Boarding

The hardest sale a real estate agent will ever make, is the sale of himself to a vendor. You must sell yourself as an agent, a person, and thirdly, as a representative and believer of the business you work for. You must sell a dream, grant a wish, and find a solution to a problem. Ultimately, we're just selling a service, but we'll never sell that house if we never have it listed. The soul must be sold first. Then we can go on to sell another soul, and then someone else's soul. Is this soulful?

Do you really want an agent's opinion?

Why do people appoint real estate agents to sell their homes? Do they think it will be a hard job to sell their biggest asset? Do they think it'll be an easy job? Don't they know how much their house is worth? Do they think they'll find out by asking an expert? Do they think they can get more for their house with an agent appointed, or less? Do they want to pay a commission? Do they want to show off their home with an agent, so that it looks more professional? Are they interested in the agent's professional opinion of the quality of their home? Do they think agents can make miracles happen? Is it for that constant flattery that they've come to expect from an agent? Do they want to be glorified by the friendly, commission hungry, and ingratiating agent? Do they just want the show with all the fluff? Are they being fluffed? Are they a piece of fluff? Are they the agent's fluff? Why do they assume that after designing, building, decorating, and maintaining their much-loved home, that the real estate agent will be able to tell them something they don't already know? The appointed agent will always tell the vendor what he wants to hear. This is how all appointments are made.

Is it all in the cost of listing?

It's for the praise. They want the praise and the marketing. They have nothing to lose. It costs nothing to list your property with a real estate agency.

This is still true up here on the Coast. It used to be true everywhere once, but Sydney agents are apparently worth more. It costs so much more when the costs aren't more, because it's harder to sell property in Sydney. That's why it costs more. Are the costs more? Are the hidden costs more? Are there more costs hidden? Hidden costs can include the following:

Costly fluff:

1. A bloke with no particular qualifications, but who carries around a little laser-measuring-gizmo that you can buy from any Dick Smith outlet, comes along to take measurements of your house. He takes it home and draws up a floor plan so that there's something fancy on your home's sales brochure.

2. A professional photographer comes along and takes photos of your house, adding new furniture, enhancing the un-enhanced, making unsightly things vanish, and improving the views etc., which provides a distorted impression for purchasers to see on the net.

3. Very special, exclusive, and expensive advertising campaigns that cost you more, the agent nothing, and creates the prestige you've only ever dreamed about. You get to be prestigious, and so does your agent, but at your expense. Publications flatter agents, and agents flatter vendors.

4. What about the aerial photographs? There's a special charter flight to search for your house from the sky. Your house is spotted amongst the land mass, and snaps are taken in order to provide a most convincing sales pitch. That's all that can be made out though, a roof and the pitch.
5. There's probably more fluff, but I'm just too unsophisticated to know about more, because I was never very good at hiding things. Do people who pay more, feel like they're worth more?

Have you been fluffed? How much did you pay for this fluff?

Why appoint a real estate agent?

Could it be that they like the idea of glossy, colour pictures, of their very special property being admired by their neighbours and friends? Do they like the idea of the brochures being circulated around the neighbourhood? Is this a reflection of their self-worth, or their property's worth? Is it a boost to self-esteem? Is it the quality or prestige of the esteemed real estate agency they've chosen, that reflects their sense of self-worth? Are they looking for the praise that comes from owning such a property? Do they want to be measured as people, by the property they own? Does the high list price make them feel especially worthy? Is it worthy of a big cost? This is about the high-end of town, but it's not that high and mighty, only a bit misguided.

Who's misguiding who?

Vendors believe their own shit. They'll believe any shit if it's good shit. They must do, otherwise they'll feel like shit. This, Ladies and Gentlemen, is why there are auctions. An auction takes four to six weeks. It's a quick and serious conditioning program that you pay for upfront. You pay, whether it sells or not. This is professional processing.

> **Process:-** n. [see PROCEED] 1. a series of changes by which something develops [the process of growth]; 2. a method of

doing something, in which there are a number of steps; 3. biol. a projecting part of a structure, or organism; 4. law. a written order, as a summons to appear in court –vt. to prepare by our subject to a special process – in process, in the course of being done – in (the) process of, during the course of.

Auctions are a process with proceeds

It's all about the proceedings. We all need pumping up and inflating now and then. Selling your house is a good way of asserting your status. Status can be inflated, and then just as quickly, be deflated. The deflation must happen prior to the auction. This is the necessary process if you want it completely processed.

Come with me on my special journey

I'm going for a ride shortly. I'll be put through the process. They'll try to process me, but I'm not part of the process. I'll be just watching the process unfold. There's a court process that's been put in place, and that eliminates me from this upcoming process. I can't wait to see the processing of the hidden processes at work.

I don't think they've read the process correctly. Will I protest to the processor? Why do I need a real estate agent, when I am one? I had the contract drawn up back in January, and it's still valid. Why did I pay for a contract that's not going to be utilized? I had this campaign organized at the beginning of the year, with a top agent who would have charged no commission. I think my ex has fallen for it – hook, line, and sinker.

The Last Hoorah

I'm not saying 'Hoorah', just yet.
I've been appointed by The Federal Court to keep The Hoorah looking presentable. I've always done this job! I've been appointed to be the one to allow access to agents and their prospective purchasers. I've done this job too! Have I been

undermined? What's my status? Will people come to see my status? Will I become a status symbol, or will my Hoorah? Who will be yelling 'Hoorah'? I couldn't give a rat's hoorah for my Hoorah. I said 'hoorah' a long time ago. I now want to say 'hoorah' to the Hoorah's other tenant in common. We are no longer joint tenants.

Her Majesty's Appointment

Her Majesty already appointed an agent.

Why was there an alternative agent appointed? This is curiouser than it sounds. Why not the agent appointed by the court? Is there a reason behind the switch? Is it discretion? Is it a discretionary tactic?

Would somebody explain to me why all this discretion, when there was no discretion before? Where did my discretionary powers go? I'm being kept out of the loop. I've been put down the loophole. This is where I'm being kept for my own good. It's quite good in a way. It's allowed me to carry on with my own interests. I'm no longer interested in other people's interests. I'm just inquisitive, considering a breach has been committed, in order to appoint an alternative agent. Is it to keep the two businesses separate? Is it to separate himself from that bad business?

Why an agent?

It's about price. It's all about money. Money is status, and no money is lack of status. My tenant in common had a lack of status and now his status is growing under the guidance of an accomplished real estate agent's methods of inflation. The tenant in common is showing the classic signs of inflation. He's all puffed out and fluffy. He's the guinea pig for this experiment.

Hypothesis

For this experiment, I've used my old tried and tested terrarium. I'll be wearing my biologist hat for this experiment, but I may need my psychologist hat on too. Put on whatever hat you have, and we can work this one out together. Put on whatever hat you can put your hands on. Any mad hat will do. We'll be going to the Mad Hatter's Tea Party. I'm The Mad Hatter, because nobody's madder than me.

How do I look?

Honestly, it doesn't matter what hat you wear. Just pick up your maddest hat for this occasion. It will be quite a mad occasion. I already know the hats that will be at this tea party. They'll be wearing some awfully mad hats too. All the hats will come out to see, because this is what an auction does. It draws tickets from a hat.

I might have this the wrong way around. An auction draws hats for a ticket. This will be my show. Everyone will want tickets to my showing. I've got tickets on myself, haven't I? Have they thought to appoint a ticket collector? I don't mind chipping in and helping with ticket collecting, because I'll need them for my books. You may want to take your hat off to me. 'Wherever I lay my hat, that's my home.' That's my sing-song for the tea party!

Seeing great results

I can watch and wait for the results I want. He'll see the results too. He's already been a result of one of my results. The result is in the wall. Have I driven him up the wall, or did our result drive him into one? I bet he wasn't expecting that. He got no result when he reported our young result for this result, because I think the police thought he deserved what resulted. The result isn't a problem though. It's only a problem for the real estate agent. He hasn't yet seen the result.

Questions not to ask the agent

(For experimental purposes only)

I have some questions for the Aldi driving agent, appointed to do the job. Where did I get that spelling from? He doesn't drive an Audi, he drives a hard bargain, doesn't he? I wonder what's in store for him. Remember, no questioning, because this is just for research purposes.

- Do you know the price you're going to achieve for my property? No.
- Does a registered valuer know the price I'll achieve for my property? No.
- Does an auctioneer know the price that will be achieved for my property?
- Does anyone know how long it will take to sell? No.
- Does the court know what I'll achieve for my property? No.
- Does the joint tenant know what I'll achieve for my property? No.
- Does anyone know anything? No.
- Does anyone know the truth? No.

But Wait! There's more. There isn't an answer to the question about the auctioneer. Did you pick up on it? I nearly missed it myself.

Questioning the auctioneer for a change

An auctioneer does however know. He knows if it will sell or not, before the auction even starts. He usually knows who will buy it, and how much he'll sell it for. He only needs to know the motivation and the reason for selling, to get the process to process it properly. This is what you call a controlled sale. If it's operated with the smooth, verbal agility of an expert showman, it will be a definite showdown. Just like the travelling showmen, with their vials of miracle health serums, and cure-alls, the auctioneer will have the guaranteed remedies for every little problem. He has it right there on his fancy wagon. Don't knock his little red wagon. It's been his experience with red wagons, that red wagons are better than black wagons. He's been a real estate agent, and now he's become a veritable strategist.

There's no panacea in real estate

Nope. That bits all bullshit too, but I had you believing me, didn't I? I think I'm starting to get some credibility back.

Why does an auctioneer have so much cred? Does 'cred' stand for credibility, or credentials?

He's all just talk

An auctioneer doesn't have to know. He doesn't really care, actually. He's out for himself only. He must ensure he makes a name for himself with the agents though, and the next lot of unsuspecting vendors. He doesn't have to ensure a sale is affected. An auctioneer will be paid, no matter what, and he gets paid his fee upfront. For the auctioneer, it's all over before the fat lady sings.

Does an auctioneer think he can make a house sell? Does he believe it's all about his style of auctioning? Is he magic? Either all the correct processing has already been done for him, and he just puts on a show, or he's just all show.

How good is his 'cred'?

What are an auctioneer's credentials? He has some rules to obey, but auctioneers are renowned for buggering them up. There isn't very many, but their egos don't have time for rules. The rules of hammer are as follows:

1. a loud and over-bearing voice;
2. an over-inflated sense of self; and
3. the ability to project confidence.

What is he confident about?

Credential:- n. 1. that which entitles to credit, confidence, etc.; 2. [pl.] a letter or certificate showing one's right to a certain position or authority.

Special alert. Breaking news item!

Just as I had finished with the definition of 'credential', I noticed the definition below, which is uncanny. Is this why people want to jump off 'The Gap'? This revelation may not be appropriate for this book, but it may have everything to do with this book.

'The Gap' is a place in Sydney that people commit suicide. It's a cliff top with a railing, and I think I visited there when I was a child. It's the infamous jumping-off point. It's well known that many people have attempted to commit suicide in this same spot. Why would everyone want this infamous location? Is it for credibility?

The definition I found is not 'uncanny'. The Dictionary follows the order of the alphabet, in case you haven't read it. After the word 'credential' is the term 'credibility gap'. I must say, I've never heard this term used in conversation before. Is it common?

> **Credibility Gap:-** an apparent disparity between what is said, and the actual facts.
>
> **Uncanny:-** adj. 1. mysterious in an eerie way, weird; 2. so remarkable as to seem unnatural.

It's remarkable, so that's why I'm remarking on it

It's uncanny how they all pick the same spot. They don't all go through with it, but it must add some credibility to their attempt. Numerous people have succeeded. It's kind of like stealing someone else's credibility, isn't it?

'The Gap' is quite a public place. It's a public recreation park overlooking the ocean. Many people use this place for recreation and enjoyment. Would people choose 'The Gap' for attention? Are they attention seekers, not suicide attempters? If you were a seeker of attention, would you feel any obligation to make a serious attempt? Would your attempt need to look serious? Would a serious position, be just the right position, for infamy?

> **Infamy:-** [see IN 2, & FAMOUS] 1. a very bad reputation, disgrace; 2. great wickedness; 3. an infamous act.

Could they be guilty of an infamous act?

> **Infamous:-** adj. 1. notorious; 2. causing a bad reputation.

Could they be in denial of an infamous act? Could the act have been committed upon them? Should they be committed? Was it to avoid being committed?

> **Commit:-** [< L. *com*, together + *mittere*, send] 1. to give in charge or trust, consign; 2. to put officially in custody or confinement [committed to prison]; 3. to do or perpetrate (an offence or crime); 4. to bind as by a promise, pledge [committed to action] – commit to memory, to learn by heart; memorize – commit to paper (or writing) to write down – commit'table adj.

I've come to a Y Junction

These are here so that I can determine which way to go. I need to find out which way it went. I think I already have The Knowing in Me. It's been spelled out for me in the past, but I've now had an order in which to put it in. An order of events will always lead to the last event. Eventually we end up dead.

What's the difference between saving your arse, and saving your soul? They're opposites aren't they? To save your soul, you must put your arse on the line. Some people will save their arse, and forsake their souls. They must face their souls to save their arses. When they can't face their own soul, they can lose the arse out of their pants. When this happens, their soul can be saved. I'm not going to be like those sorry souls. I'm saving my soul, and it's saving my arse. I've 'consouled'. (Give me a tick for this word). It's defined for you in 'The Knowing in Me' which will fill in a lot of the gaps.

Neat as a pin

The above heading is a common enough description for a house, if you're looking in the real estate classifieds. How do we classify houses? Are there heaps of houses that look as neat as a pin? How neat can a pin look? It's a pin for Christ's sake! It's a tiny metal rod for pinning up hems. What about 'as clean as a whistle'? How the hell do we compare a house, to a clean whistle? Could it be a metaphor? Could there be a message hidden in it, like wolf whistling a sexy house? Now there's a better heading!

This is one sexy house!

I've seen sexy houses. I really have. I've seen romantic houses. I've seen artistic, opulent, minimalist, retro, old-fashioned, cottage, contemporary, beach, lake, farm, doll and cubby. I've seen gothic, dated, enchanting, ugly, dirty, monstrosities, mausoleums, mansions, master built, cheaply built, sterile, cold, dank, decayed, mildewed, termite infested, rat infested, and flea infested.

Make more sense

When we write an advertisement for a property that we're hoping to sell, we need to be using all our senses. We use our eyes to pick up on the appearance. We observe the light, views, gardens, design features, floor plan, position, space, colour, cleanliness, structure and visual details.

We use our noses to pick up on the smells in the kitchen, the garden, in the home, from the dog, cigarettes, mildew, from the septic, from the ocean or the lake.

We use our ears to be alerted to the advantages and disadvantages of living in the property, such as the birdsong, animal sounds, pool filters, air conditioners, traffic noises, people noises, power stations, waves, boat motors, crackling of the wood fire, loud music, and whatever our vendor is trying to tell us.

We use our sense of touch to feel the curtain fabric, the modern wall texture, the plush floor coverings, the temperature, directional breezes, safety rails, the ease of operations, smoothness of granite bench tops and the ease of pushing buttons on remotes and alarm systems.

We use our sense of taste, to sample the vegetables from the garden, the fruit from the fruit trees, the fish from the lake, the yabbies from the dam, the fresh eggs from the chicken coop, and the cake cooked by the current owner, who cooks up a storm in the gourmet kitchen, and uses all her home grown produce.

The 'vibe'

There's a sixth sense that we could be using all the time. It's the most important sense a real estate agent can use. It's having total awareness of where you are, and what you feel you're supposed to be doing. It's the ability to help a purchaser to become aware. It's what I call 'the true gut feeling', but it's what comes from our soul, not our gut. It's our personal feeling which gives us, above all else, our personal opinion. It's the most valuable of all the senses, and it will almost always be the deal closer. It's a kind of instinct, and it's not reserved for real estate agents. It's based on all our past experiences with energies. The feeling comes from being aware of our feelings. It's about trusting what you think and feel, when others are opposing you. It's about the 'vibe'. If we have a good vibe, we're onto something good. If it's a bad vibe, it will be a shocker to sell.

Our killer instinct

Our instinct is the most valuable tool we can use, particularly with advertising. Some of us use it, and some of us don't. It's to do with emotion. That's ultimately what we're selling. We're selling you an emotion. Emotions are strong. They can be stronger than us. People will spend well over their budget for it. Emotion is also the factor that helps us to feel emotionally committed to promoting your most valuable asset. Your home will always be emotional to you, but we need to be affected by your emotions. It's personal and emotional. We are emotional beings, so put some energy into it. We all need positive energy.

Tapping into your special energy

We enter, and we become aware. We monitor our awareness inside the home. We look, we feel, we hear, we taste, and we get an impression. This can make a good impression. It's an impressionable way to start. Tapping into the energy, is like tapping into your own energy. It's about being in the moment. It's kind of like tapping into the collective subconscious. The energy we feel is manifested from the stored information we've collected over the years. It's about reading the energy of a home.

Getting the hang of it

When you get the hang of houses, you can begin to read peoples' energies too. If there's negative energy, you may feel a bit negative. This can be a problem. This is where you need your strong and pervasive energy, to turn negative energy into positive energy. This is what you bring to the job. You bring your soul. You can put your soul into this kind of work, but don't over-work it.

One of the first things to address, when you feel negativity in a house, is the light. Let in the light. Lighten up and lose the dark. You need to open windows, blinds, and curtains. Windows need to be cleaned. By doing this, you're allowing bad energy out, while you work on the good energy manifesting within. The light is the most important part, and it'll lighten the spirits of the home dwellers. Light is good for the soul.

Always vent when you can

Ventilation is the next important ingredient. Fresh air is healthy. In the same way that stagnant water can poison, so too, can stagnant air. Clean all the windows, because this will give an impression that the rest of the house is just as clean. An untidy house doesn't turn people off, but an unclean house does. Bring the outdoors in, by cutting anything growing from the garden and presenting it in a vase or pot, indoors. You can just chop a small branch from any old shrub or tree to do this. This is a sign of health inside the home. It will add good energy to the heart of it, and let nature do its trick.

A home's negative energy comes directly from people with negative energy. It's the cause, and the effect. The cause will have caused it to be there. Unhealthy people make an unhealthy home. Healing a home can be about healing the people who live there. It may only be one person that creates the energy for the rest. Always address the bad energy. If you can't change the energy, get rid of it. Energies are everywhere. They attach themselves to things. Negative energy just attracts more negative energy. Stay positive.

Some houses have a happy and positive energy. You automatically know when happy, healthy people have been dwelling in it. It's the 'vibe'. In my experience, some of the old fibro weekenders had the best energy. They were dated and a bit dilapidated, but they were full of that holiday atmosphere with a carefree, joyful, and 'devil may care' attitude emanating from within.

Always have a happy story for the house. If the vendors are unhappy sellers, don't let on to the purchasers. Happy, happy, happy! Just keep sucking in the negative energy, and blow out the positive.

The devil may not care

Some agents will look for a bad energy in the home, and take advantage of it. They'll use this shortcut to shortcut a vendor. They may be gleefully aware of the marital or financial problems that are casting out the occupants in a negative way. In my opinion, purchasers shouldn't ask the reason for the vendor selling. Agents shouldn't either, but we do.

I asked. I asked, in order to help. I didn't ask, in order to take advantage. I asked, so that I could create the appropriate service. Vendors in a crisis, need to be seen as vendors in a crisis. They're emotionally fragile. A positive approach by an agent can create a positive sale for suffering vendors.

Don't add to the bad energy

So, all houses can change their energies, or houses aren't houses. Houses aren't houses, are they? Houses are homes. When is a home not a home? When it's alone and empty.

A home should be a sanctuary. It's the very place we surround ourselves with things we like. It's personal. It's not logical. Professionals in the industry place too much logic on the processes of selling. Lives aren't logical, and neither are energies. Are agents empty of emotion?

When you're on empty

Can an empty house have a bad energy? Yes and no. Negative energy can attach itself to a home, as can positive energy. It doesn't always leave straight away. It can linger. This can be felt most palpably in a deceased estate. If you're sensitive to energies, you can pick up on the spirit itself. You can pick up on sadness, anger, and happiness. I believe it's the strong emotion of the spirit dweller and the way in which it left the body, that resonates in the dwelling. It can create the 'vibe'. I believe it to be a presence that has some power over what goes on in the house. This can be good or bad. It's best to let things take their course, and let the universe decide on the outcome. It's important not to interfere with recent spirits. Let sleeping dogs lie. When it sells, it sells. What will be, will be. You can't force it or control it. It's beyond our control. Let the powers that be, arrange it when it's time. It may not be on your time, so don't waste your time worrying about it. One day it'll be your time, and you'll know. This is what I know. Did you know?

Am I full of it?

These are some instructions on how to find the solutions. Am I filling your head with shit? Are you wiser than me? Are you none the wiser? Am I a wise guy? I've tried to look up wise chick, but it's not in the dictionary. Am I a wiseacre? This is in the dictionary.

> **Wiseacre:-** n. [< OHG. *wizzago*, prophet] a person who acts as though he were much wiser than he really is.

I'd like to be a wizzago. I was always a wizzago. I was the profit. I was the profit-maker. Am I the profit-maker in me? I was always the bit on top. Was I the fluff? A profit would be on top of everything. Wouldn't you agree? Don't agree. I wasn't a wizzago. I fluffed it. Who was the prophet of my profit? He was the wise guy.

> **Wise guy:-** [Slang] a person who is brashly and annoyingly conceited, knowing, etc., smart alec.

Does he have the wisdom to know? If he doesn't, he'll think he does. I know. I'm not being a smart alec. I must stay humble and look it up.

> **Smart aleck, smart alec:-** [< Alexander, name] [Colloq.] a conceited, cocky person.

I've known an Alex and he was a smart alec. He was no smartarse. His wife was nice, but he was a pig. He carried on like the general, but that was because he wasn't a general. Generally speaking, I could generalize his origin to the source. He was the source of much discomfort for me. He was a walking, talking, emergency. He always marched right in on my emergencies, demanding urgent attention. He can wait for the karma that I know is coming to him.

I've decided I'm a bit more of an Aussie chick, so I'll go with smartarse.

Smartarse:- n. [Aust. Vulg. Slang] an unpleasantly clever person.

Now I'm really conceited, aren't I? Is this conceit? I don't think so.

Conceit:- n. [see CONCEIVE] 1. an exaggerated opinion of oneself, one's merits, etc., vanity; 2. a fanciful or witty expression or notion.

I think so. I'm decidedly happy about being both a smart alec, and a smartarse, but I've accused the wrong person of being a wise guy. What is the opposite? Is it a wise chick?

I may be reading too much into this, but if a smartarse is an unpleasantly clever person, what is the opposite? It's obviously a pleasantly clever person? That would definitely be me. That means I'm a dumb arse! I'm sorry to bore the shit out of you, but you really need an arsehole for me to work this shit out.

Arsehole:- n. [Vulg.] 1. the anus; 2. [Vulg. Slang] a foolish or unpleasant person –vt. [Aust. Vulg. Slang], to dismiss peremptorily, fire.

This sounds all crappy now. I think the arsehole feels familiar. I'm confused with 'to dismiss peremptorily, fire'. What does an arsehole dismiss peremptorily, and what's it got to do with fire? A word fires up in my head. Chilly. That means cold, doesn't it?

Peremptory:- adj. [< L. *perimere*, destroy] 1. that cannot be denied, delayed, etc., as a command; 2. intolerantly positive; dogmatic –peremp'-torily adv. peremp'toriness n.

Oh, I get it, 'fire', as in giving someone the sack. I'm an arsehole for making people redundant. Does an arsehole make you redundant? ('You're so vain. I bet you think this song is about you, don't you?') 'Take this job and shove it!' A quick sing-song, but that's how it went, isn't it? Was it peremptorily destroyed? Was I intolerantly positive? Was I dogmatic?

Dogmatic:- adj. 1. stating opinion in a positive or arrogant manner; 2. of or like dogma; 3. asserted without proof –dogmat'ically adv.

I can't believe I've switched right back to dogs from arses. I'm staying with arses for a moment. I really have a problem with my arses, so I'll persevere with a bit more crap. I must get this arsehole business out of the way. I never know whether it's an ass, or an arse. Can you just bare it with me for a moment?

This is the story so far...

> **Arse:-** n. [< OE. *aers*] [Vulg.] the buttocks.
>
> **Ass:-** (as) n. [< L. *asinus*]1. an animal related to the horse but having longer ears; 2. a silly person.

I'm a bit of a donkey, and I'll bet I've been the butt of some jokes lately. I can joke with the best of them. I can bet with the jokes of them. That's the card I've been saving. It wasn't the Ace of Hearts. I've thrown that one down. I've had the best card up my sleeve all along. I'm saving it till last. She who laughs last, laughs best and longest. Will there be plenty of laughs before my Joker gets played?

I've missed dogmatic, but I'm asserting without proof, that I'll come back to state my opinion later.

> **Joker:-** n. [L. *jocus*] 1. a person who jokes; 2. an extra playing card used in some games; 3. [Chiefly Aust. Colloq.] a fellow; person; chap.

There are two Jokers in a full deck, and I most certainly have a full deck. I just hope I don't get decked in the process. I need to process that last sentence. I need deep contemplation before the Mad Hatter's Tea Party. I'm a joker. I'm not a fellow, or a chap. I'm just a person who jokes with an extra playing card.

Am I a good vendor?

Now this question could be a good opportunity, couldn't it? I'm no longer an agent. I'm now my own agent. Am I 99? Agent 99 could be my role model. She's smart. She's not 'Smart'. That's

Max. She's 99. She's the wise one, isn't she? Is this the sort of agent I am? Why was she the sidekick? Why are the smart ones, always the sidekicks? I'll kick that aside for a minute.

I'm reminiscing about my job as an agent. Shall we go back now for another look?

Let's gamble

The big problem arises when an agent hasn't got the trust of the vendor. He'll offer valuable and factual information on price, give his expert opinion and advice, but it's invariably ignored. The real estate agent has a dilemma.

Does he list the property at the ('tell him he's dreamin'') vendor's idea of a list price? Does he pay all advertising expenses over the next three months, knowing the property is highly unlikely to sell?

Does he take the listing and gamble with it?

Does he gamble with the ideal that he can condition the vendor to his way of thinking, and sell the property before the time runs out? He has three to four months of talking, convincing, proving, and building rapport with the vendor.

He's up for the challenge, because he doesn't want the listing to go to another agent, and he wants to win the day. He now has a limited amount of time to build enough trust, to bring about a reduction in price, and the chance of a sale.

The inspections are happening, and the open houses are being conducted. The agent's petrol is being used, and he's on the phone to purchasers. The costs associated with keeping a business open, and keeping staff over the term of the agency agreement, are adding up. Time is of the essence. The pressure is on.

The risk

Will the agent be able to save the day? Will the agency time expire, before he can safely sell the house and make commission to cover his costs? Will his hard earned commission from his last sale, be flushed down the toilet with this new listing? Will the vendor list with an alternative agent, if there's no sale? If a sale is achieved, will the vendor get cold feet at the last moment and withdraw his property from the market? Will the vendor get off scot-free, and pay nothing for the four months of service? Will the vendor suddenly decide to take the house off the market altogether, and promise to try again next year with the agent? Will the agent look forward to flushing more money down the toilet next year, when the vendor wants to have another crack at it, at a higher price? Will the agent waste all his time, money, and energy, and be labelled with an unjustified and poor evaluation of his sales ability? Will the vendor finally listen to the agent, and take his expert advice?

The last hand to be dealt

Is the agent holding enough royalty in his hands? I mean 'loyalty'. Is he sweating on an offer? Is he encouraging any offers at all? Is he still pushing the property at the eleventh hour, or has he developed a limp, and stepped backwards with his head hung low? Is the agent still holding on by his finger nails waiting for a miracle, or is he awaiting the grim death of another Agency Agreement? Has he ceased paying for any further hard copy advertising, hoping the internet will do the job at the last minute? Has he changed the advertisement to create more urgency? MUST BE SOLD! URGENT SALE REQUIRED!

The cliff-hanger

Who makes the call?

It's not that easy, is it? It's a hard game to be in. It's a game of chance every time. There's no pattern to it. You can have a screamer of a listing, one that any agent would consider buying himself, but it can end up sitting on the market with no sale. You pull your hair out wondering why it hasn't sold. You don't know what to tell the vendors, so you tell them anything. Anything is better than nothing. You're the expert and you should know. You'll blame it on the market, or on bad luck. Will you have enough guts to tell the vendor that the price is too high? The vendor doesn't want to know this, because he wants a miracle. That's why he's paying you to do the job.

You'll need to write it off now as a bad debt, and get busy with your next listing. You've got to cut your losses and look for your next wager.

I know now what it is you need. You have two choices, but they both have to do with the same thing – luck. You can just rely on existential luck, or you can improve your luck.

Is it just luck?

That's what gambling is. Everyone's looking for luck. What's the agent gambling on? He was gambling on luck, but what he could have been doing, is improving the odds. This is the second choice. It means getting not double the listings, not even triple the listings. It means getting more and more listings, for more and more chances. It means improving your odds. It means hard yakka. Yakkity yak, yakkity yak. Yuk! Let's take a look through the arch window, and see what happened in 'The Cliff Hanger'. Who makes the call?

The winner takes it all

Do you want to know who ultimately makes the call? It's the third choice. It's the Trinity. It's always the last caller. It's all in *The Worker in Me*. Is it working now? There's simply no call for any of us to make that call. What's it called? It's called having no control. The way to place your bets is to bet your all on luck, and then pray to God.

Is this The Dreamer in You?

People can be so personally committed to their homes that when they come to sell them, they're convinced a sale will happen overnight. They imagine hordes of people arriving the next day for inspections. They have very high expectations. They'll be disappointed easily. They'll also feel insulted. This is a hard one. The agent's taken note of how devoted to the home the vendor is, and must replicate that devotion in his devotional presentation. This is what the vendor wants to note. The vendor must see the devotion reflected in her agent. She'll demand the same devotion that she has for her marvellous property.

> **Devotion:-** n. 1. piety; 2. religious worship; 3. [pl.] prayers; 4. loyalty or deep affection.

A sleep-out at the rear is an asset

The agent doesn't feel inclined at this point, to tell the vendor that her home is mediocre. She's been regaling him with all her special features, substantiating the added value of the sleep-out at the rear. She has illusions of her grandeur. The agent has no choice but to agree with the value of her two beautiful assets. All he can think of is how he's going to get his money's worth out of them.

Insist on full exposure

She wants to be assured of the agent's feelings towards her best assets, so she takes plenty of time showing him how wonderful they are. She wants the agent to have the same feelings for her best assets, as she does. He agrees that she has incredible assets. He's even wondering if she has more to sell than her two biggest assets on show. She's flattered beyond repair when the agent asks to see more.

Exposing the competition

The agent knows that there's going to be a second agent arriving soon, to give his impressions of her appealing assets, and possibly a third, and a fourth. He doesn't want those agents cutting the grass out from under him. He knows there'll be lots of agents appealing to her lovely assets. He knows they'll all be inspecting the vendor's assets with devotion. Everyone's showing devotion and worshipping assets in this business. It's all about how much the assets are flattered and valued. It will be an asset test. Have you ever applied for the asset test?

Using your best assets

How do you think this vendor will choose her agent? Can you know how, if you don't see her? You know her. You might even be 'her'. You might be him, with his larger than life asset appraisal techniques. You can imagine 'her' from my description, but can you imagine the agents? Which ones are easier to imagine? Why can we imagine them, when we don't know them? We imagine them because we've experienced them. We can only know, because we already know. We know so much more than we think we know. Think about what you know. I know too. Do we already know it all?

Know thy Vendor

How does anyone choose an agent? It's most important that an agent understands how a vendor will choose an agent. The only way an agent can know how the choice will be made, is to know the vendor. Don't worry about knowing what the other agents will do or say. The only relationship an agent needs to be concerned with, is his private relationship with his vendor. An agent needs to take up ownership fast.

Egos are attracted to other egos

You must find the ego. Not your own ego, the vendor's ego. It's probably smaller than yours, but it'll be easy to find. The ego will always be the weakest spot. You'll see the vendor go weak at the knees when you find it. This spot is exquisite to both the vendor and the agent. When it's been discovered, both parties can enjoy a great trip. It's a much smoother trip throughout the process of transacting, if this spot can be found early. The earlier it's found, the better the end result. It forms the bond between vendor and agent. It's the all-important button, if you're into pressing the right buttons. Once the agent has put this powerful bond in place, he'll have complete control of his vendor. It can lay the foundations for laying down a lot of listings well into the future.

Be careful of whose buttons you press

I can determine straight away how a vendor will choose. I don't always care for the weak spot. I wanted to find a nice spot, not a weak one. I haven't always been able to meet the criterion. I'm a woman. There's a fine line here, with what the right thing to do is, and what the wrong thing to do is. I have a spot myself, but I guard it very carefully. I don't just let anyone push my buttons.

Personal boundaries are boundaries that protect you against vendors getting too personal. A vendor can detect a personal boundary, and will either be repelled by it, or have respect for it. I wanted my buttons respected. If you can gain the vendor's respect, there's respect across the board.

Conducting the rules of the Act

How many listings would you suppose an agent would be able to sign up, if they conducted themselves in a completely ethical manner? If an agent followed the Rules of Conduct under the Act, could he be as successful?

If only…

If there were no competing agents, it would be a breeze. It would be a walk in the park. There would be no problem obtaining listings in an ethical manner. It's hard to compete when everyone's playing by different rules of conduct. It's hard to win against rule breakers. I didn't break rules, but I've been known to bend them. Whether my intentions were good or bad, is what I'm most concerned with now.

Concerning our intentions

What's a good intention? Is it the intention to get the job done that you were appointed to do? Is it with the intention that everyone thinks kindly of you? Is it with the intention that the vendor remain in charge, or the purchaser? Who's in charge of intention? Whose intention is the best intention?

Competition exists

Competition is good for the consumer. Competition is the deal breaker. It's just not feasible to follow all the rules. I don't care how shiny and clean you think you are. If you're a real estate agent, you're a rule bender. It wouldn't matter if you took a copy of the Property Stock and Business Agents Act with you, and showed your vendor all the rules you're required to follow. They simply wouldn't care for you, or your style of workmanship. They're not interested in your rules. They don't want rules either. They want what they want. They want a quick sale and a high price. They want it to go their way. They don't care what you do to make it go their way, and they ultimately don't care what rules you break. It won't be on their conscience. They're passing the buck to the agent. An agent won't buck up. It's a bucked up system.

Agents are bucked from the outset

Vendors are fickle. Vendors are self-absorbed. They're your boss. Can you back up a bit, and find that heading 'The cliffhanger'. The question about who makes the call. The vendor will always make the call. The vendor calls all the shots. The vendor takes it all. The vendor will love you and leave you, and you've just lost your spot.

'Dream maker, you heart breaker'

Those are the lyrics to a song I like. It's a very old song, and I've liked it since I was a girl. It's called 'Moon River'. Was I a dream maker, or a heart breaker? Was I a dream faker, or a half baker? It's a bit half-baked, isn't it? It can't be a half-baked plan. It must be fully baked. I bake on special occasions. 'I can bake a cherry pie Billy boy, Billy boy. I can bake a cherry pie, charming Billy. I can bake a cherry pie…' I can never remember the next line of this nursery song. There's something more to it – about his mother. Is it 'I'm a young thing and cannot be his mother'? It just came from out of nowhere, but I'm fully aware of where it was going.

Hoping my condition's right

I believe that vendors want to be sold hope. If I can give them that, I feel justified in my behaviour. We all want to be sold hope. I want someone to sell hope to me. Hope can be a comfort. It can give one confidence, and peace of mind. Is hope enough?

Is hope a humble hope?

It may not be enough for people who have experienced a lot of disappointment in their lives. They'll be harder to sell hope to. They don't seem to trust hope. They tend to be more diffident about their situation. They don't have high expectations. They don't want to get their hopes up. They're humble.

These are the people that an agent can do his best work for. These are the people he'll strive for. These are honest people. An agent will always be dedicated to a better result for these kinds of vendors. These are the vendors that will listen to their agent, and they'll take his advice. They're the people that acknowledge their own limitations. These are the people who inspire an agent's respect. This sentence can be read in two ways.

Respecting the un-knowable

There are ways to respect people. You can respect who they are, and you can respect why they are. I'm talking about the agent too. Why does an agent want respect? An agent needs respect, in order to be respectful. Respect is the conditional amount. All contracts have a condition. This is Contract Law at its most basic level. I did the most basic level. When the condition isn't money, the condition must be respect, and the terms and conditions respected. They were my conditions, but I wasn't conditioned to getting them.

Not getting my conditions met

These were my working conditions. If there's respect, is hope necessary? If there's no respect, then there's only hope. I believe it's got to do with the degree of hope that you've sold them. Hope is good, but it can be the opposite. If you give too much hope, disappointment can occur, and you'll be blamed for dashing their hopes. If you give too much hope, you take away your own hopes of getting a sale.

Hopelessly devoted, and hopelessly addicted, to you

At the start, the vendor wants to be given extensive hope. High hopes. That's what they expect. If you don't give them enough high hope with your market appraisal, your hopes of a listing will be dashed. I told you it was a fine line. There are so many fine lines in the real estate industry, that it's hard not to get tangled up in them.

Don't sell me a line

They're like a web, and it's hard not to get caught in a wrong line. You have your own lines to be careful of too. It's a good thing to have your main lines in place, even if they do get stretched occasionally. It's all about keeping the lines of communication open. The lines cannot be broken, no matter what.

If you're talking to your vendor every week, you're keeping in line. You're also keeping them in line. Don't just rely on online communication, because it's not enough of a line. Lines get lost, and they get broken. Lines sent online can be misinterpreted. Don't hide behind the online lines. Go out of the lines for better communication. Put it all on the line. Be personal, because it is personal. Personal is the best line to pick up on.

It's getting personal

Personal is a strong line. It's a supportive line, and an intimate line. You'll understand the lines that they're on about, with personal lines. I've used personal lines. Personal lines are good. They can take up more of your personal time, but you'll find they can affect both of you personally. These are sensitive lines, and rewarding lines. They're also hurtful lines. These are the lines, that when broken, can hurt an agent personally. They can also hurt the vendor personally. When they haven't been broken, they're personally rewarding lines.

I put myself on these lines most of the time. Sometimes it was painful.

Painfully personal

Should business be so personal? This is a question I've just added out of the blue. It hasn't come out of the blue, because it's been a question sitting inside me for a long time. Why was my business so personal? That's what I want to say, because I know it to be the truth. Some people won't know it's the truth, until they experience impersonal. This is when they'll find out what's missing.

We only know what we had when it's gone. I know what I had, and it's gone. Maybe I crossed a line. I may have got too personal with my lines. My person was personal. I'm my person. What makes someone want to be personal? It's the difference between being on the surface, or in the deep. Is it the difference between being in debt, and indebted? Here it is. I need the answer to this question. Is there one answer or two, or even three? Is there just one?

Was I bankrupt?

Was I personally bankrupt? What do you do, when you're empty? You try to fill up, don't you? Why was I trying to fill up with all these personal lines? If I had all this personal communication, where was the reward for me? Why didn't I fill up? I think it was a one-way street. Did I let anyone in? I just let a couple of people in towards the end, really.

I blurted in an unguarded moment. I hope it's been guarded. It's all about dynamics. I had a dynamic personality. This isn't boasting. It was nothing to boast about. I'm not boasting now. I'm toasting to better dynamics.

A telephone line to give me a sign

Maintaining all these lines can be utterly exhausting. Lines are coming in, and lines are going out. You want the phones to ring, but you also want them to stop. Your ears get sore, your throat gets sore, and your poor head gets sore. Your brain will get very sore. Be careful of a sore head, it could be too many mobile phone calls. I knew someone who got a sore head and had to have it fixed. He realized what was causing it. He waited on those mobile calls with bated breath, and it nearly took his breath.

Finding a good enough line for a vendor

It's all very well to make the call to the vendor, but then you've got to have something to say. You must have a story ready. You've got to make a report and feed them the feedback. Feedback must be good to feed on. It must be appetizing and interesting. It must be feedback that feeds back to you, the agent.

A priority takes priority

You must allocate enough time for this feedback, because you want the vendor to feel he's the priority. He expects to be the priority. The vendor will always forget how many other priorities there are. He'll not understand your order of priority. An agent can't always understand his own order of priority. All his priorities are a priority, unless there's been a prior arrangement.

Keep your priorities to yourself

You must never talk to a vendor about your other priorities, because he can become very jealous. When many vendors are sharing the one agent, it's normal for jealousies to arise. An agent must pretend devotion to each priority separately. An agent must know how to look after the affairs of all his priorities at the same time. This is the reason we have a little black book. Taking the little black book everywhere is a priority.

Having so many affairs at the same time, can be stressful

It can turn your job into a love/hate relationship. It can be a bit like the movie *Fatal Attraction*. The agent can put himself into a position of powerlessness, against what has now become too high a power play. He's now successful. He has stacks of listings, and no time to play. It's now all or nothing. He must play it to the beat.

When the mood takes you

Making calls to vendors when you're not in the mood for talking, can be a bit difficult. Difficult is what they'll get though, if you don't talk to them enough. Vendors don't wait, they demand. They don't listen either. They're only listening to themselves. All conversations must be about them, and their affairs. An agent cannot have his own private affairs. This can never be a priority. This goes against a vendor's assumed privileges.

> **Privilege:-** n. [< L. *privus*, separate + *lex*, a law] a right, advantage, favour, etc. specially granted to a certain person, group, or class – vt. -leged, -leg-ing, to grant a privilege to.

Let us have a gander at the origin of their assumed privilege.

> [*privus*, separate + a law, *lex*].

Just as I thought! Vendors are a law unto themselves. Where does it say this in an Agency Agreement? Does it set out the times you can call your agent? It should. A vendor selling his house isn't an emergency. I know this, because I've had real emergencies. Privileged vendors have rung me during emergencies. They've not recognized my emergency, nor have they listened to me.

What has emerged?

It has emerged that vendors aren't able to acknowledge any emergency but their own house emergency. House = money. Is money an emergency? Are vendors emotionally merged with money? Can money and emotion, be merged? Is this what they call a Merger? Is it a Merger of Acquisitions?

A universal question

Can an agent have an emergency of her own? This question is universal. It's bigger than any one of the questions I've written so far. Couldn't I have been a priority? Could I have been a priority for a vendor? Just once, and only in an emergency, couldn't I have been more important than them? Wasn't I only human? Was I a human or an agent?

I know this question to be one of the biggest questions of my life. What happens in an emergency? It's a question that will be answered throughout my life, so throughout my books. My emergency was a high-emotion emergency. High emotion is a life emergency. My emergency pissed off some vendors. My emergency pissed off some landlords. My emergency pissed off a lot of people. It was my emergency. Nobody, but nobody... I repeat, no-fucking-body...

> **Emergency:-** n., pl. [orig. sense, an *emergein*] an unexpected occurrence or situation demanding immediate action adj. for use in case of sudden necessity [an emergency exit].

... was more pissed off than me!

Dear pissed-off vendors

Making calls to disappoint your vendor is hard. Making calls as the disappointed agent is hard. A sale has died. Breaking bad news is hard. I've become proficient at breaking bad news. I've had to do a lot of it. Not just vendor news. I've conquered breaking the worst news, not just once, but many times. Too many fucking times! You must be careful as an agent not to break under the pressure of bad news.

Remaining your agent

I'm trying to stay with you here. I'm trying to remain your agent. But why do I always get the fucking job of giving people I love, the bad fucking news? Tragic news! Am I that fucking good at it? Is it because I've had so much fucking experience? Is it because I'm assumed to have no fucking feeling left? Well fuck you!

Sorry. I've said it. I'm sorry if I've pissed you off. Everyone gets pissed off sometimes. It takes a lot to piss me off. I've said it before. I'm an 'all in, or nothing' kind of a person.

Am I 'all' or 'nothing'?

I was all done in. Now I'm nothing. Is it piss, weak to be pissed off? Am I as weak as piss for telling you all? I got the call! When you get the call, don't call it off. Now I'm really pissed off, because my computer keeps putting one of those green wiggly lines under the 'piss', next to 'weak'. I've very rarely used this word phonetically, but it's in the dictionary and my dictionary says it's fine to use it, but not all the time.

> **Piss:-** vi. [prob. echoic] [Vulg.] to urinate –vt. to discharge as or with the urine –n. 1. urine; 2. [Vulg. Slang] beer –piss about [Vulg. Slang] to waste (someone's) time –piss off [Vulg. Slang] to go away; depart –pissed off [Vulg. Slang] annoyed.
>
> **Pissed:-** adj. [Vulg Slang] drunk, intoxicated.

I'm not pissed, I'm just pissed off. I can't figure it out. I can put a comma after 'piss', and the 'weak', and the wiggly line disappears. So that's the way it will have to be, 'piss weak' will have a comma between. There's now a quick pause.

> **Comma:-** n. [< Gr. *komma*, clause <*koptein*, cutoff] a mark of punctuation (,) used to indicate a slight separation of sentence elements.

Now this really gets my goat. I just typed 'piss weak', and didn't put the comma between, and now there's no wiggly line. Where does this wiggly line come from? Maybe it's a sign, that I'm not piss weak. Is it a separation of the elements of a sentence? Aha. Was I seen to be piss weak, when I was sentenced? Yes/no. There's that wiggly line again! Well, I shall prepare myself to address that accusation later. Be prepared. Be very prepared. Am I just pissing in your pocket? Are you pissing yourself laughing? I hope not, because I was deadly serious about being pissed off. You'll see why (Y), soon.

Breaking the connection

Making a break can sometimes feel like the better alternative. Making calls to rude and intolerant vendors is hard. It's hardest when you're innocent of the crime. I had no say. The customer is always right. The only thing you have left is your skills in dispute resolution.

I got skinned alive

There are a few tools you can use, but you'll need to have grown a thick skin. This is important if you want to protect yourself. A thick skin still feels the sting of the attack, but it's better insulation than thin skin. When you grow a thick skin, the idea is to insulate yourself within, from the outside attack.

A skin for all occasions

You can be putting this skin on so often, that you eventually stop taking it off, and just leave it on all the time. It sticks to you for the duration of your life, no matter where you are, or what you're doing. The problem is, while it keeps out the unwanted attention, it also keeps out the wanted attention. You don't even see that you need attention. Nothing can penetrate it. You grow so used to it, until you can't see that it's formed a barrier to yourself. You can't see out of it, and people can't see through it. They can't see through to you. They'll never glimpse the real person underneath.

This happened to me. It happened to me before I was in real estate. I started to grow my thick skin early, when I was a small child. As I grew older, it grew with me. When I became a real estate agent, I just grew it thicker again. It was so thick, I couldn't recognize myself. I couldn't penetrate it either. It was only able to be penetrated on a number of occasions, and only then, because the attack was so great. The attack to my senses was so savage, that it wore down that thick skin of mine, and got in.

It does get in

It got into a most sensitive place. It was such a sensitive a place, because it wasn't used to being touched. When it did get touched, it really hurt. It was rawness, like the rawness of a newborn baby or an innocent child. It hit the inner child. That inner child was already sensitive. It was the sensitive child guarding her senses for survival. I am diverse. I have diverse personalities. It's not a personality disorder. It's all in order of my diversity.

Diversity:- n., pl. -ties 1. a being diverse, difference; 2. variety.

I'm a being, diverse. We're all diverse. We're made up of diversities. We have our diversity for a reason. It's for adversity. We need to be diverse for all the diverse experiences we have, and will continue to have. The more diverse the experience, the more diverse you'll be. Being diverse is good. It gives you the strategies you need for life. Finding your diversity is hard. A diverse personality is hard to predict.

Diverse:- adj. [< L. *dis-*, apart + *vertere*, to turn] 1. different; 2. varied –diverse'ly adv.

I was a diverse real estate agent. I could divert the conversation in any direction I wanted, whenever I wanted.

Divert:- vt. [see DIVERSE] 1. to turn aside; 2. to amuse; 3. to distract –divert'ing adj.

Diverting the vendor was my specialty. I had plenty of diversions, but they were good diversions. When things go wrong in the sale process, you need a quick diversion. Negotiating commission was the first on my list of diversions. I felt that the vendor should be paid for his loyalty to me. Providing extra advertising, editorials, gifts and flattery, were my diversions. Sucking up, sucking up, and more and more sucking up, were vital diversions on my list of diversionary tools. This is how diverse I was.

Don't do it forever

You can do this forever. It's the most important prerequisite to becoming a successful real estate agent. One must know how to suck up. One must learn how to be battered, how to take insults, abuse, accusations, and slander, all with a ready smile. This is the way to success. You'll not be classified as a smooth operator without these skills. Be diverse. Be, and do, anything the vendor wants. This was my catch cry, 'whatever it takes'.

Sharing a hold

Holding on to the market share of listings in your area is a hard slog. It must be slogged out continuously, foot-slogged, phone-slogged, and self-flogged, or you can lose your share. If you lose your share, you've been flogged, because whoever has the biggest share will continue to get the bigger share. Once you lose your share to their share, you have less of a share. It's not sharing. You simply don't want to share. You can't afford to share a listing.

You can always flog one

When can you afford to share a listing? When there are barely any listings. Then you'll take any share. Beggars can't be choosers. You'll even take the worst share. You'll even pinch someone else's share, so you'll be able to share with your own. Is this taking responsibility for your share of the work? What's the intention? Is it for survival? Ethics can't survive under tough conditions. Tough market conditions, will get rid of ethical real estate agents quick smart. When the going gets rough, the fluffy get going. Are you tough, or are you going? This is in The Knowing.

Ensure you're covered

Can you choose a share by its cover? Your signage is coverage. This is one of the most important lessons you can learn in real estate. If your share covers the area, you'll be seen to be an active and successful agent. This is what vendors want to see. They want the best agent. They want a popular agent. They want to be seen in the popular group. This is all about the peer signage. It can look like you hold the biggest share if you get the signage in the right place. This is what's called high-exposure positioning. Main road signage can give you this sort of a cover. 'It's the place to be seen.' If you've got the main road positions, you've got great coverage. You've covered all your bases.

Was I branded hard enough?

It's just branding. Branding properties with your signs is a good strategy. Brand awareness is what you're aiming for. It's what they're looking at. They'll just remember the brand. What brand was I? I was my own brand. People liked my branding. They liked the look of my signs. They stood out. I don't think anyone will pinch my branding now. I think my branding has taken a battering.

I was used to my signs taking a battering. They were kicked, burnt, drawn on, slashed and thrown. The old ones were used again, and no doubt I'll see the backs of them from time to time. They'll no doubt be seen being used for a community project or whatnot. They'll only be seeing the back of me though, and they'll be advertising something else entirely.

How much did I pay for those signs? This is not a mathematical question. It's a personal question. I would, in all honesty, and as I sum it all up, have much preferred the math question.

It's easier said than done

Being a real estate agent is a tough gig. It's tough if you're not good at it. If you're not good at it, you're out the door as quick as lightning. Someone either turns the lights out on you, or you turn the lights on.

You must measure up. If you haven't got the right measurement of listings on the board at the end of the quarter, you'll be out on your ear. Forget about the sales, let someone else in the office sell them. Just make sure they're all your listings. You always get more for a listing. You get more listings with a listing. It's not sales that make a decent real estate agent. It's the listings. If you don't have the listings, you don't make the sales. It's why you meet so many people that used to be one, a real estate agent, I mean. They used to be. That's a good place to be.

I used to be. But I'm not anymore. I'm now my own person again, and I answer to no-one.

What's there to know?

You're not required to know a lot. A one-week training course can give you a certificate, and you're on your way. The rest is on the job training. It's training the soul to keep quiet. Not everyone can be a good real estate agent. Some personality types just can't hack it. Some personality types are too healthy to hack it. They know what's good for their health and wellbeing.

I've always said that being a real estate agent isn't so much about the real estate, as it is about the people. I've never said any truer words. It has barely anything to do with the property. It's all about knowing the kinds of people that have it, buy it, and sell it. It's about recognizing the good in people, and the bad in people. It's about working with both kinds. The good and the bad, that is.

It's black and white

It's not bad, but it's not good either. It's the working in, and amongst it, that's bad. It's about changing the bad to good, and the good to bad. That's the balance I'm afraid. It's soluble.

Soluble:- adj. [see SOLVE] 1. that can be dissolved; 2. that can be solved.

The dilution camp

I'm a dilutor. I can dilute. This is important. You can dilute any situation. You may have to dilute the emotion in people. You must dilute the strong emotion, and make it easier to handle. If you can do this, you can take away peoples' worries. You can alleviate a situation. You can relieve people of sleepless nights, and high blood pressure. You can take away anger, and any other distressing emotions. You can allay fear. You can put it into a truer perspective, for the prospective purchaser with a perspective all out of proportion.

Dilute:- vt. -lut'ed, -lut'ing [< L. *dis-*, off + *lavare*, wash] to thin down or weaken by mixing with water, etc. -adj. diluted -dilute'ness n. -dilut'-er, dilu'tor n. -dilu'tion n.

Distorted vendor problems

When a vendor or purchaser make a mountain out of a molehill, it's the agent's job to change it back into a molehill again. This is what people do with problems. They get a small problem, and without being aware of it, they grow it into a whopping big mountain. They add all this other shit to it, until it's big enough to get the attention they need. This is really what they want in the long run. They want somebody to attend to their problems.

I've always believed that problems are easier to deal with, when they're small. This is the job of an agent. Whether it's a big or small problem, you must make it soluble. You must take all the unknown factors out first.

Shit is always the unknown factor

This is the shit the vendor or purchaser will add to it, just for full effect. Once you've taken the shit out, it becomes a problem you can solve. This is no shit! If you can take the shit out of the equation, you'll be a hero, not a zero. This is as long as you weren't the one, that put the shit into it, in the first place.

Just keep swimming, just keep swimming…

Some agents get a kick out of adding their own shit to a problem. They do this primarily, so that their shit will stick to someone else, and not them. In order for you to get rid of the problem, you have to immerse yourself in the shit. You've got to learn how to swim through it, before you can find the way out of it.

God Stone the crows

Real estate agents (I'm thinking of the Aldi driver), who dive into people's shit, must do so bravely. Most agents will try to blame the shit on someone else, or declare that they haven't got the time for this sort of shit. Shit can ruin a sale, so you must get rid of it. Someone needs to take responsibility for the shit that's happened. In the end, someone's got to scoop up all the shit, and put it somewhere else. The further away you put the shit, the better. You don't want it sneaking back up on you later.

This bit's for that shit head

But if you've been the shit head adding to the problem, the shit will find its own way back to you. That's karmic shit. You can't hide from it, because it invariably finds you. Being found is just a lesson, but if you don't learn your lesson, you'll just cop another lashing of it.

This is what an agent is folks. He's a professional shit-kicker. I'm not a 'he', but I am kicking the shit out of him, metaphorically speaking.

Reading between the lines

We're the facilitators. We're the facilitators of fortunes. Good fortune, bad fortune, but rarely our fortune. If the Act was ethical, we'd be classified as mediators. But the Act isn't ethical, and we do in fact only act for the vendor. We don't owe allegiance to any purchaser, whether they wish to think it, or not. We take advantage of the purchaser, for the advantage of the vendor. That's the job. It sounds crook, doesn't it? It depends on what side of the fence you're sitting on.

Showing your allegiance

If you're a vendor, you'll be happy with the advantage. If you're a purchaser, you're a bit pissed off with the agent. That's only if you become aware of where the agent's allegiance lies, and only if that's where the agent's allegiance lies. Lies are lies.

Some agents get confused with showing their allegiance. This is when their strongest allegiance is to their own egos. They'll pick the side where their egos will get the most stroking. Keep the egos out, because egos can't be allowed full control. Keep control of your ego, and you won't lose control. Your ego wants full control, but you must be aware of its motives. Its motives aren't always right. Mostly, your ego will be motivated by greed. Egos are greedy things, and they want all the control.

Egoism is a work fetish

How's your appetite? Have you got an appetite for what I'm about to tell you? You may have already had your fill of my definitive delights.

I can define in a line, or in a one-liner. I can sign to align, and make everything finer. I can sting like brine, when I speak in Strine. When I dine on my spine, it's not to recline. It's a sign of what's mine, which I intertwine. I've been unwinding the twine, from an old forest pine, and digging a hole, in an old buried mine. I'm cleaning and scrubbing, with turpentine. I'm just making me shine. Do you want to give me a shiner? You will shortly. It's karmic logic.

The very best screws

If you're relocating, you'll usually be selling and buying simultaneously. You're screwing someone down for a sale, and getting screwed back when you purchase. This is what you call a mutually satisfying screw. You can't go wrong with this kind of a screw, because what you do is reciprocated. If you've screwed someone down, you're bound to be screwed right back. It's the best sort of screwing, because there's a good result at either end.

Totally screwed

The agents are the facilitators of these screws, and they'll be out in force, showing you how to do it. They'll help you to do one, for the sake of the other. The first screw always helps the reciprocated screw. It's often better for the agent, if you've purchased first. You've screwed first, and now you need a quick screw before you're screwed over by the bridging loan. You'll be out looking to be screwed. You won't care who screws you, or for how much, because you've screwed things up for yourself, by purchasing before you've sold. Screw that!

Worst screws

If you're forced to sell your property for financial reasons, you're being screwed twice. This is a double storey screw. You have a financial screw, and he's being screwed by a real estate screw, or is it vice versa? This is heavy screwing. You've got the two coming down on you at once. They both want their pound of flesh from you. You end up just skin and bones. They'll be left with slim pickings, screwing you. Looking on the bright side, this is usually the last real estate screw you'll ever have, and your screwing days are over.

Top screws

If you're a collector of real estate, and have an investment portfolio, you're being screwed left, right, and centre. You think you're an important screw, but you're screwing up your life. You'll expect the agent to jump on demand, and the agent will have to drop all his other screwing, to come and screw you. You think you're doing all the screwing, and that's why the agent's jumping up and down. Take another look and see who really does all the screwing. Who's making the moves?

The agent knows he'll get more screwing done with you in the future, if he keeps screwing you the way you like it. The agent likes to let you think you're doing the screwing, so that you feel good. The agent will invariably let you be on top. You're a top screw. You're a screw-top he's keen to reopen.

An ignorant screw

When you're a purchaser, you'll be screwed, and it'll be an unconsenting screw. You won't necessarily know that you were screwed. You may still think you've negotiated the greatest deal of the century. That's what a good vendor's agent will tell you. The agent wants to keep you unawares, so that you'll stay loyal. He likes to keep you feeling committed to him, and him only. He wants his bit on the side for later. The agent's predicting another screw, way into the future, when you one day become a vendor.

Keeping the screwing secret

The agent won't want anyone to know how he secretly screwed you down, but sometimes he'll whisper it to his vendor. His vendor will know about the screw, and be delighted with his agent. He'll want to know all the details to prolong his excitement. This usually makes a vendor feel a lot bigger, when all is said and done.

Your very first screw

Agents love a virgin. Agents love real estate virgins. They love first-timers. Real estate agents even look virginal, to real estate virgins. Agents love to look virginal. If you're a purchaser, never let on it's your first time. If an agent suspects you're still a virgin, he'll try anything to get you into a house. He'll even take you in his shiny new car. He'll be charming, as he asks whether you're hooked up with another. If you are, he'll down-talk his competition, in order to get you onside, and inside. Once he gets you inside, he'll try to screw you. Once he's screwed you down, he's also screwing the agent with the house you were previously hooked on. This is the agent with the most notches. He can screw in two places at once. He's great at what he does, but he's also a home wrecker.

Am I getting too rude? I'm finding myself a bit rude. I feel offended by my rudeness. Is this how a lady discusses her workday? Those days are over. I turned myself off. I might turn a few real estate agents off themselves, now. That's always a turn on.

Screwing an old flame

But one day, that purchaser will want to sell that same house that he purchased from you all those years ago. He remembers the good rapport he had with you at that time, and he hasn't had to deal with an agent since. In fact, he really doesn't know any other agents as well as he knew you. He knows that you're the agent that already knows his house. He remembers all the wonderful things you told him back then, about the house. He remembers how good you were at convincing him it was the right house to buy, and how big a bargain he got.

Qualifying the screw

The former purchaser wants to show you his, and you want to show him yours. This former purchaser, and soon to be vendor, shows you all the improvements he's made to his property since you screwed him, and you get yours out and show him all the screws you've been having ever since. He's convinced that he's onto a very fine specimen, and he appoints you as his selling agent.

Screwing is private

This time he's a vendor, and he gets to direct the screwing. He directs you to go out there and screw someone down, on his house.

He'd really like to watch this screwing, or even listen to the screwing when you're in the middle of doing it, but you're an agent and you like to keep your screwing private.

You need to keep your vendor in suspense, and get him all excited. You try to prolong the excitement for a while, and then return to him with the offer, and as the hero. This is when you try to consummate the deal with one last screw between you. By this time, the vendor's happy to give in to a little screw at the end, just for old-time's sake.

Screwing with the lines

Now all this screwing must be done while maintaining the fine lines. This is at the agent's discretion. There are so many lines that can't be stepped on, or screwed with. The more listings you have, the more bloody lines to maintain. If the vendor and purchaser think I'm just screwing with them, think again.

You may have had a few more screws than you wish to admit. Nobody tells the truth about how many screws they've had. That's a lie, I think agents do. They want to be the best, and most successful, at it. Be careful of the best agents, better is always best. Less is more.

I'm a bit disturbed

If any of the above is a bit disturbing, have a thought for the poor agent. The agent is, and should be, the most disturbed. He's almost certainly screwing himself!

Screw karma

When agents set about selling their privately-owned homes, they must declare 'agent interest'. We must have the words 'Agent Interest Declared' posted on all advertising, in accordance with our industry regulations. All advertising must have this notice, whether it's on a signboard, window display, real estate magazine, or in a newspaper.

Agents don't want to do this because it's discriminatory, but it's the regulations under the Act.

An agent is a shrewd vendor. Is it fair to the agent's wife when she's just the tenant in common? She has no say as to whether a declaration of this nature is advertised? She's not an agent, but she's worked hard for her half share of that property. Shouldn't the declaration be, 'Agent's Half-Share Interest Declared'? This is an unfair regulation, and I'll show you why.

'Warning – Expert Dealer on Site'

When a purchaser sees this said notice on a property he wishes to inspect, he'll instantly be suspicious. He'll be on full alert, and start considering all the angles. He knows he'll have to watch his back, because this is an agent's property, and he'll be dealing with an expert. The purchaser already suspects the price is too high to start with.

There's got to be a screw loose somewhere

He'll be considering whether there's something wrong with the house, questioning why the agent is selling, and he'll be looking for all the hidden catches. He's like a dog with a bone. He can sniff that there might be something a bit off, but he's not sure where it is.

Where's the catch?

While he's sniffing, he gets a whiff that he could be onto a house that's better than the rest, because an expert owns it. There must be some special benefits with this house. It must be in a pretty good position. It's got to be well built, and structurally sound. It must be a pretty good house for the agent to have bought it in the first place. He surmises that an agent would be pretty discriminating when it comes to buying his own property.

Selling yourself short of an agent

During the inspections, carried out by the owner/agent, with the prospective purchaser, the owner/agent has put himself in an unprotected place. There's no other place to be, for an agent selling his own property. He's not exactly spoiled for choice.

He's left himself wide open

He's left his house wide open. The only thing shut, is his mouth. He has no cover now, and the firing squad has an easy target. There's no place to hide, from the shots being fired. He must take them head on, and learn to turn the other cheek. He's still under the obligation of the Agency he works for. His choice of agency is his only choice, if he wants to continue working there, by choice.

No fairer options

He's put his property for sale with the Agency he works for, because he can't be seen to be supporting any of the opposition agencies. He'll get a discount on commission with this agency, but he'll do all the work. Everyone in his agency will know his business.

The purchaser feels a sense of power because he's the customer, and the agent's taken on the role of the owner. Suddenly there's no facilitating, mediating, arbitrating agent, because he's now the owner, and acting like one. He's sensitive about his personal space.

The purchaser feels the best course of action is to treat the owner like he'd treat the real estate agent. He's not used to dealing with the owner direct, and he's only in the habit of talking to agents in a situation like this. Agents listen to him. He wants an agent to listen to him, so the owner turns back into the agent. The purchaser ignores the owner, because that's just what purchasers do.

A defective agent

The purchaser thoroughly inspects the property, investigating inside pantries, and built-in robes. He inspects the stove top, the bathroom plumbing underneath the hand-basins, and inside vanities, (literally). Since the agent has the owner persona on, it's worth the purchaser's while, to regale him with all the defects he's found, and the ways that he'd need to improve on them. The purchaser is thoroughly enjoying himself, knowing he has the owner/agent by the balls, and starts to twist further. The purchaser's now catching on to the Catch-22 situation he's in.

Just getting started

The purchaser states his dislike of the garage set up, the landscaping design, the broken pool fence, the busted downpipe and the fact that he's surprised the agent hadn't bought a north facing home. The purchaser gets the knife in, and turns it again, with some quick costing calculations on fixing what's broke. He goes on to inspect the lousy tiling job in the toilet, after being told that it was a DIY job. He goes on to give a quick lesson to the owner/agent on how tiling should be done correctly. The purchaser is catching on fast. He's caught on to the fact that he holds the balance of power in this situation. His ego is set to get the high it so rightly deserves.

The purchaser can't believe he's getting on so well with the owner/agent, because the bloke still appears friendly and seems to be taking in all this professional advice with obvious interest. He feels unable to break the connection, and continues with the lengthy inspection, knowing how important this house is for the agent/owner to sell. He's generous with his tips on selling this piece of real estate.

He'll give it a bit more thought

The purchaser feels it's his duty to qualify himself now, because after all, the agent is the owner. He doesn't want the owner to think he's wasting his time on an unqualified purchaser. The purchaser has no time to waste. His time is precious. He must qualify his quality.

The tyre-kicker kicks in

The purchaser knows that the owner/agent is happy to spend a lot of time on this very important inspection. The purchaser feels it's a sign of respect to linger longer. In fact, the purchaser is wondering why he hasn't yet been offered a cup of tea, especially because he could potentially be the all-important new owner of this home. His ego is now expecting the red-carpet treatment.

I think I can, I think I can…

He knows he doesn't want to buy the home, but he could. He can, if he decides, and would, if he wanted to. The purchaser's sense of empowerment increases. The purchaser's chest has swelled, and so has his head. It's a long and thorough inspection. The agent is struggling in his dual role. He's back-flipping from owner to agent, and from agent to owner. He's confused. The pain of the ever-hopeful owner persona, is mixed with that of a wise and knowing agent. A hard-arsed agent.

The hustle

The two personas are squabbling inside. One is vulnerable and hopeful, and the other is knowledgeable and experienced. Knowledgeable and experienced, equals cynical. Either way, he must have hope. He can't get rid of it. The vendor side to him needs it. He knows this bloke's probably a tyre-kicker, but he just can't take the risk of pissing him off. He could, potentially, be his buyer. He could even be a buyer for another listing altogether.

The motions of power

The purchaser is wielding his long sword around now. He's left the firing squad for later, and takes a different angle.

The purchaser now feels the need to ask 'the all-important questions' like:

- "How long has the house been on the market?"
- "Have you had many lookers?"
- "Why are you selling?"
- "Has anyone made you an offer yet?"
- "What was the offer?"

Here's an agent, right where you want him. He's on the right side of the fence for a change, and caught right in the beam of the headlights. Who's being screwed now? The purchaser feels it's his duty to give the agent some tips on selling his home.

It has some kick in it

- "I thought you'd have more photos on the internet."
- "I notice you didn't take the shot with the broken gutter."
- "That can all be negotiated in the price though, can't it?"

The purchaser requests a copy of the contract and all the building certificates. He just wants to check everything's above board.

"You can never be too careful, you know. How negotiable is the price? Will you take an offer for it? I'll have to start down low. I'm just giving you the heads-up. I always throw a low offer. You never know if someone's desperate. Can I come back at seven o'clock tonight, and show the missus? She hated this one, but I told her we should look at absolutely everything. I told her we wouldn't be paying top price for it, anyway. It's not as good as the pictures in the paper. There's a lot of work I'd have to do, to get it up to scratch. They always look better in the ads, don't they? You should have installed an air conditioner. That can make all difference in getting it sold. When I sold my joint, I high-pressure water washed all the mildew off my south wall. I wouldn't try it on this one though. I reckon the paint would peel off."

All the while, the owner has a job to do. He's still the agent. He has a smile plastered across his face. The plaster is cracking under the strain. There's enough pain here now, so we'll fast forward to the new purchaser.

The never-ending screw, it just goes on, and on, my friends...

Once there's a sale, if anything goes wrong with the house in the years following, it is the agent's fault. The agent has ripped off the unwary purchaser, and is a lowly scoundrel. The agent will always be the deviate. Your status will leave a trail of destruction behind you. You won't even need to be destructive. It just goes with the territory. An agent will always be to blame.

This situation would not occur for the average vendor.
I might be pulling hairs here, but there's more...

Karma from both barrels

Have a thought for when an agent wants to buy something. He'll try to keep it on the quiet. He won't want it to get out, that he's an agent, and he's purchasing. This isn't always easy when you're so well known, especially if you're inspecting the prized property with an agent from a different agency. If you're this well known, you're a bloody good agent. If you're such a bloody good agent, you're undoubtedly going down!

In unknown territory

This is the competition, as it were, showing you through the property and trying to be friendly. They smell the enemy, but they also smell a sale. They smell revenge. This is kind of like watching two large saltwater crocodiles fighting for dominance over a patch of ground. The patch of ground is someone's lounge room, and the owner of the lounge room wants the agents to play nice, especially when one agent could be her purchaser. Smiles are on the crocodiles.

This is the competition the agent screwed in the past. It never gets forgotten.

A Never Forgotten Blot

Both know, what's not forgot.

It could be time, for a parting shot.

The agent wants to give him the lot.

He wants to get rid of the not forgotten blot,

It ruined his top copybook spot.

He wants to get even, and he wants it a lot.

He wants to sell this plot, why not?

He hopes it'll besot and be got, for a lot.

He wants to get him to sign on the dot,

Then he'll swallow his lot,

But his anger's still hot.

He wants him to rot, as he leads the trot.

This is one deal, he cannot boycott.

By Ms T.L. Mock-the-croc.

Can you imagine who will come off second best, in this dealer-drome? It doesn't matter how good you are at negotiating, because once that vendor knows a real estate agent is interested in buying her house, she's smiling.

Like a Cheshire cat

Come in spinner! She knows a real estate agent is an expert in property, so she suddenly gets the idea that her house must be worth a lot more after all. An expert is interested. The compliment is priceless. If the real estate agent wants to buy it, it must be really good!

State your status

So we're continually fighting our status. Our status is taken advantage of, and we pay more for the house than we feel it to be worth. Any house, once the vendor knows we're an agent. Any house an agent wants to buy, just goes up, up, up. The vendor knows an agent's buying, and the vendor's agent knows an opposition agent is buying. This is stiff competition for an agent buying.

Non-disclosure is a must

I wouldn't ever disclose that I was a real estate agent. I filled in forms with my occupation as 'Sales'. I'd never disclose the fact to a doctor, hospital, at a school meeting, or any other social event, where I was meeting people. I was in love with the idea of 'it' when I first started, but when I inherited the reputation of the industry, I was ashamed. I was ashamed, not for how I operated, but just because of people's instant assumptions.

Maybe even for operating

I guess I made assumptions too. Did I start to believe the public's assumptions? Did I make the wrong assumptions, because of the public's general assumptions?

Did I assume the position?

I was very rarely able to keep up the charade, and either had to be honest, when they asked me outright what I did in sales, or it would somehow come to light, one way or another.

My mother would divulge it to the doctors she knew and worked with. You don't attract much sympathy when this happens. In the pre-theatre room, while being prepped for a major operation, it's real estate that they want to talk. You're no longer a vulnerable, nervous lady, waiting for the knife. You've suddenly transformed in to a 'hard as nails' woman of substance, who must entertain and perform the sales patter once again.

I couldn't win over a rattle from a baby

I didn't want to be that person on that day. I didn't feel like that person on that day. It was too much of a strain, but I gave them what they wanted. I performed. I rose to the occasion, and so did my real estate persona. You get less care when this happens. You become a stronger personality type.

Medical personnel don't worry about our type. We're seen to be tough enough to take care of ourselves. We don't look vulnerable. We just look like we want to win you over. I couldn't though. I wasn't well. I was in terrible pain, weak, and unable to advocate for myself. I didn't have my real estate patter with me during the ten days in hospital after this operation. I was expected to have it, but I couldn't find it. I was disabled. I was not myself. If I was not feeling myself, who was I feeling? I was feeling just like you would, in a similar situation. I was at the mercy of others. I was desperate for mercy.

The Goddess of Mercy

The story of The Goddess, goes way back. Way back, but not just way back, all over the place, far and wide. She is the deity who was originally china's contribution to the Buddhist world, and known as Guanyin. Love and compassion is what she's revered for. She has the power though.

The goddess of Mercy, also known as The Goddess of Love and compassion, has endured. Not only has she endured, she has travelled throughout Asia. Some would say she has had the power to traverse countries, cultures, time, and gender. Her name is Bodhisattva, Avalokitesvara/Guanyin. She's up there with buddha himself.

Guanyin is her original name from China, but I'm still having trouble pronouncing it. I don't think it matters what we call her. Sometimes she's depicted with all the arms, but if you look her up, she has evolved to take on many different forms.

I want to go far and wide

Avalokitesvara translates to 'hearer of voices of the suffering beings' conveying the existence of a higher force able to observe all of humanity. She reigned supreme, and just like the Arch Angel Gabriel, is known in both male and female form, or no gender at all. That's how she got entry into both Chinese and Indian culture. She transformed.

She's armed with compassion

I worry about what's gone on. In China they had the one child policy. A one child policy seems fine, considering the over population of China and its problematic economics. The main problem arises from the lack of importance placed on gender equality. I mean, Noah didn't take one of everything. He had pairs. Mates. So where are all the mates?

Mateship

Where is the love? A man is more important in China than a woman. His responsibility is to his parents, first and foremost.

He's expected to support them in their old age. That's the culture. A son works. A son provides. A daughter marries and leaves her parents.

It's a social experiment which will change China forever. I watched something on TV about there being 34 million more men in China than women. What happened to all the women? As far as I know, there isn't such a thing as a deadly epidemic, which only kills female babies. And as far as I know, we don't yet have a special contraceptive that prevents the mother from conceiving a girl instead of a boy. Are women being wiped out?

As far as I know

How do they get all those boys? Are they begetting the girls? Are they forgetting the girls?

> **Beget:-** [< O.E. begitan, acquire] 1. to be the father of 2. to produce [tyranny begets rebellion]

Is it a disaster waiting to happen? Where's the balance? Where am I going with this?

I mean, didn't yin and yang come from China? It's as obvious as black and white. They now have a supply and demand situation. They're top heavy. Have the girls become more valuable? The girls have become a commodity on which their parents can trade, but only if the value stays in control of the parents.

Getting ready for a big match

They're at the parks, and they're at the gatherings, looking for the best mate for their daughters. They're intervening for a wealthy male to support them. Not a healthy male, but a wealthy one. Wealthy ones are the only ones that will get a mate.

Is it genocide?

> **Genocide:-** n. [< Gr. Genos, race + -CIDE] the systematic killing of a whole national or ethnic group.

Could I make a new word up here? I'd like to propose the word 'gendercide'. Let's face it, the same thing could happen to blokes, couldn't it? What's in a word? What gender are we really talking about?

It's not a new word!

This is getting heavy, but what I'm really talking about is infanticide. It shouldn't even be a word, because my research shows that it only ever applies to one gender.

Is it a cultural revolution?

What is a need? A need is the forerunner of a want. We all want happiness. We all want security. We all want love. To create these things in our lives, we must do the needs first. What does China need? What does China need for happiness and security?

China needs more room

China's population is exploding. Did they stop the explosion by adopting the one child policy? They no longer have this law. Have they managed to create a culture of smaller families through adopting the use of the one child policy? Is everyone in China now used to the idea of smaller families? Were there other reasons for bringing in the one child policy? China is fully aware of how their population is growing. China has a growing army of men. How would you set out to create the greatest army in the world? Would you breed soldiers?

I'll now change the channelling

What is freedom of speech? 'the right to express any opinions without censorship or restraint'. There's more to it, but I'll quote from Wikipedia as follows:

> 'any act of seeking, receiving and imparting information or ideas, regardless of the medium used.'

The Goddess of Real Estate

If there had been a Goddess of Real Estate when I was an agent, I would have worshipped her. I would have prayed to her for forgiveness, and asked her for guidance. I would've had someone to air my problems with. I'd get so stuck on morals, motives, and intention. There are no real estate books to help with these intricate people problems. These are the tenuous problems that a real estate career throws up, that make you want to throw up, or throw in the towel.

Laws are narrowly minded

Can we work by rules alone? Are rules all we need, to equip us for the journeys of a real estate agent? Are we assumed to have already at our disposal, the morals and virtues, that are also needed? What virtues should our goddess possess, and what commandments would she offer to us poor unworthy souls?

Your wish is my command

Would she have stood by a list of holy commandments to keep us lost souls from wandering in the darkness? Could there be a place worth seeking, where holiness and purity could thrive in our industry? We need a powerful goddess of exceptional beauty, with a heart full of mercy, for her yet undaunted foot soldiers. This goddess of real estate could be our shining light, and our hope of redemption. She could be our path to sales of purity and truth. Maybe even of prosperity and inner wealth.

The great redeemer of real estate agents

She'd be the light shining over us, as we negotiate the right path through an industry dominated by obstacles and ethics. She could be sworn on, and shrines could be erected in all real estate agencies across the world. She could be there to remind us of her eternal protection, and to give us hope for a better life, and a better workday. She could lead us not into temptation and deliver us from evil.

A real estate heaven

Our real estate industry could honour her with a pledge, and she'd be the symbol of our nobility. The real estate regulators would uphold her holy commandments, and no longer be the toothless tigers that they are today. It could be an institution of learning, with great scholars and theosophists, scribing the new rules for a better industry and for the saving of lost souls.

I'm still holding a valid real estate license

I've appointed myself the Goddess of Real Estate. You knew I would! I did hold back, but nobody else came to mind. Someone's got to do it. I've named her with the letters that make up the words 'real', and 'estate'. Her highness has been named by me. I give her the name 'Lisatrace'. Does this sound Greek? Maybe it's Latin. It sounds like 'Harry Potter'. Could it be Aussie? Its place of origin, is in the book *The Maker in Me*, by me.

Lisatrace: (You see, this is where I'm limited. Dictionaries won't give me any of the Goddesses. I knew she wouldn't be there, but I was looking for the definition of Aphrodite. This would have given me a clue as to how to create Lisatrace's persona. The closest I came to it, was aphrodisiac. I'm open to anything.)

> **Aphrodisiac:-** adj. [< Aphrodite, Gr. goddess of love] arousing or increasing sexual desire –n. an aphrodisiac substance.

Do you think Aphrodite would mind sharing? She already shares with Venus, so I hardly think she'll mind me squeezing Lisatrace in. Do you think Venus will get offended?

> **Venus:-** [L., love] 1. Rom. Myth. the goddess of love and beauty 2. a planet in the solar system, second in distance from the sun.

Not to be confused with the 'Venus flytrap'

> **Venus' flytrap:-** a swamp plant having leaves with two hinged blades that snap shut and so trap insects.

She's far from being any sort of Goddess of Mercy, no matter what she's said.

I don't possess any books on Greek mythology. If Lisatrace is Gnostic, this means I can use other mediums to create her many attributes. Let's see, I have the following reference books for reference:

A random choice from my randomly meagre stock pile

- *The Complete Book of Astrology*. Caitlin Johnstone.
- *The Complete Works of William Shakespeare*. William Shakespeare.
- *Crystals, Gems & Minerals Guide*. Pamela Robbins.
- The Thirst for Wholeness. Christina Grof.
- *Sophie's World*. Jostein Gaarder.
- Healing, Secrets of Ancient China. Pier Tsui-Po.
- The Bible. God.
- *The People of the Lie*. M. Scott Peck.
- *Freedom: The End of the Human Condition* (autographed). Jeremy Griffith
- *The Descent of Man, and Selection in Relation to Sex*. Charles Darwin.
- *Sharing the Universe*. Seth Shostak.
- *The Crucible of Consciousness*. Zoltan Torey.
- *Some Unrecognized Factors in Medicine*. L.J. Bendit, P.D. Bendit, H.T. Edmunds, A. Gardner and M.B. Bayly.
- *From Creation to Chaos: Classic Writings in Science*. Edited by Bernard Dixon.
- *The Wealth Within*. Ainslie Meares.
- *Passages*. Gail Sheehy.
- *Forgotten Wisdom*. Kerry Cue
- *The Stormy Search for the Self*. Christina Grof and Stanislav Grof.

- *Collins Australian Pocket Dictionary of the English Language.* Marian Makins, Margaret Martin, Pamela Breckenridge, Diana Adams, Michael Munro, Danielle McGrath, Kay Cullen and Nancy Marshall.
- *Reader's Digest Word Finder*, The Australian Thesaurus.
- *The Dance of Intimacy.* Harriet Lerner.
- *Concerning You and Me.* C.R. McRae.
- *In the Words of Nelson Mandela.* Jennifer Crwys-Williams
- *Man and His World* (autographed). Clark Blaise.
- *The Light Fantastic.* Peter Mason.
- *The Knowing in Me.* Vanilla Extract.

What's missing from the references?

Do you want to know what happened to *The Maker in Me* by Vanilla Extract? It hasn't been acknowledged. It sits here on my shelf. It's finished. It was my first book. It's highly controversial. I was less discriminate with this book, and it's got a whole host of people I know featured in it. It has evidential proof of my story. It was the maker of me, but it could be the unmaking of me. I've made my bed, but I haven't slept in it yet. I contemplate sleeping in it now.

The Maker in Me - A good bedtime gem

Who will be in bed with me? Will being in bed with me, wake some people up? Who will awaken beside me? Who will awaken behind me? Who will awaken from a lazy slumber? I could awaken a whole village. It's just the villagers I'm waking, and maybe the village people. I might put them on the map. Is this what they want? Can a backwash, be washed back up? I want to wash it. I have always wanted to wash it up. This is what I'm doing. I'm washing away the dirt. It's my dirt, and I'm washing it away. I see it as my duty. It's the least I can do, after getting washed up myself. You should always clean up after yourself, I say. Cleanliness is next to Goddessliness.

There's been a big mix up

Do authors ever write lots of books, and then release them one by one, when they're needed? Is this a good plan? I'm waiting for a direction, and considering in what order to release my books. They're a series. They follow on from one another. What can happen if I release them out of order? Will people get mixed up? The only people confused by the mix up, would be the people who've had some input into it. The mix up, that is!

Are you getting a feeling for the story?

They'll be the ones that won't want the truth. The remainder of you won't really care about the order of things, because you'll have nothing to compare the truth to. It's all the truth, and it's all out of order. You'll get a feel for the order I've been given. You'll only get a feel. Sometimes that's all you get, is the feel. Are you copping a feel right now? How big a feel are you getting? Do you feel me? Do you feel that I'm real? Can you tell that by feeling, or reading? What do you feel? Are you feeling for me? You'll feel a lot more if you read *The Maker in Me*.

You'll make your own assumptions. Remember to feel from your gut, soul, instinct and intuition, or wherever that place is, that gives you real honesty. These are all good ways open to you, for knowing the truth, but maybe not. There's more in *The Maker in Me*. You haven't been told the whole sorry story yet. I'm not as sorry as I could be.

How did it all start?

Only the people who heard, and contributed to the various stories of my story, will be confused. They're the people that will be most desperate to read *The Maker in Me*, because they'll probably recognize themselves in the story. They'll barely be able to recognize themselves, because to do so, will be horrifying. Can one always know what one has done?

I've lost my train of thought, so I'll just remind myself.

There's a train coming to deliver on time

I used to have so many more books. I've had hundreds of them, but I've donated them to the Salvation Army. I thought that in this way they could go to the people who most need them. These people will know who donated to their cause. Not me. I credited the people who helped make my story. It makes for good reading, if you're not the person being read about. I dropped my bundle. Have I dropped my cover?

Is this illegal? Is it illegal for books to be sold on like this? Is it against copyright law, to on-sell second-hand books for profit?

[Except in the United States of America, this book is sold subject to the condition that it shall not, by way of trade or otherwise, be lent, resold, hired out, or otherwise circulated without the publisher's prior consent in any form of binding or cover other than that in which it is published and without a similar condition including this condition being imposed on the subsequent purchaser.]

Is this ambiguous? Does this mean it just can't be resold, or does it mean it can't be resold with a different cover, other than the cover it was first published in?

You see I've written in, and on, the covers. I thought I had it covered.

I'm 'out there'

The Goddess Lisatrace has virtues of compassion, resistance, persistence and holy negotia... hang on... I'm not so sure where I'm going with this. Let me get my bearings.

> **Gnostic:-** adj. [< Gr. *gnosis*, knowledge] 1. of or having knowledge; 2. [G-] of the gnostics, or gnosticism, -n. [G-] a believer in Gnosticism.
>
> **Gnosticism:-** n. a system of belief combining ideas derived from Greek philosophy, Oriental mysticism, and, ultimately, Christianity.

Now I'm on the right track. Have I got the knowledge to keep going? Carl Jung taught me a lot about Gnosticism, so I'll be testing myself, won't I? I may be testing you. My Goddess Lisatrace, is a multidimensional woman. She's multidenominational too. Of course, she's a multitasker. She's a woman!

That's a cover!

Let's see, what does she look like? She's not tall, but kind of solid. Well she would be. I'm imagining the marble statue of her. She's graceful looking, not fat, but with soft curves and a warm, friendly smile. She's standing with a blackberry in her left hand, or is it a serpent? Nah, make that an Apple i Phone with a glamorous, black glomesh cover. She has a badge of honour pinned to her left lapel. Oh, and she's in a business suit. Now I'm not sure... Should it be the skirt, or the trousers? I'm going with the skirt because she's got good legs. I'm going to go for the middle ground with the shoes. They're sensible because she gets around, but they have a medium-sized heel. She's got a decent cleavage, but decent coverage. In her right hand, she holds a large ring with many keys dangling from it. She holds the keys to all our big real estate problems. It's the bloody rent roll keys. She has her smokes hidden in her skirt pocket. She's well equipped. She's wise, and she has The Knowing. She's a Gnostic, so she sees and knows all, and she's pious. She has many pathways to the top, so she can take her pick. They all lead to the one place. She's monotheistic.

> **Pious:-** adj. [L. pius] 1. having or showing, religious devotion; 2. hypocritically virtuous.

She has a past, but she's overcome it in a brave and solitary manner. She works alone. She rose from her slavery to find her freedom. She's been oppressed and manipulated in her past life. She now wants to save other souls and guide them to the great light of Agency.

Let's shine a light on this

Agency:- [see AGENT] 1. an organization offering a particular kind of service; 2. the business or place of business of any person, firm, etc. authorized to act for another; 3. action; power 4. means.

She has the means

She wants to take them by the hand, and free them from the dark night of suppression and guilt. She'll lead them to authenticity and consoul (I get a tick for that!). She knows of the many pitfalls, but dances a fancy pirouette around them. She'll show you the dance of the Gods. She'll show you the correct way of waltzing with vendors, without treading on any toes.

THE SWEARING-IN PLEDGE TO THE GODDESS LISATRACE

1. Thou shalt not kill a sale for thy brother;
2. Thou shalt not walk in the valley of thy competition, and steal from his shepherded stock;
3. Thou shalt honour and obey thy soul for the resurrection of listings;
4. Thou shalt not bother, nor hinder thine prospect, when not invited;
5. Thy soul, shall see the goodness in another's soul;
6. Bring not evil to the table of negotiation;
7. Do not yield to riches, unless offered in holy matrimony;
8. Love thine enemy, as shown by organized and honourable battle;
9. Bravely face the wrath and weakness of such foe, as is your sustenance;
10. He who hath taken from you, taketh in hand, and pledge noble reconciliation with the divine Goddess of Real Estate;
11. Resolveth to share the bounty of men from the larynx, and not from the ego;

12. Worship in sorrow, and also in exalted gratitude, the Goddess of Real Estate and the providence bestowed from her mercenary soul.

Is this okay? Did it touch something in you? It's my first time. The first time's always the hardest, but you can always learn from experience. I haven't been a goddess long, just a day.

I'm an aphrodisiac talking, virginal Goddess of Real Estate, with love in my heart and a Gnostic's freedom of speech. I pledge my soul to save the unenlightened. Your CPD points will never be the same again.

CPD. Continued Professional Development

Criminal Programming Day, Cursing People Dealings, Crook Professional Dosing, Crime Pays Development, Conditional Property Ditching, Crediting Personal Deliberations, Copying Pathological Damage, Capital Punishment Duty, Clever Pompous Dribble, Claiming Pathetic Decimals, Collecting Preening Dopes, Cramming Putrid Diatribe, Controlling Petulant Dealers, Crazy Preschool Dummies, Classic Preventative Dynamics, Constant Poop Droning, Crappy Pontificating Dialogue, Credibility Proving Dysentery.

The list is getting too long, but I wanted to describe what goes on when we attend these training sessions for our twelve points per year. People get paid. That's it! The trainers get paid. Does anyone learn anything other than how to avoid litigation? No. You only learn how to avoid being blamed. You learn about new rules. You don't learn good rules, or fair rules. You learn the rules of the game, and how to play them shrewdly. You learn how not to get caught out.

Pre-schoolers are noisy

You get to listen to how our biggest mouths play the game. They love standing up in these training sessions to captivate you all with their inspiring words. I'm sure the trainers love them too. They love having you there to listen to their boring stories, of who did what, and why should I, and what happens when. They love hearing themselves talk, and prolonging the life of the party. Why do they think we're all vendors? We're the agents dopey! Stop preaching to the enlightened ones.

I rejected those training sessions and did my CPD points online. It's a no-brainer. I don't know who makes up this shit, because these comprehension tests are absolutely ridiculous. They're Constant Poop Droning. I'll give you an example of the kind of typical scenario they feed you. Apparently we're meant to learn something about our real estate industry.

Risk analysis

Betty trips over an electrical cord in the office. What should Betty have done? What precautions should have been taken prior to Betty tripping over the electrical cord? How could you prevent Betty falling again? What preventions could you have in place in the future, so that John won't fall either? Make a list of all the preventative solutions for your office so that John and Betty don't hurt themselves.

It's always about signage

It's written for pre-schoolers, because we are pre-schoolers. What happens if you aren't a pre-schooler? If Betty and John weren't pre-schoolers, they wouldn't feel the need to trip over the electrical cord, and nobody would have to do CPD (Crazy Preschool Dummies) points. This is the point I'm making. It's one of my points of no return. I've finished with the pre-school. My pre-school days are over.

> **Pledge:-** n. [? < OS. *plegan*, to guarantee] 1. a promise or agreement; 2. the condition of being given or held as security for a contract, payment, etc.; 3. a person or thing given or held as such security; 4. a token; 5. the drinking of a toast; 6. something promised, esp.

> money -vt. pledged, pledg'ing 1. to promise to give; 2. to bind by a promise; 3. to present as security; 4. to drink a toast to - take the pledge to vow not to drink alcohol -pledge'er n.

I'm not sure about number twelve of The Swearing in Pledge of the Goddess Lisatrace. It's my mercenary soul that I'm concerned about.

> **Mercenary:-** adj [< L. *merces*, wages] 1. working or done for payment only; 2. designating a soldier serving for pay in a foreign army -n., pl. -naries, a mercenary soldier -mer'ce-narily, adv.

I have an idea. If I'm mercenary, then I could get all my foot soldiers (all my fellow real estate agents), to pledge a donation to the cause. This could be a fund for the disadvantaged souls. It could help rebuild the souls of our fallen comrades. Throw me a donation. Throw the Goddess a gold medallion and we shall have a cause to support. We'll support the fallen. We can support our comrades that have fallen in the line of duty. We know who they are.

A license to print money

Is it a health fund the Goddess is talking about? Are you getting the mental picture? Let's see it on Facebook. The Goddess knows of one such face, and has wept for it. She knows the honour of a battle well matched, and she believes in putting her hand out to the enemy. Competition has its good side too.

I'm thinking of a Tree in his honour, with a Set of Allen keys for opening up the office of ill repute.

My office was reputed to be ill, but it wasn't. My real estate license is in perfect order, and this is what I'm using it for. It's poetic license now. It's to be used in the art of war.

All is fair in love and war. It's not a war to be fought in the open. This is a fair and just cause.

> **Comrade:-** n. [< Sp. *camarada*, roommate < L. camera] 1. a friend, close companion; 2. an associate; 3. a fellow-member of

a political party, esp. a fellow communist or socialist -com'-radely adj. -com'radship' n.

Now, what else do I need? What do you need? You need respect. This respect I speak of, needs some contemplation. I shall commune with the great goddess and find the answer I'm looking for. It needs to be a soul-saving respect. When was I respected? She said there's no getting out of it, that I must first consider the respect I've shown others. This sounds like karmic logic to me. This might hurt a bit.

> **Respect:-** vt. [< L. *re-*, back + *specere*, look at] 1. to hold in high regard, show honour or courtesy to; 2. to show consideration for [respect others' privacy] -n. 1. high regard, esteem; 2. deference or dutiful regard [respect for law]; 3. courteous consideration; 4. a point or detail, [right in every respect]; 5. reference; relation [with respect to this]; 6. [pl.] courteous expressions of regard: chiefly in, pay one's respects, to show polite regard as by visiting and, pay one's last respects, to attend someone's funeral.

Did I wipe my feet?

I understand respect. This shouldn't sound as good as it does. I know when I haven't respected others. I know when I've been disrespectful of another's privacy and rights. What made me disrespect these people? Was it the chicken or the egg? Was it the rules? What inspires respect in me? Is it the correct standard to apply, and where did I get my standards from? Are our standards disrespectful? Are our industry standards disrespectful?

Getting my comeuppance

Let's jump over the fence and see. Hindsight is a dirty word. Don't look at my behind!

I'm going to get some, aren't I? Will I be a tenant? I'll surely be a tenant by the way things are looking right now. Karma is right on my tale (leave spelling). I'll be back riding by the seat of my pants. Where are all my tenants?

ATTENTION: ALL PAST TENANTS

I, Vanilla Extract, hereby give notice of my impending tenanthood. This is my statutory declaration of apology to all the parts I missed.

I wish to acknowledge any wrongdoing on my part, while at your part, or at any time, before we parted. I'm sorry for any parting words, when you departed. I'm sorry for the bad part I might have had, in making your part worse.

Now that we're apart, I can see where I'd parted from the right part. I should have taken the right part all the time, but I couldn't see a way apart, from the part I took. It's all a part of it. There were too many parts to it. This isn't a parting excuse, but it's a better part to play.

I part now with my strongest and most sincere apologies, for taking away any good part in your part. This is said in part, for some, and in whole part, for others.

The other parts working under me weren't always seen by me, when they were doing their part, so it might not have come from my part, in it. All parts are to blame though. It's a shame it fell apart, but not my shame. My shame is only for your part in it.

I hope you can take some parting pleasure in knowing that I too, will now have to play a part like you. I'll no doubt be up against you, in getting a part. I have no past to rely on, so I probably won't get a good part. It might be a slow start.

I'll be reminded of the part I took now. I'll be reminded of you as I hunt for a little part somewhere to live in. I'll have to keep my little part tidy, and keep my part of the bargain with the main party.

As we part now, and before I depart, I'm sorry for any disrespect on my part. This is *The Worker in Me*, but there are other books, and I will remember the part you took, if you've played a part in my story. It might have just been a small part, but I remember most parts, no matter how small or insignificant. Small and insignificant is my part now. I've been parted with all that was big and significant.

Yours truly, and sorrily, for the bad parts

Were my standards a learned behaviour, or did I create my own standards? Whose standards did I adopt as my own? Did I ever lower my standards? I did.

I tried to, so many times. What happens when you start to lower your standards? What can be perceived by others? Does it affect their standards? Can it take away their respect, or give it back to them?

This is a double-sided tape. It's a double standard. It can stick on either side. Is lowering your standards seen as weakness or compassion? Can weakness be taken advantage of? Can compassion? Where's the advantage? Should the disadvantaged get the advantage? To what advantage?

Give an inch, and they'll take a mile

Standards are very important in relationships. They pertain to values and principles for living. If you have differing standards from your close circle of friends, can you be circled out? Is it likely to change the circle? When you don't want the circle changed, do you reinforce your standards with their differing standards? When standards are in question, all standards are weakened.

Should someone else's standards affect your own standards? Yes, but only when you know they're the right standards. Keep the right standards close. Your standards can be threatened by another's standards, particularly when you don't understand the importance of your own standards.

A stand can be 'ard' sometimes

It's like politics. If you're particularly interested in it, and vehement about the policies you support, your standards will be hard to shift. They'll be rigid standards if you're vehement.

> **Vehement:-** adj. [< L. *vehemens*, eager] full of or showing very strong feeling; intense, fervent, impassioned, etc.

Do we celebrate vehemence these days? Do we celebrate the greats who fought for what they believed in? The brilliant farsighted people with clear vision, strong resolve, and the determination to see change, are fast disappearing. Where are they going? Where did they go? Are they there all the while, but we're the ones with short-sighted vision? Can't we see them in the distance?

Where's my glasses?

This is the way of change, isn't it? We need the fanatics to stir up chaos, so that we'll take notice and consider. Once they have the attention of the people, there can be understanding. Once there's understanding, there can be change. So many great campaigns have been waged in pursuit of change. Much has been good change, but ultimately, it's been brought about by the voice of the people. Was it your voice?

Are you the voice of change?

What change has your voice brought about? Has your voice done any determined resolving? Have you got resolve? Will you resolve to do better, and allow your voice to make change? Will your voice change? My voice has changed. There's a voice inside me that wants change, and I'll be voicing whatever it wants. I have a free voice. We're all free with our voices. We can say whatever we like, can't we?

Will my voice be shut down?

Can our voices be censured by the law? I must look into this, because I'm pretty sure swearing in public is illegal, and you can get into trouble with the police for doing it. I'm pretty sure my swearing is an art form. I've sworn in my books, so it's of literary merit.

Getting to the common senses of people

It's about getting in front of the eyes of people. It's also about getting inside the ears of people. It's about getting up the noses of people, and putting a bad taste in their mouth. This is what people will notice. They won't like it, but all their senses will be alerted to something not right. Once a bad taste is in their mouth, they'll spit it out and voice their concerns.

Inspiring talk

How do you get the attention of the people? You do something radical so that it's noticed. Do you do something out of the ordinary, so that people notice non-ordinary?

To get the people talking and discussing the issues, you must do something extraordinary. You must get into their psyche and affect their conscience. You need to activate their consciences to get things changed. What you're aiming for, is a collective conscience.

Don't just talk about it

You can't do it by talking. You must do it by showing. You'll need to get people talking to each other. Once the issue gets some circulation, more people will jump on board. It gathers speed, power, and momentum. We watch the issue enlarge as more people get into it. The issue gets bigger, as more people gather around it. Once it's a decent-sized issue, it starts to get noticed by more important people.

This is an important issue

These aren't more important people, but they're people that want to look important. They get more important just by turning up to important issues. They jump on the bandwagon and start playing in the band. They usually take a leading role in the band, and this helps the band to get noticed even more. The more important the important person is, with the issue, the more people will get excited. They're excited that it's now become an important issue for everyone.

Is the top brass interested?

Finally, the top brass get interested, and wonder whether the issue is now worth changing. They work out what is wanted by the majority, and get to fix the issue in front of masses of people. This is what they wait for. They wait for a full audience before they use their energies on something big. This is how they get their brass. This is how they keep their brass shiny.

Mass action is a peaceful form of channelling the anger of people. Nelson Mandela (known by his countrymen and women, as Madiba).

I have a protest

We don't protest enough! That's a fat lie. We have too many protesters. These are isolated protests, and petty protests. These are unworthy protests. We are trivial protesters. We protest about trivial things. We protest about things that aren't worth protesting about. We protest about irritations and silly concerns. They aren't really concerns. We shouldn't be concerned with silly protests.

Don't waste energy

We protest when we buy an out-of-date jar of mayonnaise at the supermarket. We make a huge song and dance about it, tell our friends and family, boycott the shop, harass the shop assistant, and bad-mouth the business. We carry on about it for ages. All this energy is wasted on approximately four dollars. We take the item back, get a replacement, insist on an apology and still, we keep up the protest. We'll remember the protest until we have another protest to take its place.

Why protest? Are we that angry about the mayonnaise? Did we miss eating potato salad that evening?

A timely experiment

1. Empty out the out-of-date mayonnaise from the jar, and rinse the jar under hot running water.
2. Look closely inside the jar to see how much volume it can hold.
3. Measure out the energy expended during this common protest.
4. Put it all in the jar.
5. Imagine the protesting energy expended from this one trivial protest, and consider how long it lasted.
6. Put four dollars in the jar.
7. Pack a suitcase for a week, and pack the jar in the suitcase.
8. Get on a flight to any of the many war-torn, famine-affected, or Third World countries.
9. Once you've arrived, get on your soap box in front of the crowd of desperate refugees. Explain to them your plight in a loud voice.
10. Hold the jar out to them, and show them what you've suffered. Tell them about the potato salad you wanted to make. Don't forget to tell them not to shop at that store.

To jar or not to jar

Will you gain the support of the people? Did you gain the support of the people back at home? Did they support you 100%? Do you feel the need for a real protest now? Is there a need for a real-life protest? How much support could you garner for a real-life protest? Is it worth protesting about? Are lives worth protesting about? Is the life of the mayonnaise worth protesting about?

What's worth a protest?

Did you bring the jar back with you? Don't open the jar. Keep all the energy, and the four dollars inside. You have a protest on your hands now, and it's about time you protested where it counts, because it really counts. Go around to every petty protester, and gather up all their jars with their four dollar notes.

Give them to charity

Give them to an overseas charity for the people who really are suffering. They won't ever get to taste potato salad, but they may get a meal of rice out of it. They'll know real happiness from it. You can bet your four dollars that there won't be a protest if the rice is out-of-date.

Are we out-of-date, or out of line?

We're refugees in this country. All of us are. We're misplaced persons. We've misplaced our persons. We live in a world of our own making. We make it too small. We can't fit anything but ourselves in it. We can't see past our own noses, or in this case, mouths. We have big mouths and small brains. Can we see how trivial our lives have become? Can we see how trivial, our protests?

Broaden your horizons

Let's get worldly with our protests. Think big! Think about the others. Think about what you do, and what you say. Think. Think about a decent protest, and gather as many small-time protesters as you can. Get massive. Get that jar out, and pass it around at your next family gathering, at your next celebration, or dinner party. Take it to work with you. People won't mind adding their four bucks to the cause. Tell them it's an experiment. Tell them you're doing a study on mayonnaise. They probably didn't like your potato salad anyway. They might agree that you should do more experimenting with it.

Make a rice salad

Get them to put their mayonnaise worth in, and you can send it to the suffering people. There's plenty to choose from.

Suffering people I mean. There are millions of them. Pluck a ticket out of a hat. You'll need a big hat. Get some other hats to help you. Market your protest. It's the Mayonnaise Fund. Get up to date. Get sophisticated and advertise how important the protest is. Tell them you're important. Tell everyone you're important. Tell everyone they're important. This is an important protest, so it needs important people. It's important. It's a worthy protest.

This is my new hat

I'm wearing a new hat. I'm wearing the hat of a big protester. It's a bit big for me right now, but I'll grow into it. I've found a really big hat to wear, because I want to pass it around from time to time.

Every book's a protest

I want to pass it around every time, just to get up your nose. I'll be in your ear, and I'm sure to get in your mouth too. I might take it out of your mouth, and put it into a hungrier mouth. I won't need to get in front of your eyes, because that might be a waste of time.

You are blind

We're all blind. We have blinkers on like a horse wears, so it doesn't get spooked. We don't want to see past our own hay bale. Our hay bale is the only one we can see.

I want to make hay while the sun shines

When my grandfather was alive, I used to ask him "how are you Pop?" I used to love asking this question of him. It's the first question I'd ask, because I always loved his answer. I was always ready and waiting for it, because I knew it would make me feel good. He'd answer with great sentiment, and with a gravity that was heartfelt. He'd respond with, "I've never seen the sun shine brighter". He meant it. He meant it at that moment, upon talking to me. I knew it, and I knew I had made the sun shine brighter for him. I'd made the sun shine brighter for him, and he'd made the sun shine brighter for me.

Just one word

I loved making the sun shine brighter. How hard is it? It's not hard to make the sun shine brighter for someone. It's not hard to make the sun shine brighter for a lot of people. How many people do you think one person can make the sun shine brighter for?

To make the sun shine the brightest, it's best to take it to the darkest places. It will light up so much brighter when it shines out of the darkness. This is the light I want to cast. I'm casting it now, and I hope you're getting warmed by it.

Horsing around

A man on a horse rides casually into town. He's a stranger, and the town's people come out to see who goes there. They watch as he makes his way up the main street, and towards the saloon. They watch him dismount and tether his horse out front. He has a slow and steady way about him, and the town's people are mesmerized. They watch on, as he walks around to the back of his horse and raises its tail. Not caring who might be watching, he leans in, and plants a big lingering kiss fair on his horse's arse.

The sudden intake of breath, spluttering of disgust, and coughs of disapproval, reverberate down the main street. The town's people are stunned. There's faces grimacing at the saloon windows, as the watchers are suddenly taken aback by this stranger's intimate act with his horse.

All is silent, except for the sound of the stranger's spurs as he ascends the steps, and pushes through the saloon doors approaching the bar with an air of confidence. With a slow and steady drawl, he requests a neat whisky. He swigs the whisky straight down, without a drop touching his lips.

The barman can't help himself, as barmen can't, and says to the odd stranger. "Mate, why in the blazes did you just kiss your horse's arse?"

The stranger takes his time, and raises his head to face the barman with the look of the wise and knowing. He raises a finger to his lips, and in a gingerly fashion, he says to the barman, "Chapped lips!"

"What do you mean 'chapped lips'?" quizzes the barman, completely perplexed with the queer response.

The stranger directs his gaze at the barman once again, answering the question with a pertinent question of his own "Well mate, would you lick your lips, if you just kissed your horse's arse?"

Can girls tell jokes?

This was a classic old joke that I used to love telling. It was part of my repertoire of jokes that I told at parties and such. I told them well, and people thought they were funny, but not always. Can girls tell jokes? This isn't the question I'm asking, because I know that they can. Some of the funniest people I've ever known, are girls.

What I'm really asking is... Do men approve of girls telling jokes? Do men like funny girls? I'll change this a bit, because I've grown up. Do men like funny women? Do men like funny women, or is it strange and unseemly? Is it unladylike? I'm asking a lot of questions, because I think I want a modern and up-to-date answer.

Will you pay me lip service?

I know men have enjoyed my jokes in the past, because they've laughed. I'm pretty sure less men than women, liked my jokes. It wasn't the jokes. It was more to do with who was telling them. Is telling jokes, a blokey thing to do? Are jokes just for blokes?

It's for the birds

Does it have anything to do with whether the jokes are rude or not? I didn't tell rude jokes in mixed company. I only felt comfortable telling dirty jokes in women's company. Women can sometimes be the dirtiest company, when it comes to being funny. We're more comfortable with our own gender when telling dirty jokes or stories, and I think this is the same for men too. I think it can be too personal between men and women. It's personal because it can be seen to be a reflection. Is it our morals being reflected to the opposite gender? Will assumptions be made? What are we advertising? Is it sort of like 'wearing your heart on your sleeve'? Would it be like 'wearing your sex on your dress', and does it advertise that you're liberated? How liberated is telling a joke these days?

> **Liberate:-** [< L. *liber*, free] to release from slavery, enemy occupation, etc.

Are women really liberated? Are we free to advertise how free we are? I could pop up on my horse here, so hold on to the reins for me, while I get comfortable in the saddle. It's not a comfortable saddle, so I don't want to be sitting on it too long. Sitting on this saddle for too long, gives me saddle sores. Should I be riding side-saddle?

I don't think side-saddle is a very balanced way of riding a high horse. A straddle is much more balanced, and it's safer. It's putting your arse in the middle ground. This is what being liberated means for a woman. It just means balance. The weight is equal. You can't fall off as easily when you have a leg either side.

Is straddling your mount ladylike? I'm a lady, but I know what I like. I just want to know what the horse likes. Is a horse more balanced with someone astride it? Is it comfortable for the horse?

Can you lead a horse to water?

I'm not sure about this heading, and I'm not sure how the rest of the saying goes. I think it's something about not being able to make the horse drink. I don't know too much about horses, but I'm on my high horse now and it's a long way down, so I'll tell you what I do know.

There are horses for courses. Horse flies hurt when they bite. Have you ever heard of a talking horse?

> Ride a cock-horse to Banbury Cross
> To see a fine lady upon a white horse;
> With rings on her fingers and bells on her toes,
> She shall have music wherever she goes.

Here comes Brumby Jack, bringing the horses down the track. See him come as he wheels them around. He keeps them together safe and sound.

It's just me horsing around. Can you read 'horse'? Yes, or nay?

I think that's all I know about that

It's not! It's not all I know, but I'm uncomfortable thinking about this next subject. It's triggered some memories, and some pain. It's climbing to the surface now, so I'll let it climb up onto these pages and then they'll be right up where I can see them. I'm not keen on horses. It's not that I don't like them. They haven't got brakes, for starters.

> There was movement at the station,
> for the word had passed around
> That the colt from old Regret had got away,
> And had joined the wild bush horses
> – he was worth a thousand pound,
> So all the cracks had gathered to the fray.
> All the tried and noted riders from stations near and far,
> Had mustered at the homestead overnight,

> For the bushmen love hard riding,
> where the wild bush horses are,
> And the stock-horse snuffs the battle with delight.
>
> This is from *The Man from Snowy River*
> **by Banjo Paterson.**

It was a poem that I heard recited by my mother on numerous occasions, as I was growing up. She learnt it off by heart as a girl, for her father. He promised her a sum of money if she could learn it, and she did. He never paid her the money. I paid for it. I paid for it every time she recited it, because it was usually when she was drunk. I thought she was amazing remembering all the words to this poem.

Moving on at a canter

I rode a horse from early dawn until dusk for a few consecutive days, when I was nineteen years old. It was on a cattle station in North West Queensland. We were mustering cattle. We mustered all kinds, Hereford cattle, and Brahman cattle. They're the only kinds I can remember, but I remember the Brahman cattle weren't kind. They were wild and angry bastards.

This was the classic 'city girl comes to the bush', kind of story. It lasted a week. I lasted a week. I was bruised, sore, dirty, exhausted, and culture-shocked, from rounding up stock. I was not stock standard for out there in the bush. It was a huge property, and it was rough and hard going. I loved it! I loved what I'd learned, and I appreciated the opportunity of experiencing it. It was, and still is, one of the most important experiences of my life.

These are the experiences that you never forget. I wasn't a horse rider, but I got the hang of it quickly, because I had to. I galloped up ravines and down steep gullies, as the cattle stampeded for water. I was terrified half the time. The great horns of Hereford bulls, just inches from my legs as I moved with the mob.

I'm still most grateful to the people who invited us for that stay. They made us very welcome, and I still remember the stories and the history of their pioneering family. We drank billy tea from the muddy river and sat around camp fires. We went to an outback rodeo, sang songs in the evening on the verandah, and sensed the utter wildness of outback life. I was wild in those days.

I know what saddle sores are. After three days of mustering, I could barely walk. I couldn't straighten my legs, and I could barely sit down. I felt sorry for my horse too, because it was almost twenty years old. Its name was Firefly. This is what I remember about horses, but I'm really remembering some good times had. I'm remembering that there were good times, and it hurts. It hurts to admit it. It hurts to know the truth of it. It was in the beginning.

> **Liberal:-** adj. [L. *liber*, free] 1. favouring reform or progress, specif., favouring political reforms; 2. broadminded; 3. giving freely, generous; 4. ample, abundant; 5. not restricted to the literal meaning -n. 1. a person favouring reform; 2. [L-] a member of a Liberal Party.

This is not a political statement. I mean this literally. The definition doesn't mean it literally. I'm going to tell another joke, just to get us back on track. My horse headed for home, but I've got him back under control. He thought he was home free.

Extremely Educating

I've been enjoying some lectures on 'The Varieties of Religious Experience' By William James. I haven't been anywhere, other than my own inner sanctum. I've chosen to read what William James has to say about it all, because he was so knowledgeable in both science and religion. He was president of both the American Society of Church History and the American Catholic Historical Association. I've decided on William James, because he was a great scholar in the fields of chemistry, anatomy, physiology, philosophy and psychology, with an MD from Harvard where he was assistant professor. He's also got some great connections, because his brother was the famous author Henry James.

I'm not going to start lecturing, or name dropping, because I'm just a reader. I'm writing about this book, because it has many examples of religious experiences from people all over the world, and from every walk of life. Something miraculous has happened to them, and conversion has occurred. Conversion to a faith in something much bigger than themselves. A force so powerful, it leaves them rocked to their very core, and precipitates the incredible change in their lives. Some describe the experience as a kind of euphoria, madness and intensity, never imagined. So something that wasn't there, suddenly is there. Some of these experiences have happened at a time of great suffering or despair. Were you aware?

Could there be something to it all?

Have you had a sign? Do you have personal experience of phenomenon that you can't explain? Does everyone? Where do you go with phenomena? Where can we research it? How do we make sense of it? How does one make sense of it, when one doesn't believe in the unknown? Do we discuss phenomena? Do we discuss miracles? Are we game enough to discuss the supernatural? I'm about to do it, and I feel somewhat nervous about it. I'm nervous about sharing anything with you, because it might seem a bit unnatural.

> **Supernatural:-** adj. existing outside man's normal experience or the known laws of nature; specif., of or involving God or a god, or ghosts, the occult, etc. –the supernatural, supernatural beings, forces, happenings, etc.

Are we spooked by what we don't know? Would we rather not know? Would we rather know what we know, and leave it at that? You can't just start raving on to people about unnatural and supernatural occurrences that you can't explain, because people could suspect you're going nuts. They'd think you're a bit weird. It may not be you, or your fault. It maybe the occurrence itself, that's seemingly weird. Who is to say what's weird, and what's not?

Weird happens to be my fate

> **Weird:-** adj. [< OE. wyrd, fate] 1. of or suggestive of ghosts or other supernatural things; 2. [Colloq.] Strikingly odd, strange, etc. –weird'ly adv. –weird'ness n.

My dictionary appears to be fairly enlightened on this subject, and in the past six months, it's alluded to some interesting phenomena. My dictionary is unnatural, supernatural and weird, but I don't think it's mad. I think it's trying to teach me something. I'm more open to the weird and wonderful, now days.

Can weird be wonderful?

I think it must be wonderful for the scientists. I think during their discoveries, they must happen upon some weird and wonderful phenomenon. They don't have the answers either, but at least they're looking for them. They often happen upon chance discoveries, when they've been searching in another direction. They're trying to put knowledge in the place of unknowing, and all sorts of things can manifest.

All life is supernatural phenomena, until we attach our knowledge to it. Think about the birth of a baby. Is it not the most amazing phenomenon of all? New life is to wonder at. To have the recipe to create human beings, that we'll call our children, is quite miraculous. It's a miracle. To create a replica of a human being out of marble is hard enough, and a work of great beauty and art, but to create a living organism like a new-born baby child, is beyond reason. It is truly awe-inspiring, when you really think about it. We are all creators, but we do create from something.

Sex education

I'm not that good at this subject, because I forget the names of all the organs involved, but I'll give you a quick run-down on how to do it.

> "You put your right hand in. You put your right hand out. You put your right hand in, and you shake it all about."

How did we know how to do it in the first place? I wondered about this, while watching that movie *Blue Lagoon*. Those kids grew up on the island with nobody to tell them about the birds and the bees.

If Adam and Eve were given instructions by God on how to do it, what would he have said? I can't imagine him giving them picture books, like I got when I was a kid. I hardly think he would have given them a film to watch, which is what we were shown in high school. Are you thinking what I'm thinking? Would he have said, "go and watch the animals?"

The birds and the bees don't do it

Who showed the animals how to do it? I think God just left them to it. I think they just experimented, and did what felt good at the time. I bet Adam and Eve didn't know what the effect would be. I wonder how long it took them to work out the cause. Did they just credit God for their offspring? God's the original creator.

Courage under fire

Primitive people thought that fire was a magic phenomenon sent from the heavens. I still believe it is. We've just attached some knowledge to it, so that we can take ownership of it, control it, and not be frightened of it. We generally fear the unknown. Some of us face our fears, and try to know the unknown. You don't always need a science degree to acquire knowledge and understanding – however you do need courage.

Superstition:- n. [< L. *super-*, over + *stare*, to stand] 1. any belief, based on fear or ignorance, that is not in accord with the known facts or rational thought; esp., such a belief in charms, the supernatural, etc.; 2. any action or practice based on such a belief 3. such beliefs collectively –su'persti'-tious adj.

All religious denominations, whether they're Christian, Muslim, Seventh Day Adventist, Buddhist, Baptist, Lutheran, Amish, Zoroastrians, Taoism, Hari Krishna, or Hindu are superstitious. (There's shit loads of others, but I'm not a theologist or a theosophist). Are people with no beliefs, superstitious? Of course they are. They simply don't know what they don't know. If we weren't superstitious, we'd be all pushing the boundaries. We'd be risking our life and doing everything we wanted, and bugger the consequences. Often we can't be sure of the consequences. Can consequences be a known fact?

It's a soldier's life

Kids jumping off a high rocky outcrop into the water below, don't know what's underneath the surface. They can't see what's lurking down deep. They just jump off in the hope that they'll be safe. Some people haven't been safe. Some people have incurred spinal injuries jumping off that rock. Why is it okay for some, but not for others? A very superstitious person would not risk jumping off this rock, or maybe they would, if the conditions were right. Is it about belief or non-belief?

Is it about the conditions?

Are we all superstitious? Do we do little things, like check the depth, check how many people have made the jump safely, check the waves coming in, cross our fingers, say a prayer, and jump? Is this a tried and tested formula for guaranteed success? So many things can go wrong. You could slip before launching yourself clear, or a shark may be waiting in the vicinity.

We all know of deaths that shouldn't have occurred. These are deaths that have no rhyme, nor reason. We simply don't understand why they happened, and how they could have been prevented. Why? There must be a reason why, but are we so sure we want to know the real reason why, to anything on earth? We can reason things out, but what about the reason behind the reasoning? Is my reasoning getting a bit unreasonable?

Don't step on the cracks

Is this a superstitious technique? Is crossing your fingers, the same as making the sign of the cross? One is luck, and the other is a divine blessing. Is one science and the other spiritual? Do we really have the knowing of these two? Have we tried to rationalize luck, or a divine blessing? We have, but we're not getting anywhere, are we? So we're surrounded every day, by things we just don't know. They're supernatural things, and unnatural things, but they're perfectly natural. We're all perfectly natural. Whatever happens to you, could quite possibly happen to all of us, and vice versa. We may not have the same experience, and that's what makes it all so un-knowable.

The un-knowable must stay un-knowable, to be un-knowable

You simply can't know if you haven't experienced it. Just because you've experienced it, and others haven't, doesn't mean that you should deny the experience. The experience has probably happened for a reason. You're the reason. Just because we haven't found or understood the reasons behind it, doesn't mean that we must rely on someone else's opinion, to be able to rationalize it. Everyone's reasons are different, because we're all so different. Don't put the wrong label on it.

Touch wood

I guess I'm really trying to encourage you to take ownership of your experiences. Your experiences are for you, and may not be understood by others. If this is the case, then we could reason that you alone can only know the reason, and nobody else can. Your understanding and reasoning is probably as close as you'll come to understanding. Don't take on another's understanding of it, because they aren't you.

If you're wracking your brain trying to find a memory of something weird that's happened to you, and you can't seem to find any phenomena at all, you're now aware. You're in a position to recognize what you don't know, and what could be passing you by every day. This is good, because now you're open to new and wonderful phenomena. All life is a phenomenon, and our individual experiences, are meant to be our very own.

Are you seriously taking this in?

I can already hear some of your responses. It's your mind just going through the same old habits of denial, and you're shutting off to something you don't believe in. Is it fear of the unknown, causing you to react in this way? Think about it. We shut off to things we don't know. We generally shut off to things we don't want to know. Are you habitually shutting off, something that should be turned on? Flick the switch, and be open to what you don't know. Listen to others, and be open. When you're open, more information can flow in, and then you'll have something to help you reason with.

Subliminal questioning

You've probably already listened to other peoples' experiences of supernatural phenomena. If you deny it's true, why are you referring to it now? Has your mind brought something to the surface? Did something resonate for a reason? Have things just popped into your head to remind you of what others already think they know? Our brains are clever, but our habits are old, and they've mostly been taught to us as we've grown up. Get a new mind. Or better still, take proper ownership of your own mind and let it roam wherever it wants. Think whatever you want, and seek the answers for yourself. Go alone.

That's not the answer

Your mind is perfect for your life's purpose. If you're reading this now, there's a reason for it. This book has happened for a reason, because all of life has happened for a reason. Our universe has come into creation for a reason. Cause and effect is the answer. Now that's science!

Nothing happens for nothing

You can't make something from nothing. Even if you think you can conjure up wonderful things just because of an idea that's come into your head, you're wrong. That idea has come from somewhere. If you decide that you're going to create something from nothing, you can't. If you decide to make something with bits of wood, and turn it into something else, you're just changing something. If you decide to be a different person, and change things about yourself, you're just changing what's already there. You may have been inspired by somebody or something, but you've started with something, and used something else. Each of us have something in common. All is common that starts with an idea.

Where have the ideas come from? Did you create the idea from nothing? Can you take sole credit for the idea, or has it come from existing information? 'Nothing' simply can't make 'something' other than 'nothing'. Nothing + nothing = nothing. Is this physics?

Sweet nothings in your ear

All the answers must be attainable. If there's a question, it's reasonable to assume that there must be an answer. If we are questioning, then we must also be answering. Everything has its opposite. [***God***] or whoever you'd like to put in this space, has thought of everything. He's given it all to us to work out. He's given us a *Whitman's Activity Book* to keep our minds occupied with finding the answers. It's for growth. It's for spiritual reckoning.

I reckon some people have come across some answers, but it's hard to test your answers when not enough people are seeking them. I'm talking of the studies and research that scientists do, when they come across the answer and can't back it up. The way it gets substantiated is to have other scientists do their own tests, and try to prove them wrong. It's kind of like a tribunal or panel of experts. The theory must be rigorously tried and tested, before it can be celebrated as being factual. Other scientists are obliged to look for the faults and to try to prove its falseness, just in case. The original theory is positive, but it must now be processed by a negative to ascertain its authenticity.

Three strikes and you're out

Is there enough incentive for the negatives? That's just my question. Do they just apply the Law of Probability? The Law of Probability reminds me of luck. Do ratios get worked out? I mean, it would be easy, if there were only ten possible results, but what if there were hundreds? This process of elimination is fine, if you know all the elements. My education is elementary, isn't it? I don't know all the elements involved. I'm just working with what I do know. I know questions. If I know the questions, does this mean I'm waiting for the answers?

If you undo your belly button, will your bum with fall off?

I've come across some interesting material that helps me to rationalize a question I have about God. I've never been interested in dinosaurs. I know some kids just love the subject, but I've always hated it, and I still do. When I think of dinosaurs, I think of an old 60s TV program *Land of the Giants*. Anyway, I found it quite depressing. I couldn't quite get how primitive man could have existed in any great population, with a pack of dinosaurs in the vicinity. Now I'm telling you right here, that my education is rudimentary when it comes to the era of dinosaurs. I told you I wasn't much interested. Man may never have existed at the same time as the prehistoric animals. Leave my ignorance, just for a moment, and I'll continue.

I know we have fossils and such to prove their existence, but is it a story just like Greek mythology? Greek mythology goes back a long way. Anyway, I won't keep you in suspense, but I've got to tell you now, that I'm quite partial to this man's theory.

From *From Creation to Chaos, Classic Writings in Science* (edited by Bernard Dixon):

> "The ample fig leaf served our artistic forefathers well as a botanical shield against indecent exposure for Adam and Eve, our naked parents in the primeval bliss and innocence of Eden. Yet, in many ancient paintings, foliage hides more than Adam's genitalia; a wandering vine covers his navel as well. If modesty enjoined the genital shroud, a very different motive – mystery – placed a plant over his belly. In a theological debate more portentous than the old argument about angels on pinheads, many earnest people of faith had wondered whether Adam had a navel.
>
> He was, after all, not born of a woman and required no remnant of his non-existent umbilical cord. Yet, in creating a prototype, would not god make his first man like all the rest to follow? Would god, in other words, not create with the appearance of pre-existence?"

I'm coming to the dinosaur bit now

"This argument, so often cited as a premier example of reason at its most perfectly and preciously ridiculous, was most seriously and comprehensively set forth by the British naturalist Philip Henry Gosse in 1857. Gosse paid proper homage to the historical context of his argument in choosing a title for his volume. He named it *Omphalos* (Greek for navel), in Adam's honour, and added as a subtitle: *An Attempt to Untie the Geological Knot*.

Since Omphalos is such spectacular nonsense, readers may rightly ask why I choose to discuss it at all. I do so, first of all, because its author was such a serious and fascinating man, not a hopeless crank or malcontent. Any honest passion merits our attention, if only for the oldest of stated reasons – Terence's celebrated *Homo sum: humani nihil a me alienum puto* (I am human, and am therefore indifferent to nothing done by humans).

To understand Omphalos, we must begin with a paradox. The argument that strata and fossils were created all at once with the earth, and only present an illusion of elapsed time, might be easier to appreciate if its author had been an urban armchair theologian with no feeling or affection for nature's works. But how could a keen naturalist, who had spent days, nay months, on geological excursions, and who had studied fossils hour after hour, learning their distinctions and memorizing their names, possibly be content with the prospect that these objects of his devoted attention had never existed – were, indeed, a kind of grand joke perpetrated upon us by the Lord of All?"

Adam was created already an adult

I won't go on with the detail outlined in this most interesting book, but the gist of it is, where could God have started? You can't start with nothing. We create illusions for ourselves so that we can live happy lives. We paint nice pictures to live in and this helps us to feel secure. When we don't have the answer, we just make one up. We usually pick a nice one. It doesn't matter if it's correct or not, it just helps us to get along.

Dinosaurs are not mentioned in the Bible. I've always wondered about this. Did God start off with Adam and Eve, and just paint the illusion of a past? Was Charles Darwin sent on a wild goose chase?

There's one other idea that I've come up with on my own, and that is, where are all the stories? My archaeologist's hat doesn't fit me, but I wonder if prehistoric man is fossilized too, and if so, do any of the fossils show signs of man being eaten by dinosaurs? I know this is lame, but what about rock paintings? The aboriginal people have ancient rock art, and old stories that are passed down. I've seen aboriginal rock art, and some of it looks pretty supernatural. It's weird, isn't it? It's a hell of a theory, but who can disprove it?

I like the sound of this Gosse fellow's theory. I like the idea of God crossing all his T's and dotting his I's. We need history, to learn about the present, and the future. God didn't want to throw us in the deep end, and hold back the answers. God has provided Adam, so he must provide Adam's background. Now I've got you confused. I'm mixing science with theology. I just reckon that if it's questioned, then there must be an answer. Why do we have science in the first place, if not to work things out?

Is it pocket-money?

Is the money I'm going to get when I leave the Hoorah, pocket money? I won't be putting it in the bank, because I haven't got an account. I could put it under my mattress, but I won't have my mattress to hide it under. Even if I did, I know it wouldn't be safe. Does everyone look under a mattress for valuables? I keep valuables under my mattress. They'll never be stolen. They're for personal use only, but they're very valuable. Do you hide things under your mattress?

What's a bed for?

A bed is where we retire to at the end of the evening. It's where we can stretch out and relax our bodies. It's a place to luxuriate in peace, and a place for dreaming. It can be a place for worrying. A bed should be used to get comfortable, and be comfortable. A bed is where we rest our brains and stimulate our bodies. It shouldn't be a place to worry. Our brains are being used all day long, as are our bodies. A bed is for pleasurable pursuits. If you're in bed with someone, the pursuit is over. Work and worry should be over too. Why go to bed to work? We should go to bed to play.

A bed is a playpen for adults

A single bed can be a lonely place for one adult. A double is for young adults in training. A queen is for married adults. A king-size bed is for when the marriage is over. A king-size bed is for keeping away from each other. It's a bed that two people can sleep in, without touching. It's too big for intimacy. A king-size bed is a bed to end all pillow talk.

An intimate bed

Intimacy is touching, even when you don't feel like it. It's an apology. It's a kick in the back, by accident. It's hearing the breathing of your partner, and smelling your partner. It's being able to tell your partner that they stink. It's curling up to one another to keep warm. It's waking up from sleep to find security in awake. It's not being alone in the dark. It's mostly about being wide awake to each other. It's wanting to be awakened from sleep, if the other is awake too. That's why couples sleep together. It's to go to sleep together, and to wake up together. If you both get this schedule out of balance, beware of the rest of the balances.

> **Wake:-** vi. woke, wok'en or, occas. woke, wak'ing [< OE. *wacian*, be awake & *wacan*, arise] 1. to come out of sleep (often with up); 2. to be or stay awake; 3. to become active again (often with up); 4. to become alert (to a danger, etc.) -vt. 1. to cause to wake from or as from sleep (often with up); 2. to arouse or excite (passions, etc.) -n. 1. an all night vigil over a corpse before burial; 2. [usually pl.] [N Eng. Dial.] an annual holiday.

Wake:- n. [ON. *vok*, hole in the ice] 1. the track left in the water by a moving ship; 2. any track left behind – in the wake of, following close behind.

My king size bed was a wake and I'm now doing the after math.

The Lion King

What does it feel like when you wake up alone in mid-life, in a king-size bed? It's feels like emptiness. It feels like too much emptiness. It's waking up to wide open spaces. It's a trip. It's a harsh awakening. It's the harsh reality of daylight. Is it just the circle of life?

It's never the same again. It's a bed to be rid of. It's too big to fill. How do you fill all the surplus space? I don't want to have to dilute anything in it ever again. I bought this bed. I can't call it our bed anymore. It was never our bed, it was my bed. I spent more time in it, resting and reading. This bed was my sanctuary. It was my safe nest, but only with just me in it. It's a nest that I collected for, and decorated. I made it, and clothed it. Beds have clothes. My bed was always clothed, it was never naked. I made this nest look nice. I wanted it to look inviting. I put expensive sheets on it, and continued to update it. I made this lovely nest. What the hell was I building?

How are nests built?

They have to have a base, and a strong support. They're moulded by our bodies into the shape we need. We leave imprints in them. Imprints are evidence of a good relationship or a bad one. I was embarrassed by the imprints in my bed. They were very far apart. I wanted there to be a big hollow in the middle. I was always cold. I wondered at my coldness. Was it bad circulation, or not enough warmth? Why couldn't I keep warm?

Good rules for nests

They need to be cosy and soft to keep in the warmth. They need to be kept fresh and clean. There are a lot of different nest building materials around, and you have to pick out what suits your nest and your needs. I like a certain style of nest. I'm fussy about my nest. I wanted it to be luxurious. I'm a sensual being, and I love to feel things against my skin. I'm into skin and touch. That's the Taurus in me. There are so many great Manchester stores to satisfy the nest-maker in you. I love Manchester and always have. I love looking at the catalogues and admiring the bedroom suites and accompanying apparel.

I'm stuck on this word Manchester, and I don't know why. My computer is okay with the spelling, and doesn't display the red wiggly line underneath it, although it is insisting on a capital 'm'. I've looked it up in the dictionary but it's not there. It might be a sign.

> **Man:-** n., pl. men (men) [OE. *mann*] 1. an adult male human being; 2. a human being, person; 3. the human race, mankind; 4. an adult male servant, employee, etc.; 5. a husband or a lover; 6. any of the pieces used in chess, draughts, etc.; 7. [Colloq.] fellow; chap –vt. manned, man'ning 1. to furnish with men for work, defence etc. [to man a ship]; 2. to take assigned places in or at [man the guns!] –adj. male –as a (or one) man in unison – he is your man, he can accommodate you, - to a man, with no one as an exception.
>
> **Chest:-** n. [< Gr. *kiste*, box] 1. a) the part of the body enclosed by the ribs b) the outside front of this; 2. a box with a lid and, often, a lock; 3. same as, chest of drawers; 4. a cabinet for medicines, etc. –get (something) off one's chest [Colloq.] to unburden oneself of (some trouble, etc.) by talking about it.

Why did I have such a love for Manchester? Is this why I had to substitute 'Man' and 'Chest'? Was Manchester a substitute? My dictionary knows me.

Guarding your nest

Other birds get ideas from your nest. They want to try out your nest. They decide that your nest is best, and they want to take over your nest. Sometimes birds take over other birds' nests. This is what can happen when you don't guard your nest. You fly off to get things to line your nest with, and find that when you get back, you have an empty nest.

My little birds no longer come into my nest to get warm. They're busy building their own nests. I think it's time for me to abandon my nest. I'm an empty nester. I might have to take my nest on the road. I might have to build a smaller nest, or look for an abandoned nest. I might have to fight over my own nest first. Possession is nine-tenths of the law. What is the other tenth? Is that tenth, breaking the law? Who takes possession, if you haven't paid the down-payments on the nest? I think my nesting days are almost over.

Who gets the nest of tables?

I was never any good at my times tables. Are there three tables in a nest? I need to table my possessions. Have my possessions already been tabled? There were six tables in my Hoorah, and I think that's a double nest of tables. These tables are nesting at my little birds' nest, way off in the forest.

Tabling is a hard job for me

I have too many possessions to add up. I don't want the possessions anymore. They're possessed. They have bad energies attached to them. I don't want any of the bad energies attached to me. I want to find some good energy to attach to me. I want to have some good energy to take to my new nest.

How big should a one-person nest be? Should I get a single nest? Should I have hope, and get a double nest? Should I leave some space for a hopeful nest, or a listless rest? I'm a bit depressed. It's not been assessed, and I haven't been blessed. It could be a test. Could it take a guest? Where would my nest take them?

I dream of an energetic nest. If I can't have this, I can use my own energy. This could be wasting my energy. I'm all out of energy, but I still have long life energy. I must remember the possessions under my nest. There's only positive energy there.

They're the only possessions I require. They have positive energy for a positive result. This is keeping me positive, in a negative world.

Am I as positive as I feel?

I'm positive I can share this energy with someone as positive as me. Positivity is the key to negativity. Opposites attract. Is this a positive statement? Stating something is positive isn't enough to make it positive. Positive is a plus not a minus. Will my minuses deflect a positive arrival?

I am minus many things now. Will this leave me out in the cold? Can a negative attract a positive guest? Every thing's been negative. I negate that I've been the cause. For every cause, there's an effect. I am the effect. I am the last special effect. I want to have an effect on the causes to my effects. Effects are also possessions. These will not be my effects anymore. I'll have to find something more effective. I have one big effect that I've been saving. It's the largest effect I've ever possessed. They're in my possession and will need to be in yours, for full effect.

It's the Trinity

I'll have to consider the effects of it first. I don't know whether it'll be a positive effect or a negative effect. It will affect some more than others.

Have I got the gift?

Have you got the gift of the gab? It's been said, that you must have this gift to be a gifted real estate agent. The best-known rule in our real estate industry is to use our ears and our mouth, to the proportion that we have them. We have two ears and only one mouth, so it stands to reason, that the reason for this is to tell us to listen more than we talk. What happens if our mouths are bigger than our two ears put together?

> **Gab:-** [< ON. Gabba, mock] [Colloq.] to talk idly; chatter –n. [Colloq.] idle talk – gift of the gab [Colloq.] the ability to speak glibly.

> **Glib:-** [< or akin to Du. glibberig, slippery] speaking or spoken in a smooth, fluent manner, often too smooth and easy, to be convincing.

How glib is your gab?

You can learn how to be a good real estate agent by reading the dictionary. Learning to be a good real estate agent is learning how to use words. Words are your greatest tool. The written word and the spoken word are your tools in trade. If you're not good at making words work for you, you'll have to learn the hard way. The hard way is not my way.

I shall be your Maker

This is *The Teacher in Me*. It's not written yet, but it will be. It's been written.

I trust my dictionary

Your words will need to inspire trust. You'll first need to have trust in yourself. Trusting yourself is about knowing yourself. Do you trust me? Don't trust me, trust yourself. Ask yourself the question. Always know your limitations. That was one, right there.

No limitations

Don't promise what you can't deliver. Know what you can promise, and what you can't. These are inspiring words, but don't tell these ones to your clients. Your words must first inspire the best in you. Inspire yourself with your words. When you're inspired, it's time to inspire your clients. You must believe in your own words.

Don't perspire while you inspire, or your clients will conspire. They must trust that you have the inspiration to do what you all desire. They must be able to trust that your words are not another's words. They don't want copied words. They want your special words. If you get hired, don't get tired, or you'll be fired. It's as simple, or as hard, as that. Don't let your words get tired. If they get tired, put them back in the dictionary, and get another batch. It's good to refresh your batch regularly. You don't want to sound like a broken record. "It's got the WOW factor." Don't sell this to anyone! It's been done to death. I'll die right on the spot, if I have to read it again. I'll give you the arse for it. She's in here somewhere.

Don't run out of words

Do you know how many words there are in my *Collins Australian Dictionary*? I've just done a rough calculation and I think there would be around 40,000 words. That's just the basic words, but there's more being made every day. Get an updated dictionary and you'll have plenty of words to choose from. Think about the stories you could tell, and the new words you can try out. You'll need some patter. This is sales patter, or a spiel.

> **Patter:-** vi. [< PAT] to make or move so as to make, a patter –n. a series of quick, light taps.

This isn't the patter I mean, but you'll need this for the doors you'll want to open.

> **Patter:-** vi. [PATERNOSTER] to speak rapidly or glibly, –n. 1. glib, rapid speech, as of salesmen, comedians, etc.; 2. language peculiar to a group, class, etc.

Yep, this is what you want, and you'll need to be good at it. You'll use a language peculiar to your group and class. You're in a class of your own.

> **Spiel:-** n. [G., play] a talk or harangue, as in selling –vi. to give a spiel –spiel'-er n.

The contestants are…

Being a real estate agent is like being in a constant popularity contest. It can sometimes be a beauty contest. It can be a mathematical contest. It can be a contest of charms, and a magic contest. It can be a contest of tricks, but mostly it's a contest of sorts.

All sorts of contests have to be won, before you'll be given the business. Will they give you the business? Some really do give you the business. You'll wish you never set eyes on the business. You most often have to compete with other competitors for the business. They'll be all business, and they'll mean business. In the time that you're allocated, you'll have to win as many contests as you can.

Cheating the contest

If you cheat by trying to have other contestants disqualified, you may win the business, but you need to be undetected. You don't want the client to see you cheat for the business. He'll think that you'll cheat at his business. Don't cheat in the mathematics contest either, because the client will want to see all your workings out. If you've cheated with the mathematics contest, you'll only have to go back and confess it, when it hasn't calculated up to a sale.

Winning the contest

The only way to win all these contests is with words. You'll need many words for all these contests. You'll need a different patter for each contest. Don't keep using the same words because it'll be no contest, and you'll lose the contest altogether. You need to win the majority of contests.

The most common contest

Always claim the common ground. The more common ground you find with the client, the closer you'll both become. Don't lie about common ground, or you'll be lost on the grounds. This is quite common, and you'll look and feel a bit common, especially when you can't talk your way out of it. It's common sense, even though common sense is the least common of the senses.

You need to have a lot in common. You need to have so much in common, that you'll be commoner than any commoner. Having things in common, means you share the same things. Being in common is sharing.

> **Commoner:-** n. 1. one who is not of the nobility; 2. at some universities, a student who is not supported by a university or college scholarship.

You don't need a college scholarship or a university degree, to be a commoner. Thinking up ways of being in common with someone, is a talent. It can be finely honed with practice. You have to understand that we're all the same and all equal. We are all common.

It won't matter how different someone is to you, you'll always have common ground. It won't matter how rich or poor someone is, or how nasty, or good. It won't matter how irritating or how ugly. It just won't matter. You just need some brain matter to think about it. We all have brain matter so it all matters. Is it a matter of making things matter? Does a bear shit in the woods?

Common brain matter

You have to look for it and find it. Once you've started finding common ground with everyone you come across, you'll realize that we're really just the same. We are, all of us, just as common as the next fellow. We're all human beings, and we all share a lot in common. We all have common needs.

Don't isolate yourself from either mankind or womankind. They're both of a kind, so just be kind to both. When you have a pair to contend with, don't side with one kind. Don't side with the kind one, because you'll tip the scales. Put more work into the unkind one so that they're balanced. I must warn you that sometimes when this kind of a situation exists no amount of kindness on your part will attract kindness in the other part.

An unkindly parting

I reminisce here about a situation, wherein my hand was injured by a large man of about sixty. He was a very unkind man, and no amount of kindness on my part could rub off on him. He was a bully of a man, and don't think for one moment, that this man didn't intend to physically hurt me. Don't think kindly of him, because I know. It was my hand he almost broke, and I almost cried when he crushed it on purpose as I cordially shook his hand. I'd proffered my hand to shake his hand, as a show of kindness, but he only wanted to subdue me. This is a low act from somebody who had invited me to their home. It reminds me of that song from the 60s 'My Name is Sue'. That wasn't his name, but he'll know who I'm talking about, because he took on the name of a woman. It was a cowardly act, and I suppose you might think writing it down is a cowardly act, but it's just balancing the unkindness.

A common myth

We shouldn't feel intimidated by anyone. We shouldn't feel inferior to anyone. Everyone is just as common as everyone else. When you find out eventually that everyone is the same, no matter how educated they are, or how important they think they are, you'll see that they're just as intimidated as you. This is a battle. There will always be battles of intimidation going on. Intimidation is insecurity. If you're intimidating someone, you're insecure. If you're being intimidated by someone, you're insecure. Intimidation isn't necessary in finding common ground.

Check out if you have this in common. Check out anything you have in common because this will be your 'in'. This is something you know about in yourself, so it'll be just like talking with yourself. We are, when all is said and done, just reflections of each other. The more common you are, the more popular you'll be. This is a common fact.

Common ground is for common use

The common ground is an immense land of common traits, experiences, and personalities. The common ground is a colossal expanse of land to run around on, and to find all the opportunities you're looking for. Everyone resides on common ground with each other. We're all equal once we're on common ground. Common ground is the middle ground. It's the best grounding you can have. It's the grounds of communication. We all get grounded here together.

You must have the knowing

Good real estate agents have big mouths. They have small ears in comparison. They must know all there is to know already. They have the knowing in them. To know is to know when, where, and who. Are you listening for this information? You won't have to listen too hard for it, because you'll just need to be in hearing of it. You have to have your ear to the ground all the time. You have to be in common hearing of everyone. Everything you hear bears thinking about, so that you can use it to hear more. Hear all there is to hear, and wait for it to come back up, when the need arises.

You have to know what you're hearing

Being a successful agent is purely about how many people you know. You have to know as many people as you can. You have to know people you don't know. You have to know people. You have to know of all sorts of people. You have to know of them, and from them. These are the people that will be working for you. They'll be doing lots of the knowing for you. They'll be sending people they know, that you don't know. It's all in The Know.

You must ask them to work for you, but they must never know that they are. If they know they have, they must be paid. This is like pyramid selling, only not as complicated. The people you know, should lead to people you don't know. These are the connections that will work the furthest.

You'll need connections

Your closest connections are your furthest connections. If you've buggered up a connection, and this can happen from time to time, you must never sever the connection. You must immediately repair the connection. One broken connection can ruin too many other connections. This is what they call networking. You must keep your network intact.

Quality connections are said to be close connections, like friendly connections, or family connections, but these are the trickiest connections of all. This is where you must use all the tricks of the trade. These are the very connections you'll get lazy with. These are very expectant connections. They're also expensive, and personally sensitive, connections. Spare no expense with these special connections and all expectations will be achieved.

Just connect

You're likely to come across compromising connections. These are connections you're not supposed to be connecting with. These are connections that your other connections don't want you to be connected to. Some connections must be secret connections. You may need to sell out some connections for better connections. The best way, is to weigh up your connections. This is about rich connections and poor connections. It's also about harder connections. Harder and richer connections, don't always add up to easy cash connections, they may just mean fast and furious connections. They sure as hell aren't loyal connections. They've had too many connections too.

Always look for the money connections, and you'll be well connected. When you can no longer feel the connection to yourself, you'll know that you're doing a great job and shaping up to be a really successful real estate agent. Don't get too connected to the job. It's better to be a mediocre real estate agent. This is a good balance. The only balance that won't be that flash will be your bank balance.

What's for sale?

Being a good real estate agent is selling your soul for the job. It's just not worth your soul. It can be soul destroying. Get another job. I should have got another job a long time ago. I should have got another job, one soul ago. I don't know why I didn't. People should never have said to me back when I was studying for my license, that I wouldn't be able to do the job with two small children to care for. That's like a red rag to a bull. I'm a Taurus. I'm determined and I'm stubborn. Once I'd got stuck into it, I was stuck in it.

Did real estate feed the hunger in me?

I knew early on that it was, and is, a ruthless industry. It didn't make me feel good, nor did it make me feel secure. I believe it was my ego that kept me in the industry. My ego has always gotten me into trouble. Ego is a dirty word. Ego can make you play dirty. Your ego can make you want to stand up to everything. Ego is the mother of pride. She bosses people around. She bossed me around. She won't see that she's doing the wrong thing. My ego was in denial. An ego can inflate your head, and inflate your mouth. You must keep your ego in check, and be aware of her shortcomings. Nobody likes a big ego.

Deflate your ego

Don't boast how good you are. Show your evidence in a subtle way. Don't believe your own ego. Never, ever, believe your own ego. Egos can be bullshit artists. My ego was a bullshit artist. I mean a really talented artist. My ego was extremely artistic when it came to bullshit. If your ego starts to do this, you're a goner. Bullshit is made-up stories, or factual stories with too much embellishment. You'll start to believe in the big stories and then you'll be disappointed when they don't come true. Don't leave yourself open to disappointment in yourself. It'll be your ego's fault. Your ego feeds on big stories.

Expected patter

Real estate agents are expected to be familiar with every detail of each of their listings. This can be an impossible expectation. It's better to have stock standard responses to purchasers' queries. You can't possibly know all the details pertaining to thirty properties. If you have thirty listings, you don't have time to write all this stuff down either. The trick to this, is improvisation. You learn to be a good guesser, investigator of the moment, or, you get back to them on it. You won't be able to get back to them on it, because you simply won't have the time. They'll ring you if they're interested. Let the purchasers come to you. It's important that you get your priorities right. List, list, list!

Getting the pyramid built

For every sale you make, you must be sure to list three others. There's always a fair chance that a listing will be withdrawn, go to another agent, or be too hard to sell because the owner is resisting price reductions. It's imperative that 70% of your time be spent getting listings. (Do not tell your vendors this.) If you don't have listings, you have nothing to sell. This is supply and demand. If you have no supply, you'll not be in demand. If you're not in demand, you'll be made redundant.

A quick little pyramid

Make sure you do most of the work at the bottom, and just chip a little at the top. Each time you chip a bit off the top, you have to replace it with another four listings at the bottom. This is the ideal shape, and the Egyptians knew this too. What am I talking about? The Egyptians knew nothing about structure.

> **Pyramid selling:-** a method of selling in which the right to sell certain goods is purchased by people who then sell this right to other people.

Maybe the Egyptians knew more about this pyramid selling after all. This is how their pyramids got ransacked and pilfered. Make sure you look after your entire pyramid.

> **Pyramid:-** n. [Gr. *pyramis*] 1. any huge structure with a square base and four sloping, triangular sides meeting at the top, as those built in ancient Egypt; 2. Geom. a solid figure the base of which is a polygon whose sides are the bases of triangular surfaces meeting at a common vertex – pyramidal adj. – pyram'idally adv.

So you're supposed to be running through the chambers and secret passages, and attending to all the listings, and negotiating the sales. This is why there are secret chambers, because you don't want anyone knowing too much about what you're doing. This is now your system, and you don't want the other agents in the office to get a glance at it. This is how you'll earn your reputation as a smooth operator. You'll make it all look easy and the competition will lose heart and confidence when they go up against you for a listing. They'll wander back from a lost listing, wondering how you did it. This is good. Keep them wondering. You can build a reputation of mythical proportions.

Keep your own private leads list

I can't stress this enough. This is the stressful part. I know all about in-house computer data bases now. It has everyone's contact details, but this just means that the whole house can look at them. Your leads list is top secret. Keep a book, and just jot down everything. As the years go by and you're contacting everyone on your leads list personally, your leads list will start working for you. Personal contact is vital, so forget all those annual anniversary cards and crappy real estate mailouts. Just get on the bloody phone and have a yak. By all means, send them a Christmas card, but don't send it if you're not going to write a personal note and sign your own name. Leads are your secret weapon. A mass of leads is your only congregation.

Whenever you speak to anyone on your leads list, note the date and any important information. When you're chatting, don't forget to let them know you're looking for listings, and see if any of their friends or relatives would like a free market appraisal. This is better than asking if any of them want to sell, because they won't want to divulge this sort of information to you. They will however pass on to you their friend's details, or yours to them, if it's just a market appraisal. See, this is a gift from you. It's a freebie, and that's how you sell it. If you operate your personal leads list correctly, you won't just have your immediate contacts, you'll also have all your immediate contact's contacts.

My leads list was my list of my people

I had a leads list, and it went back over fifteen years of people. I had fifteen years of leads on that list. It was a wad of paper bound together with one mother of a bulldog clip. I miss my leads list. I can't believe it, but I do. There was a long history in that leads list. There were many stories and many commissions. There were many lives. That leads list of mine was my bread and butter. It was my crust. It was what I did for a crust. I could come in to work at any given day and know I could get a listing from that leads list, but that was only because that leads list had been worked by me for many years, and I was meticulous and dedicated to it. When I needed more leads to add to my list of thousands, I would get in my car and get out there amongst it. If I saw someone in the garden, I got out and had a chat. Sometimes I'd take stuff with me and give out pens, brochures, my business card or just my innate charm. All these people went on my list. I even told them I'd be putting them on my list, and I think they liked that.

I was nosey

I had a nose for leads, and if I saw really old people occupying a two storey house – bingo! They went on my list too. Those were the people I wanted to talk to, because I knew they would tell me that the stairs were getting too much for them, or their knees were playing up. Is this bad form, or just wise thinking? This is what's called the 'intensification method'. I'd create the visual for their worst case scenario, describing their fall down the staircase and the consequences. Most people have already considered the solution to their problem, but are waiting for someone to come along and make it easy for them. Some of them are waiting for the push. Not the fall, the relocation.

There were other ways of working out who should be on my leads list, but I'm not going to tell you all my secrets. I was a private investigator. Don't think for one second that your information is private. There are plenty of ways to find information.

Sources for courses

When you think of a gossip, who do you think of first? Do you think of a neighbour? Neighbours are the greatest source of information you can get. All information is good information, as long as you keep it to yourself. I'll tell you who else to get friendly with, and a great connection to have, and that's the local deliverer of information. This may only work in small suburbs, and it sure as hell worked for me, in more ways than one.

Who opened my mail?

I was told who had died, who was sick, who was thinking of selling, who was cranky with their current agent, who was thinking of renting their house out, who had lost their job, and whose marriage had just broken up. I was lucky really. I despised the source, but I kept my ears open. I guess I could be seen to be as bad as the source, but that's only if I had no feeling for the people being talked about, and only if I'd added my two cents worth.

Small town talk

I guess this was one of the ways I kept up to date with the community, and it did prompt me to send cards when I felt these people needed one. I believe my intentions were pure, and not just motivated by business. These were people I knew and liked. They were my community. I believe I'm confessing, and it feels bad. If I feel bad about it, then hopefully it's doing me some good.

Is this more karma? I'm sorry I had this job. I'm sorry I was so good at it. If I hadn't had this job, would my life have been better? Did I have the job, or did the job have me? Did the nature of the job do a job on me?

I'm sorry I was a real estate agent

We aren't the only industry whose standards are arse-up. What about your information being passed on to us by solicitors and conveyancers? Who do you think refers the work to them? We hatch a plan between us, to get you to do what we want. Yeah sure, they're acting for you as experts in their field, but their performance must be for the real estate agent if they want more clients referred to them. They're talking behind your backs.

What a crazy network!

Now I'm blowing the whistle, so I'll throw the finance consultants in too. Private? Did you say private? Are your financial affairs private? They probably are, if the agent hasn't referred the finance broker to you. If you think agents don't refer finance brokers to purchasers, you're mistaken. Maybe the lousy ones don't, but this is how the wheels keep turning. If you're relying on a real estate agent to put you on to someone that can get you a loan to buy a house, then you probably should be thinking twice about buying the house.

It's not our fault that people don't think for themselves. They want the agent to do all their thinking. They just want someone else to take care of it all for them. Thank God I'm not talking about all our clients, because if that were the case, I reckon agents would have lawsuits coming out their ears.

There's no kickbacks

It's more a matter of 'you scratch my back, and I'll scratch yours'. There used to be substantial kickbacks, but the industry's now tightened up and kickbacks are hard to get.

I hope one Greek God reads these pages carefully. One must stay human, and not get too high and mighty, when it comes to serving the people. I'm sermonizing now, but I can't help it because a chap that I worked with is taking some shortcuts. He may be in desperate need of a good sermon. I know the inner God is there, because I've glimpsed him from time to time. I should have known that if something doesn't feel right, you shouldn't do it.

What am I qualified for now?

If you think this is an ugly picture of a real estate agent's job, you're mistaken. This is a good job. I had made a good job of it. I just did a real job on myself, trying to do it right.

It's a reality check for all you agents out there. You'll speak my language, if you're any good at your job. The hard reality hurts when you look over it properly. It's like looking in the mirror for me. I want to deny it exists. I do want to deny that I ever existed as a real estate agent. It's strictly an in-between job.

I'm qualified for the following jobs:-

1. Prostitute;
2. Cab driver;
3. Counsellor;
4. Profiler;
5. Chess player.

I can't decide. They all look like too much hard work, to me. What about…

6. Writer?

Squeezing in between

Have you ever been the meat in the sandwich? You're now the agent, and this means you're dead meat. You'll always find yourself between a rock and a hard place.

You'll be between a landlord and a tenant, or a landlord and a tradesman. You're between a vendor and a purchaser. You're between a vendor and your boss. You're between your boss and a purchaser. You're between solicitors and their clients. You can find yourself between the bank and a vendor, or a bank and a purchaser. You can find yourself squeezing between a bank and a vendor who's unable to pay. You can find yourself between an auctioneer and the bidders, or an auctioneer and your vendor. Sometimes you don't even come between.

Coming last

This is when you must come after, or when your family and friends can't come before. A listing will always come before everything else. It's what you've been waiting and hoping for. It's what you've been working towards. It will come on your day off, or in the middle of your kid's concert. It will come late at night, or while you're shopping for the family. Listings wait for no man. Listings just go and find another agent to list with. Listings can slip through your fingers like chocolate melts in your mouth. You can do everything to try and stop it melting away, and you can't help sucking. You'll suck. You'll try not to suck, but you won't be able to help yourself. Your family won't understand why you're home late, or have to dash out to an appointment in the middle of your day off. You'll always be competing. The competition just continues. It's never over. You never leave the competition, even after you've won a listing. You must start the next race immediately. There's no time for a breather, and if you happen to take two weeks' holiday, you've lost dough. You've lost your spot and lost ground.

You've lost a lot of ground

Nobody will look after your ground for you. You'll come back to find the listings you've missed, and the sales that someone else has claimed, that should have been yours. You weren't there to cover your bases, so you've lost your footing. Your vendors won't be happy you left them to go on holiday, either.

Learning to deal

Know when to holdem! You must learn how to hold them. You're just like The Gambler. You're just like the song. This is our industry's theme song. You must learn to hold fire. You must learn not to shoot your mouth off, and don't run off at the mouth. You can't mouth off at someone. You can't mouth off at anyone. Everyone's a connection now. Your mouth will always be the first thing that gets you into trouble.

Shut up your face!

Shut your mouth and be done with it. This is the best advice I can give you. Negotiation is about your mouth, first and foremost. Don't open it. For most, it's the first skill you'll learn. You can practice this skill by saying nothing. I used to write 'shut up' on my desk pad to remind me of what I should be doing when I was on the phone negotiating a deal. Always write this word down in front of you, before picking up the phone to your vendor with an offer. I can't stress this enough. Just shut the fuck up. You're listening for the combination to open the vault. Whatever you do, don't get the numbers wrong. Don't use the wrong words. Remember what has, and hasn't been, said. In fact, or unfact, write it down.

Let's negotiate

An offer to buy is not necessarily a sale. The first offer on a house is most often an insult. You must take the insult and hit your vendor with it. You have to be very careful not to be charged with this insult. You have to disguise the insult as a compliment. If your vendor gets upset with the purchaser, they can't be friends, and there can be no friendly deal. It rarely ends up in a deal when this happens, but if it does get to be a deal, it's a shitty deal all round. You'll get dealt some of this shit too.

    You can't refuse to inflict insults on your vendor, because our industry regulations stipulate that you must submit all insults. All insults are good insults. The worst insults are the best insults. These are conditioning insults, and you need them early on in the process. This will help the vendor condition himself to the full array of his defects. Once he's been made defective by the insults, you're likely to be complimented by an acceptance of an insult. It's usually a nicer insult than the original insult. It makes the vendor feel a bit nicer too. In order for the vendor to feel nicer, you have to make him feel bad first. It's the balance.

A newborn sale

The vendor has gratefully accepted the invitation to sell, and you have conducted the delivery single-handedly. Don't forget, you've had instructions the whole way through, so I should get some credit too.

You sit there, put the phone down, and lean back in your chair with a sigh of relief. You have sweat marks under each of your armpits, and beads of perspiration on your forehead. You look down on your desk pad and smile in sublime satisfaction. You were able to shut up when you needed to. You let nature take its course. Knowing your vendor's nature, and your purchaser's nature, was the nature of the business. Allowing the purchaser to do all the pushing, and letting the vendor do all the pulling, made the whole process more rewarding for everyone. You were just the mid-man, overseeing the birth of the sale.

Learning to control what you can control, which is only yourself, is your final battle. You'll always have this battle going on. You can only control what you say, or don't say. You don't say!

A sale is born and a salesman is born, or saleswoman. I still believe women are better in this role, for obvious reasons. It's all about delivering a happy, healthy, sale.

Celebration of the past

Whenever a sale is born, it's an occasion for celebrating. You must always join in the celebration otherwise the vendor will not know what he's celebrating. If he's celebrating, there must be something worth celebrating. He'll see this as a good sign. Signs are important, but we'll get to the signage later. You can attach your sold sign onto your 'For Sale' sign, as a sign to attract your next sign. Your next vendor will see it as a sign for them. This sold sign is a sign of things to come.

The future celebration

The main celebration should be with your purchaser. This is the big celebration. This is the celebration that will lead, one day, to another celebration. If you conduct this celebration with great aplomb, you'll have listings landing in your lap.

It's hard to look this far into the future, but remember the future isn't always bright. There may be many sales in this property's future. Never write off a property once you've sold it. I've sold the same properties three times within ten years. I've sold many, many, properties, more than once. Some properties are cursed. Look out for these ones, because you won't know whose being cursed by them. If they've been cursed to turn over regularly, you get to benefit.

Inspecting the expected

Make sure you're always the M.C. This is another important title you must hold. You must be Master of Ceremonies. When you ceremoniously invite a purchaser to inspect your listing, you must be the master. The mistress of the home must know who the master is, just in case she unceremoniously puts off the purchaser. Be careful of the mistress who reveals too much. It can sometimes be very off-putting, especially if it's old or dated. It's better to evict vendors before any inspections.

Vendors should listen to your 'vendor patter', and purchasers should listen to your 'purchaser patter'. The vendor and purchaser should not be within earshot of each other's patter respectively. You don't want to hear the wrong patter being repeated back to you.

The inspection is in progress, and your honesty is being appreciated by the purchaser, but it may not be appreciated by the vendor. Once you start hiding a vendor's mistake, you've made a mistake. Don't let the emotions of the vendor, and the emotions of the purchaser, pull down a sale. This is emotional blackmail. One will hold the other accountable.

Sad to be going, and happy to be coming

The best sale is an emotional sale. It must be your emotional sale. Don't let it be a vendor's emotional sale, or a purchaser's emotional sale. I haven't expressed that very well, but it's best to have your purchaser and vendor as emotional as possible. The emotion must be the emotion you have fed them. You can work with emotion. What you don't want is angry emotion between a vendor and a purchaser, and this is hard when money is involved, especially big amounts of money. Keep the angry words in the middle. You're in the middle. You're the filter, and you need to filter out the bad, and turn it into nice, in the nicest possible way. This will avoid a conflict of emotions. I'll give you an example:

No I won't, because you have to learn this all by yourself. You have to learn to think first. Look before you leap. Assess. Consider all the angles. Look at the board. Know your players. Shut up for a while, and go back to the office and think. Run the whole process through in your mind first. Think of who you're dealing with, and try to predict their thinking. Think about best-case scenario, and think of worst-case scenario. Think of the risk. You are the balance beam. You have to keep them on that tight rope. You're also the net below.

The delicate trades of information

When you're walking on common ground, it's of extreme importance that you walk on eggshells. The more you walk on eggshells, the softer your fall will be, if you happen to leak the wrong information.

Trading information is a portfolio you want to keep private. Once you start trading with your vendor and purchaser, you can lose sight of who traded what, and for whom.

You must remember the order of your trades, and how big they were. You can easily get mixed up with all these trades, and before you know it, your portfolio will have been blown. Your clients will know you've been a secret trader. The trade will be over, and they'll trade you in. Don't let vendors and purchasers become friends, because they could start a trading portfolio against you. They may tell your other connections about your trading job. Information is secret trading.

The best way to avoid exposing your trades is to trade nothing. If you don't trade, you don't lose, but you won't gain as much either. A better way to trade information is to stay with small trading. Being a small trader is less risky. It's all about considering what to trade and what not to trade. Less is definitely more. The less information you trade, the more sales you'll make.

Don't let anyone trade you anything different. This was my job, I should know. It's about being in the know, not about letting others know. It's not something that people want to know, that you know. Your catchphrase should be 'to know me is to love me'.

I know, I'm telling you, aren't I? It's good to finally get it off my chest. It's no treasure chest.

An enterprising appraisal

Your market appraisal should be an open appraisal. You must be very careful to praise with an appraisal. Your appraisal should not be your opinion. It must be more the vendor's opinion. You can't be held accountable for their opinion, but you will be, for yours. Opinions don't cut ice. Keep your opinions to yourself. Don't be opinionated, and your opinion will count for more.

Appraising the competition

All opinions are different. This is the best result you can get. This is when not having an opinion, will give them a better opinion of you. Never ride pinion on another agent's opinion. You'll end up open to competition. This is an open listing competition. All it does is open up the competition. You don't want a competition, because there's too much competition already.

You can take another opinion with you, and I used to do this all the time. I used to say that two heads are better than one. Two of the right heads, are better than one. Two heads must be of the same opinion, but with two different ways to substantiate it. Two heads are always more credible than one, but only if the two heads are on the same page. One can't be above the other.

Mending your ways

If there's a listing the competition has sewn up, you can unstitch it. This is called stitching up the competition. The timing is everything with this strategy. You must wait up, until the competition's vendor gets tired. When a vendor gets tired of waiting up, they're waiting for a new competitor. Move in with stealth. You want to wake up the vendor in the nicest way, but not the competition.

Waking up the vendor is easy. You wake them up by talking to them. Your competition has stopped doing this, because they don't want to awaken their vendor to the fact that nothing much is happening. It's quiet. The market is too quiet. An awakening can take place at this quiet time, and you've woken up to a new listing. Remember to keep your new listing awake. Make plenty of noise, and rest assured, you won't lose the listing.

A lousy erection

Never hit signs. This is unethical. Signs don't like you hitting them. Hitting a sign will not hurt the sign. Signs are strong if they've been erected properly, and maintained.

A poorly erected sign will blow down in the first puff of wind. A poorly erected sign is a great indicator of a weak sign. This is always a good sign. A sign of weakness will strengthen your position. You'll go from strength to strength on weak signs.

When you're erecting a sign, it's good physical activity. The more signs you erect, the more activity you'll have. It's a strong sign that you're active in the area. All activity is good activity. Your sign is your star sign. You need many stars to shine. You must shine the brightest, to be recognized as the best. The best star should be shiny in appearance. This means the full attire. Don't get slack and tire of the attire or people will think you've retired.

The principles of a principal

Have I tired you out yet? It's tiring to learn. Not everyone can learn these principles fast. I was a slow learner. I didn't like the principles. They were not my principles. When I refused to learn these principles in my first real estate job, I was told off by the principal. The principal is the licensee of the business. He's referred to as the Principal on Agency Agreements. Your principal will always remind you of your school principal, especially if you were sent to him for punishment.

My first principal was a bit of a careers' advisor. He told me "If you don't learn to lie, you can go and get a job at Grace Brothers". These were his exact words to me. I didn't want to work for Grace Brothers. It wasn't what I had visualized for myself. I realized that I'd have to change my principles for my job. I was keeping my job, but losing my principles. This was the school of hard knocks. My principles were soon to be knocked out of me, and I was on my way. I was on my way to knocking around, and knocking on doors. I got knocked around in the process.

The upright principles

I didn't have any problems kicking goals, but every time I did it, the principal would move the uprights. He would post a commission target and before you could kick another goal, he would move the posts. It was hard to score points in this way, so I went looking for a sturdier set of goal posts.

This was the second field I worked from. I didn't want to get hooked with the first set, they were on the game. There were plenty of goal posts around, and another one with a similar name just down the road. I thought they seemed professional but they got called a name for short.

I'm not naming names

Some people just fit straight into a name, don't they? Some people move from name to name in real estate. They're known by a real estate name, because they nearly wear out. You might get wet and stimulated if I tell you the name of another. I'm about to blow it! Have a guess whose name went there? What's in a name?

The second little piggy

Anyway, the name I eventually chose was an old name. There were two names, and one was a partnership. This is where I went wrong. I got invited to be a partner. I accepted, but realized I'd got partnership mixed up with silent partner. I was kept in the dark like a mushroom. I grew like a mushroom though. That compost heap was a big area and I almost had it all to myself. I already knew a lot of people living in that patch of compost. It proved to be a nutritious patch of ground. Winterground Tip.

The third little piggy

These third set of goal posts were harder than the rest, but they were designed by me. I didn't make them as high for everyone else, as I did for myself. I made them really high, just for me. I was ambitious. I liked a challenge. I was challenged, because no one kicked goals like I did. It was made of the right stuff though.

The greatest goal I ever kicked

My goal kicking days are over. I get no kick out of it anymore. I kicked it to kingdom come. There was no kickback at the end, but there was no kick off at the beginning either. I've now kicked the habit. I've just kicked the greatest goal of all time. I kicked a goal, and there was no goalkeeper at the other end. He was a lousy catch.

Kicking things around

When you kick something away from you, you must be sure that it won't come back. I keep kicking boomerangs. These are a bad invention if they're not used in the correct manner. They were designed for hunting. You throw them at your prey until you hit them. It's really handy if you're a lousy shot because they return right back to you for a handy second attempt. I'm an expert boomerang thrower. It's an easy sport to be an expert in, because hardly anyone competes. This is a good strategy for success. It's well taught.

I don't compete anymore, because people keep throwing down the gauntlet, but I just keep throwing it back at them. I don't react. Reactions are distractions. My reactions are the opposite now. People keep expecting me to do things, but I don't do it. I don't have to do it. I never did have to do it. I won't ever do it again. I'm the opposite of a real estate agent now. That would be good, wouldn't it?

I'm the opposite of a real estate agent because I can see myself going backwards fast. I'm an 'agent estate real'.

> **Agent:-** n. [< L. *agree*, do] 1. a person, firm, etc. authorized to act for another; 2. [Colloq.] a travelling representative, as for an insurance company; 3. a person or thing that performs an action or produces an effect –agen-tial adj.
>
> **Estate:-** n. [< OFr. *Estat*] 1. landed property containing a residence; 2. a large area of new property development, esp. of houses or of industrial premises; 3. property, possessions; 4. a large area growing rubber, tea, grapes, etc.; 5. formerly, any of the three classes having specific powers: the clergy (first estate) nobility (second estate), and commons (third estate); 6. a) a stage of life [man's estate] b) status or rank.

Real:- adj. [< L. *res*, thing] 1. existing as or in fact, actual, true; 2. a) genuine b) sincere; 3. designating income as measured by purchasing power; 4. Law. of or relating to permanent, immovable things [real property].

Agent

In Latin, I'm agreeable and firm. I just do, because I have authority. I can perform an action, and produce an effect.

Estate

According to the Trinity of estates, I now have powers over the clergy, nobility and the commons, and this is now my status and rank.

Real

I exist in fact, and I'm genuine and sincere. My income is now being measured by my purchasing power. I'm permanent and immovable.

What does it all mean? It means karma is doing some balancing.

He wants the house

Is there any reason why I can't quote some legal documents submitted to The Federal Magistrates Court of Australia? From what I can see, I have no Orders restraining me from telling my side of the story. I'm under no restriction in appointing you my legal aid, and asking you to consider my case. I have the documents in front of me, and I'll site them word for word. I've just changed the identifying words, so you can't identify with anyone. I'm asking you to peruse them carefully, and decide whether you'd like to act for me, or not.

THE FEDERAL MAGISTRATES COURT OF AUSTRALIA
REGISTRY:

BLAND

Applicant

BLANK

Respondent

APPLICATION IN A CASE

This application is made by (name): **BLAND**

Court date

This application is listed for hearing at the Court location on the date and at the time specified in the 'Court Use Only' box above.

All parties or their legal representatives should attend this hearing, at which the Court may hear and determine relevant issues or may give directions for the future conduct of the proceedings.

....

(for) Registrar

Date:

Orders sought (state precisely each order sought)

That the parties do all acts and execute all documents necessary to sell at market value the property known as 'The Last Hoorah' being the land in Certificate of Title Volume Folio Identifier No: 666 ('the Property') by public auction with the reserve price to be determined by the Applicant Husband in consultation with 'Up Yours Real Estate'.

1. The Applicant Husband is to have the conduct of the sale on behalf of the parties and instruct solicitors and agents to act on his behalf.

2. The agent for the sale is to be Mr Wealthy, Principal and Licensee of Up Yours Real Estate of Specific Highway, Duck Ocean and the Solicitor acting in relation to the Conveyancing will be Mr Key of Bird. Bird. Lies and Associates of Master Road, Handy.

3. Within 21 days of these Orders, the Wife and all other occupiers of the property must vacate the property, must not remove any fixtures from the property and must leave the property tidy, clean and in good repair having regard to its present condition.

4. The proceeds of the sale of the Property are to be deposited into the Trust account of Bird. Bird. Lies and Associates and payment distribution made as follows:
    (i) All reasonable expenses of the sale including agent's commission and legal costs and disbursements;
    (ii) Discharge of Mortgages secured upon the Property
    (iii) Rate adjustments and other outstanding debts relating to the Property paid and
    (iv) The remainder to the Applicant Husband

5. The Applicant Husband is declared to have no interest in any interest in any superannuation fund in the name of Blank.

6. The Respondent Wife is declared to have no interest in any interest in any superannuation fund in the name of Bland.

7. Except as otherwise provided in these orders each party is declared to have no interest in the items of property in the possession of the other.

8. Within 14 days of the date of these Orders, the Respondent Wife is to provide valuations of the three vehicles owned by the Business or purchased with funds obtained from the Business accounts being the CAR 1, CAR 2, and the CAR 3.

9. That after the Business known as 'Jerry Mindings Pty Ltd' trading as Blank Real Estate, is wound up and all debts and accounts associated with it are paid in full; the Respondent Wife is to receive the balance of any remaining funds in full and final settlement.

Affidavit/s (Provide details of the affidavit(s) supporting this application)

This application is supported by an affidavit made by BLAND, and filed in the Court on 03112011 in support of the Application in a Case of Bland.

Signature of person applying or lawyer
....

Signed by (print name) Bland

THE FEDERAL MAGISTRATES COURT OF AUSTRALIA

REGISTRY:

BLAND

Applicant

BLANK

Respondent

AFFIDAVIT

Name of deponent: Bland

Date: 02022011

I, Bland of C/- Bird. Bird. Lies & Associates of Master Road, Handy, in the State of New South Wales, make oath and say / affirm:

I am the Applicant Husband and I seek to also rely upon my Affidavit filed on 04102011. The Respondent Wife is referred to as

1. 'Blank'. Our children are Hermione and Shark Boy.

<u>THE BUSINESS</u>

2. At the time of our separation, our company known as 'Jerry Mindings Pty Ltd trading as Blank Real Estate' ('the Business') was successful and increasing in value and employed eight staff members. A copy of the Business advertisement is attached as Annexure "A".

3. The Rent Roll alone was valued at $225,600. A copy of the Business Valuation at 31012011 is attached as Annexure "B".

4. The Business Cheque Account had a balance of $143,852.23 at 01122010. A copy of the Transaction History is attached as Annexure "C".

5. I am extremely shocked that directly through Blank's actions, the Business is now almost worthless. I do not know where the monies withdrawn from the Business or Trust Accounts are or if Blank has spent all the funds. A copy of the business account is attached as Annexure "D" showing a closing balance on 21092011 of $0.00.

6. This annexure shows two withdrawals dated 07072011 of Statement 143 at page 2 of $6,180.00 and $6,000 from Middle Edge Car at Gossy. As I have seen both Shark Boy and Hermione driving around in new vehicles, I reasonably believe that these vehicles were purchased using funds from the Business.

7. I have been working closely with the Headquarters of Unfair Swapping who have been appointed to wind up the Business. I am concerned that even after the sale of all the assets, business equipment, furniture and other assets, that there will be insufficient funds left to cover the outstanding costs which will now include payment due to the Headquarters of Unfair Swapping for their costs.

THE PROPERTY

8. Given the actions of Blank in withdrawing and closing the Business Bank Accounts, I became concerned that she may also attempt to obtain money from the Property and I instructed my Solicitors to lodge a Caveat against the Title. A copy of this is attached as Annexure marked "E".

9. Whilst sorting out the offices of the Business, I discovered a 'Sales Inspection' Contract which is attached as Annexure "F". I recognize the handwriting as that of

Blank's. I agree that the estimated selling price should be $750,000.

LEGAL REPRESENTATION

10. We received a letter from Blank's former Solicitors Two Dopey People Lawyers requesting our consent to them acting for Hermione. A copy of their letter is attached as Annexure "G".
11. I was very pleased that Hermione would have some legal assistance even if it meant a possible conflict of interests. I was extremely distressed that Hermione had to attend Court and that Blank was not present. I love Hermione very much and I would not have wanted her to have to be involved in any way in this matter. A copy of our letter in reply is attached as Annexure "H".
12. My Solicitor then received a letter saying that Two Dopey People Lawyers had been contacted by Blank and could not act for Hermione. A copy of this letter is attached as Annexure "I".
13. I do not know if Two Dopey People Lawyers are again acting for Blank or if Hermione has been able to obtain alternate legal representation.

SERVICE OF DOCUMENTS

14. Further to the Orders made on 11102011, my Solicitors arranged for a Process Server to serve the documents personally upon Blank and Hermione. I understand that the Affidavits of Service have now been tendered as evidence in this matter.
15. Further to the Orders made on 19112011, my Solicitors arranged for a Process Server to personally serve those Orders upon Hermione and the Property address. I understand that his occurred on 27102011 after previous

attempts had been unsuccessful. To date we have not been provided with the affidavit of service.

16. Prior to receiving the letter from Two Dopey People Lawyers at annexure H, my Solicitors had provided Two Dopey People Lawyers also with a copy of the Orders dated 19102011 as they had requested.

PROPERTY SETTLEMENT DISTRIBUTION

17. The asset pool at the time of separation was $1,173,700 according to correspondence received from the Solicitors who formerly acted for Blank. Their letter dated 16022011 has been tendered in Court as evidence in these proceedings.

18. Due to actions of Blank, the Business is almost worthless. I have been working closely with the Headquarters of Unfair swapping in trying to sort out the book work, the transfer of the existing client base and trying to assist former staff members and clients who continue to contact me seeking assistance.

19. I have recently been advised that clients have attempted to deposit payments and rent into the Business Trust accounts but as it has been closed, such payments have been unable to be made. I have felt totally out of my depth in dealing with such matters and the winding up and selling of Business assets including furniture and the like whilst also working full-time so as to be able to make my own rental payments.

20. At the time of our separation, we had ensured that we were significantly ahead of our Mortgage payments and had some $80,000 available in a 'Line of Credit' and portfolio account. I have been advised by the Bank that Blank has not made any Mortgage payments since approximately the end of 092011. I do not know if the Rates are up to date or not.

21. I have offered to both Shark Boy and Hermione that they are more than welcome to live with me at any time if they would like to do so. I am very upset that the children have had to be involved in this matter. This was never my intention. I had hoped Blank and I would have been able to finalize all the financial details after our separation without this expense or conflict.

22. I understand that the Settlement I am proposing in my Application in a Case represents a split of the asset pool in my favour. However, given that Blank has retained the Business accounts, Trust accounts, cars, has remained living in the Property and is responsible for the loss of the Business and has left me to deal with settling the debts and winding up, I believe that this is just and equitable in these circumstances.

Sworn/Affirmed by **BLAND**)

the deponent at **HANDY**   )

On the 02102011   )

....

Before Me:

....

Signature of Witness

Full name of witness: Gorge Happiness Burntbee

Qualification of witness: Solicitor

I felt like a legal secretary again back there, but I've never worked in Family Law. Guess what areas of law I used to work in? I worked in the areas of Property Law, and Litigation.

As you can see, because of Privacy Laws, I've had to change the names and any identifying persons just in case. Just in case of another case. Who knows how many cases could be opened. I hope you can understand the case now, because cases of this nature don't get much airplay. They usually fly under the radar. It's a very private case.

You're my legal eagle

If you're a real legal eagle, you'll pick out some anomalies but I don't know what you'll do with them. What happens when false Affidavits are tendered to the court? Who checks for truth? I think someone should invent a scanner that can detect lies in legal documents. This is the only way that anyone can sort the shit from the clay.

Incidentally, I've just finished another sculpture. It's the long hand of the law. It's a man's arm from just below the elbow. It's large and powerful, but the hand is flaccid. There's defined muscle and sinew in the forearm but a piss-weak positioning of the hand. Where did it come from? I didn't set out to sculpt it. I just let my hands do the talking. Where did my hands get the talk? It wasn't me, because I was talking to someone the whole time. I was talking with a friend who was also sculpting. She doesn't know where her sculpture came from either. It hadn't been previously imagined. Neither of our sculptures had been in our imaginations. Neither of us set out to sculpt what we ended up creating. It's creation. It's recreation.

Flaccid:- adj. [< L. *flaccus*, flabby] 1. flabby; 2. weak; feeble –flac-cid'ity n. –flac'cidly adv.

Withholding evidence

But wait! There's more. There is, but it's for later. It's perjury.

> **Perjury:-** n., pl. –ries [< L. *perjurus*, false] the willful telling of a lie while under oath.

I want my case to be heard, of course I do. I'm next in line. You have to take turns, and he went first. I've been very patient, and the more patient I've been, the bigger my case is getting. He's having a long turn, because he's never really taken his turn before. He never wanted to take a turn. He left me all the turns. I'm burnt out. I need him to take a turn for a change. He's having a long turn, because he has a lot of catching up to do. Don't worry I'll catch up. This will all catch up with him. It's karma. You can't outrun karma.

It's a cat-o'-nine-tails

I feel someone should warn him about karma, but I think that might happen quite soon. I've let the cat out of the bag, and I'm waiting to see where the cat goes. If the cat got out of the bag because I opened my mouth, where will the cat end up? This is a different experiment, and I'm using cats this time.

> **Cat-o'-nine-tails:-** n. a whip made of nine knotted cords attached to a handle.

Do you ever say certain things on purpose, just so that it gets moved from one person to another? About you, I mean. Would you talk about yourself to someone, in the hope that they'll tell it to someone else? This isn't gossip, is it? Is gossiping talking about yours truly? Have I talked about 'yours truly'?

Fighting fire with one bright spark

I'm spreading my own gossip about myself now. I'm getting my own back. Will it come right back? Will it hit me in the back? Will it be the push from behind that I've been waiting for? Could this be karma? I've looked it up again. I've definitely told the right person.

> **Gossip:-** n. [< OE. *godsibbe*, godparent] 1. one who chatters or repeats idle talk, esp. about others' private affairs; 2. such talk or rumours –vi. to indulge in idle talk –gos'siper n. –gos'sipy adj.

Yep! I've got two special people in my life to do this job. One is better than the other, but you never know, do you? God's on my side. He's a powerful talker, is God. I need some powerful talking now. I need some strong talk. I need strong supporting words. Then I'll need some strong shelves. The shelves I can sort out for myself. I just need to be strong enough to keep my books on my shelves, for as long as possible. I need to resist the temptation of blurting it all out too early. This is what you call holding your breath for a long time.

I can't blow it

I've been under water all this time, and I haven't been able to let out my breath. I haven't had any airing. I'll need to get some air soon. My books have been kept in isolation for too long now. I can't keep them close forever. I have to set them free. This is what they were written for. I want to take them out into the wild, and put them into their natural habitat.

I want to watch them go

They need to find their purpose. I'm proud of them, and I'll miss them when they go off into the great blue yonder. I'll be worried for them. I'll be more worried for me. I think I'll have separation anxiety. 'Detach with love.' I've heard this said, and I'm doing it. I'm going to detach. I hope they find their match, and open the hatch. They'll undo the latch. I wonder who they'll catch. There's one particular patch. Don't snatch!

>Yonder:- adj. [ME.] 1. more distant (with the); 2. being at a distance, but within sight –adv. over there.

I'll need to know how they're doing out there, when I let them go. How will I know? I'll know, from *The Knowing in Me*. Send me an angel. Send me a book review. I want to hear your response. I want to hear all the responses. I mainly want certain responses. Just the responses I deserve. I want responses to my questions from me, the respondent. I'll feel despondent with no respondent. I want the knowing responses from all the knowing people. Those are the ones who knew me, and the ones I want to know about. I want me to know, and them to find out. You know what? You're mad and I'm not!

Where do we go from here?

I've just been reclining on a banana chair on the verandah, which is just outside my bedroom. It's just coming on to dusk. There's a slight mist in the air from the big ocean swells today, and it smells nice.

I look up to see what the buzzing sound is. I tilt my head back to the beams overhead, and see a large dragonfly busily trying to find it's way out from under the eaves. It keeps banging into the beams and getting stuck in the corners. Above me is a sheltered cover from the rain and it's made of Perspex sheeting, so we can both see through it to the clouds above. This is where the dragonfly is headed for. It sees freedom, but it just can't get to it. I'm frustrated just watching it dizzily bouncing from one barrier to another.

It finally stops to rest. I'm hoping it will slow down now, and get its bearings. I'm hoping it will just get itself grounded, and assess the situation properly. I want it to take time, and calm itself, and still its mind. I know for sure this will work, if it just takes the time to be aware of where it is. It only needs to consider where it's come from. It needs to remember how it got there in the first place. It needs to consider where it ultimately wants to go. It can't want to head for the clouds because dragonflies don't do that, do they?

It just needs to go back downwards, to find some foliage to buzz around in. It's flown two stories up. It's too high up for the foliage that it seeks. Why did it fly this high? It's going to have to come down to earth. It's started buzzing and bumping into things again, and it's stuck between two beams, flicking its gossamer wings through the spider webs. It's dangerous behaviour. It's risky behaviour. What causes risky behaviour?

Take a walk on the wild side

When is risk, worth the risk? When is risk, less of a risk? What have we got to lose, really? Things are lost all the time without us even being aware of it. Valuable things are lost from our life, and we don't see them disappearing. We forget the value of them. Chasing after valuable things is risking the value we already have.

I was thinking about this tonight, while I was enjoying a sumptuous evening meal of peanut butter on toast. Believe it or not, it was truly sumptuous, and tasted delicious. I hadn't ever realized just how tasty peanut butter on toast can be. I'm not exaggerating, because I hadn't eaten anything, in over twenty-four hours. This is what you call fasting.

> **Fast:-** adj. [OE. *faest*] 1. swift, quick; 2. ahead of the correct time [his watch is fast]; 3. a) reckless, wild; b) sexually promiscuous; 4. firm, fixed; 5. firmly fastened; 6. loyal, devoted; 7. that will not fade [fast colours]; 8. Photog. adapted to very short exposure time –adv. 1. rapidly, swiftly; 2. soundly [fast asleep]; 3. firmly, fixedly; 4. ahead of time; 5. in a reckless way; 6. [Obs.] near [fast by the river] –a fast one [Slang] a deceptive act [to pull a fast one] –play fast and loose, to behave with duplicity.
>
> **Fast:-** vi. [OE. *faestan*] 1. to abstain from all or certain foods, as in observing a holy day; 2. to eat very little or nothing –n. the act or period of fasting.

'Fast' is a good word. I like fast. I don't like fast as much as I used to, though. Fast isn't always best, slow can be better. I better slow up here, because I'm going to be onto another subject before I finish the last one. I'm a bit too fast and furious sometimes. This is when I get too fast.

When I'm furious, I speed up. When I'm happy, I think I tend to slow down. Do you slow down when you're angry, or speed up? Did I pull a fast one on you?

I wasn't fasting for any biblical reason. I was fasting for a bilious reason.

> **Bilious:-** adj. 1. of the bile; 2. having or resulting from some ailment of the bile or the liver; 3. bad-tempered –bil'liously adv. –bil'iousness n.

Yes, all of the above. Anyway, whatever it was that was making me feel vile, I thought I'd starve it out of me. I thought I could detox my way out of feeling lousy. I just drank plenty of water and green tea. When I knew my stomach was completely empty, I threw down a couple of soluble aspirin to kill any lingering bugs. When I eventually ate, I was so hungry that the toast tasted exquisite. I'm easily pleased when I've fasted. I'm easy to please, when I've gone without.

Have you gone without?

Have you ever had this experience and gone without something for a long time? If you've had a drought, it might be time to break it. You may not know what you're missing. You may have even forgotten that you're missing out on something. You might now be able to see what you've missed. Don't miss out.

Fasting was what Buddha did to assist him to reach enlightenment. I always thought that through feeling faint, nauseas, and delirious with hunger, the Buddha's mind would have been more open to what is. His mind would be in a weakened state, and possibly not able to function in its usual way. Is fasting unsound?

> **Unsound:-** adj. 1. Not normal or healthy; 2. Not safe or secure; 3. Not safe and secure financially; 4. Not accurate, sensible, etc.

I think Buddha gained enlightenment through suffering. I question this seriously, because of the obvious factors surrounding this assumption, that beg me to re-examine my assumption.

Buddha was fat. Is that why he was fasting? Was he given a direction to lose some weight? I think not, because the diet wasn't working. Does the suffering have something to do with it? I was suffering. I was hungry as all get out, but I chose abstinence for my own health.

I was suffering in order to get well again. I did get well again, because I feel fine now. I suffered the pain in the short term, for the long-term gain. It was a gain, in reality. It's not a loss.

I'm at a loss to explain it

Leave Buddha alone for a moment and consider the starving people all over the world.

Some parts of the world just don't produce enough food for the population they have to support. Some of these places endure plagues, disease, famine, and other natural catastrophes, which makes matters even worse. These are the people who have only ever had less than basic sustenance, and security. They only survive on staples, like rice and grains. Their lives are hard lives. They can't predict their futures and often can't change them.

I can't be any plainer

Their food is plain food. When there's famine and crisis, and food becomes scarce, does plain food become more valuable and more enjoyable? Is it joyous to eat rice when rice has been taken from you? This is a sad story, but I want to continue with my thoughts for a moment more. I want to enlighten you.

When Muslim people fast during Ramadan, are they suffering? They have food available, but they choose to go without for the sake of their faith.

Why suffer the hardships of others?

A lot of us from Western societies don't understand this sacrifice. We don't understand, because we don't understand what comes from it. We won't understand until we try it. It seems odd, but it's not. It's just trying to even things up for a while. Until you've had something basic taken away, you cannot concede that it's not basic.

Concede:- vt. [< L. *com-*, with + *cedere*, cede] 1. to admit as true or certain; 2. to grant as a right -vi. 1. to make a concession; 2. to acknowledge defeat in an election, etc.

A bowl of rice can look basic when you've so much of it, and you can choose to eat it whenever you're so inclined. But when it's your only source of food and it's taken away, or there's so little of it to go around, will you ever truly understand its value.

It's only then that we suddenly understand how wonderful that bowl of rice really is. It tastes great, because we're starving, and it gives sustenance so that we can live. That bowl of rice can take away our pain and suffering for a while. It gives relief to minds and bodies. It's life. We can now contemplate that bowl of rice in a whole new light.

We are now grateful and offer up a million thanks. We're humbled by our food bounty. We're so joyous to have it in our bellies, because our bellies now *know* the feeling of being empty. We see things differently. We see the truth of the matter. We see the basic truth of life. If we miss the basic truth to life, what are we missing? We miss life. There's no time like the present for finding your life.

I gave praise for the toast and peanut butter. I was euphoric eating that meal. I munched it down in no time and felt completely satiated when I'd finished. It made me think of all the wonderful rich and expensive meals that I'd eaten in the past. It made me ask myself, did I really enjoy them as I should have? Could I have enjoyed them more than I did? Were those meals not enjoyed as they should have been, because I'd been spoiled for choice? Could plenty of other less fortunate people have enjoyed a meal on me and appreciated what I couldn't properly appreciate?

Had I taken away my own pleasure? You can only get pleasure from a meal, to the extent that you haven't had the pleasure of one. Do we miss pleasure for not having tried something? Always try for pleasure, because it might be just there waiting for you to get to know it. Risk a pleasure now and then. Risk a famine. This is how you'll know real pleasure. It will be in the now, and you get to look forward to it again, in the then.

Is the pleasure in less?

What I'm trying to express is less is more, and more is less. I've been spoiled for choice, and I've made the wrong choices. I can get the most tremendous pleasure with less. Can you believe I just said that? It's true.

I haven't known pleasure like I'm experiencing pleasure now. I truly see the good in less. I feel it, and see it. I really experience it. In my past, I wasn't truly experiencing anything. I didn't notice where joy could be found. Joy can be found anywhere, as long as you put it on its own, and make room for it. You don't have to fast, just slow down. Slow down, and experience the yin and yang of life. This was Buddha. He loved food, but he also loved going without. This was his extreme joy. He had to suffer it, in order to celebrate it. Have you ever tried it?

What about the starving people, I can hear you say? They'll only get to feel an extreme, if we're extreme in our generosity. If we give more, we get to feel more. When they get more, they get to feel more. Can you see the extreme point I'm making? They don't get it, if we don't give it. Should one side of the world be balanced by the other side of the world? What could we learn from their side of the world? Are we missing out from their missing out, and vice versa?

Extreme enlightenment

You're extreme. You have all the extremes. You may need to go a bit the other way. You may need to go all the way. It depends on how extreme you are. Just get balanced. You get so much, but how much do you give? You're one sided. Find the balance. Balance your up with your down, and the in, with the out.

Balance your sing, with your sang

This is the present and past tense, isn't it? Think about it. So, this is the present, and you're singing. You sang, in the past. What sort of singing did you do, in the past? Did it help your present? Was your past tense? Is your present tense? Don't tense up, when I ask you to look inward. I'm only bringing my inward out. You don't have to look at my innards. Look directly at your own innards. Clean them up, and you'll feel much better. It's a great paradox for detox.

I've got all my innards out on the table and I'll be practicing what I'm preaching. I believe. I've been preaching to the unconverted for a while now. Now I've converted. I haven't had anyone preaching to me. I've just been preaching to myself. I've found all this preaching inside and it wants to go outside.

I'll teach you a few tricks

I won't be outside preaching, because that's not as far-reaching as my book preaching. I've shown you my teaching. No I haven't, that's coming up. That's *The Teacher in Me*. It's already started preaching, because that's the job of teaching. I'm looking forward to getting even with teaching. They're an odd bunch.

I've been at odds with teachers in the past. I'd like to even up some odds. I'm going to even up the score. It's due. I've paid my dues. I've earned my right to a say. Some bad press might not go astray. I won't digress.

My Directions.

North, South, East and West.

You're in my heart,

you are my test.

South, West, North and East.

You're of the one,

that I know the least.

East, North, West and South.

All that I say,

Comes not, from my mouth.

The north is the point,

Encompassing all.

South is the point,

Of which I could fall.

The cross of the compass,

Will spell it all out.

A compass is true

And there's no room for doubt.

I wait for the arrow,

To teach and to guide.

Wherever it lands,

I'll follow my stride.

I am a mere follower.

By Ms T.L. Learner

I didn't recognize my value

If you get something for free, how do you receive it? Do you snatch it quickly, before it can be withdrawn? Do you protest the generous gift, and offer to pay for it? Do you offer to pay half? Do you accept it gratefully, and consider how you can pay it back in some other way? Do you tell others of your windfall, and let them know of the generosity of the giver? Do you boast about your free something, and about your cleverness in getting it, as if you had orchestrated it? Do you boast that you were worthy of it, and had earned that free something? Can you recognize when you've earned something, and when you haven't?

The big question, is indeed, a big ask. Did you enjoy it? This is a question of honesty. Have you been honest with yourself first? Were you accepting it, because you wanted to? Did you accept it, because you had to?

> **Windfall:-** n. 1. something blown down by the wind, as fruit from a tree; 2. any unexpected gain, esp. financial.

Which way is the wind blowing?

Do you ever consider that you should pay it back in some other way, to the universe? This is what good karma is. When I've been lucky, I've acknowledged my windfall as a bonus. It's the fluff on top. I've not seen myself as deserving, because I wasn't striving for it. I haven't earned it, and I didn't look for it. I see a windfall as something to be shared, because I had nothing, and it was turned into something. It's a magic moment. Should you share the moment? Do people want to share magic moments? Do they, and can they recognize the magic moments? If you've had too many magic moments, do they lose their magic? Has the magic I provided, lost its magic? What sort of free gifts lose their magic the quickest? Are they small magic, or big magic?

Magic is an illusion

Things appear and disappear, and you wonder where the magic went. I lost a lot of magic. I'd had some free magic, but most of my magic was hard earned. I thought I was magic, when I shared my magic around. I'd be happy with some reciprocated magic. I'm waiting for the magic to magically appear.

Working with black magic

Was it fair magic? Was it seen as pure magic? Was the magic in it, ignored? Was it demanded magic? Do you forget all the magic? I like helping people out. That's magic! Too much magic can spoil everyone's magic. I've got no more magic left. There's no more magic in me. Can I feel the real magic? I can feel magic. It's black magic.

Once a magic trick has been shown, it loses its magic. You can't keep repeating the same tricks. You end up with no more tricks up your sleeves. The tricks are over. Did you take a trick from me? There are no tricks left. I'm used up. Nothing up my sleeve, hey presto! I think I'm going to need another sleeve. Where does The General keep her armies? Up her sleevies.

No new magic

Who wanted more from me? Who wanted to work harder, and longer for me? Did we all hold each other back? When somebody does more, they'll naturally expect more. They'll usually demand more. Do they want what's fair, or just more? If you just want what's fair, you just do a fair day's work. That's fair!

Are market forces fair?

If people do more, does more income get generated? If there's more work done, there's more money being generated, isn't there? What about the market forces? If it's a poor market, we'll all just have to do more, in order to remain in a job. It's not the fault of the boss. He's not making anymore money in a poor market. It doesn't matter how much harder he works, or how much harder he works you. If there's no extra funds, there's no extra funds. These are the facts. You can't give something, if there isn't something to give. Did you ever give me something? Did I earn it? Was I worthy of it? Did I accept it gratefully? What was meant by it? Was it freely given, or was it expected to be returned in some other way? I don't accept gifts anymore, because I can't be sure as to whether it's white magic or black magic.

Painting magic white

At the moment, my magic is in the red. It's all red magic. How will I turn my red magic into white magic? This is the magic I've been waiting for all my life. This is karmic magic. It's going to depend on how much magic I've given out so far. This will be the magic moment. This could be the magic that finds its way back to me. I don't care how much magic there is, just as long as it's my magic. I may have to try and make some more magic, so remember how magic works. If you want some of my magic, you have to give out some magic of your own. You've got stacks of magic, and it's all stacked up, and not making an ounce of magic for you. Send your magic where it can do the most magic, and try and make someone's day magic. Look for people with no magic in their life, and where a little bit of magic goes much further. There will always be further magic made in this way. This will make you feel like magic! I'm not made of magic, but I was self-made magic. I made it, and then I un-made it. Now I have to make it again. I'll make it different. I want to make more of magic, and more magic, magic. I want to put my new magic in the right places, and take it back from places it wasn't magic in. It should have been magic, but I'm not a magician.

Magically employed

I must start making some magic first. This is magic right here. I can make magic with my words. Magic can come from good words, and bad words. Magic can come from truthful words. Magic is the realm in between.

I'm between jobs at the moment. This is an unemployed statement. So, it's not my statement. I'm employed. I'm fully employed. I'm employed for overtime too. I'm employed doing some night shifts, and day shifts. I'm also on call. I get called on to work in the middle of the night. I'm used to this.

I'm working. I'm working my magic on you. This is the job of a writer, and I'll be in it for the long run

Heartless callers

I used to do this all the time in my last job. My last job had me permanently on call. I was on call on public holidays, and even on Christmas day. I was on call at my mother's funeral, even when I called out what I was doing. When you're on call, you can never call it off. If you call it off, the client will call it a day, or just call somebody else. They're just constant non-stop callers.

I don't get paid for being on call. Shouldn't people just call it off, sometimes? You'd think they would, but they don't. I suspect that if I was dying in a hospital bed from a sudden heart attack, I would still have been called on. That's the calling I was in. It's an attack on the heart.

A magical vocation

Was my job a calling? Was my job a spiritual calling? I believe so. I believe it was the wrong calling. I think the calling was from down below, and not from up above. It was a bad calling. I think that's why so many real estate agents get burnt out from the job. It's purgatory!

> **Purgatory:-** n., pl. -ries [see ff.] 1. [often P-], in R.C. and other Christian doctrine, a state or place in which those who have died in the grace of God expiate their sins; 2. any state or place of temporary punishment.

I didn't burn out completely, because I never stepped right in. If somebody told you to put your head in a fire, would you do it?

This is a spiritual question, and a childish question. Most kids would say no. Some of us are still kids, and we were the kids that wanted to say yes, just out of spite. This is a question asked of me, when I was a child. I explained away my crime by saying that my friends told me to do it, and they were doing it too. I blamed my decision on others. Everyone does it!

Does this make it alright? Just because others do it, doesn't mean that you should do it too. Why, why, why, did I ever do it? I'm still a child. I didn't learn that lesson. Am I in that burnt-out place now expiating my sins?

Expialladocious

I was under a spell. There were some things I did, that I wish I hadn't. I felt ashamed of them, so I justified. I had a good imagination, so my justifications were very convincing. I was able to convince myself, that it was a good job and that I liked it. I didn't like, that I was good at it. I was ashamed that I was so good at it.

Why was I so good at it? This being clever at it, was where the shame was. I was surely capable. What was I capable of? What is anyone ever capable of? We are all capable, but to different degrees.

Am I culpable?

Did I teach others the power? Is the power to persuade, a force now to be reckoned with? Did this power go into the wrong hands? Powerful forces are at work. Is the power out of control? Is it being used for good, or evil?

Culpable:- adj. [< L. *culpa*, fault] deserving blame.

This isn't a power-trip for me. I never took such a trip because I was wary of the power. I didn't let power go to my head. I'd seen what it could do to other heads. It's terrible what some power can do to heads.

Magic powers

I knew more than other people, about people. I could work them out and work them over. This is despicable, but it's good business? It's good business acumen, but poor business practice. It's kind of cheating. What kind of cheating? Was I cheating myself? Was I stealing from the rich, and giving to the poor? Was that for my poor soul? Do the poor want dirty money? Is this how you clean money? Is this money laundering? Did I launder my powers?

Would you be cheated if a hypnotist made you do something you wouldn't normally do? This is a hypnotizing statement. Watch the pendulum closely, watch it sway backwards and forwards, backwards and forwards, and now you're getting sleepy. STOP!!!

I'm not a hypnotist, but I'm almost a mind-reader. I've been studying minds for a long time, and I've had many years of experience watching minds in action. I've contemplated our minds for many years. I've contemplated your mind and I've contemplated mine. I've contemplated information I've read about minds. I've researched minds. It's mind-boggling. I don't always believe everything I read. I listen to my own mind. I let my mind sort it out. If it doesn't ring true, I don't pay any mind to it. I wait for the ring tone.

I'm specialized, so I only know about the buying and selling minds. This is one enormous mind frame, but it's specialized. I've specialized in how minds tick in relation to real estate, real estate sales, and purchases, real estate renters and the real estate obstacles. Obstacles are just mindsets. All these minds are just your minds. Hardly any minds are left out of this mind frame.

I've figured out minds working out figures. I've figured out wives, figuring out ways to change their husband's minds. I'd figured out ways of helping them. I knew how they'd make up their minds, lose their minds, and say their minds. I knew what was on their mind. I worked out who minds what, and which ones they don't mind. I could see who the minders were, and who didn't have a mind of their own.

I watched minds working overtime, and their workings on my master mind. I witnessed some minds resenting, disregarding, and ridiculing other minds. I could see some minds minding their own business. Minding your own business is good if it's not your business, but some minds don't know what business is theirs, and what isn't. My mind didn't mind because I kept an open mind. I worked out smart minds and simple minds. I could prove that all minds can think alike if they liked. Most minds didn't like to use their minds. They liked to rely on other minds for thinking. This is where I would get into the minds of others. I liked being in their mind, and it was good for my mind. I liked to remind. Who do I remind you of? Who do the minds, remind you of? Were you on my mind, or was I on yours?

I created mind-altering situations, and mindless decisions. It was all just mind over matter. I had to bear in mind that sometimes I could be in two minds at once. Being in two minds at once, was just keeping it in my mind's eye. I had to keep an eye on each mind. It can be mind-blowing for my own mind. As long as my mind had the knowing, I could keep the other two minds in line.

I had to be mindful of who I could share a piece of my mind with. I knew my own mind on this, and I'd made up my mind. I thought I knew my own mind, but I didn't. I should have been more mindful, and not as mind full. I should have been minding my own business. This is where I always feel like I'm losing my mind. This was for the business. It was all in my mind, my business. It was always playing on my mind.

The business was playing

I had a team to support. They were all in support of my great mind. They would have minded very much if I wasn't supporting them. I had jobs to support with my mind. That was always on my mind. I had many people to support. I was their minder. Mind-numbing, isn't it? I bet you've blown your mind in this job, or I've just blown it for you! I'm not blowing the whistle, and I'm certainly not blowing my own trumpet. I'm just blowing it out of the water. Am I blowing it out of my arse? Am I purging?

Thank your lucky stars

You must know how to talk underwater too. This is mindless patter. Is this what client's want? Do some people really want to be hypnotized? Do they want to be spellbound? Do you read your star signs? If they say it's your lucky day, do you buy a lottery ticket? If someone gives you a sure tip for the Melbourne Cup, do you have a bet on it? When we ask for advice, do we have to take it? Are you a sure bet? Come in spinner! Roll up, roll up, and place your bets.

The punters

Do you take your winnings when you win? How do you take your losses? I win, you lose! You don't take it, do you? You blame. I don't win all the time. I lose a lot of the time. Win, lose, or draw. I lost. I lost most of the time. I lost it this time! It's a risky business. I don't blame you, when I lose. I blame fate. It wasn't meant to be. I blame bad luck. We all should blame bad luck. When we have a win we're in luck. It's not hard, luck. It's not you, making the luck. Luck is beyond our control. Did you know? Sometimes luck has all the control, and yet we think we can control it.

> **Luck:-** n. [prob. < MDu. *luk*] 1. the seemingly chance happening of events which affect one; fortune; 2. good fortune, success, etc. –down on one's luck, unlucky –in luck, lucky –out of luck, unlucky –push one's luck [Colloq.] to take superfluous risks – worse luck, unfortunately –luck'less adj.

Do we try to take the credit for our luck? What about our bad luck? Can we take the good with the bad? Everyone talks about the real estate losses they've suffered. I'm sick of hearing about their missed opportunities, or their missing money. They always moan about their losses, and they keep looking back and blaming someone else.

Do they count their wins? I didn't have to talk long, to find out where their wins were. They were always there. They were winners, but they couldn't see it. I just had to remind them. I fought a losing battle over wins and losses. Just put it down to bad luck, I'd say. Get on with it, and get over it. The longer they looked back for the missing ingredients, the longer they stayed where they were. The loss held them back. The losses always had a hold. That's because they held onto the blame. They blamed. They blamed someone else for their bad luck. This was just a little bad luck story. It's just your luck, I told it to you.

I don't blame anyone for my bad luck. I'm going to turn my bad luck into good luck. I'm lucky. I have The Knowing. It's the Maker in Me.

Was my bad luck, a lucky break?

When we have a win, we have such great luck. It's not bad luck. When we have a win, we're in luck. It's not hard luck. It's not you that makes the luck. You can't boast about good luck. You can boast about how hard you've worked for it, if you've worked for it. Sometimes you just get lucky and it's easy luck. That's the luck of the draw.

What's the draw card? Is there always a risk? Always, there's risk. You won't always be able to see the risk. You'll declare that there was no risk made. There probably wasn't. It was just pure luck.

Risk is a permanent

You live with permanent risk in your life. It's your life. It's in everyone's life. If there were no risks, there wouldn't be a draw. You won't be drawn in without the risk.

Write down everything at risk in your life today. You'll see that it's everything. It's all up for grabs. It's sitting in the hands of luck. It's resting in the hands of providence. Get over the risk. It's a hurdle, but you can leap it in a single bound. Is it a bird, is it a plane? Yes, there's another plane. It's as plain as day.

A supercalifragilistic risk

All real estate is a risk, just like any other investment you make. There's no such thing as a sure thing. When we see others with so much, we think there's a secret recipe for their success. We seek the recipe for our own success. We may be lured to investment seminars, and money-making schemes. These are not the place to find the recipes. These places only offer the ingredients. The ingredients will ultimately come from you. That's how they make a success. They make money out of showing you, success stories. So they make up a few good stories to show you, and you pay them more money to find new stories that show you how lucky some people are. They may not be making them all up, but they'll only show the good luck stories. They won't show you any of the bad luck stories. It's bad luck!

Success is just a good luck story

These are what they label the success stories, but they're just good luck stories. They're based on good luck. Sometimes they're founded on bad luck stories first. These are hard luck to riches stories. There's only one get rich quick scheme.

Lady Luck

That's the scheme! She's a bit shonky too. If there really were 'get rich quick schemes', wouldn't everyone be rich? We'd all be lining up for this sort of a scheme.

Most people with much of the wealth today, have enjoyed a shit load of good luck, but with good luck, there'll always be bad. You won't see the bad. They'll never show you that. They're only proud of the good luck, because they're claiming they created it all. They often won't see the bad luck either, until it's too late. They lose their sense of self, for their wealth.

A wealthy dynasty

Some people are born into wealth, and inherit their wealth. They may have inherited the wealth-building system. They've been born into a system where they can't see past their wealth. These are people born into family business systems. These are the people born to wealth builders, who have expectations of their wealth building abilities. They may achieve great wealth, but they'll never know the wealth within. Many will have sold their soul for this wealth, and that's like throwing the baby out with the bath water.

By stealth or by wealth, you'll be risking your health

There are those that are wealthy by stealth, and some that are stealthy from wealth. Wealth can ruin your health. Stealth is just as bad.

Once you have wealth, you can threaten your health by trying to keep it in health. Wealth is a huge responsibility. The bigger the wealth, the bigger the responsibility is. It can be too much responsibility.

I've seen what wealth can do to health. I've seen what bad health can do to wealth. Can you have one without the other? Which one? There's no point to wealth, if you haven't got your health. It's easy to get your priorities out of alignment, but you'll always get a wake-up call, so wake up when it comes.

Wealth is relative, not a relative

Wealth is only relative. This means that we're only as wealthy as who we compare ourselves to. To be satisfied with your wealth, you need to consider other people's wealth. You need to consider the happiness of people with much less wealth than you. If we allow ourselves to see real wealth, we'll be able to acknowledge and find the true wealth within ourselves.

Don't compete with a relative. It's not relative. You're not your relative. You don't have to match your relative, or better them. Relatives are just related. We're not related by wealth. Don't be pressured into wealth by your relatives. Pressured wealth is pressured health.

Don't wait for wealth from a relative. This is not healthy. It's not healthy for the relative either. The relative shouldn't have saved the wealth for you. You shouldn't bank on the wealth of a relative. This is stealth. It won't feel like real wealth, and you'll get no inner wealth from it.

My first parable

The person with only the ragged clothes on his back can see that he's rich, only when he sees his comrade with no clothes on at all.

His naked comrade will see that he is indeed rich, next to his dead comrade. Were they any richer for seeing?

> **Parable:-** n. [< Gr. *para-*, beside + *ballein*, throw] a simple story teaching a moral or religious lesson.

Do you get what my parable is about? It's about the picture you choose for yourself. You can choose any picture you want. You don't have to choose the harder picture. You don't have to choose too hard, a picture.

Those two blokes relied on other, to show them whether they were rich or poor. If they couldn't see each other, they wouldn't have had cause to consider where they stood. Is wealth about how and where we stand? What caused them to consider? What causes us to consider? Is wealth consideration, a painful consideration?

Have you considered who was the richest?

The richest one of all was the dead man. He wasn't in any pain. He didn't have to consider. He didn't have to compare, and he didn't have to suffer. He was free from competitive thoughts. He was free of stupid thoughts. He's finished with thinking and comparing. He was at peace. He was oblivious.

Am I allowed?

I wrote a parable, and I'm wondering if it's a conceited thing to do. Is it righteous? I'm trying to change that about myself. I'm wondering which man I am. Am I the dead man? Am I the dead man walking? Am I the dead man talking? I'm not in this trinity, because I'm a woman, and it's a woman's prerogative to change her mind.

What wasn't considered?

I wrote nothing about food. They all had food in their tummies, but you couldn't know that, because I didn't tell you. They couldn't see that either. They only saw what they wanted to see. It was all about the outer, and not about the inner.

Can this parable be applied to anyone? Can you apply it to yourself? Are you richer or poorer for reading it?

The healthy balance

What's a healthy bank balance? If we had one, would we feel any healthier? How much would we need the balance to be, for us to feel healthy? Would we know when we had a healthy bank balance?

This is a good question for me. Did I ever have a healthy bank balance? I didn't have a personal balance. I had a personal debt. I did however, have a healthy balance in my business account. This balance never made me feel healthy, because it was relied on to keep a lot of people feeling healthy. It had a lot of mouths to feed. It wasn't money that could be used like a windfall. It wasn't a windfall. It didn't just fall out of a tree. It was capital. Was it capital punishment?

> **Capital:-** n. [< L. *caput*, head] 1. a city that is the official seat of government of a state, nation, etc.; 2. money or property owned or used in business; 3. an accumulation of such wealth; 4. wealth used to produce more wealth; 5. [often C-] capitalists collectively; 6. same as CAPITAL LETTER –adj. 1. involving or punishable by death; 2. principal, chief; 3. being the seat of government; 4. of capital or wealth; 5. excellent –make capital of, to make the most of, exploit.
>
> **Capital:-** n. [< L. *caput*, head] the top part of a column or pilaster.

This capital was security. It wasn't security for me. It was only security for the business. It was securing the running of the business. I had to keep running. I was the capital too.

Capital punishment

This isn't a good balance. I was secured to the business for others. I was part of the capital. I was the capital. I was secured to that business by the capital letters on the door. I finally cut myself loose from that business. There were heavy mooring ropes holding me fast. I was in a noose. I found a loophole in that rope. Once I'd found one hole, I could see all the other holes. These were the weakest points in the rope, so I took up the slack and struggled out. Many people saw me struggling to get away, but they all wanted to lasso me back in. I'm still dodging the nooses they made for me.

That balance was in the balance

Trying to keep that bank balance up, was taking me down, one notch at a time. That business had been taking me down for a long time, and I was running out of rope. Was it enough rope? Ask Andrew Denton. He knows about roping people in. He knows when to throw the rope, and when to haul it back in again. He knows when to cut the rope. I like watching *Enough Rope* because it's honest interviewing. Andrew Denton conducts an honest interview. I need an honest interview. I haven't been given enough rope.

Asset rich

> **Asset:-** n. [< L. *ad*, to + *satis*, enough] 1. anything owned that has exchange value; 2. a valuable or desirable thing; 3.[pl.] a) all the resources of a person or business, as accounts and notes receivable, cash, property, etc. b) Law, property, as of a bankrupt.

An asset can be sold. My business was not an asset. It couldn't be sold. It would've been one hell of a hard sale. My business had no debt, but it did have assets. The assets could be sold, but not the business. I was the most valuable asset in that business, and I couldn't be sold. That's the answer.

What does a real estate business really have that's worth selling? The rent roll wasn't mine. The rent roll is a collection of landlords. They have no obligation to me. They just give thirty days written notice, and they say goodbye. I couldn't sell that to somebody? It's not a good asset, is it? It's not a sure thing. I'd be selling them a risk.

Did I risk too much?

A rent roll is always a risk. It's risky, both personally and professionally, and for more reasons than you suspect. A rent roll is people, not property. You take on its people, and they include landlords and tenants. These are people from all walks of life, and you never really know who they are, and where they've walked. I was always worried about my rent roll, because I was the agent. I was the go-between, and I was the authority.

You can end up between some angry people, and angry people are unpredictable people. These are people who are strangers. I didn't know them, and they didn't know me. Tenants would ring me in the middle of the night. This is a bad time to call, because usually emergency calls come in the middle of the night. My tenants just wanted to know how to turn the gas off. I had lots of stupid calls like this, and I wasn't the concierge. Would you want to buy a rent roll?

Was it honest accounting?

I know what you're saying. Other people do it. Well, another person could have done it, but he didn't. He didn't know anything about it. He must have wanted to wash his hands of it pretty quickly. He should have asked me first. I could have told him what he had on his hands. I could have given him an honest account, which is more than he's ever given me.

Selling words

Did I want to sell my name? What's a name worth? Mine isn't worth what I thought it was worth. A name can be a good name, or a bad name. A name is a risk. My name's now a liability. My name would have been a shame, had I sold it.

I didn't want to be asset poor. I didn't want to be asset rich

The valuation of the business was wrong. It was false. The business was a liability, not an asset. It was my job and my wage, I grant you, but it shouldn't have been a life sentence. I'd have been stuck in it for life. It would have become my life. It would have become my life's asset and a life sentence.

The business was valued at $260,000. With the addition of the capital in it, I was likely to achieve a minimal amount from the proceeds of the one true asset, the Hoorah. This was the only true asset. That's not true. It was a liability too. It was too much for me. It had always been too big, and too hard to maintain on my own.

What was the difference?

The settlement didn't look fair. I ran a business for ten years, but had no equity.

> **Equity:-** [< L. *aequus*, equal] 1. fairness, justice; 2. [pl.] the ordinary shares of a limited company; 3. [E-] the Actors' Trade Union; 4. Law, a system of rules as in Britain, supplementing common and statute law.

Suddenly I see what fair really is. I never understood fair, because I'd never had it. I want fair now. I want a rest from running up the hill. It's only now, that I can see a way down the other side.

My most valuable asset

Me. The real me, the one and only me, the original me, the authentic me, the wonderful me, the middle-ground me. Me, me, me, me, me, me…

The effects of a balance

What's a good account balance? I went off on a rant back there, but I'm back with you again to sort out your balancing. A good balance is one that doesn't change. Would you agree?

Would it make you feel secure? Yep! It's the ups and downs of the balance which cause the bad affect, isn't it? It's possibly not the ups, but certainly it's the downs. It might also be the ups, especially when you've seen how quickly the ups can go down. I'll give you the up and up, on this. This is what I'm up to. You can give me the thumbs up.

A casualty of causality

This is cause and effect. Don't be affected by the cause, be effectual for a cause. Don't be affected by the cause, and you won't feel the effect. Is this piece of writing ineffectual? I think I'm admitting the cause, and not worrying about the effect.

> **Causality:-** 1. causal quality or agency; 2. the interrelation of principle of cause and effect.

It's the balance you want to look at. You only need to balance yourself. Don't look for the ups and downs. What goes up must come down. Just look for the balance. Don't look at the statement. Bank statements are boring. A bank's statement is boring. They're not nearly as interesting as my statements. Banks don't tell you what to do with your statement. I do. Fuck it off!

I have a rude statement for my bank

This is a legal statement. The bank has acted illegally. My bank has acted on my behalf without my permission. I've had no correspondence from my bank. It doesn't communicate with me anymore. It hasn't listened to me, because it's been listening to others. I'm nothing to my bank now. We've been together for twenty-eight years. No explanation necessary.

How necessary was I?

A rude awakening statement

I hate to think of all the money my bank has made out of me. I want to know what money I made from it. Maybe I did make some money out of some of the loans I took, but I worked a lot bloody harder for it. I was never late, and I never missed a beat. I still got beat up though. They beat me up, without any evidence. I'll beat the bank in the long run. I'm here for the long run. I'm going to run with it.

An unenlightened bank

My bank is no saint, but it's full of dragons! It works for the other side. My bank is just a workplace for some. Who takes responsibility in a bank? It's a black hole. It's nothing, because it hasn't got a soul. There's no one soul responsible.

This is the way to run a business, isn't it? Does the devil have a soul? If you haven't got a soul, you have no feeling. There's no point in fighting my bank because it just wouldn't feel the blows. I could take stabs at it, but it just wouldn't register the pain. That's why you can't hurt a bank.

Is your number up?

Can a bank hurt the people that work for it? Definitely not! You can't hurt numbers. Numbers are just nouns. Numbers are tools. Numbers are just phonetic sounds. What can numbers do? They just add up and subtract, don't they? Do they do much multiplying? I hate numbers. I was never a number lover. I hate math. Numbers are logic. Logic is boring.

> **Logic:-** n. [ult. < Gr. *logos*, word] 1. the science of correct reasoning; 2. a book on this science; 3. correct reasoning; 4. way of reasoning [poor logic]; 5. the systemized interconnections in an electronic digital computer.

Shit! I didn't see this coming. The Greeks reckon it comes from the Greek word *logos* which means 'word'. I'm into words, but I'm as sure as hell, not into numbers.

Do banks use the Triple Filter Test?

What would Socrates have said about this? Can words be logical? Words aren't necessarily logical. Are my words all logical? What about the words that have been said about me? Are they logical? Does logic make sense?

'Sense' is a word, but it isn't tangible, is it? It's not making any sense to me. It's just a feeling. Are feelings logical? "What do you mean Socrates? Can Plato tell me?" Aristotle would have given it to me straight, if he was still around.

> **Sense:-** n. [< L. *sentire*, to feel] 1. ability to receive and react to stimuli, as light, sound, etc., specif., sight, touch, taste, smell, and hearing; 2. a) perception through the senses [a sense of warmth] b) a generalized feeling [a sense of longing]; 3. an ability to judge external conditions, sounds, etc.; 4. an ability to feel, appreciate or understand some quality [a sense of humour]; 5. a) sound thinking, judgment b) something wise or reasonable [talk sense]; 6. [pl.] normal ability to reason soundly [to come to one's senses] meaning, as of a word -vt. sensed, sens'ing 1. to be aware of, perceive; 2. to understand; 3. to detect, as by sensors –in a sense, from one aspect –make sense, to be intelligible –take the sense of the meeting, to take a vote, etc.

My dictionary's straight up with it

Words aren't as logical as numbers. Not like numbers. Which would you go for, words or numbers, when you're trying to be logical? The logical choice for Democritus would have been numbers.

The logical winner

A number is a word, you idiot! Words win. Words win hands down. Words will always win. Language wins. Language will always win any war, or argument. Language came first. Without language, we'd be dumb. Are you deaf?

> **Deaf:-** 1. unable to hear 2. unwilling to hear or listen.

Our language should come first. Our language is what separates us from animals. Our language is what makes us human, but it can also turn us into animals. Our language is our first weapon. It's our first line of defence. I've only ever used words for a battle, but words can hurt the most. I'm battling words now. I've been battling against words for a while.

You could sense where I was going, couldn't you?

Did you know? I could make my words cut you to the quick. My words could slice you up, and dice you. Words are weapons. Words will always be your best weapon. What's in a word?

A word can be so destructive. A word can have an effect. Words affect us in ways we aren't even aware of. This is how sneaky words can be. Words can be subliminal. They can sneak right into our psyche, without us even knowing they've got inside. Words are our mental fight. They're not a physical fight. Words are from our heads. They come from the top. Have you got anything up top? I've insulted you, and called you an idiot. I've insulted you with my words. How does it feel? Will you remember my words?

Which words hurt the most?

"Did she give you a good deal? Be careful there!"

These don't hurt. These words were meant to do a job, but they didn't. I know of all your words and the jobs you've had for them. Have they done a good job on me? Yep. They've given me a new job. It's the job of a reporter. I'll be reporting the words from now on. Words are so powerful. Are they more powerful coming back, than going forwards? Is a Holden better in the motion of going forward, or in the motion of reversing? I'm going to back up a bit here, because some people don't know whether they're coming or going. What's a good direction? Which way is the fair wind blowing?

I'll remember the words

The words we remember, are the words that strike at our emotions. These are words that cause our emotions to be stirred up. They're stirring words. They can stir up all sorts of other memories in us. They can hit our most sensitive spots, and make them even more sensitive. It's hard to stop words hitting these spots, and sometimes we can't ignore them. They just keep gnawing away at us.

Words can change our lives

Is it the truthful words that do the damage, or the false? True or false? Which hurt the most? I'm considering, and I just don't know. I'm in two minds about this, because some words originate from an altogether different place, from the place they eventually come out of. They're passed on without a thought for the direction they're headed in, and for the damage that can ensue. I know about the word 'ensue'. I know what might ensue, with the writing of my true words.

> **Ensue:-** [< L. *in-*, in + *sequi*, follow] 1. to follow immediately; 2. to happen as a consequence; result.

Is a launching pad a high horse?

I've analysed a lot of the words that have been launched into space about me. They haven't been launched directly at me, but I hear of them. They mustn't be for me. If these words were for me, they'd be spoken to me personally, and I'd have a chance to accept them, or reject them.

I'll have words with you over this

I'm not being spoken to, but I'm seeing the spoken words. The writing is not for me, so much as for the court. They are just tales.

"Sticks and stones may break my bones, but words can never hurt me."

I can't be hurt by words that aren't true. I can only be hurt by words that are true. True words, that cause me shame, can hurt. I'm not without shame, nobody is. I have my own private shame about certain sins I've committed, which I regret. My shame is private shame. I don't hear words that attack me truthfully. I don't have anything I'm ashamed about, since January 2011.

One man's shame is another man's glory

It just depends on the circumstances. The circumstances of the first man's shame, may not be as justified, as in the circumstances of the second man.

I'm ready to be judged, but only by the one and only judge. I don't want a jury, because a jury cannot know my circumstances. A jury doesn't know me. A jury is a forced opinion. A jury is a majority opinion. That's its purpose.

Judges shouldn't rely on a jury to make the decision for them. If you hold yourself as a judge, you should hold yourself as judge and juror. You can't go wrong, can you? Do judges and jurors, who make a wrong decision and send an innocent person off to jail, incur consequences for their mistake? The compensation money doesn't come from their pockets. Where is the incentive to make the right judgment?

I've never been chosen to do jury duty, and I never want to. I'd never want the responsibility, because I'm not responsible, and nor should I be. Who is responsible for another's life? What's the protocol for picking a jury? Do you fit the criterion? Are you so wise and knowing, that you can make the call that will affect a stranger's life forever? Be careful what job you do in life, because anything you do can cause an effect. I believe that whatever you send out into the world, you must be ready to one day receive it all back. It's a boomerang.

Feeding time at the zoo

Words are fodder. We eat up words, and sometimes we spit them out in disgust. Like fodder, we sometimes leave our words for animals. Animals aren't as discerning as humans, they just gobble up whatever fodder is put in front of them. Do humans do this? Should we more thoroughly investigate words, before we gobble them up?

Struck down by words

Look at how words have taken me down. I've been slashed by slanderous words. These are all your words about me, and against me. These are not logical words. Most of these words are without reason. You haven't used the correct words for your reasoning. Where did you come up with your words? Were they words you accepted from others? Were they your words? Were they words that came from your thinking? Did you just borrow someone else's words? Have you given them back yet? If you don't give your borrowed words back, you're stealing. Get a dictionary and come up with your own words. Your dictionary will have them all. It will help you to reason why.

My words will win. My words are the real words. They are the original words. They originate from me. No they don't! They get put together by me. I do the arranging with the help of my dictionary.

I have chosen my words carefully. Mark my words! Don't you dare mark my words! I'll be doing that in *The Teacher in Me*. I know something about teachers, and I'll have a lot to say about them too. I'll be demonstrating how powerful words can be, but teachers should already know their power. Are teachers a power unto themselves?

The wealth built-in

Built in robes are handy, aren't they? Real estate agents just refer to them as 'b/ins'. You can shorten anything. I just shortened wardrobes to robes. I'll be looking for the short version from now on. I'll want small and compact.

> Wardrobe:- n. 1. a cupboard or cabinet with hangers for holding clothes; 2. a room where clothes are kept, as in a theatre; 3. one's supply of clothes.

I am, my own wardrobe mistress. I can decide who I'll be, from my clothes. My clothes are what I'll take with me. I haven't got many clothes, but they're my new clothes.

Some are brand new, and some are second-hand. Some were expensive, and some were cheap. These clothes are the new me. They're all different, for all the differences in me. Are you with me? Can I make a difference?

> **Wardrobe mistress:-** the person in charge of the costumes of a theatrical company.

Travelling in disguise

This is my new company. It'll be full of my own theatrics. I'll be dressing me up, and dressing me down. I'll need a built-in wardrobe. I'll need suitcases. This is all I'll require. They have built-in handles for me to carry them by. I have built-in arms, and they're strong. I'll need strong arms, because there's more that I'll need to take with me. I'm not sure how I'll carry them, because they'll be quite heavy.

For my new words

I'll need a 'wordrobe'. This isn't a word yet. I'll be making this word, when I figure out how to carry all my books. These books of mine are heavy. They're heavy going. These are the books that make me feel heavy. They're heavy reading, and they supply me with some heavy thinking to do. I don't use everything I read. I don't really want to. Not everything I read is correct. Do you read stuff that you know is incorrect? Do you read into things correctly? I sometimes have trouble with this. I read too far in. I read into the depth. I read as if I'm in the book itself. I get right into the picture. Are you in my picture? Have you read as deeply into my books? I like to throw a picture or two at you, in case you fit into them. It's hard to see your own picture sometimes. A picture can paint a thousand words. I've seen a lot of pictures, and I've read a lot of words.

> **Wordrobe:-** n. 1. a cupboard or cabinet with shelves for holding books; 2. a room where books are kept, as in a library; 3. one's personal supply of books.

Slamming some words down

Right, well I'm all set then. I have my new word, and my new wordrobe to put it in.

Don't use this word, because you might get into trouble. I think there could be rules about making new words. I'm not sure what the penalty is for making a new one without asking. Do you think it's a bad practice? Will a literary genius be offended?

Offensive words

I get offended all the time by words. Some of them don't make sense. Some of them confuse me. I've been a bit offensive to some of the words in the dictionary. I've taken away their credibility. I've disputed their meaning. I've been sorting a few words out for you. They needed sorting out, because we've been relying on them when they're unreliable.

You can't believe all words. They're just not all credible. My dictionary's not infallible either. We are all fallible. Did you know that fallible comes from deceiving?

> **Fallible:-** adj. [< L. *fallere*, deceive] 1. liable to be mistaken or deceived; 2. liable to be inaccurate –fal'li-bil'ity n. –fal'libly adv.

Everything, I mean everything, is fallible. Are the words of God fallible? Yep! Is God fallible? Yep! Am I fallible? Yep! Do you want to know my theory? It's just a theory, and it's not infallible, but fallible has an opposite.

> **Infallible:-** adj. [see In- & FALLIBLE] 1. incabable of error; 2. not liable to fail, go wrong, etc.; 3. R.d. Ch. incapable of error in setting forth doctrine on faith and morals –infal'libil'ity n. –infal'libly adv.

Did you pick me up on it? God is infallible. Actually, he's both, and so are we. It's the balance. There will always be right and wrong. There will always be opposites. Everything we do is an adjustment. I reckon God makes adjustments too. Otherwise the world would be just perfect to start with, and we'd never be able to appreciate it, because we wouldn't know imperfect.

I read a quote recently, in a book called *Simple Abundance* by Sarah Ban Breathnach. The quote was from a lady by the name of Louise Bogan, but I've never heard of her. I doubt she was any kind of a bogan.

> "I cannot believe that the inscrutable universe turns on an axis of suffering; surely the strange beauty of the world must somewhere rest on pure joy."

> **Axis:-** n., pl. *ax'es* [L.] 1. a real or imaginary straight line on which an object rotates or is regarded as rotating; 2. a central line or lengthwise structure around which the parts of a thing, system, etc. are evenly arranged; 3. a straight line for reference, as in a graph –the Axis, Germany and Italy, and later Japan as allies in World War Two.

I have an axe to grind

> **Axe:-** n., pl. ax'es [OE. *eax, aex*] a tool with a long handle and a bladed head, for chopping wood, etc. –vt. axed, ax'ing 1. to trim, split, etc. with an axe; 2. a) to dismiss (employees); b) to reduce, restrict (expenditure, etc.) –get the axe, [Colloq.] to be discharged from one's job –have an axe to grind, [Colloq.] to have an object of one's own to promote.

Do you know what I'm grinding my axe on? What's your name?

This is a question, with an answer after it. What's the opposite of a question? Yep. Answer.

Does every answer, have its own question? Would you agree with me, if I said that any answer could have a series of different questions posed to it? Do you believe the opposite could also be true?

This is important thinking, and I'm hoping you'll really think about it, comprehend it, and dwell on it. It poses a great deal of thinking. I'm posing, because I came up with it all on my own. I didn't read it, or learn it. I just thought about it. I had a brainstorm. It stormed into my head out of nowhere. So where did it come from? What am I promoting? Questions or answers?

Just a word, between you and me

Can you say more in a book than you can in person? Are we more articulate and personal in books? Is a book more personal than a person? I think they are. I think I am. I'm not a book, but I'm in one. I'm not only in one, or two, or three. I'm not only in four, or five, or six. I'm in more. I'm in all of them. All mine, that is.

I wondered today – would it be possible for someone to write us into their book, without us even knowing? You might never know someone's written about you. Someone else would have to recognize you, by your story maybe, or from a pretty definite description. Could you prove that it was you? How do you prove it? How could you prove it? I can't prove anything.

A book can always tell you something

Nobody's ever told me what books have told me. There are secrets in books. Secrets don't always get told in person. It can be too personal. Through this book, I have the freedom to talk. I have the freedom to talk at you, and for you. I have the freedom to tell you, and to tell you off. I can dress you up, or I can dress you down. I can write about what I think of you. I also feel the need to write about myself. I write myself off, when I'm writing. Am I taking my writing too seriously? Is my writing serious writing? Do we all like to read serious things, or would we rather read frivolous things?

Frivolous:- adj. [L. *frivolus*] 1. trifling, trivial; 2. silly and light-minded.

I don't like the idea of my books being frivolous. I don't want my life to be frivolous anymore. That's not true. I want some frivolity.

Where will I go for frivolity? It's been a long time since I had any frivolity. It's been a long time between drinks.

My last drink was a night of frivolity. It was my girl wonder's twentieth birthday bash. I didn't join in the frivolity because I opted to enjoy more serious company.

A V.I.P.

It was the security company. I would love some security company now, but the security has gone. I wasn't that secure. I couldn't get any security from this company, so it was a pointless pursuit. I don't need the security now, but I wouldn't mind the company.

I don't have any company anymore. I barely have company. I just have three companies, two of which I see more of, but one of which I see little, but she's busy with her own company. I just have me, for company. My biggest and most important company is you. Am I leaving something out?

Thanks for your company

You've been my day-to-day company over the last six months. I made you my company before you knew you'd have my company. Now you have my company, how do you find it? I wish your company would talk back occasionally. You don't talk back to me. I'd like some back chat. How could you back chat an author? Am I asking for trouble? I'm always up for a bit of trouble.

Can you chat back?

I've had so little company for such a long time now, and I'm not sure I'd know what to say to some back chat. I'm not sure I'd be able to handle much chat. I might be all chatted out, thanks to you.

What happens if I get chatted-up? What will I do then? I've never been chatted-up. I wouldn't recognize it if it happened. I just wouldn't know the difference. I haven't had any experience of it.

Who chats-up whom? Is a chat-up, a come on? I'd have to have a chat with you first, to work out whether it was, or not.

What would I chat back? I'd need to chat about it first. I could just think about it. I don't think I can think without writing, now. I've been so used to writing all my thinking down, as I'm thinking it. I might have to write as I'm chatted. Is that too much chat? Is that ratting out a chat? I'm planning my chat. That's the best way, while I've got you here now. I'll figure out a way to chat when I get chatted. I have a few questions for you:

1. How do you know when you're being chatted-up?
2. What's the difference between being chatted-up, and just having a chat?
3. If the difference is the middle, can it make a difference?
4. How many degrees in a difference? (Remember I'm not much good at math).
5. Is it about the temperature, and if so, mine or theirs?
6. How would I measure it?
7. Should you measure it? I already know my answer to this one.

No more questions. You shouldn't question it, should you?

That could be the way of it. Would that be a private chat? I'm pretty public, as it turns out. This is an oxymoron. I feel like a moron now.

> **Moron:-** n. [< Gr. *moros*, foolish] 1. [Colloq.] a very stupid person;
> 2. a person having mild mental retardation.

Well this isn't me after all, because I'm not mild. I'm not high either. I'm moderate. I'm the middle ground.

Serve it with words

Check out my Facebook and give me a serve. Serve me some fluff. I need fluffing. I'm a vendor now. I'm selling out. I'm selling real estate agents out. I wonder if I'll cop a serve from any real estate agents. Be careful, because The Goddess Lisatrace will be watching, and she knows how to spread the word.

I've had my first open house today. I was open. I was here and working with you the whole time. I must have looked closed, because there were no openers. There wasn't an acknowledgement that I was here at all. I was ignored in my own house. That's alright, because this is how this house works. I've been ignored in this house plenty of times.

Unfairly charged

People have no manners these days. I had no manners today, because I didn't welcome the lookers or introduce myself. The agents were in charge. Am I being charged for this service? I think I am, but the agent assumes the other vendor is in charge. Who should be in charge?

I haven't had any feedback, so I'm guessing I'm not charged with being in charge. What have the agents been told my charge is? What are my charges? I think the agent is charging too much. I think he's trying to overcharge. He's over the top with his estimation on price. I might need to condition him. I feel like doing the opposite to what I would ordinarily have done. I feel like using my old tools of trade, for an opposite result. This is karmic, isn't it?

Chargeable fairness

I'm a liability in this house. I come with the job of selling it, but this time it's not my job. I'm living here, in the item to be sold. I form part of the package until the auction. I might think about how I can unwrap some of this agent's packaging. Packaging can be hard to unwrap sometimes, but I don't mess about. I'm not worried about tearing the paper, or ripping the card. This is a gift! I'm going to have the best fun getting the wrapping off this gift. I'll let you in on the ways that I can unravel it, as I unravel. An agent is a gift.

Attract me with words

Are words money? Can good words be money? Can bad words be money? Which words make the most money? I had a lengthy word to myself about this, before using any of these words. I had a long word to myself, before I put any words on paper. I thought about the words people are attracted to. I knew they'd all be in the dictionary, so I had all the words given to me free of charge. I just had to know about people. I just had to have The Knowing. I also know a bit about marketing. I've been marketed to, with words. I know what I'm attracted to, and intrigued with. The main words are as follows:

Scandal, secrets, sex, gossip, deceit, disfigurement, mystery, philosophy, comedy, conspiracy, crime, tragedy, horror, violence, happiness, knowledge, love, hate, miracles, madness, suspense, risk, trouble, beauty, cheating, resurrection, discrimination, misery and hope.

I only needed one word, didn't I? I only required one word for all these words. What's the word? Sit down, lean back and contemplate it. Think about one word that could have described all these words. Have a smoke. It always helps me to come up with the answer. Just be aware. Consider yourself sitting there contemplating, drawing in, and breathing it out, in a cloud of your own smoke. You've almost got it. You're almost there. It's you! It's life!

It's me

There's more to you than that, isn't there? Well I'm not going to write a book about it. If you're middle-aged, like me, you'll have experienced all these words yourself. You'll usually want to know something more about them, at this stage in your life. If you're living an illusion, you won't accept that you've experienced all of these words, but you're just in denial. It's the very reason you're attracted to them too. We're all in the same boat.

The subject is being suspended for a short interval

Some of us can see the boat we're in, and some of us can't. We don't always see what's in the boat with us. We may have more dangerous things in our boat, than what's over the side of the boat. Are you going to jump ship?

I did. I'm treading water. I can't swim anywhere yet, but I'm free. I'm just hanging around the boat for a while. It's alright, because I've got a rope to hold onto, and it's tethered to the boat. I won't drown. I can pull myself up at any time, but I love the freedom of the water. It's soothing. It's cool! It's not cool, as in temperature, it's just a fucking good ride. It's awesome!

It's being wholesome

> **Wholesome:-** adj. [see WHOLE] 1. good for one's health or well-being; 2. tending to improve the mind or character; 3. having or showing health and vigour; 4. suggesting health.

I feel wholesome, because I'm taking my own advice. I'm doing all the things that I've suggested in my books. These were things I was suggesting for you, but I thought I'd test them out on me too. I've tested and experimented, and the results are obvious. They're obvious to me, because I feel them. I feel wholesome. I feel luscious, lithe, healthy and free.

I've just been down to the beach for a swim. There was a crowd there, but I walked further along to a beach that was empty. I didn't have to share. Even when I'm in a crowd, I don't share. I see what I want to see. I see the environment, but first I see me. I'm just concerned with me. I'm looking inwards, and my inwards are looking outwards. I take in the smell, the fresh air, the noise of the waves, and my eyes take in the glistening water. I swim for myself and the sea. It's at the very edge of the Australian coastline that I am. I'm on the edge, looking out and over. I'm looking over it with new eyes. They're just my eyes. I don't need to share it, because I have it all to myself, with myself, and for myself. I took it and loved it. I'm alive. I feel the sun warm on me as I lay on my towel. My body feels happy. I don't need a smoke. I never need a smoke, until I come back down to earth. When I come back down to earth, it's a bump. I bump my head, and my mind starts ticking over again about things that are earthy. These are usually things I can't do anything about, in the present moment. I come back to the present moment, and it's good. It's wholesome again and I'm back enjoying myself. I'm enjoying what I have to offer myself. I've become greedy for self.

Living exclusively

Can you enjoy yourself too much? I don't mean just enjoying whatever is going on around you. I mean, just yourself, with nothing going on around you. This is when I'm not aware of anything going on around me. I've become selfish with myself. I'm careful now of sharing too much of myself with anyone else. I choose what I share of myself. I choose. I get to choose it all now. I've found every inch of my own free will. It's all in my mind. It's not outside of me. Free will is inside. This is where I'm most free. Nobody can enter, unless I say they can. Sometimes I do. When they do, they find things. They find what's inside me. I've chosen to open some of me, to only a couple of people. I think they wish they were me, because they're changing things about themselves now. They're helping themselves to what I know.

We don't always take ownership of our own decision making. We decide subject to others, when we should be deciding for ourselves. Some people base all their decisions on other people. I used to do this. I don't anymore. I don't worry about how my decisions affect others, because I'm only deciding what's good for me. If other people happen to have an issue with it, it's their issue. They're simply not my issues.

I've been suspended

I'm suspended by the buoyancy of the water. The buoyancy comes from the salt. Where does the salt come from? If we don't get enough salt, we can die. I've seen salt mines in Port Hedland. They're great hills of white glare. They're so white, that just looking at them hurts your eyes. We are salty. The water from our eyes is salty. Why isn't the water from our mouths salty too? Why are our tears always salty?

This is to tempt your taste buds

We have different tastes in us. We have different tastes from different parts of our bodies. We are walking, talking, tasting, machines. Our bodies are like the wine-tasting tours. There are some places we'd like to tour, and some places we wouldn't. There are some tastes we like, and some we don't like. What you would, and what you wouldn't, is just up to your individual tastes. Some people have a taste for certain things as opposed to others.

> **Fetish:-** n. [< Port. *feitico*, a charm] 1. any object believed to have magical power; 2. anything to which one is irrationally devoted; 3. any nonsexual object that abnormally excites erotic feelings –fet'ishism n.

Can you make your body taste better? Can we mask a taste, in order to improve it, and make it sweet? We do it all the time to food. We add sugar or honey, to sweeten a taste. It can make the food more palatable. It can make food more pleasurable. Vanilla Extract knows about this subject, but she gets jealous of the other masks.

> **Mask:-** n. [Fr. *masque* < It.] 1. a covering to conceal or disguise the face; 2. anything that conceals or disguises; 3. a) a moulded likeness of the face b) a grotesque or comic representation of a face, worn to amuse or frighten; 4. a protective covering for the face [a gas mask]; 5. a covering for the mouth and nose, as for administering and anaesthetic, etc.; 6. the face of a dog, fox, etc –vt. to conceal, cover, disguise, etc. with or as with a mask.

I've got an idea

I have a masquerade mask. It was given to me as a gift. It's a very glamorous mask, but looks a bit evil. It's black with gold edging, and has gold glitter around the eye holes. It has lots of sparkle, and it looks magical. It's my magical mask. I just tried this mask on, and looked to my left into the mirror. I don't look the same. Suddenly I look sinister. I look like I have something on my mind. I don't look innocent with this mask on. I look like I'm up to something. I can't be identified with this mask on. What can we do with a mask on, that we couldn't do without? Without one on, I mean. Would we forget who we are?

Who wears the mask?

Motorbike riders wear masks. They're built into the helmets sometimes. They're for protection in case of an accident. Balaclavas are masks too. Sometimes thieves use them, so they can't be identified. Is it for the inner identification, or the outer identification?

Actors wear masks. A mask encourages you to take on its persona. It's a natural phenomenon. This is the reason why kids love playing dress-ups. Kids often want to act grown up. Dressing-up helps them to get into the right frame of mind. Are we a good frame of reference?

What about adults? When you try on a mask, the first thing you'll do is take on the persona of the mask's image. If someone passes you a mask to put on, you see yourself in the mirror and immediately start acting the goat. You may be acting the witch, or the monster. I may be acting the clown. However we decide to act, has much to do with the type of mask we have on.

The output reflects the outfit

Do we like to play dress-ups? Are we still all growing up? Do we like to act out? Are adults acting out childhood? Are we reliving our childhood, or living it still? Is there something left over from our childhood, that needs reactivating in adulthood? Is it healthy acting? Is it good therapy?

> Masquerade:- n. [see MASK] 1. a ball at which masks are worn; 2. a disguise; pretence -vi. -ad'ed, -ad'ing 1. to take part in a masquerade; 2. to act under false pretences – mas'querad'-er n.

My mask is coming off

> Masochism:- n. [< L. von Sacher-Masoch] the getting of pleasure, specif. sexual pleasure, from being dominated or hurt – mas'ochist n. –mas'-ochis'tic adj.

Don't make assumptions that you know nothing about. I've just used this definition, to get you out of the Masquerade Ball. It's time to come home now, before anything more gets revealed. Put your mask back on, and come and play in my inner sanctum with me. I have my mask in place, and you have yours in place. I'll have to imagine what your mask is. You can be a fox. You're not a dog. I'll be the dog. A dog and a fox are in the definition of 'Mask'. It's the best two examples to use.

> Fox:- n. [OE.] 1. a small, wild mammal of the dog family, with a bushy tail: thought of as sly and crafty; 2. its fur; 3. a sly, crafty person -vt. 1. to baffle; 2. to trick by slyness; 3. to stain (book leaves, etc.) with brownish discolourations; 4. [Aust. Colloq.] to chase and retrieve (a ball) –foxed adj.

Am I outfoxed?

Am I to be outfoxed by a mask?

Scandal, secrets, sex, gossip, deceit, disfigurement, mystery, philosophy, comedy, conspiracy, crime, tragedy, horror, violence, happiness, knowledge, love, hate, miracles, madness, suspense, trouble, beauty, fox, dog, cheating, resurrection, discrimination, misery and hope.

You could be a younger reader. If you haven't reached mid-life yet, you've got all these words to look forward to. They're not all bad words. Some of these words can be both good, and bad. Each one of them should be interesting to us. They teach us about ourselves. They should teach us what's important, and what's not. They teach us about each other, and why we are what we are. If they aren't interesting to you, then you're not a thinker. You don't think about anything important. Why don't you start thinking about important things? Do you know why you don't?

You're not evolved

You're a chicken and you squawk and flap around, if you think you're being threatened. You're a dog that bails up the first intruder, growling and barking. You could be a timid rabbit that runs for its burrow at the first sign of change in the air. You might be a cockroach that prefers to live in dark corners, and scuttles away when the light gets switched on. You might be a sly and cunning fox that stays in its foxhole when it's being hunted. You could be the fox who steals the chickens when nobody's looking.

A habitat for a mask

So, be a human. Be humane. You have an intelligent brain, unlike the aforementioned creatures. You may not be a fully evolved human, but you are way more evolved than an animal. Would you prefer to be a creature? Are these creature habits? Where's your preferred habitat?

Do all creatures of the same species, share the same habitat? Are their habitats alike? What habitat would you like? Would you like to try a new habitat? Humans have many different habitats to choose from. We can have a change of habitat. This is a good habit to get into. Trying out new habitats, is the forerunner to changing from your old habitat to your new habitat. When you get sick of your habitat, you'll feel sick until you change it. This is the same for habits.

Is your habit your habitat?

Are our human habitats the same? Do all humans need the same habitat? Are we just choosing the same habitat out of habit? Are we ruled by our habitat? Does it strangle us, and hold us to ransom?

In Australia, there's a huge range of habitats on offer. Some humans in the world, are stuck in the one habitat all their life, and they don't see the advantage of changing habitats. We're spoiled for choice, but we spoil it by not choosing. Some people just accept their habitat like a prison sentence. Why sentence yourself to one habitat? A more fulfilling habitat could be just around the corner. I'm pretty sure you should try and go a bit further than that, if you really want to change your habitat. Go further than around the corner. A habitat is a habit with an 'at'. This can be where it's at!

Have all my words been in vain?

> **Vein:-** n. [L. *vena*] 1. any blood vessel bringing blood back to the heart; 2. any riblike support in an insect wing; 3. any of the fine lines in a leaf; 4. a layer of mineral, rock, etc. in a fissure or zone of different rock, lode; 5. a streak of a different colour, etc., as in marble; 6. a distinctive quality or strain [a vein of humour]; 7. a temporary state of mind, mood.

Is anyone going to want blood, from the vein of my writing? The people that are in it, might. Would you like to be written into a book? Would you want the truth written about you? I only write in truth, because I'm sick of lies. I'm sick of all the lies people tell. Tell it like it is. It's the hard facts. Just accept that it's hard. If we didn't have hard, we wouldn't know soft. Soft is easier, but that's just going soft. Don't go soft in the head from too much softness. Don't get hard in the head from too much hardness. Just strike a balance. Strike a match for yourself, and light up your life a little at a time. You might strike it lucky!

Back to the lessons

Wealth can be self-made. This is wealth built on passion. This is the best wealth you can get, but don't get passion mixed up with something else. Don't start with the idea of building wealth. Start with a purpose that makes you feel passionate. If it builds the wealth within, it can manifest the wealth without. This is me. I'm wealthy within, and I'm the wealth without. I'm without the monetary wealth. This is good, because it stops me getting mixed up with what real wealth is. I have wealth. I have $16 lined up on the kitchen bench in silver coin. I have two tomatoes, and three potatoes. I have some frozen bread left, and a small chunk of cheese. I have four eggs. I have half a lettuce and two carrots. I have half a packet of biscuits, some green tea and normal tea. I have coffee. I have about one cup of milk, and half a tub of margarine. I'm wealthier today, than I was yesterday. I'm able to appreciate my wealth.

I have a full packet of cigarettes. These are like gold. Actually, that's what they are. Twenty-five cigarettes cost me $17.80. For every cigarette I smoke, it costs me 71 cents. I've contemplated this, way too often for it to be called contemplation. I should be calling it worry. It could be an obsession. I'm so worried about it, that I've considered giving up. Should I give up food too?

Can you try and imagine for a moment how I feel? Pretend you're me, and you smoke. You can't, can you? You won't be able to understand how I feel about cigarettes, but I'll try and explain it to you. You know how we eat food, and we usually have three meals a day? I would rather give up half of the food that I eat per day, and buy a packet of cigarettes. I would rather go without food, than give up my smokes. I would rather be hungry than be without my passion.

The Smoker in Me

My grandmother used to smoke, and she used to adore drinking tea. We used to debate which one we'd give up, if we had to give up one. It was no contest for me. I'd give up tea. My grandmother just didn't want to talk about it, because she wanted both. She couldn't have one without the other. She was addicted to both. I can give up tea, not happily, but definitely, if it meant I could have a smoke instead.

I've given up a fair bit in my life for my smokes. I've calculated roughly, using an average of $8 per packet of cigarettes, over the thirty-odd years I've been smoking. Are you sitting down? Now I'm hoping my math is really bad, and the figure I've come up with is way out. The grand total to date is $87,360. This is a house, isn't it? What I see in this $87,360 worth of cigarettes is all the poor people who could have been fed, housed, and educated. I regret it, and it makes me feel ashamed. What did you do with the money you didn't spend on smokes?

I have a goal. I have a goal to repay this money to the poor people. Before I die, I want to match the amount of money I've spent on smokes, and give it to charity. This should balance me out. It doesn't balance, does it? It needs to be a Trinity.

The Smoker's Pledge

I pledge to donate the amount I've spent on cigarettes at the age of fifty, if the cigarette brand that I've supported matches my pledge. I've supported them, so it stands to reason, that they should support me in my life-saving endeavour. This would mean that my smoking wouldn't have been in vain. This is less than five years away, and this will be my new campaign. If I'm not worried about my own health, I might as well be looking after someone else's. Would this be good karma?

This would make it all worthwhile. Is this a vain attempt at raising funds?

Back to wealth creation

Is creating wealth, while employed as a real estate agent, a true passion? This is an interesting question for me to answer, so I'll take my time and reason it out with you. We shall use logic as our tool.

Did you make the real estate? Are you telling me, that you created the service, the office, or even the stock you're trying to sell? What did you create by yourself?

I can't hear you answering the question, so I'll answer for myself. I'll answer for me.

I created nothing by myself. I copied it all. I did a few things a little bit differently, but I didn't make anything from scratch by myself. I had help. I had help from my staff, help from the industry rules and procedures, and help from above. I could find all the answers I needed, from outside of me. I knew where to find resources for information, and this was all sourced from other people. I just had luck. The one thing I did do was believe in myself, and even then, I couldn't have done that without Rose Red. So, no one does anything much on their own. You can change a few things to suit yourself, but you've invented nothing. You can't invent anything new, because it's all been done before. If you think you have, you're deceiving yourself, because you've probably pinched an idea from somewhere else. We aren't that original. I did write some creative ads occasionally, but I pinched the words.

I wasn't self-made, was I? I was motivated by wealth, and the self-esteem I got from it. That's all I got out of it. I got roped in. I didn't get much happiness. I thought wealth would create happiness. I thought the self-esteem from the wealth was making me happy. I thought I was happy. The wealth and the self-esteem don't last. You've got to keep suffering for more, and more of it. It's a... never ending story that just goes on and on my friends some people started singing it not knowing what it was and then just kept on singing for ever just because it is the story that never ends it just goes on an on my friends...

STOP THE STORY!

Passion is the only thing that can't be created. You can't create it, it must be found in you. Once you've found it in you, you can create.

Your passion is both your inner, and your outer wealth. It can be realized by following your dream. Not your dream to be wealthy, your dream to be healthy. It comes from doing the very thing that you're most passionate about. We're all passionate beings and we all get passionate being something, or doing something. Passion is something you feel. It's an exquisite feeling.

Nirvana

Buddha was passionate in his search for enlightenment. He was so passionate that he meditated passionately for years. He wasn't passionate about fetching water, but he had to do it, so that his passion could be realized.

Self-realization

Just because you have a hidden **passion** for doing something, doesn't mean you'll automatically know how to do it. You may desperately want to do it, but can't yet do it. You may need to learn and study your passion. You may need to grow and develop your passion. You may need to make sacrifices for it. If you're passionate about doing it, you won't see obstacles in your way. If there are obstacles, your passion will motivate you to remove them. Let your passion be free.

Buddha was wise. He was the man people sought when they had a problem. He was the man they wanted to talk with to gain understanding. He had the insight, not the illusion.

You can have more than one passion. You can even have a shared passion. This is sharing your passion with another. A passion shared, is a passion doubled. If you can't share your passion, then don't! Don't ever trade in your passion.

People can sometimes get jealous of your passion, particularly when they don't have their own passion. They'll want to be your only passion, or they'll want to get rid of yours, to even up the score. They may put down your passion as soon as you've picked it up. Stay with your passion, and guard it passionately.

I've been guarding my passion. This bit of passion comes to you in an unguarded moment. This passion is offered to you, without me taking it away from myself. You can share it if you want to. If you criticize it, I'll know you don't have your own passion, and that's why you don't understand mine. My passion is a new passion and I'm still learning how to do it. I'm quite passionate about it. Have I been passionate enough with you?

My passion was mocked at the very beginning, by a person I employed. He had passions of his own. I could've laughed at his passions, but I admired them and him, for having them at all. He smirked at my passion, but I was too passionate to let him ruin my passion. I wonder if he's smirking now. He might be reading about himself now, and smirking.

I'm smirking

A passion for doing something you're passionate about, can be like having an intense love affair. I'm presuming this, because I've never had an intense love affair, but I want one. I've read about them and dreamt about them. It will be hard to stop thinking about, and you could become focused on one thing only. It may be all you can think of. It can take up all your thinking time. I do think about it a lot.

Reading between the lines is a passion of mine

> **Passion:-** [< L. *pati*, suffer] 1. any emotion, as hate, grief, love, etc.; 2. extreme emotion as rage, fury, enthusiasm, lust, etc.; 3. the object of strong desire or fondness; 4. [p-] the suffering of Jesus during the Crucifixion or after the Last Supper.

Reading between the lines is a passion of mine

Are you worried that you haven't found your passion yet? There's no point worrying about it, just go out and discover it. Go out immediately and look for it. Imagine living your whole life without ever finding it. Don't have a lack of passion in your life. Everyone has passion. Everyone's purpose is to find their passion in life. Things that stir you inside, are good indications of where and how, your passions need to be released.

I've been stirred up, and now I'm passionate about what I'm doing.

What can I prove?

Your life's passion can be to prove a point. Scientists from all different fields want to prove their theories. It can take many years to substantiate their passion, but when it happens, they may then move onto another passion. The substitute passion may override reaping the rewards, and accepting approval for your original passion. This is real passion, and pure passion. Pss! Add 't' and pass it on, but don't forget the 'I'.

Passion-ate my obsession

Is passion obsession? I think it can be sometimes. I've been a little obsessed, and I've sometimes been extremely obsessed. I've been really focused on what passions reside in me. I've let them come rushing out in passionate prose, and cons. I'm passionate about what comes out, and what goes in. I'm letting passion in, and letting it flow out. I'm like a transformer. My brain is the transformer. I love to transform. I'm getting mixed up with my electricity. It's understandable. I may have my transformer mixed up with my transducer.

> **Transform:-** vt. [< L. *trans-*, over + *forma*, a shape] 1. to change the form or appearance of; 2. to change the condition character, or function; of 3. Elec. to change (voltage, current, etc.) by use of a transformer; 4. Math. to change (an algebraic expression or equation) in form but not in value –transform'able adj. –trans'forma'tion n. trans'forma'tional adj.
>
> **Transducer:-** n. [< L. *transducere*, lead across] any of various devices that transmit energy from one system to another, sometimes one that converts the energy in form.

Yep, this is my mind. It's a transducer, because all the bad energy goes in, and it comes out as a different energy. It's a transducer of words. Words get sucked in and I toss them around a bit, and then I throw them back out, in a different form. I could be a transceiver.

> **Transceiver:-** n. [< TRANS (MITTER) + (RE)CEIVER] an apparatus in a single housing, functioning alternately as a radio transmitter and receiver.

Oh yes, this is me. I'm doing this all the time. I have ears everywhere, and my sanctum is the sounding board. It's all above board. No it's not, because some is below board.

There's one more Trans word that I like to dabble with, and it's kind of secret and esoteric, so don't go spreading it around.

> **Trans:-** [L. < *trans*, across] a prefix meaning: 1. over, across, through; 2. so as to change thoroughly [transliterate] 3. above and beyond.
>
> **Trans:-** 1. transaction(s); 2. transitive; 3. translated; 4. translation; 5. transport.

I'm into transcendentalism

Can you work this word out by yourself? Trans cen dental ism. At a guess, it looks like something to do with teeth. Well it's certainly something you can get your teeth into, but that's not the literal translation. It could be a hundred, but it's missing half the word, 'centum'. Let's say it's 50/50. The 'ism' is just another doctrine, philosophy, or theory. I like to define 'its' in real terms. You must be balanced in mid-life, and have all your wisdom teeth erupted, and you have to believe.

I'm a transcendentalist. It's an ancient society.

> **Transcendentalism:-** n. any of various philosophies seeking to discover the nature of reality by investigating the process of thought, rather than the things that are thought about –tran'scenden'talist n., adj.

It's deep thought. It's the thought of what's behind thought. What's behind my thought? Do you need to be a thought mechanic, engineer, doctor, analyst or processor? What qualifications are needed? You don't need anything, if you're right now reading this. You just need to have come across it. I've been through it. I'm not yet over it. Transcendentalism has a prefix and a suffix, so it has a start and an end. I'm gnawing away at the middle. I hope I haven't bitten off more than I can chew. I'm halfway. If I'm halfway, I've kind of passed already, haven't I?

Are you a transcendentalist too? Have you joined up?

Transcendental:- (tran'senden't) adj. 1. Same as: a) TRAN-SCENDENT (sense I) b) SUPERNATURAL; 2. abstract; 3. of transcendentalism.

I told you it was secret. Have we transcended when we've reached mid-life? The cups half full, isn't it? We should have filled it half way up by now. I think I achieved a half a cup full.

Where's my half a cup?

I've got the other half to fill up now. I'm going to fill it to the brim. I'm going all the way to the top. I'm going to pour into that cup... every ounce of what I've got left. This next half, is going to be filled with different stuff. It won't be the same as the first half, but I'm thirsty for the second half to start pouring into my cup. How much can a cup full hold?

Boom or Bust?

I know my cup size. I know that I need one. I know how much I need to put in it now, because I have my measure. This time I'm going to measure my cup very carefully. I'm going to put in what was taken out, and take out what was put in. Does this make any sense? I'm evening up, that's all. I'm going to try to make it add up. I'm doing the math. I'm learning the greatest mathematical equation known to man.

A passionate threat

When your passion is threatened by others, you'll become possessive and protective of it. You'll passionately defend it. We all know already what we're passionate about. We'll stand up for our passion, if we have enough passion for it. We all have our own passions in life. We can be passionate about our family, but we can't own this passion. We must have our own unique passion. My family cannot own me. I'm passionate about this. They cannot decide for me, what my passions shall be.

Are passions a purpose? Is our passion our destiny? Should we avoid our destiny? Is our destiny, our potential? Do we have the potential to reach our destiny? Is our destiny, our purpose? Is my passion for asking questions, and stirring the passion in you?

A question of passion

This is my passion. I'm passionately questioning. I'm passionate about questioning, and passionate about knowing. I'm passionate about finding the answers. I'm passionate about understanding the answers. I'm most passionate about thinking. I'm also passionate about giving you a piece of my mind, and sharing my passion with you.

Is my passion too intense?

Am I being too passionate? Am I a bit too passionate for you? I can be passionate now, because I've found all my passion again. It was lost for a long time. I love the feeling of passion. It's stirring. It's internal stirring. It stirs up the senses. It's both mental and physical. I'm wild with passion.

Is passion seen as a risk to all that you have, are, and already do? This is not the perspective you want. It's the opposite perspective to what you need. You should be with your passion first, and see all that you have, are, and do, as passionate.

Don't be afraid of passionate people

They are the free spirits. Painters are passionate about their art. Would we have such inspiring art, if there was no passion?

I have inspiring art. I have three beautiful sculptures that I've created from my imagination. I didn't just use my imagination. I used my passion. I had a passion for it, both for the forms I've created, and for what they symbolize for me. It's my passion for expression.

My sculptures make me feel passionate. My second sculpture is a nude woman in a slightly twisted pose. It's a human pose, and a languid pose. She's reaching, and opening at the same time. She's captivating and honest. She's in repose.

I'm posing again

She is me, and she expresses how I feel about parts of me. She has no head. She hasn't got feet or hands. She's truly expressive in the form that I've moulded her, with the tips of my sensitive fingers, and the senses I tapped into. I glazed her, and she's lying in a puddle of it, as if it were water. I feel emotional talking about her. She's gorgeous! I love her. I really do.

> **Repose:-** [< K, *re-*, again + LL. *Pausare*, to rest] to lay or place for rest -vi. 1. to lie at rest; 2. to rest; 3. to rest in death; 4. to be supported [the shale reposes on limestone] -n. 1. a) rest b) sleep; 2. composure; 3. calm, peace.

My latest sculpture is a man. He's larger, but he's not in repose. He's been resurrected. He's midway between lying down, and raising his body to a sitting position. I know that's what he's trying to do, but he's in shock. He's reaching with one arm out in front, so that he can raise his body. His body is in pain. He's in pain. He knows where he's been, and he's dazed. His legs are fantastic. They're strong, and his body is manly. He's nude and he has great feet.

'Forgive me father, for I have sinned'

His genitals are messy. It's hard to sculpt male genitals. Men's genitals are messy. It's not a bad mess, and not ugly, but it's sort of all over the place. It's not neat, really. It's not sculpted. Well it is sometimes, but not all the time.

Michelangelo sculpted men. He sculpted incredible muscle tissue and sinew. He loved to accentuate the tendons and veins. I love this too, and I've been able to capture it in the legs of my man sculpture. My nude man's legs look powerful. He needed powerful legs. To sculpt, you must be able to observe. You must be able to observe and feel at the same time. It's about looking closely, and imagining with your mind's eye, the form you wish to replicate. It's the detail. It's not about replicating all the perfect detail. I don't know all the detail on a body, but some parts I do. Those are the parts I concentrate on. This is ultimately what draws the eye, not the defects. Defects are a necessary evil in a sculpture. They enhance the non-defective parts. There's no such thing as defective, just comparisons.

Replicating the spirit

When you've created something wonderful, and something you're very proud of, your emotions will be affected? You're proud of the achievement, but do you marvel at your own talent? Do you think it's a fluke? It isn't a fluke. It's your true style and talent, demonstrating what your spirit is capable of. It's a demonstration of what you have inside. It's your spirit coming alive.

I'm passionate inside. I know this now. I'm passionate on the outside too. I'm so much more passionate now, than I've ever been in my life. I can now be passionate about real things, not make-believe things. I don't have to make myself believe things. I don't have to make you believe things. I just believe in true passion.

Was I a work friend?

Are friends work? This is not a good question. It doesn't explain what I really want to ask. Is being friends work? That's not quite it, either. Are real friends, part of your work? I'm almost there. Are pretend friends, work? Almost! Are pretend friends, pretend work? Aha!

This is the question I question my work about. I had it arse about. I had so, so many, so-called friends. They would only see me at work. When they came in, I would jump up. I'd put my work aside, make them coffee, or just have a chat. I'd be there to listen. I'd be the listening post. Was this work, or was this friendship? If it was friendship, wouldn't the courtesy be reciprocated?

Was I much of a friend?

Was I invited to their place? Yes I was, but just for work. I was a listening post again. It was a house call. Was I a pretend market appraisal? Was I pretending, or were they pretending? When I got the work, was it pretend work? Did I always get the work? Did I still have to work for the work? Did I work for the friendship? Did the work count as friendship? Did it count? What worked? Who was pretending? Who was I counting?

Pretend work

My office was filled with pretenders. Pretenders would come and go from my office, like a factory assembly line. I gave all that I could to that assembly line. Whatever it required, to make it work better, I gave it. I gave all that I could. Did I get back, all that I should? I got what I could. I didn't get to be understood. Who listened to me? Did I think I could? I listened to troubles, to health problems, to car problems, house problems, kid problems, money problems, husband problems, family problems, boat problems, community problems, dog problems, travel problems, work problems, and every possible problem you can think of.

I'm not pretending

I know something about problems. I know about problems. Now I have my own problems, I want a place to go like this. I'd love a place to go, where I could just stroll in and have attention immediately granted to me. No lining up, no paying money, and no gossip after I'd left. Someone would make me coffee, because they thought enough of me, to offer. I could get things off my chest and enjoy the sympathy.

Just private talking and consoling

I could get some much-needed cheering up, and a few jokes to get me smiling again. I could walk out that door feeling ten times better than when I'd walked in, and I'd have some new ideas on how to fix things. I'd have the reassurance I needed, and I'd be grateful.

It was a fabulous service. It was a public service, because it was free. It can't have been a public service, can it? The public didn't pay for it. Who pays for it? This isn't a public question. It's not a question for you. It's for me.

It's a private question

It's a private question for yours truly. I must now answer it. I pay for it. I paid for it. I am paying for it. I've never been paid enough for it. It wasn't part of the job! It was an extra. That's what I am. I'm just an extra. I was just an extra in a movie, or just the extra bit of fluff on top.

Do you pay for the extra bit, or is it complimentary? If it's complimentary, do you make sure you continue to shop there, in order to pay it back? The fluff's just to make it look nice, isn't it? That extra bit of fluff is the cream on top. I got creamed! It's not a creamy job. I was just too soft. You must be hard, to do this job. If you're hard, it's easy. If you're hard, you're hardly going to be fluffy for free. Where was the balance? You were too top heavy. You always fell over on me, and I always got hurt. I was always breaking a fall.

I wanted my opposite

It's a job of opposites. When you're soft, they want hard. When you're hard, they want soft. Forget the in between, it won't get a look in. You can't be everyone. You can try, I did.

It's almost like having a multiple personality disorder. This disorder is mandatory to do this job well. You must be able to be all people, to everyone, in an instant. They order it instantly. I must have a thousand personalities from which to choose. A lot of these were crappy, and a lot of mine were crappy too. I hated the crappy ones, because they always made me feel crappy.

You must learn to be agreeable. Being agreeable sounds quite agreeable, but it isn't. You hear yourself agreeing to things you would never agree to. You find yourself siding with sides, you're intensely opposed to. You take on their attitudes and opinions, as your own, just so you can both agree.

I never agreed to all that when I took on this job, but it agrees with the job. Agreements would include politics, religion, sexuality, racial discrimination, international affairs, community affairs, people's affairs, public affairs, private affairs, and even my affairs. I didn't have any affairs. I had no private affairs. I was always candid about my affairs. I had nothing to hide. I hid my normal affairs, because they were just normal. They weren't work affairs. Were my affairs truthful affairs, or was I just trying to be agreeable?

What did you know of my affairs?

Did anyone know me, like I knew them? This is an impossible question for me to answer by myself. I can answer half the question. Which half do you think I'll answer?

I thought I knew you. I knew a lot about you, and I thought a lot about you. I might have thought a lot of you, but did I know enough to make that call? I know now.

What call did you make about me? Did you make a call? Was it a real call, or a fake call? A fake call is making out you've called by calling someone else instead. This is called showing you've called. It's not a genuine call. A genuine, real, and honest call, is not calling at all. This is what you really feel comfortable doing. Not calling. You don't call me.

I've had to make hard calls. I've made plenty of hard calls. These are calls that call on you to call for assistance. The only assistance that's up to the job of helping you make the calls is God. God doesn't take your calls either, he just hears them coming in. Is he watching what I do? Is he watching me? Has he seen me? I don't need to ask these questions. I have the answers!

The calling

I've made the worst calls you could ever want to make to anyone. Nobody should ever be called on, to make calls of this nature. I made the calls. I did it on my own. I was called, and I fucking went. These are what you call, fucking hard calls. Those calls fractured something in me. They left a crack that wouldn't seal back up again. It's good. I can now see the light.

I'm cracked

Why did people call me when things went wrong? Am I an easy person to call on in an emergency, a tragedy, a catastrophe? What about calling me for something nice? Please don't just call me, because you think you should. Call me to get to know me. Get to know me, to see why people call on me, but don't just call on me. I'm not a call girl! It's not my calling anymore. No more calls. You can call out as loud as you want, but I won't come. I won't answer. I've answered enough calls for twenty lifetimes. No callers please! I'm calling it all off. I have my own calls waiting. It's now my call. You probably wish I'd just take the last call, but that's his call.

A silent call

I call for silence. Be silent. Just be. Relax now. I'll put all calls on hold for the rest of my life.

Have you ever been on a call out in the middle of the night? These kinds of call outs are not work. Did you think I was talking about a work call out? It is. It's a work call off. It's not really a call. I wanted to make the call, to call it all off. I think it was when an opportunity called. When an opportunity calls, to call it off, do you answer the call? I could see it needed to be answered, because I didn't have much to call on.

In 2006, my business was calling for more. It desperately needed an answer to the call. I'd been out of earshot, because of another big call, and it was trying to tell me it only had a pittance left to call on. This was a hard call. Who was taking its last calls? No one heard me call for help. I almost lost my business in that year. It was a close call. Calls were coming in, but callers don't wait for a better time to call, because they just call someone else. Even when they did call, there were not enough answerers to take the calls. They were answering their own call. It was a call to arms that was needed. My arms were elsewhere, and around other important callers.

The capital I had on call for the business was chewed up at a call rate of $30,000 per month. Within four months it was almost gone. My business was at a loss. It had lost the two best call workers, and it was grieving. We were both grieving for Red Rose. I couldn't help my business at that time, because Red Rose's callers were demanding call outs.

Two dead lines

These five young callers had their two best call takers, called away in the middle of the night. Their best two call takers, took an internal call for eternity. Both these call takers, had been killed in the line of duty. This is when you make the big calls in life. I made the right call. I only wish I'd made a bigger call, and put my business out of its misery. I should have called it a day. It would never get over the loss of its dual call team.

Rose Red was its maker too. She was its heart, and I was its soul. It eventually regained its sad soul, but its heart was forever missing. Its heart stopped beating. It was put on life support. It was barely supporting itself. I called for a support. I called for one support. She was a supporter of the cause. She was a moral support. She left her job to support mine. I don't forget a support, so I supported her.

In trust

There was also a trust fund to be supported. It was to help support the young callers. That support came from the business supporters, and Red Rose's supporters. This was from all the support that Rose Red had given in the past. It was for past support. In the past, Red Rose had supported a spiritual cause. She was the scripture teacher support every Wednesday. She loved this kind of support work. I loved providing her the time for this support work.

My business trust fund needed supporting too, because it was the only thing supporting my business. My trusted support was a good sport, and she handled a lot of the business single-handedly in my absence. There were two absent. I was absent, but I was still there, in and out, and all over the place, and as many places as I could be, but I wasn't all there.

I was grief-stricken. Nobody could see that, because I was busy being a support. I was dead inside. Nobody could see that, because I was flat out and busier than I'd ever been in my life. I was headed for a fall. Nobody could see that, because they thought I was strong and could take the calls. They probably thought I had my own people to call on. I only had one that I ever wanted to call on, but she was dead!

We'd been best mates for thirteen years. We were close. We worked together for five years. I taught Red Rose everything I knew, and she taught me everything she knew. We knew a lot about each other. We only lived up the road from one another. I guess we were too close. When you're too close, it hurts too much. It's just too close a call.

Don't purport to be a support

I don't support anymore, because one of my supports is no longer a supporter, she's a reporter. She'd never been the support that Rose Red was. She was a constant threat to the supports. She needed too much support. She wasn't the support purported. She was a rorter. She rorted the system.

> **Rort:-** n. [< E. dial. *rorty*, splendid] [Aust. Slang] 1. a rowdy party; 2. a fraud, deception.

She rorted the system and thought it was all a great rort, when she made her report. How many believed her report? People think she's a pretty good sort. She didn't have it all sorted out. Her sort can always make a clever report. Her sort will never report their rort. Did the court hear her report? All her recent reports have come to naught.

Was my business a rort?

My business has always needed honest supports. It was born with honest supports. When the dishonest support was supporting it, it wasn't supported well enough. It weakened the support in the other supports. There was less strength in its supports, and it was weak.

A fast forward to 2011

The supported break was a long time in coming. It was ten years of support, and I needed some time out. The soul of the business needed a break. It was a ten-year celebration of support.

I left the business in the hands of the support. I was still handy, and supporting the weekly meetings. Even though there was more support in the business, it was not the support it needed for life. It lived for only ten years, but it saw a lot of life in that time. It heard life, saw life, and changed life. It put life into things, and provided a life line, and a life lesson.

Its interior was bright green, but it was never green with envy. It was painted green because 'green is nice'. Green is vibrant and healthy. 'It's not easy being green.'

Have I mourned the loss of my green companion? Have I mourned the loss of my company? I'm glad it's been put out of action. They were all looking for the body. They couldn't find a body. They wanted to perform an autopsy. It's a mystery death. The body went missing in action. Nobody was a witness to its death, but they saw what happened. They saw the vultures flying low in the sky. They saw the people hovering around. They were in denial.

My company could have been saved, but no one helped it. It could have been nursed back to good health. It still had plenty of money and unseen assets. It had shown so much resilience in the past. It wasn't as sick as it had been in the past. I put it in the hands of its other shareholder, but that shareholder had been used to being cared for by it. That shareholder had never had to care for it.

A very lucky shareholder

That shareholder had always been spoiled by the company. The company had never been thanked. That shareholder never loved the company, he just used it. The company never had any help or support from the silent partner. The silent partner didn't love it like the noisy partner. The noisy partner put her heart and soul into the company and the company name.

The company had extended itself to extended family members numerous times, with lump sum loans from its capital. The accountant for the company would be required to draw up loan agreements when this happened, so that the company didn't breach any taxation laws. The company was an honest company. It never had to hide anything, because it was always upfront with whatever it did. All decisions made by the noisy partner on its behalf, were made in consultation with a professional accountant.

Death and deliverance

He was there at the birth of the company, fourteen years ago. He delivered the company into the world. Would he have known how to help my company survive? He knew who the company relied on, and what the company was missing. It wasn't trust. Actually, it was trust, but it wasn't the trust money.

It just looked that way. So many people were suspicious. The accountant was suspicious. Why would the accountant suspect any wrongdoing? He wouldn't suspect the noisy partner, would he? What had he been told? Who was running around telling everyone lies? What sort of lies were they telling, that could turn long term trusted colleagues against me?

My company's trusted accountant was called in one night, on a clandestine mission to check the company's trust account. He checked the wrong one. He should have checked one with the other, because you can never trust your intellect over your instincts. Does an accountant have an instinct for money-laundering? Can he tell the difference between clean money, and dirty money? This is a good housekeeping question. I think he'd started paying someone to do his housekeeping, because he was becoming too busy looking after the welfare of all his other companies. It's a hard call.

My company started calling the housekeeper. We loved her, she was trustworthy and honest. I was happy with his housekeeper, because I know how busy my accountant had become, and I was loathe to disturb him unless it was really important. I was respectful of his limited time. We were more than business acquaintances... I thought we were friends.

I trusted him implicitly with my company. He was a person I had great trust in. Did he trust the company I had been in, in my company? This is the deciding question. Was it the decider, for my company's death? Was my company's maker, persuaded to release my company's private business to anyone, or everyone? I thought my company's business, and my personal business, would have been kept private. I thought after fourteen years, he would have known all about my company and its honesty. He must have known instinctively, the type of company it was. It was run so differently from the rest. It stood alone in its fairness to others.

He was always happy with the results of the company, even in a bad company market. He knew my company was strong and stoic, in the face of crisis. He had seen it come back from the brink. He knew the company's circumstances of ownership. He should have known me! He knew Red Rose!

Who to believe?

They would never have got anything out of her. She would have told me everything. No matter what the circumstances, she would have believed in me. She was loyal. So is my new friend. She believes me. She doesn't believe the rest. She comes and asks me. She accepts what I tell her, and she accepts what I don't tell her. Why? She doesn't force. She hasn't known me that long, and she doesn't know me that well. She knows me. She's seen my authentic self. She didn't know real estate me. She only started to get to know me, after the event. She knew me after the first two events, but not before. She has only known me in crisis. She didn't really know me before crisis. What does this mean? Is it better to know somebody in crisis? Who would want to know me now?

What's the mean?

It means, she thinks I'm normal under the circumstances. She's the only one that knows the circumstances. She hasn't been got at, by the various circumstances. She hasn't been infiltrated. She believes the circumstances I've told her. We believe each other. Why? Because we talk to each other honestly, eyeball to eyeball. That's where the truth is. It's right between the eyes. It's the middle eye chakra. It's the middle ground. It's a balanced communication. She trusts me with her personal information, and I trust her with mine.

She's my secret agent. She brought me some information, and I gave her some information. This is a balancing of the information. It's a balancing act. It's a hard act to follow, but it created some followers. Followers can be good, but they can also be bad. Any follower is a good follower, for my purposes. This following I'm alluding to, is not a cause, it's an effect. It's another special effect. I have a deep affection for effects.

I hate to imagine

I'm imagining, trying to imagine the effects. It's hard, because there's been so many people affected. They don't know this yet, but I do.

Will some people sling off?

What's this mean? Is it to mock? Is it to denigrate? Is it to belittle something, or someone? Is it tall-poppy syndrome? It can't be that anymore, can it? Maybe it's coming from the tall poppies. Poppies have grown tall in my place. They've grown since I lost my place. Are they feeling tall now?

> **Tall poppy:-** [Aust. Colloq.] a prominent or highly paid person.
>
> **Sling:-** [prob. < ON. *slyngva*, to throw] 1. a primitive instrument for throwing stones, etc., consisting of a piece of leather tied to cords that are whirled for releasing the missile; 2. a) a looped or hanging band, used in raising or lowering a heavy object, etc. b) a wide piece of cloth looped from the neck under an injured arm for support; 3. [Aust. Slang] a bribe, tip, or kickback -vt. slung, sling'ing 1. to throw (stones, etc.) with, or as if with, to sling; 2. to hang in a sling; suspend -vi. [Aust. Slang] to pay a bribe, tip or kickback - sling off at, [Aust. Slang] to mock, deride, jeer at.

It's been a slinging match alright, but the slingers of mud, are not expecting it to be slung back at them. That's slang for sling. It could be a slanging for some slinging. If they can sling it, I'll be slinging it back. I'm not in a sling. I don't need any slings for this match. I don't need support. I wouldn't mind a well-hung support. This is not how it sounds. I wouldn't mind a hung jury, either.

> **Hung parliament:-** a parliament in which no party has an absolute majority.

I think this could be what I meant to say. Do you believe in a Freudian slip? It's a slip of the tongue. It's when you say something that surprises you, because you didn't mean to say it. Sometimes it's just a word out of the blue, but Freud, the great mind reader from above, believed it came from the unconscious. He believed that when you make a Freudian slip, that you've got something more to say, but you refuse to acknowledge it. I've made many Freudian slips during my writings. I leave them in when I do it, and build something around it. I'm not sure I've built the right things around it, but who knows? Who knows where any of it comes from?

One slung slow

There's a big difference between their slinging and my slinging. It's all in the difference. A difference is a minus, isn't it? I do remember something from school math. I'm not sure what it is, but Freud might have a clue. What is the difference? Is it a problem? Is it a problem-solving word? If I had a $1 and I gave you 50 cents, how much would I have? That's not the difference, is it? What's the difference between a hare, and a tortoise? What's the difference between night and day? What's the difference between being rich or being poor?

Half, half, half, half

This is the difference. It's getting even, isn't it? It's getting even. I love evens. I don't like odds. Odd is odd. Even is neat. Evens are tidy. Evens are fair. Odds aren't fair. Was that an odd way to calculate it? I'm not a good calculator. I have a calculator. I've always needed a calculator. I've owned many calculators, and they've calculated for me. I'm calculating, aren't I? I could be better at math than I thought. If my calculations are right, I have four answers to my difference questions. I have half + half + half + half = four. Four is even, so I'm correct. I'm getting even with four. If there's any more I'm getting even with, they're just the remainders. Did I get that wrong? Are you questioning my math? Is it two or four? My mind isn't made up.

What do you do with remainders? Long division comes to mind, and I want it out of my mind. My mind says no to long division. Can you just throw the remainders away, or do I have to carry them? I think that's what I used to do. I threw them away. In fact, I still do it. All the remainders that I have left, I'll just chuck out. I think I've got a place for them. I'll chuck them on the 'fuck off pile'. I have one in my backyard. It's now four metres high and six metres in diameter. It just keeps getting bigger. It's what you call 'growth'. This is the pile you might relate to, but you'll read more about it in *The Knowing in Me*.

The bigger, the better

It's a wicked pile, and I made it. I've made it all by myself. It's become a bit of a hobby. I'm very proud of it. I think it's become a bit of a passion. I'm chucking all the remainder effects in it, and it's a cocktail for the senses. Everything you can imagine, is going onto this pile. There's garden refuse, lawn clippings, old tools, old clothing, bric-a-brac, nick-nacks, linen, furniture, pictures, photos, crockery, cutlery, ornaments, appliances, and all manner of rubbish. Everything from my old life is in it. I look at it, and just wonder at it.

I've been feeding myself shit

I think I've been full of shit most of my life. I've been fed a lot of shit, and I've been feeding myself a load of shit. When you've had so much shit fed to you, it's hard to tell the difference. You can't see what's real, and what's not real. I could smell it, but I could never see it. I got whiffs of it, but when I asked if anyone could smell what I could smell, no one owned up. There was a fair bit of shit hidden. There were a fair few people who could smell it though.

It reminds me of the classic situation, where somebody gets a whiff of some foul odour, and declares it out loud. Everyone immediately starts checking their shoes. Nobody wants to be the culprit. They're praying they won't be the one with the dog shit squashed into the sole of their shoe. They're praying that they're not the one guilty of walking it into the carpet. You might try to hide the fact, and deny it was on your shoe.

"No, it's not me!"
"It wasn't me, either."
"I never ruined anything."

Everywhere you go with your dog now, you're expected to take a plastic bag with you. You're meant to scoop up their shit, and put it in a bin somewhere. This is good practice. Treading in dog shit is less likely to occur now, than it once was. People have to clean up the shit they're responsible for.

A lot of it, is unused shit

A lot of it was expensive shit, but nevertheless it was reduced to matter.

> **Matter:-** n. [< L. *material*, material] 1. what a thing is made of; constituent material; 2. whatever occupies space and is perceptible to the senses; 3. any specified sort of substance [colouring matter]; 4. content of thought or expression, as distinguished from style or form; 5. an amount or quantity [a matter of a few days]; 6. a) a thing or affair [business matters] b) cause or occasion [no laughing matter]; 7. importance [it's of no matter]; 8. trouble [what's the matter?]; 9. Pus –vi. to have significance –as a matter of fact, really –for that matter 1. as far as that is concerned; 2. indeed on consideration –no matter 1. it is of no importance; 2. regardless of [no matter what you say].

It doesn't matter anymore

In amongst the layers is shit. It's the dog's shit. I've been throwing every bit of shit in there, that I can lay my hands on. Not my hands, the shovel. I've been shovelling shit. It stinks like shit now, too. I'm going to burn the shit. I've got some petrol. I've got heaps of boat motor fuel. I'll need to build up the fuel a bit more yet, and then I'm going to ignite. I'm a bit worried about the tree that's standing in the middle of it though. It's a type of pine tree and it stands about twenty metres tall.

It could be a fire hazard

I wouldn't burn it down. I've loved all the trees in my yard. I loved this yard as soon as I saw it. It's a private oasis yard. It's got some massive trees, and they've kept me private. Some people hate trees in their yard, but I love them. I love trees. I love big trees. I don't care about leaves, they're natural. Leaves are natural.

We all have leaves

We all leave our leaves lying around. The hair from our head falls off, and it's just left lying around. We notice it on our clothes, on the floor tiles, in our hairbrushes, on our pillow, in the shower recess, and in the vacuum cleaner. We shed, just like a tree. We need to shed, because it makes way for new growth.

I've got a shed. It's disguised by black timber. It looks nice from the outside, but the inside is a bit messy. It's just more of his mess. The evidence for this mess, can be found in his mess. I find empty beer cans stashed in hidden places. I find them wrapped up in brown paper bags, or crushed to fit in dark corners, and on the top of messy shelves. This isn't where you put old beer cans, is it? He was hiding the evidence of his messiness. He was so very messy. Is this what's supposed to go on in a Men's Shed?

Some peoples' sheds

Some people shed, but don't get the new growth. It's a strange phenomenon, baldness. What does it mean? I know it's supposed to be hereditary, but could it be psychological? What does baldness mean? I didn't ask where it originates. What does it mean for the bald person? It's just the hair on the scalp, isn't it? I mean no hair on the scalp. Is baldness special? Is it extraordinary? It's a minority, isn't it? It's not common. I like uncommon phenomenon. Is this an oxymoron?

> **Phenomena:-** n. pl. of PHENOMENON
>
> **Phenomenal:-** adj. 1. of or constituting a phenomenon or phenomena; 2. extraordinary – phenom'enally adv.
>
> **Phenomenalism:-** n. the philosophic theory that all knowledge comes from sense perceptions.
>
> **Phenomenon:-** n., pl. -na; also, esp. for 3 and 4. -nons [< Gr. phainesthai, appear] 1. any observable fact that can be scientifically described; 2. the appearance of something as distinguished from the thing in itself; 3. anything extremely unusual; 4. [Colloq.] a person who is extraordinary.

I'll put that subject to bed now. I can't put it to bed, because it just won't stay down.

Same shit, but different day

They'll be slinging off in private. I'm the public, because nothing is ever private. This book isn't private, is it? It's all public. It has all my private information, but it'll be put out to the public. It just needs to be read privately, but in public. The public will need to see it being read, to know it has indeed gone public.

> **Indeed:-** adv. [see IN & DEED] certainly; truly – interj. an exclamation of surprise, doubt, etc.

The public will think I've done it privately. Is a privately published book public property? This is a serious question, and you know the answer. I just think I know the answer. If you're reading this book, you're one step ahead of me. As I write this, I'm still devising a plan. I've got my calculator out, and I'm calculating the plan. It's a curious plan. I'm curious as to what to do next. My calculator knows the plan, because it keeps giving me the same answer. I have a basic plan, but not the details yet. You may, by now know the details, but maybe you don't. If you don't, you'll be curious, and vice versa.

I need a vice squad

Can you tell a book by its cover? This question must be the most important question for all the answers in my books. It's the most important question for any book. There's no question more questionable than this one. It's not illegal, what I've planned to do. It's a cunning plan.

> **Cunning:-** [< ME. *cunnen*, know] 1. sly; crafty; 2. made with skill or ingenuity; 3. [U.S.] pretty, –n. slyness, craftiness.

Can you have a sling off version first? Can you sling off about the first version, while your other version is being slung around? Can *The Worker in Me* do the slinging off, while *The Knowing in Me* does the rounds for *The Maker in Me*? Can the Trinity support *The Dreamer in Me* and *The Teacher in Me*, before I have the others? I have *The Thinker in Me*, and that's worth thinking about.

I have a plan hatched, because I'm not a chicken. It's a long-term plan. This plan matches my long-term dreams. Is it possible for me to have short dreams come true, during a long-term plan? This is a motivational question that I need to answer for myself. Can we realize our dreams without making them a reality? The reality for me is in the making. Should I be watching my dreams come to life?

Does a book have a life?

Does the shelf have a life? Both are objects that need each other. Does a book have a shelf life? The more it stays in the public eye, the more shelf life it'll have. Does this mean putting more life into the shelves? If it's been shelved, is it out of life, or in life? I think it depends on the life of the shelf. Some shelves sell lives off. When the lives are sold, the shelves need more lives to replace the last lives. Whose life is being sold off? I'm selling my life. My life will be sold off. My life will go to other lives.

Left on the shelf

Am I being shelved for a while, till I can have a better life? Have my dreams been shelved until my life has been sold? Is this the way it goes for writers? If this is so, it'll have to be the way I'll go. I don't have any way I know to go. Do other writers feel this way? Is it their way to go? I feel like a bit of a goer.

I just go, and go, and go

I haven't stopped the flow, and I go, go, go, to know. I don't go too fast, and I don't go too slow, so what's the go? When do I get to show, my go, go, go? I just don't know when I'll get it on the go. When I've finished my go, it'll get its go. I don't know how far it will go. When my go is finished, and I've given it a big enough go, where shall I go? Will I have any dough? I'm not in The Know. I'm in *The Dreamer in Me*.

Advance to Go

This is what a book advance is. This is quite an advanced statement. I have advanced. I have two books down, and two on the go, but nothing yet to show. I need another advance. I'll need to have another go. I don't want to start another book, until one is on show. I feel a bit low. I'm about to be taken for a row. Row, row, row your boat, gently down the stream, throw your 'teacher' overboard and listen to her scream. I am screaming! My head is screaming no, no, no! Not another blow. I sound like an old crow. I'm having a crow. I'm crowing about my next in a row. I want to press go. Can I possibly be this advanced?

I have advanced on the board to Go. Am I going somewhere? Would you like to know? I've got no dough, I haven't passed Go. Is *The Teacher in Me*? Is it my next go? Go, go, go, and three books on the go. Ho, ho, ho, all I want for Christmas is another bloody go. All Christmas, go, go, and go! I'm writing Christmas off. This is how I'll go. My wonders will think it's a blow! I'll be blowing them off for my go. Christmas will be a no show. I don't want to stop the flow. It flowed into The Maker and into The Know. It's all in the Worker, and in *The Dreamer in Me*. It'll be in The Teacher, and I'll teach you what I know. There'll be more of me than you'll ever want to know. There's more there than you'll ever see in you. Or is there? I might be able to teach you something about yourself in The Thinker I've tried to stow.

Ask me a question?

You are not of me, but you will know of me. Where will I be? I ask this question of me, because I don't know the answer. Many of my questions don't have the answers. This is the reason I write them down. If I write them down, I'm asking you. Because I don't get your answer, I'm forced to look for the answer myself. Sometimes I just use my own reasoning. Is reasoning the best way to answer questions? Is reasoning like seasoning? Do you add a bit of this, and add a bit of that? You need to be careful about what seasoning you use. Some are quite strong, and some quite spicy. Some can barely be acknowledged. When your seasoning is barely perceptible, it's best to add a bit more, for the full effect.

Play it again, Sam

Have you ever read the same book twice? Is it better the first time around, or the second? I think you can sometimes pick up on things you missed the first time around, on your second time around. You can't always take it all in at once. You find yourself going back for seconds. You may even go back for thirds, especially if you're a glutton for punishment. This is when you want to check you have it right in your head. It's to make sure you properly understand the meaning. This is called refreshing. It's also called referencing. I have referenced in my books. I have used my memory as a reference guide. It's a clear sign that I have a memory. My memory may, or may not correspond with your memory of events.

If this book is hard to read, spare a thought for the writer. It wasn't easy to write. It's not easy to right something that's wrong. I haven't been able to write what I want to write, because of what's been written. It's too hard to write it. This book has been written with wisdom. I have the wisdom to know what to right, and what not to write. How do I rate as a writer?

I can answer that. I'm pretty average. That's neither here nor there, but it's somewhere. I'm always going somewhere with it. Somewhere is the middle ground.

Evidently a memory

It's the memory of events leading up to an event. This is where the frightening memory is. This is what frightened me. This is what frightened everyone else. How did I remember? It wasn't a memory. It was evidence.

> **Evident:-** adj. [< L. e-, from + *videre*, see] easy to see or perceive; clear; obvious; plain – ev'idently adv.
>
> **Evidential:-** adj. of, serving as, or providing evidence.

What if there's no end to the events? What if there's no lasting event? The last event should be the big event, shouldn't it? I need an event organizer. Is this a real title? Everyone has this title, don't they? It's like Real Estate Agent. Everyone has this title too. If you are the person between real estate, and a real estate agent, you are an agent.

> **Agent:-** [< L. *agree, do*] 1. a person, firm, etc. authorized to act for another; 2. [Colloq.] a travelling representative, as for an insurance company; 3. a person or thing that performs an action or produces an effect.

You produce the effect, not the real estate agent. Who are you an agent for? You! You are your own agent. We are all our own agents. I'm my own agent too. Have I appointed anyone else as my agent? Yes, but only if I'm incapacitated.

Incapacitate:- 1. to make unable or unfit; disable 2. law to disqualify.

Incapacity:- 1. lack of capacity, power, or fitness; disability 2. legal ineligibility.

This is where I was going

It has been written. It wasn't written for the purpose purposed. It was written for someone else's proposed purpose. I made it on the proposal of what had been proposed for me. I had made my purpose clear, when I had my solicitor draw it up. I made it clear what my purpose was, and in case of the worst purpose coming to pass. He was not a witness to it having been witnessed. Even if he was, he would have been mistaken. The document was an Enduring Power of Attorney.

It gave no power to an attorney. It gave no power to anyone. It deemed my two wonders equally, as my agents in the event of my incapacitation. I didn't want to be incapacitated, but others did. This was the scheme. I was protecting my legal rights against such a scheme.

In case of a scheme

The document in question, was null and void (ab initio = from the beginning). This is because one of the appointed is not old enough to have been an appointed, nor to act as a witness. My instructions were for my girl wonder and my attorney to be powers until my other wonder was of age, and my attorney would in time pass his power on to him. My under-aged power was with me at the time I was giving my instructions. He understood the nature of the document, because he'd seen the nature of the beast. I'd explained the nature of the beast to my attorney, but he turned me in, when he met the beast.

A beastly scheme

Should I be paying for such a service? Is it a true service? Should you have to pay for something that's not worth the paper it was written on? It was not in working order. It was never in working order. My privacy was not in working order.

My attorney acted out of order. I was in working order. I wasn't out of order. 'OUT OF ORDER.' Who put this sign on me?

Dirty fuel for the fire

Are you a service provider? An event organizer is a service provider, and so is a real estate agent. That's all they provide.

What is a service? I feel I could do with a good service. My fuel is low. I'm dirty about something, and I need an injection of money. I'm having an injection today, but they'll be taking it out, not putting it in. This is *The Giver in Me*, giving you the heads up.

Another one of my serves

I'm donating my blood to the Red Cross Blood Service. I don't have to pay for this service. I hope this service doesn't make any mistakes. Is it a risky service? Is this service worth my risk? Is my health or my privacy the risk? The last service was more of a risk. Will my not giving blood be noticed? Is it better to be noticed by giving, or by not giving? I'll give my blood, but I won't be giving anything else away. I won't disclose any details, only the relevant ones. What are the relevant details? Will my details serve their end, or my ends? Will they serve my purpose?

An inherited purpose

It's been my special purpose to give blood every three months. It became my service in 2006 when the service lost another one of its servers. I had never given blood before 2006, but I always admired one dedicated to giving to this service. He gave enduringly to this service, in case of his family ever needing a service. Since his untimely death, I've taken his place and serve regularly in place of him. It's just a little service I feel I need to endure for him. It didn't end up helping him in the end, but I bet he helped lots of others. It's a good service. Give blood, you're not a stone.

It's far too deep

I'll play it to the beat. I'll play it by ear. I can always hear the beat. Is there no end to the music in my head? It's the song that never ends. It's a song I've almost forgotten. It's a vague memory. I need to hear this song play again, before I can write *The Music in Me*.

I want the music to start in my life again, but it's hasn't yet. The music isn't ready to come out. There's a time for music. What could make it flow? This is the book I've been longing to right (leave the spelling) from the start.

Longing:- n. a yearning - adj feeling a yearning.

Am I yearning for a long shot? Is it a shot in the dark?

Long shot:- [Colloq.] a betting choice that has little chance of winning - not by a long shot [Colloq.] not at all.

This book I long to write, may be a bit of a long shot. It's been long-standing.

Long-standing:- adj. having continued for a long time.

It hasn't just been a long-standing goal, it's been more like a long-suffering goal.

Long-suffering:- adj. bearing trouble patiently for a long time -n. long and patient endurance.

How long can one person take? Is it a test of endurance? Haven't I passed the test? Have I run out of time, or is there still time in which to be tested? Has your patience been tested? Have a thought for mine. If I'm the testee, who is the testor? I'm a test case.

Test case:- Law, a case that is likely to be used as a precedent.

Testa:- [< L., shell] Bot. the hard outer covering of a seed.

The testa has a hard shell. I do not. Now don't get all excited when I define testy for you. I'm not a ball that can keep bouncing back.

> **Testy:-** [< OFr. *Teste*, head] irritable; touchy; peevish – tes'tily adv. –tes'tiness n.
>
> **Ballocks:-** [OE. *beallucas*, testicles] [Vulg. Slang] the testicles – interj [Vulg. Slang] nonsense.

Are testicles nonsense?

Watch the bouncing ball. The little bouncing ball can teach us to sing. I could never get this timing right. I was always out of time with the ball. I was never on the ball when it came to singing, but I love doing it. I just don't always love the sound I make.

I can sing quite well when I'm drunk. This is a rare occasion. Singing well, is the rare occasion. You may have had occasion to hear me sing, but I doubt it. My drunken singing partner is gone. She was my partner in crime. We would always end the evening singing old hymns. Was it a crime to sing hymns like this? Will I have to pay for my singing? Did she pay for her crimes? Were they crimes against hymn? Who is hymn?

> **Hymn:-** (him) n. [< Gr. *hymnos*] a song of praise; esp. in honour of God –vt. to praise in a hymn.

Why did I have to be drunk to sing an old hymn? They weren't just any old hymns, they were remembered hymns. These are the songs I remember the words to. How do you think I felt when I sang these songs at the end of the evening? Did I feel melancholy or morbid? I think I felt maudlin.

> **Maudlin:-** adj. [< ME. *Maudeleyne*, (Mary) Magdalene] foolishly and tearfully, or weakly sentimental.

My drunken singing partner Red Rose and I (a rose by any other name), loved all the songs from the rock musical *Jesus Christ Superstar*. We went to see it together at the Civil in the Castle of old. We'd both been to see it when we were kids. We'd both grown up with it in our childhoods. I had the soundtrack, and we both knew the words off by heart. This is because they were in our hearts. When you have a song in your heart, you're moved by it. It moves you emotionally. This can happen easily when you're drunk.

> **Drunk:-** pp. + archaic pt. of DRINK –adj 1. intoxicated; 2. overcome by a powerful emotion –n. [Slang] as drunken person.

I'm not intoxicating

You see, one can be drunk on emotion alone. It doesn't necessarily mean that you've been drinking alcohol. This is not what you were assuming is it? Can you be drunk with happiness? If it's very powerful happiness, you can be overcome with emotion. When we laugh uncontrollably, we can look like we're drunk. That's enough drunken talk for now. When you are a rose by any other name, you are not red. She was a red, but now she's dead. Is this a dead end? Should I deadhead the rose bush? That's nipping off all the old buds that are dead to encourage new growth. I don't want to be the last rose. I want to be the one and only. I can't think of the words to the song, and I'm not too sure of the story, but I know it's sad. It will always make me feel sad.

My new drink

I know of the drink Rosé. I like this drop. It's a mix between red wine and white wine. It shall be my special drink. Is this the wine they use for the offering in church? Why? I want to know why. Is it the medium? Is it used like a medium? Is it a medium with which we commune with God? It's the middle ground.

What is the middle ground for drinking? What's the balance? I'm not a drinker. I enjoy wine with dinner. I can drink too much if I'm nervous. I don't ever want to drink too much. I just want there to be a medium. I want to have a balance for drinking. I think a good wine should be savoured. I think it should be sipped. I believe it should be sipped and enjoyed with good food. I think it's for special occasions. This is the occasion I'm waiting for. I haven't had a drink for five months. I want to have a nice drink, and a nice occasion to drink it for. Good wine tastes nice. It's an acquired taste. Too much acquiring, can ruin the taste. I want to savour the taste of my next drink. I'm waiting for a taste.

I'm a medium

I went to a medium. She told me things about myself and my future. She was like a spring flower. Her words flowed over me like spring Jasmine grows over an old paling fence. I was paling into insignificance, as she contacted and spoke with the spirits I asked her to contact. They were there, and they spoke to me through her. It was divine. I knew it was them. I knew it was real. I knew what they were talking about. I knew what they meant. My mother wasn't angry with me. She wasn't even there yet. She was at the in between level. She was neither here nor there. She hadn't crossed. Could she have been in limbo?

> **Limbo:-** [< L. (in) *limbo*, (on) the border] 1. [often L.-] in some Christian theologies, a region bordering on hell, the abode after death of unbaptized children and righteous people who lived before Jesus; 2. a place of oblivion; 3. an indeterminate state.
>
> **Limbo:-** n., pl. -bos [<?] a West Indian dance in which the dancers pass, while leaning backwards, under a low bar.

I'm trying to fathom the idea of limbo. I have two definitions, but I'm opting for the second. I rather like the idea of the dance. This is the only dance I can think of, that you do while looking straight up. If you're looking up, you're not looking down. If you were already up, you'd have to be looking down. If you were in the middle, wouldn't you be looking straight ahead?

Going forwards

Thank God I'm lousy at doing the limbo. I have a cheating technique. When the bar starts to get a bit low for me, I assume the appropriate position, and as soon as my torso gets near the bar, I angle sideways and throw my head forward to get under. So, I kind of do a bit of looking up, looking down, and looking forward as I negotiate my body under the bar. Is this cheating? It is, and I always get disqualified. I think it's best to make the attempt, no matter what. Is it the strength in your legs that's needed, or balance? It's about strength and balance, isn't it? You need strength in all parts of your mind and body. You can even put your arms out in front to help balance your bent torso. It looks like we're reaching out in front for balance. Listen to what I'm telling you.

She disqualified herself

Life is a balancing act all in all. What is death? What is the opposite to balance? That's an unbalanced line of questioning. What happens when you're unbalanced? Are you mad? Are you mad, as in angry? No. When you're unbalanced, you're falling. Bang! You hit the deck. I can't say more than that, because it's not nice. It doesn't feel right. You shouldn't speak ill of the dead. I didn't know. This is not *The Knowing in Me*. It's just *The Worker in Me*. I'm still working it all out. I'm working on it. If I work it the right way, I'll feel good about it all, when all is said and done. What if I don't work it all out right? Will I know? How can one know if one has it all worked out correctly? Should it be correct, or can it be worked out to assuage our guilt?

She was toxic

Why do we get left with guilt once someone dies? Shouldn't they take it all with them when they go? What's the point in leaving it behind? Guilt isn't grieving, is it? Is it just grieving for lost opportunities to assuage our guilt? I'd been given plenty of opportunities, but there was just way too much guilt. How does guilt get created? Are we all capable of making it? How much can one person make? How much can one person take? Guilt takes a long time to create. No it doesn't!

Have you been to see your mother recently?

Did you get it? Did you feel it? Think about it, or think about her. Did you get it off me? Was I able to tap into it? I'll try a bit harder. She misses you and she'd love to see you. You know all this already. Should you go and see her? I think she needs a couple of things done. Did you feel the guilt I just offered you? Did you take it on board? Not the obligation, just the guilt. Are they the same? Obligation is created from guilt, but you can choose whether to oblige or not. Choosing takes guilt away. Choosing takes guts. This is what psychologists will tell you. Make a choice. It's not against the law. It's not criminal. When your mother cared for you as a child, was she under obligation or did she make a choice? Did she love you and want to do those things for you? She always had choice. We all have choice. There's no binding contract in place.

Liberate her

Psychologists will ask us to determine whether our choices are made because of a need, or a want. This is hard to work out, but we only need to survive. What we don't want to do, are the things that make us feel guilty, if we don't do them. We don't need guilt to survive. Some people have guilt till the day they die. It's an addiction. It's a habit that can be too hard to break. We'll all be guilty of something when we die. We're all just guilty.

I'm sorry if I'm making you feel guilty, or if I'm boring you. I feel a bit guilty for bringing all this up, but I just want to figure this guilt mystery out once and for all. I'll explain.

Did God make guilt, so that we'd do good things for others? Is guilt a punishment for sin? Is guilt a punishment for unseen sins? Is our problem with guilt, based on a problem of sin? What I mean to say is… Are we labelling things we do as sins, when they're not? Are our perceptions wrong? Are we getting our sins mixed up?

Guilt:- n. [OE. Gylt, sin] 1. the act or state of having done a wrong or committed an offence 2. a feeling of self-reproach resulting from a belief that one, has done something wrong.

It's not just a noun. It's a verb too. It's a doing word. I did it. I kept feeling it. My mother did it to me first. When she wasn't around, I just kept doing it. I gave myself the feeling via my beliefs. She gave me the beliefs. She was a good teacher. 'It must have been me'. 'It was probably me'. 'It would have been me'. Was it me? Was I the scapegoat?

Guilty if I did, and guilty if I didn't

I've done this. I was too harsh on myself most of the time, and I was too harsh on others because of it. Some of my sinning was not, and never had been, sinning. My sinning days are over. Can some of us recognize true sins, and some of us not? Who judges whether it's a sin or not, when we're alive? I get my sins now. I get what they are, and why I do them. I get which are, and which are not. I'd been so wrong about sins. My worst and most despicable sins were committed against myself, for thinking I'd sinned when I hadn't.

I sit in judgment of myself throughout my books. I'll continue to do this throughout my life. It's an important judgment time, being alive. And now I am alive.

Sins are about our intention. If we do a good deed for self-aggrandizement, it's a sin. It's not the right intention. Even if the good deed was indeed helping another, but the intention was to show off, it's a sin. This is where I've found some loopholes, thank God. If we do the deed with self-serving in mind, but we also wanted to help by doing the good deed, is this a sin? This one's a tricky one. It's not a sin, and it's not a good deed. One will cancel out the other. You've done nothing. It hasn't been counted as a good deed, but it hasn't been counted as a sin either. It's probably not worth doing. You won't get anything out of it. You might think you're getting something out of it, but personally, you're not. What's missing is the good feeling. The purely good feeling that comes from self-sacrifice and truth. Try the real thing for a change.

Inflicting a hurt on another is always a sin. I used to think this, but it's wrong too.

I didn't want to be hurt, so I tried not to hurt others. When I had been hurt by another, it was simpler just to turn the other cheek. I was probably angry for a while, but I just moved on and forgot about it. I pushed the anger aside, and got on with what I had to do. I had no time for indulging in anger. I didn't have my say. I didn't allow myself to have a say. It would have upset the apple cart. I thought this was a virtue. It was a sin. It was a sin against nature. My nature.

Energy must go somewhere

When anger raises its ugly head, I push its head back down. I've pushed lots of angry heads back down in my life, but only inside me. I rarely do it on the outside of me. We shouldn't be pushing anger back down all the time. Anger won't always stay down. Sometimes when the anger rises back up, we take our anger out on innocent others, and we don't recognize where this anger came from in the first place. We're using anger from something else, and throwing it where it shouldn't be thrown. Often, we take this anger out on ourselves. This is called self-abuse. It can be self-defeating, and it needs self-examination.

Self-defence is an important lesson

There was my problem. I didn't recognize that I could defend myself. You can fight a war, if you're defending yourself. If you're defending what's right and what is truth, you can defend till the cows come home, but you can't deceive yourself. You must be able to be honest with yourself first. Fight the good fight, with all you have and do, but make sure it's a fair fight.

It's a noble war

The reason I got this wrong, is because I didn't learn it as a child. It didn't matter who was right or who was wrong in our family.

It still doesn't

How does one learn, if one is never taught to defend one's own position? Did I get taught to stand up for myself, when I was wronged or persecuted? No. I just got told to shut up. It just didn't matter who created the problem, because the problem was invariably swept under the carpet.

When you're in the wrong, you shouldn't defend your ground. This is not self-defence. It's self-denial. In the long run, self-denial can't be denied. Karma makes certain of it. Karma balances the books.

Self-defence:- n. 1. defence of oneself, one's rights, etc; 2. boxing: usually in manly art of self-defence.

If you think it is self-defence, you're into self-governing. You may be self-delusional, because self-defence is defending rights. We must be self-disciplined, not self-complacent, to know what our rights are. It's about the rights, and what's genuinely right. It's about everyone's rights.

This is my defence

Many people lose sight of this self-rule. They have a habit of defending themselves, even when they know they've committed the sin. They probably know that they were in the wrong, but they habitually defend their position anyway. Is this for self-preservation, or self-interest? It's more like self-deception. This sort of a person has a false sense of self-regard. They tend to be self-satisfied, and are just self-seeking. They're only interested in serving their own ends. They're self-serving, and self-appointed. They choose their own rules, and that's self-evident.

A self-portrait

They should say sorry and ask for forgiveness. I was told all the time that I was in the wrong. I was told for so long, that I continually believed it. I just believed it, when I wasn't. It was easier for me to accept the wrong position. This was a habit. This was self-destruction.

By the time I was an adult, it didn't matter whether I was in the wrong or not, I just apologized. I was a walking apology. An apology was the easiest thing to offer. I was full of apologies. I always felt I had heaps to apologize for. It just makes everything go away. It fixed everything up for me. I just said sorry all the time. I've never had a problem with it, because I'm so used to it. I feel sorry all the time, and don't even recognize it. I'm a sorry excuse for a person. Sorry.

No wonder I felt guilty

What I didn't do, and what I had a huge problem with, was to tell anyone else, that they were in the wrong. I could voice it to another, and justify it in a private conversation, but I didn't have the self-confidence to stand up against the wrongdoer.

I'm still apologizing now. I'm self-justifying. Am I the self-same? I think I've changed. I think you're hearing me changing right now. This is me learning to change. You've read me like a book.

I don't want self-pity, and I don't want self-denial. I'm being self-taught. I don't want any more self-abnegation or self-restraint. I am self-employed, self-fulfilled and self-determined. I'm self-sufficient, self-reliant and self-propelled. I now have self-possession, I'm a self-starter, and am self-sustaining. I am self-willed and want something for myself now.

I want self-realization. I may need to get self-styled, so I'll need some self-support.

> **Self-righteous:-** adj. thinking oneself more righteous or moral than others.

Are there degrees of self-righteousness? If we set the bar too high for ourselves, then it's fair to say, that we've overstepped the mark, and we're trying too hard. It's also fair to say that we've set the bar too high for others too.

My dictionary is self-absorbed. It has all these selves, and I want to share them with you. Are they you, too?

Self-abnegation, self-absorption, self-abuse, self-addressed, self-aggrandizement, self-appointed, self-assertion, self-assurance, self-centred, self-complacent, self-conceit, self-confessed, self-confidence, self-conscious, self-contained, self-contradiction, self-control, self-deception, self-defeating, self-defence, self-denial, self-destruction, self-determination, self-discipline, self-educated, self-effacement, self-employed, self-esteem, self-evident, self-examination, self-existent, self-explanatory, self-expression, self-fulfilment, self-government, selfheal, self-help, self-hypnosis, self-important, self-imposed, self-improvement, self-incrimination, self-induced, self-indulgence, self-inflicted, self-interest, selfish, self-justification, selfless, self-made, self-opinionated, self-pity, self-portrait, self-possession, self-preservation, self-propelled, self-raising, self-realization, self-recording, self-regard, self-regulating, self-reliance, self-reproach, self-respect, self-restraint, self-revealing, self-righteous, self-sacrifice, selfsame, self-satisfied, self-sealing, self-seeker, self-service, self-serving, self-starter, self-styled, self-sufficient, self-support, self-sustaining, self-taught, self-ward, self-willed, self-winding.

Am I self-absorbed or self-righteous?

I'm sitting here on my bed writing, and it's quite early in the evening. Right at this moment I ask myself, does anyone carry any guilt which relates to me? Can I acknowledge that I've caused someone's guilt? I only want true guilt to be acknowledged. I don't want to cause false guilt. Will I? Will I cause a shit load of guilt with my books? Am I creating more guilt for the universe?

If guilt is a motivator, can it be a good motivator? Can it help people to change their ways? Can it be a teacher? Will it be written? Can I get rid of all your unwanted guilt in *The Teacher in Me*?

I've changed my ways

My new faith makes me feel guilty for the right reasons, and not the wrong reasons. This is new for me. My faith is new, but my guilt is old. When I was eleven, I gave up my Catholic faith for this very reason. Have I gone backwards again? I don't think so, because while I'd got rid of my faith at eleven, I didn't get rid of the guilt. The guilt came from other sources. Who else did I have faith in? I've never been without guilt. I never will be without guilt. We never can be without guilt, no matter what faith we have.

We're all guilty

The only thing we can do, is to try to reduce our guilt. First, I need to become aware of what I'm truly guilty of. I'm guilty of everything. I'm probably guilty of every misdemeanour known to man. I've done it. I've just done it to different degrees.

I've killed a spider in self-defence

I've believed all my guilty feelings. I've just believed I must have been guilty of a wrong doing. I just thought that whatever it was, that caused me to feel guilty, needed to be paid for. I believed I must have had a hand in it. It was no use denying all this guilt, because the guilt was driving me. It drove me to do more than my fair share. It drove me to give more than my fair share. Guilt was driving me over a cliff.

I know who planted the first seed of guilt in me. I know who tended it, and what they got in return. People can control other people by sowing the seeds of guilt. Other people saw the benefits of growing guilt, and wanted to get in on the act. I was oblivious.

Do you think I could be this guilty?

I'll apologize now for apologizing. Sorry self. Self has accepted my apology, and has forgiven me. Self says that I need to undo some things I did. Self says this will balance the guilt in me.

Doing it, and undoing it

I'm undoing it all. I'm relinquishing it all. I'm giving it back. I'm also giving the guilt back. I'm offering someone else my guilty conscience. I'm offering it up to the universe. This is transferring the guilt. It's karma. It's good karma. It's good karma for someone else. It's good karma for me too. Let karma taketh away, what I shalt not have taken on.

Don't taketh my tree of knowledge

I look out my window and meditate on my grandfather tree. My grandfather tree is a protector. My grandfather tree is tall. It's taller than my three-storey house. I'm looking at it from my second storey. I'm on the middle ground. This is a good place to meditate from.

A preacher is a reacher

The tree's branches are straight out to the side. It's a reacher. It reaches out. It reaches under. It uplifts me. It's uplifting this house. It's a tall tree, and its roots are spread wide in the sandy soil for stability. It takes on the coastal winds. My grandfather tree is a Norfolk pine. It's the one thing that I'll truly miss about this home. This tree watches me contemplate. It helps me to contemplate. When I sit on my verandah to smoke, I start by contemplating the tree. I'm contemplating everything, but I always start with this beautiful tree. It always reminds me to think. It gives me all the subjects I need.

The tale of Pocahontas

I've observed everything about this tree. I know of the lichen that covers its main trunk, and the shape of its fronds as they uncurl and stretch out. I watch growth. I watch the birds sit on my tree. I watch the spiders make their webs in it. I watch it sway in big winds. I scoop up all the pine needles that it sheds over the front yard. I notice sap coming from under its bark, and wonder at the reason for it. Is it tree blood? It's that dark red colour. It's like liquid glass and I can see through it. It's beautiful sap, and it's the resin. Like gloss or two-pack enamel, it helps to glue things together. It's a preserver, and a repair substance. It could be repairing the tree's wounds.

> 'Deep in thought, Pocahontas went to a very special glade in the forest inhabited by Grandmother Willow, a magical and wise tree. The Indian maiden told her enchanted friend about her dream.
>
> "I am running through the woods," began Pocahontas, "and then, right there in front of me, is an arrow. It spins faster and faster until suddenly, it stops! Then I wake up. What does it mean, Grandmother Willow?"
>
> "Well, it seems to me this spinning arrow is pointing you down your path," the old tree replied.
>
> "But what is my path? How am I ever going to find it?" continued Pocahontas.
>
> "Your mother asked me the very same question. I told her to listen," Grandmother Willow went on. "All around you are spirits, child. They live in the earth, the water, the sky. If you listen, they will guide you."
>
>> From Disney's Pocahontas. Published in Australia by Reed For Kids, a division of Reed International Books Australia Pty Ltd., 1995. The Walt Disney Company. Printed by Southbank Book. All rights reserved. No part of this book may be reproduced without the written permission from the copyright owner.
>>
>> (Don't sue me first. Just ask me, for whatever it is you feel entitled to.)

Pocahontas (born Matoaka, and later known as Rebecca Rolfe, c. 1595 – March 1617) was a Virginia Indian notable for her association with the colonial settlement at Jamestown, Virginia. She was the daughter of Powhatan, the paramount chief of a network of tributary tribal nations in the Tidewater region of Virginia. In a well-known historical anecdote, she is said to have saved the life of an Indian captive, Englishman John Smith, in 1607 by placing her head upon his own when her father raised his war club to execute him.

Pocahontas was captured by the English during Anglo-Indian hostilities in 1613, and held for ransom. During her captivity, she converted to Christianity and took the name Rebecca. When the opportunity arose for her to return to her people, she chose to remain with the English. In April 1614, she married tobacco planter John Rolfe, and in January 1615, bore him a son, Thomas Rolfe.

In 1616, the Rolfes travelled to London. Pocahontas was presented to English society as an example of the civilized 'savage' in hopes of stimulating investment in the Jamestown settlement. She became something of a celebrity, was elegantly fêted, and attended a masque at Whitehall Palace. In 1617, the Rolfes set sail for home, but Pocahontas died at Gravesend of unknown causes. She was buried in a church in Gravesend, but the exact location of her grave is unknown.

Numerous places, landmarks, and products in the United States have been named after Pocahontas. Her story has been romanticized over the years, and she is a subject of art, literature, and film. Her descendants through her son Thomas include members of the First Families of Virginia, First Ladies Edith Wilson and Nancy Reagan, and astronomer Percival Lowell.

Thanks to Wikipedia, I now know that Pocahontas was a real woman and not a fictional character. Figuring out what's fictional and what's non-fictional is what I'm about to find out. I'll get back to you on this in *The Dreamer in Me*.

A wiser word was never said

Yes, I'll miss this big old tree. I hate to leave this tree here, but I can't take it with me. I suspect the new owners will want to chop it down. They may want to improve their view of the ocean. It will be a dangerous thing to do.

This tree of mine has a special purpose. It helps to diffuse the orgone energy from the large electrical transducer on the telegraph pole at the front of the house. There are special things to be careful about, in this house. There are bad energies in and around this dwelling place. This house is on ancient tribal land and there are grid lines running under it. This block is sand-based, so water runs under the house all the time which is a conductor. This can attract negative spirits and negative energy. This is the reason why I keep organites. This property is high voltage. This could be why I have lumps in both my breasts.

I don't know whether to warn anyone. This could make me sound strange. I don't know whether I should leave the organites with the house, but I think not. As part of this organite system, there's also crystals placed over the door frames. These are cornerstones. They're to protect the arches. I've had to take many precautions while living in this house. This house attracts evil, if you don't take precaution. I took the scientific approach. This is *The Science in Me*.

Possession is nine-tenths of the law

I also called in a psychic to help me with this house. She helped me understand the reason for the presence. I understand the spiritual significance of the reason. I had a spirit that was protective. He was protective of his home. He was possessive. There was a combat of sorts that took place here. There's an ongoing battle of sorts. There's also a higher power now. This is the other approach I took, and it's been written. It's in *The Spirit in Me*.

There will be reminders of me in this house. I won't be leaving the house as I found it. It has left its mark. I've left my marks on it, and it's left its marks on me. It's an indelible mark.

Indelible:- adj [< L. *in-*, not + *delere*, destroy] 1. that cannot be erased, blotted out, etc.; 2. leaving an indelible mark.

An indelible sign

The first night I spent in this house was a stormy night, just weeks before we were to move into it. We had a camp-out, or rather, a camp-in, with fold-up mattresses and sleeping bags. I had a dream that night, that wasn't quite a dream. It was a nightmare to beat all nightmares. It was one mother of a nightmare! It was the worst nightmare of my life. I was rocked by it.

The Hoorah was a nightmare

When I think of that nightmare, I think of the terrible feeling it gave me. I'd never experienced a feeling like it, nor close to it. I'll never forget the horrific feeling. The closest I can come to explaining it, is comparing it to the dementors in *Harry Potter*. Just like the dementors, this demon sucked the very life out of me. The dementors are said to be able to suck every bit of happiness out of your soul. This is how I felt. It was a dementor clawing into me, and it sucked like a heavy-duty vacuum. Everything good in me went out of me. It felt like horror. It caused a vile and strangulating anguish within me. It was a feeling of horrid and sickening possession. It was attached to me in a way that was like a dreadful growth. It reached right into the heart of me. It overtook me, and was changing me. It wanted possession.

The Knowing of the scene

The scene of the nightmare was eerie, set on a grassy verge on a hill above the ocean. There was a shack, and I've always thought of Catherine Mount Bay when I'm remembering it. It's a place I've always found eerie, particularly because there's a very old cemetery right by the beach. I've felt the energy at Catherine Mount Bay, and I think I always will. There were other people in my nightmare. My ex husband was there, but he was behind me, as I tried to climb the slope with this thing digging right through my shoulder blades. I was trying to reach around to pull it off me, but I couldn't get rid of it.

Red Rose was further up and across from me, and I was trying to reach her. She just stood there staring at me, willing me onwards. There were a few other people, but I can't put names to them. I feel I know them, but I can't identify them. I have the knowing now.

They were only halfway up

I had this nightmare in the winter of 2005. It haunted me a great deal, and for a long time. It was a dream I was worried about. I had a feeling of foreboding. I understand this dream now, and it no longer holds that same foreboding feeling. I've put this dream to bed now. It's already happened. It's history.

A bedtime story

I knew that nightmare was an omen. It cast a dark cloud over this house from the beginning. I knew it was a bad sign. I read the signs with my instinct, and felt them in the house that weekend. I chose to ignore it. I was a sceptic then, and a strict atheist. I didn't have any strong beliefs. I just had the feelings.

I believe that sometimes we're just destined for our destiny. Do I believe it all the time? No. I believe that we can change our own destiny. I believe that we just don't know that we can. It's a hard call to make, but it's a call that's makeable. It's a makeable call. I hope you make the call for a good destiny, and call when you need to. This is sincere. It's from yours sincerely. Who is 'yours sincerely'?

> **Sincere:-** adj. [< L. *sincerus*, clean] 1. without deceit or pretence, honest; 2. genuine, real [sincere grief].

It's yours cleanly, and yours without deceit. It's yours, without pretension, and yours honestly. It's always yours genuinely, and yours truly, and surely. It's all yours, if you want it.

Yours authentically

Who is yours? I know who mine is. I know who yours is. What's mine is yours, and what's yours is mine. Can 'yours' be 'everyone's'? When do we know 'yours' is ours? We can know this, when we're on our own. We know this when we're alone. When we're just one with ourselves, there's room for our spirit. It's the Holy Spirit in us. We are never ever all by ourselves if we don't want to be.

Don't wanna be all by myself

Great song, but it's bloody sad when I'm by myself. I mean, really by myself. Christ, I'm so by myself right now, that I'm grateful for this song's company.

I can sing this song with great pitch, and great strength. I know how to sing this song with pure passion. I sing it with tears running down my face, but it's a song for my lonely soul. I sing it with great gusto. I sang it in my car today. It's a wonder you didn't hear me. I hope I've been heard.

> **Gusto:-** n. [< L. *gustus*, taste] 1. great vigour; 2. zest, relish; 3. [Obs.] taste; liking.

I couldn't have sung this song before. I couldn't have sung this song a year ago, before all the strife. I had very few moments of being alone. I was barely ever alone, but that just goes to show you how alone I was. I had people around me all the time. The only time I didn't, was in bed, and I wasn't alone there either. I could be alone in the toilet. I could be alone when I had my head in a book. Reading a book isn't really being alone. Being in the toilet doesn't last long enough for it to be quality time. If you take too long in the toilet, people start to talk.

I'm all alone inside my head

Are we self-conscious about being alone? This isn't the question I'm asking. When we're alone, are we feeling conscious of it? Do we find a connection point, and become aware that we are being conscious of ourselves again? Being aware you're alone, is the most important thing about being alone. This is when thinking is your own. It's when you hear your own questions being asked, and you feel yourself trying to answer the questions for yourself. You can be aware that you're thinking and reasoning for yourself. You find the answers. The answers always come when you take this time. Most times, we don't.

There's a chicken inside my head

We run around like chooks with their heads cut off. We listen to all the other chooks running around squawking at us, and telling us what to do. We know what to do for ourselves, because we are ourselves. The only one able to reason properly, and from the one true perspective, is our self. Having faith in ourselves can only come from knowing and thinking about ourselves. We must reason with ourselves. Start like this:

- Find a quiet place with no interruptions. It could be in nature or in a quiet room, but there must be no distractions. Turn your phone off. Just sit. Do nothing.
- What is the nature of the problem? Ask the question of yourself. Ask it in articulate speech. This means writing it down. You can write down the problem if you want, but make it clear. Don't forget the question mark, because you alone are going to answer it. You are going to work on it by yourself and work it out.
- It's hard to know where to start, because problems are bombarding your mind now, and they're all fighting for the frontline position. You must prioritize. You're only solving one problem today. Choose the easiest problem first. You want success, because this is a learning curve, and we want to improve over time and excel at problem solving.
- There, it's now written out or verbalized. Walk around it a couple of times. Read over it a few times and assess

it. Check out how strong or weak it is. Assess how it makes you feel. What emotions has it released in you? Write them down.
- This is an important question to ask yourself, but it's of vital importance to solving this problem you have: ask yourself if it is indeed, your problem. If you now see that it isn't your problem, give yourself a tick and your work is done for today. Move on, and vow to yourself that you will leave other people's problems alone, and not let them interfere with your life.
- If you believe it's your very own problem, you haven't picked correctly. You might have picked a hard problem after all. It could mean that you'll be able to solve all your problems with the one answer. It could mean that you do have a problem with problems. You're the problem. You need to break down the problem, slowly, and with small steps. Examine the problem. That means look within. Where did the problem first manifest?

Let's move ahead to some examples of problems, and I'll give you a list of categories so we can define your problem better.

<u>Categories</u>

Health   Personal   Money

This is a short list, but these are the only three words we need. All problems fall into these categories. You may have a problem that will fall into all three.

That's not the answer

All problems arise from one word. They're also fixed with the one word. They can't be fixed by saying the word, but they can surely be fixed by using it. There's a common denominator in all of us. It's the common denominator in all our problems. It can be a real problem, but it's also a problem solver.

I think I've solved this one by myself, but I guess heaps of people know it already. Could I fix all problems with it? Yes, but only real problems. This is where people get mixed up. A real problem isn't a broken machine. If you can't do your job because the machine's broken, it's not your problem. If you're the machine repairer, it's only your problem if you don't like your job. The machine is not the problem though, your job is. It may not in fact be the job that's the problem. You may have another underlying problem, and you're blaming it on your job. You can always go and get a different job, or strive for the job you've always wanted. That's just self-love.

Have I just given you the answer to all life's problems?

A problem example

One such example is the problem of the forty-five-year-old woman with three teenage kids, who works full-time. She's married and has a mortgage with her husband, which they're trying hard to pay off, before they reach fifty. She weighs a hundred kilos and her knees are playing up. This is affecting her happiness, because she can't see how she can continue to work. It's affecting her marriage, because she's grumpy and fatigued. She eats too much, but she can't help it, because eating is the only joy easily accessible to her. Let's see if we can help.

We can't help her

She'll have to help herself. Her question to herself is:

1. Why am I so unhappy?

There isn't any need for more questions, because this is the problem. Her problem happens to be all three of the categories. Which category is the most important? It's the first one, isn't it? You can't get personal if you haven't got your health. She needs to piss the other two off until she gets her health in order. This means stop work. It might only mean take six months off. Suddenly she sees more problems in doing this. She goes straight to the money category and starts working on it. She gets tied up with the personal category, because she's now thinking about what her husband will say about less money coming in.

Your own person

Personal doesn't mean him. Personal is personal. Everyone is responsible for their own person. She must get personal with herself for a change, and concentrate on that. Health is very personal, because it can affect your personal relationships if it isn't in good shape. She needs to have a think about how well her personal relationships will be, once she has a good personal relationship with herself. The way to a good personal relationship with her self will be in looking after herself.

This is cause and effect

She takes the time off work and gets fit. In order to get fit, one must gift one's self the fitness. She needs to enjoy her fitness. It just means taking walks in beautiful places. It means gifting yourself wonderful fitness experiences. Forget the gym, it costs money. Nature is free. Nature is also good for this lady's nature. She needs to walk twice a day and increase the length of time. She also needs to increase the number of environments that she walks in.

With more time off work, she has time to eat nutritiously, and has time to provide for herself first. Her problem is a priority for her. It's her problem. Her diet is the most important diet in the home. She needs to demonstrate to others around her, that her life is the most important to her out of everyone's, because it is. Her responsibility to herself must come first. This will have a lasting effect on her kids. This effect can go either way, but it will always be up to the kids. It's their choice as to how they want to be affected.

I can hear her carrying on about her knees, and I've just suggested small walks to start with, but more swimming. She needs to swim every day. Her knees have been very responsible.

They've alerted her to her problems. This is what the body does, if only we would listen and do something about it. Her knees said "help". She's now helping her knees, because she's just lost three kilos in her first week.

It's a win, win situation

Everyone at home has congratulated her, and they admire her spirit because they can see how determined she is. They're respecting her more. They respect her determination, and the respect she's giving to herself. She's taken more of an interest in cooking healthy food, and she's found time to indulge in other pursuits that make her happy.

Time to deal with other problems

She's started sorting a few things out at home that she's never had the time for. This is taking away another few problems that have always given her the feeling of frustration. She's gone through her own wardrobe and thrown out all the clothes she looks terrible in. She's now discovering other styles of clothes, and buying the opposite to what she used to buy. She's spending more and more time on her own, and she's beginning to get to know herself. She's listening to herself. She's enjoying listening to herself think. Ideas are popping into her head now, and they're uplifting ideas. They're great ideas for her.

It's not a problem

As part of her new regime for becoming healthy, she's developed a pleasing routine. She wakes in the morning and before doing anything, she has a shower, washes her hair and takes her time enjoying the water. She takes time for herself. She looks after her skin by applying the body lotion that she's had sitting there since last Christmas. She uses it all over her body and then dresses. She applies make-up every day, for no other reason than for her to feel good. She takes time to do her hair as if she's going out somewhere special. She is special, and needs to feel special all the time. She wants every day to feel special. Every day feels more special than the last.

I can hear you

You're still worried about the money. I can hear you saying the mortgage isn't getting paid. The mortgage is getting paid, because she's sold her car. She's also sold some gold jewellery that she didn't wear. These items aren't anywhere near as important as being healthy and happy. Get your perspective right. Did the car and the jewellery make her happy before? No. They just didn't cut it. They didn't cut ice. That's what she used to be, a block of ice. Personally, she's now thawing out.

Don't be blind to options

We always have options, but we just don't see what our options are. Options are the open doors. We look at the doors, but we don't enter. Options are our hand-holds. Everyone has options. Options are the very things that allow us to change our lives.

This lady is feeling happier. She loves loving herself. It's making her feel good. She looks in the mirror every day now, because she can see what she likes about herself. She now has more time to consider her attributes and how lovely she really is. She'd forgotten. She's had time to remember who she used to be. She starts to see that person coming back. She's lost ten kilos, and people are noticing.

It's like the good old days

She starts to consider the things she used to like, and all the things she always wanted to do, but didn't have time for. She buys some paints and gets painting. She's having fun. She's also taken an interest in the garden and is growing vegetables. She's thrilled with the flowers blooming now, and they bring her a ridiculous amount of joy. A packet of seeds has created a beanstalk. She puts something tiny in, and gets something huge back. She's already sprouted some rocket, to go into her special signature dish. She makes a fresh beetroot, walnut, and rocket salad. Yum!

Happy is healthy

Her family is enjoying coming home to a happy house. They see how happy mum is now, and they like the look of her. They're proud of her. The home is happier and is a nicer environment to come home to. They're all getting more active now.

This lady has developed self-confidence and self-esteem. She weighs eighty-two kilos. She's considering a change in career, and doing some part-time study. She recognizes the range of options opening up to her. She sees all the open doors. She doesn't think she wants full-time work anymore, because she's discovered that there's more to life. She realizes that she'd had her priorities wrong, and why she'd become so unhealthy. She realizes that personally, she's so much happier, and this in turn has made others happier to be around her.

Liking your person

They don't know what she'll do next, because she's getting more interesting by the day. She's become a bit unpredictable, and she's full of surprises. Her husband is surprised too. He's a bit jealous, and wants to join in the fun. This is good, because this is where it gets more personal.

Pipe down, I'm getting to him...

Now, I can hear your voices again, and I know what you're thinking. Her husband may have reacted in the opposite way. Her change is getting to him. This is true, because some husbands do react badly to change. There's always a bit of a reshuffle when one person makes changes. It's cause and effect. She could have caused a bit of a rough effect on him. She's only ruffled his feathers though. She hasn't hurt anybody. He's just an old chook. Let's have a look from the chook's perspective.

The chook or the rooster?

Suddenly she's having time off, and he's still working like a dog. This isn't her problem. This is her husband's problem. He has the same options. He can also put himself first. He could put himself first, at his expense. He can't put himself first, at her expense. She won't let him. Her expense is her expense. We all own our own expense. We must stay rigid with our expense account. Every one of us is more important to ourselves than to any other.

Compromise is an option. It's all about discussing happiness. It's about who wants it, and how bad. He has the same options as her. He could take six months off. They're in advance with their mortgage payments. It could be life reassessment time. Each must assess their own life. One cannot be responsible for the other's life, under any circumstances. This is the law you know. We must take responsibility for ourselves.

We walk alone

I can't stress enough, that you must be number one. You are one. You are your own one. No one belongs to you, and you don't belong to another. This is the big mistake that we commonly make. This is the answer to our problems, most of the time.

Anyway, this lady goes on to lose twenty kilos in six months. She looks twenty years younger. Her life has changed, and she hasn't known happiness like this since she was a young girl. She's really living. Her husband agreed to sell the house, and they got rid of the two eldest kids who have now moved in with friends. The fifteen-year-old is happy in her new home and loves her new life. She's learned an incredible life lesson. Instead of being a slave to everyone else, she's growing into an independent, self-sufficient, and self-confident young woman, with a part-time job of her own. Everyone is happy. Everyone now knows how to be happy.

Her husband didn't pipe down

The alternative scenario is still happy, for this formerly unhappy lady. Her change had an effect on her family, who were most dependent on her, and super demanding of her. They got the shits, gave her a hard time, and pissed off. They took Dad's side. Her husband got the shits too, and went off and found another lady to be dependent with. He has control back, and he thinks he's the winner. Nothing much has changed in his life.

His fit, beautiful, and lively ex-wife, went north to a new life, new job, and a new lover. Not a live-in lover, just an unrestricted love fest, when she wants. No obligations anymore. She has a completely new life, and a new identity. She has an identity that she's grateful to identify with. She's found her talents, and her purpose. She's happy that her knees don't hurt anymore. She's as healthy as a bull. This is no bull.

Is this a happy story too? What perspective are you taking? Everyone has their own perspective. This is our right. We always have a right to our own personal perspective.

Oh, and incidentally, the ex-husband died of a heart attack at age fifty five.

But he needn't have!

Don't be repelled by change. Be open and accept it. It's a natural part of life. It's our life's purpose.

Do you look around you at the environment, and think nothing has changed over the last ten years? You aren't looking closely enough. Everything has changed. You may be the only thing that hasn't. Get a move on. You're wasting precious time. Look how much time hubby had.

I told you I was a good storyteller.

What is a New Year's resolution?

> **Resolution:-** n. 1. a) a resolving b) the result of this; 2. a decision as to future action; 3. a resolute quality of mind; 4. a formal statement

of opinion adopted by a group; 5. a solving or answering, solution; 6. music, the process in harmony where a dissonant note or chord is followed by a consonant one; 7. Physics. the ability of a lens to distinguish between adjoining points.

Did you make a New Year's resolution? How many of us made a pledge to ourselves for change, on the eve of 2012, or on the morning of 2012? I waited for 1.1.2012. It wasn't at the eleventh hour. It was at the twelfth hour. It wasn't a resolution. It was a New Year's dissolution.

What is a New Year's dissolution?

It was the lucky hour. The date: $1 + 1 + 2 + 0 + 1 + 2 = 7$. It was the lucky number. It was odd, because I thought it would be an even number. Oops!

My mistake

The real date: $1 + 1 + 20 + 12 = 34$. That's better. Half of $34 = 17$. Yep, that makes a lot more sense to me now. I'd forgotten the 1. I'd forgotten the one. I forgot me. I'm starting to like math. I just make up my own formulas, and they just make heaps more sense. It's always a Formula 1 that wins. It always takes the line honours. I'm at the beginning of the race. It's a race for time. I want time honours. I want an honest time for my date.

Dissolution:- n. a dissolving or being dissolved, specif., a) a breaking up or into parts b) termination c) death d) the dismissal of parliament before a general election.

At the twelfth hour, I made a request to the universe. I made a wish, and wished with all my heart and soul, that it be granted. I then got a text message. It was from my daughter. She was sending me her best wishes for 2012. I could tell it had a lot of heart behind it. I knew she really wished it for me. She's passionate about what she wishes for. I felt the magic when I read her message.

It's been spelled out

I sent her a spell in reply. I know she likes spells, so I cast a special spell on us for the New Year. It went like this…

> Abrica Dabra,
> Abrica Sendous.
> Make this New Year
> Fucking Tremendous!

I'm not a witch, but I feel like it sometimes. I can make things happen. I've made things happen to other people. They've only been able to happen, because those people had always relied on my magic. Those people depended on my magic. How many people rely on your magic? How many people depend on you to provide magic?

The question is asked of me now – whose magic did I rely on? Did I rely on other people's magic, or did I go out and find my own magic?

The magic business

Making magic can be a tricky business. It's all about spell making. It's about casting good spells. I always try to cast good spells over people, but someone came along when I wasn't around, and cast a greater spell. It was a big spell. It was quite a powerful spell, so I'm assuming it's come from a powerful witch. I didn't know this spell was being used. If I had known a witch would cast a spell over my people, I would have cast a protective spell. I could have gone to the sacred house of spell making, and asked for a spell to stop her spell from working. You really should check to see whose spell you could be under. Could you be under her spell?

The magic grotto

I'm having a lengthy spell now. I'm busy casting. I'm spelling it all out. Are you in the cast? I know I've put a spell on someone I like. Actually, I've cast a spell over two people I like. I've cast subtle spells. These are spells that these people won't know about. They'll be unaware they're under my spells. A spell can be just a suggestion or an idea. It can be a subliminal message. A spell is cast out, into a murky depth. It can hook something deep down, and then it drags it back up to the surface. It becomes more than mere suggestion or a new idea. It becomes a reality. I'm casting good spells, and I cast around in my mind, on where to cast my next one.

Checking the wand direction

I've got to look at it from the right angle. I must cast from a perspective. My perspective is a changed perspective now. It's a balanced perspective. When things aren't balanced, they need a new perspective.

My inside perspective has changed. I don't have a lounge suite perspective anymore, nor a coffee table perspective. I don't have my big dining suite perspective. I have no furniture perspective. I have less of the old perspectives, so I have my perspective more in perspective. It's clearer now than it was. I have two perspectives that are comfortable for me. I have my bedroom suite perspective, and I have my desk perspective. This means I have my work and rest perspectives, in perspective. I have balance, because they're both in focus.

Sustaining my perspective

I sit on the floor to eat my meals, just like the Japanese of old. I know that it's the culture in many countries to sit on the floor to eat meals. Everyone is at the same low level as each other to share sustenance. There's no head of the table when you sit on the floor, there's just tales. I won't be sharing, but I would be happy to share if anybody was interested.

A wand pointing south

Sitting on the floor to eat a meal is a humble feeling. It seems more relaxed. When we go on a picnic and sit at a picnic table, it's not the same as spreading everything out on a picnic blanket on the ground. Sitting on a picnic blanket is way more relaxed. One can recline on a picnic blanket. That's the first inclination we have, when sitting on a picnic blanket.

Picnics are relaxing. Stretching out and feeling and smelling the ground underneath is relaxing. It's also restorative. Have we forgotten the art of picnicking? Are we becoming too sophisticated for picnics? A picnic is simple, and it's cost effective. It doesn't cost much, and it's very effective.

The smell of fresh air

There are many affects to be had from going on picnics. You have time to smell the grass and watch the clouds as you lay on your back. You watch branches swaying in the breeze, and the leaves as they fall to the ground. You watch the bugs and butterflies. You notice. You notice all kinds of shit. You notice that it's the shit that you miss. It's free shit. We're all as dumb as dog shit. It's better shit than what we'd be watching on television. It's better for us, in every way. It's better for our kids to know about shit like this. Make some room for some good shit, because life's no picnic!

Defining my picnic

When I think of an ideal picnic spot, I don't think of a designated picnic area. I think of a natural bushland surrounding with a grassy clearing and shady trees. I think of a creek or a river, and I think of swimming. I think of privacy, and being away from everyone else. I think of the peace and quiet. I imagine a fresh water river and swimming nude. This is what they did in the olden days. They just got their gear off and went in, but they kept it private. It sounds sophisticated, doesn't it? I might find this hard to arrange, because it's not easy finding a spot like this, all for one, and not one for all. It may need some careful planning.

Picnic:- n. [< Fr. *pique-nique*] 1. a pleasure outing, with an outdoor meal; 2. [Slang] a) a pleasant experience b) an easy task 3. [Slang] a troublesome situation or experience used ironically –vi. –nicked, -nicking, to hold or attend a picnic –pic'nicker n.

I have a new and sophisticated idea, and it's just manifesting as I write. I have an idea. I have an enchanting idea. I want to buy myself a picnic spot such as this. I want seclusion. I'm not sure how much seclusion will cost, but I now have a dream to strive for. I want to live by a river somewhere in the bush.

I've lived in the suburbs, and I've lived on the lakefront. I've lived by the ocean. I haven't lived in the bush or on acreage. In the past, I haven't considered living on acreage. I was frightened. I thought I'd feel frightened living in an isolated place. I felt scared of being away from people. I thought I'd feel insecure. I now feel it is more secure. I want to live closer to nature. I want to be closer to my own nature. This is only natural. I might be able to live more naturally, and grow vegetables. I think that's all I'll do. I'll just grow.

I'm finally growing up

I want a garden. I want time in a garden of my own making. I've never had enough time for a garden. I've had gardens, but I've never had time to grow anything myself. Is a garden creating? I'll have to ask *The Maker in Me*. *The Maker in Me* says to ask *The Dreamer in Me*. *The Dreamer in Me* has the job. I want time in a garden of my own making. I want to create my own Garden of Eden. I want to tend my own personal garden. I want to watch it flourish and grow lush. I want a lush garden.

> **Lush:-** adj. [< OFr. *lasche*, lax] 1. of or characterized, by rich growth; 2. tender and full of juice; 3. rich, abundant, extravagant, etc.
>
> **Luscious:-** adj. [ME. *lucius*, infl. by ff] 1. very pleasing to taste or smell; 2. delighting any of the senses.

I love this word. I love it's very sound. I love how it slips off the tongue as you say it. Luscious is juicy. I dream of lusciousness. I dream of a hot steamy day, a swim, and a juicy mango to devour afterwards. I dream of a luscious garden, damp aromatic earth, and overripe tomatoes with a glorious smell. I want my hair to grow long, and luscious. Black luscious hair left wild and untamed, but shiny, and smelling sweet. That's me. I can do the hair, but I'm not sure how luscious I can really be. I'd like to feel luscious. I think I'd like to luxuriate in all things lush, and luscious.

Oh, wouldn't it be nice!

> **Luxuriate:-** [< L. luxuria, luxury] 1. to revel (in) 2. to grow in great abundance 3. to live in great luxury etc.

What is a luxury? Is a luxury a feeling? Is it an emotion? Is it a sense? It's not a cost. It's a frame of mind. I've learnt this the hard way. It's not what it's cracked up to be. Luxury is simple really.

I've learned that a luxury is to be indulged in. I don't want it to become mediocre. I want it to stay lush and luscious. I want it to be simple abundance.

Can I afford the luxury?

Luxuriating in the love of all things natural, is the only way to experience pure love. It has no dependency, guilt or payment. The only condition is free love. I sound like a hippie now, but I think it's a philosophy. I like the sound of it. I'm getting into the moment.

Love is a reward. This reward is a celebration of all that is good, and nothing that is bad. It's natural. Our feelings are always natural. They are within us, so they can't be faked. Our feelings must rely on ourselves, and we must rely on our feelings. Our feelings shouldn't rely on anyone else's feelings. They're not our feelings. Our feelings shouldn't depend on another's feelings. Love can't flourish when feelings are dependent. Love can't flourish when feelings aren't honest. Love is measured by degrees. Love doesn't have to be a hundred degrees centigrade, to be lovely. There can be different degrees. You can enjoy your own temperature, and the outside temperature on offer.

> **Centigrade:-** adj. [< L. *centum*, hundred + *gradus*, degree] 1. consisting of or divided into 100 degrees; 2. same as CELSIUS.
>
> **Celsius:-** adj. [A. Celsius] designating or of a thermometer on which 0 degrees is the freezing point and 100 degrees is the boiling point of water; centigrade: abbrev. C.

Love doesn't need any further intentions other than to be felt. You can feel love in the moment. Love can take place in the moment of loving, without any other considerations, expectations, or obligations. Love can be given and taken freely, in a place of freedom. Freedom is a natural feeling, and doesn't need to be complicated with a 'should' or a 'shouldn't'. It just needs a 'want'. If a 'want' is all that love needs, then it can flourish without the need for measurements or tests. Love doesn't have needs.

Don't test it

It doesn't need to be tested. We test love out of habit. We test it, because we've grown to expect things from it. We've been groomed to expect. We go on testing to see how much it's going to offer us. We test love, as a way of measuring our own sense of self-worth.

By middle age, we're meant to be over the testing. A child will test. A child tests, to find his limits. A child will test your limits too. These are limiting times. They are the times that we need limits, so that we can grow slowly. We need to grow this slowly, for survival. The tallest and strongest trees, almost always grow the slowest. These are the trees that live for a very long time.

By middle age, there are few limits left. The limitations are almost, or already gone. You can be limitless. You've now earned your limitlessness. I want to be limitless.

Don't be greedy

We can get greedy for love. We can become greedy, because we enjoy the feeling of love, and we don't want it to disappear. We test and compare it, so that we can feel secure. We are comparing it, weighing it, and often we're trying to contain it. We don't need to compare anymore. We've already made it. We should have already made it. You have made it. You've made it, whether you want to acknowledge the fact or not. You're still comparing, aren't you? If you're in your forties, you've made it, because you're still alive. You've really made it, if you're reading and understanding this book. It's working for you. It's *The Worker in Me*.

What a miracle!

You've survived forty years or more of life. You are who you are, now. Right at this moment, you are you, at middle age. Don't look outside of you for the answers. They're now all inside you. You have wisdom at your disposal, if you seek it. If you don't seek it, you'll miss out on your reward. You must be able to reward yourself.

It's a time of going forward by looking backwards. It's the midway point. At the midway point, it's important to see where you've come from, and where you're headed. You can't see where you're headed until you've looked back in your past. You need to have learned from your past. You have the wisdom now, and you have the knowledge. You've already been taught. This is *The Teacher in Me* trying to teach you.

I'm not a threat

As soon as we have enjoyed this feeling of love, we're threatened by its removal. It isn't immoveable, because it needs to move. We all need to move. You can't threaten love. Don't threaten the removal of your own love, to get more love. This isn't truth. This isn't honest love. It's threatening love.

The love bubble

You'll always think about love. It's understandable that we'll think about it, because it's a nice feeling. Thinking about it won't hurt it. If it's mutual, it will come back of its own accord, when the time is right. Love can't be pressured. If it gets pressured, it will find a way to expand. Love can't hold too much pressure. It can burst with too much pressure, just like a bubble.

> **Combustion:-** n. [< L. *com-*, intens. + *urere*, burn] 1. the act or process of burning; 2. rapid chemical combination accompanied by heat and, usually, light.

We think of ways to keep it, and we fire it up to make it brighter. We think of ways to improve it and make it stronger, by adding too many ingredients. We add so much to it, that we can't taste its purity anymore. We've lost the original taste. We want the original taste to come back. We don't want it to leave us. Leave the feeling alone. It's a feeling. Don't ruin it with ambition and terms. The conditions should be free. You can't lock love in. It's natural, and will do what it wants. Natural love is the most valuable love we can experience. It's real, and it's pure. It doesn't have the impurities in it. It's as non-toxic as you can get.

It's non-toxic

It will give what it can. You can't force love. You've got to learn to accept what comes from it. You can feel what you feel you want to give to it. It must be true. It must be based on true feelings and honesty. This is the real thing without the appendages. I don't want appendages. I don't want to be an appendage. I want to be able to see it honestly, and feel it honestly. I want the truth from it this time. I don't want to pretend it's something it's not. I don't want to pretend I'm something I'm not. The truth will do.

Append:- vt. [< L. *ad-*, to + *pendere*, to suspend] to attach or affix; add as an appendix –append'age n.

Appendix:- n., pl. –dixes, -dices' [see APPEND] 1. additional material at the end of a book; 2. Anat. an outgrowth of an organ; esp., a small sac (vermiform appendix) extending from the large intestine.

Have we outgrown our appendices?

It doesn't mean I wouldn't accept what love might offer. Love can be beneficial and bring happiness, laughter, gifts, companionship and help. It can bring it, but it can also take it away. It's free and clear of obligation.

Love won't rely on an Appendix. It can't be relied on, because it doesn't need it anymore. By middle age, we should have outgrown our needs. You need love, but you don't need the expectations that you used to attach to it. Your feelings are free to change if they want to. Your feelings can change. You have no control of your feelings changing, they just do. You do have control over recognizing the change, and acting on it. This is truth.

In true spirit

When we try to rely on love, it's because we have insecurities. One must get rid of the insecurities and neediness, to find true spiritual love.

I want to go up a notch from what I've had in the past. I might want to go up more than a notch or two. I might want to go right up there. I'm banking on the idea that the higher you go, the longer it will take, to come down. I don't think you can really control the love you feel. It's either there, or it isn't. Whatever it is you feel, you just feel. It can't be interfered with. It's just the pure form of love.

Willing it to come to life

My garden will be tended by me. I'll be tending my garden. I'll water my garden and turn the soil, and when nature brings its own gifts, I'll gratefully receive them. I'll be open to nature's gifts and love will thrive in my garden. Eden is bliss.

> **Eden:-** [< heb. *Edhen*, delight] any delightful place: after the garden where Adam and Eve lived.

Will I have an Adam? I wouldn't mind a part-time Adam. Could I be a part-time Eve? What would I do with the other parts of the time? This is an odd time to be contemplating this, because I'm not there yet.

I'll get there in time

How many parts of time are there? I think I'll have lots of time. I think I'll just take lots of time. If I make lots of time, I'll need to fill some parts. Could there be a Trinity? This isn't how it sounds. It's not a three-way split, or whatever that French word is.

Ménage à trois

Fuck! I didn't expect to find this word in my dictionary. It's here right under ménage. My dictionary speaks French, and it speaks in the language of love.

> **Menage:-** n. [Fr. < L. *mansion*, dwelling] a household.
>
> **Menage a trios:-** [Fr., household of three] an arrangement by which a married couple and the lover of one of them live together.

It's a bit of a tame definition but I thought it was a bit less serious than that. I wasn't aware there had to be a married couple involved. This sounds more like swinging. Would it be swinging? This is all too complicated for me. I can't quite imagine this working out. I can't imagine which would be what. I mean would there be two of a kind, and one of another kind? Would it be better to be the odd man out? I mean woman. I hope you're getting what I'm throwing you. "Are ya catchin what I'm throwin?" If you were the odd one out, you could end up the meat in the sandwich.

Part-time love

I can only concentrate on one thing at a time. While I can boast of my multitasking talents, I just don't think I could be that talented. I don't think I'd like to spread myself that thinly. I've always done my best work when I concentrate on the task at hand. I do tend to work better alone, but I do love company when I'm working. Is this work-share?

Sharing the load

When you have a part-time job, you sometimes only work a couple of days a week. You may only work one evening a week. They're just bit parts. They're small parts to play. You may only work on a casual basis, so you could be called in, if and only if, you're required. This is what I'm concerned about.

I was oblivious

I can see why people choose to do two part-time jobs, but there must be a way to some better security, for part-timers. What I'm getting at, is Adam. If I had a part-time Adam, and I mean only part-time mind you, would I be getting enough? Are you really getting enough with just one part-time job? This would be the reason you'd get two, wouldn't it? The benefit would be the varied work you could have. It wouldn't get boring having two different part-time jobs. You'd be more satisfied with the income this way, wouldn't you? This is the way of it, because this is *The Worker in Me*. I'm doing some homework and seeking the right answers on this part-time gig. Would two part-time jobs add up to one full-time job? Would two part-time jobs, be more than enough? I'm in love with the sound of these calculations. My math is improving by the day. Good work love!

I'm in a fish bowl

I see out and people look in. People watch, and they think it's an empty fish bowl. They talk about the fish bowl. It inspires more talk now that the sign is up. I hear all their chatter. It's not nice chatter. It's judgmental chatter. My sign reads 'For Sale'. Apparently, it's a crime. I'm being judged for a crime. I listen to their comments. They're derogatory comments, but they don't know my story. They don't know the occupant.

I've heard the story going around, and it's all in the receivership. This is the information being received by my neighbours. Who are they deceiving? Peoples' powers of observation are poor. The glass sliding doors are open. Do they suspect there's an occupant inside? Do they care for the occupant? What about if the fish bowl wasn't in receivership? What if the truth were told about who had been receiving who, in this here fishbowl?

The neighbour wants receivership

The word 'receivership' doesn't appear in my dictionary, so I refuse to acknowledge it. The dictionary says it's a more modern word, and it's getting more popular by the day. I know what it means. It means the bank hasn't received its loan repayments. You don't need to miss many, for the bank to take control. It doesn't matter how many payments you've made, or for how long. The bank doesn't care who has, or hasn't made the payments, when it's in both names. It's a breach of the loan agreement to be late with payments. There's always a penalty.

Is breaching, a fair way to go?

I think there should be a penalty. I believe my loan agreement has been breached from the word go. My loan agreement was between the bank, myself, and another party. That third party breached an earlier agreement, and had a party without my consent. He took his party elsewhere.

He wanted half the share of this party house, but he hadn't paid anything towards it for nearly twelve months. He was twelve months late with his loan repayment and he always paid less. He'd paid very little towards it from the word go.

Is this fair? I mean, fair go! I passed Go, and I paid it. He couldn't afford to pay it. If you can't afford to pay it, how do you get it in the first place? Do you have to steal it? Do you get it given to you? Nothing is given to you without a security. This is how a bank works. The bank will give you a loan on the condition that it holds the security. I shared with this party on the basis that certain conditions were met. I shared, on the proviso that there was security. It was in an agreement that we signed together. This was the first breach of agreement.

How do you get it, if you can't afford it?

The law gives it to you. It just lets you have it. The law just gives half, whether you've paid half or not. The law hasn't got time for fairness. The law isn't fair. I haven't been fair either. I always paid too much and got less. That's not fair. I know what's fair now.

A fair fight

Do you know how much a fair fight costs? A fair fight isn't fair. A fair fight costs a lot. It costs you time and energy, and it can cost you your health. It can cost you too much in the scheme of things, and you won't get what's fair. You'll never get what's fair. What's fair is incalculable. There's a pair of shares to calculate, and the pair can't agree on what's fair.

An unfair advantage

Certain people get a share in what's fair. They'll do their fair share of sharing the fight. They'll tell you they care, that you get what's fair. They often tell you, they'll get you some spare. They really won't care if it's fair. Those lawyers don't make it fair, and the courts don't care. It's just not fair. Getting your share is their job from a chair. Do you think they care, whose getting what's fair? They won't be splitting a hair. They'll do what they dare. Are you scratching your hair? How much is fair, for an unfair affair?

The affair won't wear

You tell them what you dare, about a disloyal affair, and their happy to share. They want to know how, why, and where, but you don't go there. They'll just compare. What you want is your fair share. Just get on with the job, and get me my share. It's costing me a fair bit more than my fare. I say a prayer for my fair share, but I'm under the glare.

The bare share

If you tell them they're not playing fair, it just won't wear. They won't wear anything, because they already wear the pants. They'll just wear the pair out, and pick up their share. They'll pick up their share, when the pair's had their fair share, of more wear and tear. Eventually the pair goes spare and one is left bare.

The more you fight for fair, the more fight you'll lose. You lose your fight for what's fair, and you lose your share in the fight. You end up losing the bulk of your share, while fighting for it. You lose your fair share, in the fight for your fair share. Is this fair?

A fair disadvantage

They've got a bit of a flair for it, those solicitors. They get a fair old share of the fare for themselves. Suddenly the fight between two, becomes a fight between four. That's doubly fair. Who pays the share? That part's fair, because it's shared fair and square. He pays his, and she pays hers, and they get theirs. It really tears you up. It tears it to pieces. Who cares? I didn't take a share in a fair fight, because I didn't dare. I was avoiding a snare. I'd had a scare, so I let them do their share, without my being there. They didn't get to stare. This was a bit of a dare, but I didn't care. Are they aware? They need to beware. This case was a bit rare. It certainly got a glare. I stayed in my lair, and let it all go pear. That's fair!

Is fair, poor?

So just be aware, that you'll never get a share that's fair, with a fight like the fight, back there. You're better off bare. Just grin and bear it. This sounds like a song from *Jungle Book*. It's a jungle out there. There's a rumble in the jungle.

That's what I'm doing now. I'm being the tortoise, not the hare. They're in for a scare, so they better beware. I'm working on my own snare. They're not so well aware. Not like you. You're in The Know. No you're not. You're in *The Worker in Me*, with me, working it out. So there!

Liquid Assets

Are liquid assets the best assets? How many people have liquid assets? I had a liquid asset. It didn't last. It got liquidated.

> **Liquid:-** adj. [< L. *liquidus*] 1. readily flowing, fluid; 2. clear, limpid; 3. flowing smoothly and gracefully [liquid verse]; 4. readily convertible into cash; 5. like a vowel, as the consonants l and r –n. a liquid substance.

I'm liquidating the assets. Liquidating assets is like changing gears from drive to reverse.

> **Liquidate:-** [< ML. *liquidare*, to make clear] 1. to settle the accounts of (a bankrupt business, etc.) by apportioning assets and debts; 2. to pay (a debt); 3. to convert (assets) into cash; 4. to get rid of, as by killing.

Playing fair should be automatic

I can only drive an automatic. I start from a parked position. I'm stationary. I've turned on the ignition and my car has come alive. The motor is running, and I change the gears to drive, with my foot still on the brake. I let off the handbrake, take my foot off the brake, and push down on the accelerator pedal. I move off gradually.

As I get going, my gears automatically change up, and I'm driving faster. I cruise down the street at 50 km, onto the main road at 80 km, and onto the expressway for 110 km. I'm in the fast lane. I have more control of the car at this speed. It's quicker to react, and I have the brake when I need to slow down. I'm observing the road conditions, and I check my rear vision mirror for what's happening behind me.

I have cruise control, and I use it to save me worrying about speeding. This speed is most relaxing when I don't have to monitor how fast I'm going, and when there's less traffic to worry about. I can take my foot off the accelerator and give my foot a rest. Where am I going?

I'm here. I haven't gone far

I put my foot on the brake pedal and ease down slowly. I put my blinker on, and pull over to the left. I stop the car completely. What am I doing? I'm just sitting. I'm aware that I've stopped, and it's good to stop like this in the middle of a trip. You just take a breather. I breathe. I know where I am. I know where I've come from, because I have the rear vision mirror. I look up at the rear vision mirror. I don't see myself. I see behind me. I'm thinking. What am I thinking about?

> **Interval:-** n. [< L. *inter-*, between + *yallum*, wall] 1. a period of time between two events; 2. a space between two things; 3. music, the difference in pitch.

This is where I am. It's mid-life. It's the middle ground. I like it here. It's balanced. It's the best place to be. They say life begins at forty. I believe it does, but I had to put it off a bit. I was put off my fortieth birthday.

A turning point

I had arranged a party for my fortieth. I had arranged it, and sent the invitations out. It was to be a big party. That's sad, isn't it? I was arranging my own fortieth birthday party. I did it, because I wanted to have more friends. I did it, because I felt a strong need to have more friends than just Red Rose and Black Irish. I wanted us all to have time for more friends. I wanted things to change. I wanted to broaden my life, and my horizons. I was restless. I think I was in a rut. I wanted to have a social life. I knew so many people that I liked, but I didn't have many friends, because I had little time left over. I didn't get invited anywhere. I didn't realize that I had all the friends I needed. I had the best friends anyone could ever want. Red Rose and Black Irish were my true friends, in every sense of the word.

True

Do you want to know what I see in my rear vision mirror? My best friends Red Rose and Black Irish were killed in a car accident, less than two weeks before that party was to take place, and they were only in their early forties. They were just starting their mid-life. They only got to mid-life.

I didn't celebrate my fortieth. I didn't celebrate a thing for over a year. I had no celebration in me. I couldn't celebrate their life. They didn't have it all. They lost half their lives. They only got half. They didn't get what's fair.

I stop and ponder whether they really did get their share. Did they do double their share? They had a pair each, and one over. They got double the pair in there. It's hard to know why or where.

I didn't yet have the knowing then, but I'd got my first taste of it. I spat it out. I didn't want to swallow it. It was too hard to swallow it, when I was way back there.

> **Interlude:-** n. [< L. *inter*, between + *ludus*, play] 1. a period of different activity between two events; 2. an interval; 3. music played between the parts of a song, play, etc.; 4. any performance between the acts of a play; 5. a short play formerly presented between the parts of a miracle play.

This is a play on words, isn't it? What am I playing at? I'm playing it back. I pressed the rewind button. It's a performance really. I'm putting on the best performance of my life. It's a live performance. You'll see if I make a mistake, but hopefully you'll forgive me and turn a blind eye. If you're turning a blind eye, what's the seeing eye seeing? Is the 'all knowing', the 'all seeing'? Is he seeing? I'll be judged on my performance, won't I?

As You Like It

> All the world's a stage,
> And all the men and women merely players:
> They have their exits and their entrances;
> And one man in his time plays many parts.
>
> **Performance:-** n. 1. the act of performing; execution, accomplishment, etc.; 2. functional effectiveness, as of a machine; 3. a deed or feat 4. a) a formal presentation before an audience, as a play b) one's part in this.

Come along for the ride

I now put the car in reverse. I can only reverse at a slow speed. It's difficult going backwards when you're a forwards person. Going backwards is hard. It's uncomfortable, and I've got to stop now and then, to straighten out again. I just can't go backwards in the same way as I went forwards, so it'll be a dismal trip back. I want to go all the way back, the same way that I've come. I want to go back to where I came from. I want to go back to where I was. I'll go back to where it all started. I want to go back to me.

A trip through yesteryear in my time machine

We all hit the button on our time machines from time to time. Sometimes we hit it by accident. Sometimes others hit it for us. We get reminded of things from the past. Sometimes we're brave enough to look at them properly, but most times we're not. We just put it behind us and forget about it. We try to put it back to bed. When we do this, we're putting ourselves back to bed. We haven't woken up yet. We need to wake up in mid-life. This is the time for awakening. It's a time for learning. It's the right time for studying your time. It's a good time, and a bad time, but one will cancel out the other, and you're left in a time warp. This is when there's plenty of time. It's time that we need to get organized for the next half of life. This is an important time. It's at around this time, that we can finally get our shit together, for the first time. Take the time.

> From *The Road Less Travelled* by M. Scott Peck.
>
> 'A life of total dedication to the truth also means a life of willingness to be personally challenged'.
>
> 'Otherwise we live in a closed system – within a bell jar, to use Sylvia Plath's analogy, rebreathing only our fetid air, more and more subject to delusion.'

Just me and nothing

This is where we all start from. We start from nothing.

I haven't got as much time to go backwards, as I did when I went forwards. I believe it's a lot quicker on the downhill run. I'm pretty sure you can lose everything much quicker, than you can win it. I haven't had to make much of an effort, because I've got other people wanting to do this work for me. I've been watching their efforts. Have their efforts been in vein? Is this sort of work in their blood? Are they out for blood?

Unconscious or fully conscious?

Can you go forward and in reverse at the same time? Does one cancel out the other? Would this be mutual, or would it be neutral?

> **Neutral:-** adj. [see prec.] 1. not taking part in either side of a quarrel or war; 2. not one thing or the other, indifferent; 3. having little or no decided colour; 4. Biol. same as NEUTER; 5. Chem. neither acid nor alkaline; 6. Elec. neither negative nor positive -n. 1. a nation not taking part in a war; 2. a neutral person; 3. a neutral colour; 4. Mech. A disengaged position of gears: also called neutral gear.

I feel neutral. I feel disengaged from it all. I'm neither here nor there about it. I'm unmoved. I haven't moved yet. I don't want to move yet, and I can't move yet. What would move me? Would money move me?

Excuse me for moving

I have the greatest excuse for not moving. I have no money. You need money to move. You need money to move from one place to another.

Moving money for a problem

I understand this problem, and I've understood this problem for others. This was a problem I could fix. I had provided for this problem when it arose in other people's lives. I knew how to fix their problems. It wasn't a problem. Some people asked me for help to solve their problems, and I helped. I provided the money for their move, before their property settlement day. It was my money, but it was agreed to be paid back afterwards. This was a service that was easy to provide at the time, but it's not easy now. I haven't got a service anymore. It may not be on offer to me. I might have a problem. Are there any problem fixers out there? What would you say my chances are, of my agent, doing this for me? Am I a problem now? Could there be some good karma owed to me?

The Story of a Killing

Am I a problem, that won't go away?
At the open house viewing, I insist that I stay.

I'm an ear to the ground, and a flea in their ear,
But they all ignore me, and don't come too near.

They all see the wall, with the bloody big hole.
And they assume someone's missed kicking a goal.

They can see that the furniture, has all gone amiss.
"Something's not right – it's a divorce", they hiss!

They wonder what's happened, and see it looks bad.
They listen for gossip, and hear that I'm MAD.

But madder am I, and still working on words.
The more that they say, is more for the birds.

And more for my story, if that can make sense.
It's the build-up I need, it's making me tense.

So roll up, be heard, and spread what you will,
My books are still climbing, to the top of the hill.

They'll never stop coming, and they'll be coming still,
When my books tell the story, and your story, they'll kill.

By Ms T.L. Massacre

Moving along nicely

You need transport to move. Will I have transport? Will my transport need money? Everything needs money.

I don't need much money to stay here. I've needed less than I thought. I have my money tied up in the last Hoorah. I can't sell my transport, because my transport is wound up in something else. It might get wound back in soon.

Is it time to wind this all up now? I need a wind up first. I need to be wound up, by an auction.

How's the competition looking?

An auction is a competition between purchasers. When there aren't any purchasers at an auction, is it still an auction?

There can't be an auction with no purchasers, because there's no competition. You can't have a sale if there isn't a purchaser, because there isn't any bidding. There's usually a vendor bid, but the vendor doesn't want to buy. The vendor wants to trick a purchaser into bidding with his secret bid. A vendor's bid must be declared publicly these days, but what point does it make?

I'm making a point

Is the vendor saying to the potential purchaser, "I'm going to give you a run for your money"? Or is he saying, "Buy this, because I want to buy it too"? I know it's to start the bidding off, but why would the vendor start bidding? I can't see how the purchaser's going to feel that biddable about it.

> **Bid:-** [< OE. *biddan*, urge & OE. *beodan*, command] 1. to offer (a certain amount) as the price that one will pay or accept; 2. to express in greeting or taking leave [to bid farewell]; 3. to command, ask or tell; 4. to declare openly; 5. Card Games, to state (the number of tricks one expects to take) and declare (trumps) –vi. to make a bid –n. 1. a bidding of an amount; 2. the amount bid; 3. a chance to bid; 4. an attempt or try; 5. Card Games, the act of bidding –bid fair, to seem likely –bid'der n.

Who will do my bidding?

A purchaser is a bidder. Purchasers are not the people standing around gawking at the auction. Purchasers aren't all the people you've had coming through the property.

A true purchaser must be registered to bid. Not only that, but they must make a bid. Not only that, a purchaser needs to make the winning bid. If not that, then the purchaser needs to be the last one negotiating with the vendor. Even at this point, the purchaser is not the purchaser until he signs on the dotted line and pays his deposit.

> **Purchase:-** [Ofr. *Pour*, for + *chacier*, to chase] 1. to buy; 2. to get at a cost, as of suffering –n. 1. anything obtained by buying; 2. a buying; 3. a fast hold applied to move something mechanically or to keep from slipping.

I have a pretty firm purchase on it

This is the only time you can properly identify a purchaser. Not before. The rest of the time, they shouldn't be called purchasers. They should be called hopefuls, but only if they're hopeful of buying, not just because the vendor calls them hopeful.

The vendor will want to call everyone a hopeful. The vendor is always, way too hopeful. The agent is a hopeful too. He likes to think all the lookers are hopefuls. They're exactly that, most of the time. They wish they had the money, or they're just hopeful that one day they'll be able to afford to do whatever it is that they want to do. This is a hopeful. They're usually full of it, but it's just hope. Hope won't buy the property. Hope won't even bid. Hopefuls can be a bit too hopeful and register to bid, but then they don't make a bid. This is someone who knows how to be a purchaser, but isn't a purchaser. It's all 'make believe' at auctions.

It's just an action

'Auction' is a funny word. If you take the 'u' out of it, it becomes action. I've been taken out of action, and I won't be the 'u' in it. I'll have no say at this auction, so maybe we'll get some action. It's all up to the actions of the agent. I've told him about the actions of the other party, and repeated what the actions of the court were. I think he might start getting into the action now. Are my actions actionable?

The agent has now been informed of both side's actions, and he'll now have to consider his own actions. There's only one course of action for him to take. He'll make his own actions, and try to action a sale. Any sale is a good sale for him. I bet he's taking immediate action now.

The auction process is like the legal process, because they can use discretion at their own discretion. I've used a bit of discretion myself. I'm not missing in action, I'm appearing in action. Lights, camera, action!

Signing up for an auction

When you sign up for an auction, you're signing up for an upfront cost. It can be costly, depending on how much cost you want to get back. If you're not expecting much, it won't cost you as much as when you're expecting much more. It's much of a muchness. This is the reason they're sometimes called 'campaigns'. A campaign sounds way better than a program. Does a package sound better than a campaign?

> **Campaign:-** n. [< Fr. < L. *campus*, field] 1. a series of organized, planned actions for a particular purpose; 2. a series of military operations with a particular objective in a war –vi. to participate in, or go on, a campaign.

The auction packaged

The auction campaign is a packaged deal. It's no big deal! It's packaged differently at different real estate agencies. You can package it however you like, but the agent won't tell you that. An agent will package it however he likes. He'll want a pretty penny for his package. Is his package worth that much? How big is his package? How big is his mouth? If he's a top agent, he'll have a big mouth, and a big package. These two things usually go together, I find.

How valuable is the package?

There are questions you should ask about an auction campaign before you sign up for one. You really should find out how much you're getting in this package, because you'll be the one paying for it. You'll get a quick look at his package, before he asks you to pay for it upfront. You need to ask him to put his package out on the table, so you can get a good close look at it. You want to see exactly what you're paying for.

Tell him to whack it out on the table

Firstly, you want to ask if his package can pack a big enough punch. Secondly, you need to ask if his package always works.

Thirdly, ask him what would happen if his package didn't work, and whether you'd be refunded your money back. These are the questions he won't like you asking, because he's very proud of his package, and he'll feel you don't trust his pretty package. He loves his package. His package is very important to him personally, professionally, and for the agency he works for. His package is his reputation.

It's all in the packaging

He likes to advertise his package wherever he goes, because he may get another opportunity to use it. His package will include advertising. He likes expensive advertising, because he gets his package advertised along with it. His package will include an auctioneer of his choice, and the auctioneer's fee. There may also be a special signboard included in the package. Everything he's offering, he's selling you. He loves to sell his package. It's best if he offers his package to the right vendors. Not everyone will go for his package. They may not want a package deal. They may decide on another smaller package.

There are so many packages out there to choose from. They're a dime a dozen. A dozen packages would cost you more than a dime, but perhaps not. It depends on what sort of package we're talking about.

Bingo! Uneducated and desperate

The agent will prefer to show his package to an uneducated vendor, or a desperate vendor. These are the best vendors for his package.

The first vendor won't have seen an agent's package before, and he'll be just grateful for a look at it. He'll feel chuffed, just to be considered good enough to gaze at the package. He'll start thinking he's better than good. He'll get talked into it without understanding that the cost isn't optional. He'll probably realize later, that he could have kept this option open, because it didn't get him anywhere but poorer.

Do you really get what you pay for?

The second vendor will reluctantly think the package is the right one. He can barely bear to look, but will take any package he can get. He just wants to take the package, and get it over with as quickly as possible. He knows what's coming. He can see he has to swallow this package, whether he wants to or not. Either way, the agent's package is looking like the only option. It won't look like a big package, or a small package, it'll just look like the end of all the vendor's worries if he closes his eyes.

Housie

There are two vendors arranging the auction for the last Hoorah. It's not me and him, it's him and him. The last two vendors I just described above. I don't know if his agent has a good package or not, because I haven't seen it. There was no offer to show it to me. I wouldn't have minded a look at his package. I don't think he wanted to show it to me, because I might have seen better ones. He might not have wanted me to see through his packaging. You see, I know how these packages work. This is *The Worker in Me*. It wouldn't have worked on me. I wouldn't have swallowed it like the other vendor.

Eyeing-off the package

Anyone can get a package whenever they like, but you must be prepared to pay through the eye for it. I wouldn't have minded casting an eye over it, before the uneducated, and the uninformed, signed up for it. I've closed my eyes to it, because I've got a little package of my own , and I'm playing around with it too. I'm working on this package when I get the time.

The catch

He got caught up in things he doesn't know anything about. The agent has rung me for the money for the package. The uneducated, and uninformed vendor, asked the agent to ring me for it. That's a bit rich, isn't it? It's a bit rich for me, because I can barely afford to feed myself. I can't afford to save myself. I can see a package forming, that I might be able to make a packet out of. It's only my packet I'll be making, but at least I'll have a say. I may have to break the law to do it.

Are laws meant to be broken?

I've been asked to breach the Orders, made by the Federal Magistrate under the Family Law Act of 1975. These were the Orders he paid a lot of money to have enforced. I'm restrained from signing away anything. The Magistrate has appointed herself signatory for me, and I haven't even met her. What does this signify?

> **Auction:-** n. [< L. *augere*, increase] a public sale at which each item is sold to the highest bidder –vt. to sell at auction.

The agent hasn't been fully informed. I hope he gets informed before auction day. I hope the Magistrate's thought of this, and is coming to the auction with her signature. I won't be signing anything. What are the ramifications for breaching the Orders?

It's so depreciating

You can't have a sale if there isn't a buyer. How do you make something sell? I know about this, because I know about sales. I know about good sales and bad sales. This proposed sale of the Hoorah is what you call a bad sale. It's a good sale for the agent, but a bad sale for the vendor. Not this vendor, that vendor.

This vendor just wants a sale. That vendor just wants more. That vendor wants more than me. That greedy vendor wants all of it! This is what he has applied to the court for. He wants everything! He feels he deserves all. I don't think he wants my super, because that's less. What a super idea it was of mine! Paying him a wage plus super, when he never earned a cent of it!

It's just super

This is the answer to the question of how you make something sell. You advertise the motivation. You talk about it, and tantalize with the predicament. Predicaments are great motivators. This predicament might be decent enough to motivate some hopefuls into being bidders. It might be big enough to convert a bidder into a purchaser. There tends to be more hopeful bidders with a predicament. Agents and auctioneers love predicaments. They can make the predicament seem much bigger. They won't have to try too hard with this predicament, because it's already predicated.

> **Predicate:-** [see PREACH] 1. Orig., to affirm; 2. to affirm as a quality, attribute, etc. −n. 1. Gram. the verb or verbal phrase that makes a statement about the subject of a sentence or clause; 2. Logic, something that is affirmed or denied about the subject of a proposition (Ex.: green, in "grass is green").

Preaching to the faint-hearted

> **Predicament:-** n. [see PREACH] a situation, esp. one that is difficult, embarrassing, or comical.

Embarrassing

I'm not embarrassed about the predicament, and why should I be? I didn't cause the predicament in the first place, but it's a hell of a predicament now. Do you see the predicament?

Difficult

I don't think the predicament is difficult. It won't be difficult for me, because I won't be doing anything. I have no role in it. I'm not involved. It's no difficulty doing nothing.

Comical

Now comical, I most certainly agree with. This predicament does have its funny side. This is the side I'm on. I see the funny side, because I'm the funny side to it. Everybody thinks I've gone a bit funny. This isn't the funny part. The funny part is what they think. They think they know.

What they're thinking is different to what is. I won't disagree that I can be very funny. I am, first and foremost, my biggest fan. I'm a comic. Did you know I was this funny?

I'm a comic strip

I can strip the comedy away from them, and have it for myself. They won't be laughing at my comic strip. It's a pretty common comic strip. There's a commotion, and the villain is wreaking havoc, but then the hero arrives and saves the day.

Can a comic strip?

Can a comic, or a comedian, strip? If they stripped, would they be taken seriously? How could they be taken seriously, if they've been a comedy act? Do they strip away the comedy persona first? Is there another side to my comedy? Are we funny on one side, and serious on the other? I'm trying to find my way to the middle ground.

The striptease was no act

This Hoorah has been stripped. I stripped it. I stripped it down, and cleaned it out. I've been stripping all emotion from this Hoorah. I've washed it down and stripped searched it. I haven't cleaned it as well as I normally could, because I haven't the money for cleaning products. I've done the best I can with what I've got. It looks like I've stripped a bit more than what I have, because the photographs being advertised have magically revealed the most beautiful modern furniture that I've **never** set eyes on before. Will people assume I've bought all this new furniture, and stripped the bank accounts? Is this throwing more fuel into the fire? I didn't fuel it, the agent did. Shouldn't he declare, "This is not the vendor's furniture"?

Do photographs lie?

Furniture doesn't go with the house when it sells. The furniture should have no bearing on the sale. If it has no bearing on the sale, why has the agent gone to the trouble of supplying my photos with all these ostentatious appointments? Is it a misrepresentation? Has he misrepresented me? This is what lies do, ladies and gentlemen. Lies are the webs we weave. These are webs not being weaved by me, but they will be used against me. I'm bound to get caught up in them.

I think there's more magic in the agent's photos, but it could be that of my spatially challenged female brain. My lounge room looks three times larger than it did. It's been stretched right out of proportion. This is common law now, isn't it? Everything gets stretched out of proportion.

My story's been stretched

The view I have, has been altered. The view is something that shouldn't have been tampered with. The view is good enough from where I'm standing. Zoom. Zoom! Why want for more? It's bullshit! Agents lie. They'll lie through their teeth. This is lying while they're smiling at you. These are the hardest lies to pick up on.

Some people lie back

Some people lie back and think of England. They don't want to know what's really going on. They want to believe the best in people. They want to believe good things, because good things are better than bad. I haven't lied back, because I believe that the truth will come out in its own good time.

It's all very well for me to form judgments about other people's wisdom, when it comes to making big decisions, but I now ask myself the question. When have I been laying back and thinking of England?

Stiff upper what?

I need to ask myself some more questions, but I think I'll ask you first. When you're laying back and thinking of England, should you be thinking of something else? Shouldn't you be in the moment, and thinking about where you are? Is laying back and thinking of England, a diversion? What are we avoiding?

I haven't been to England, but I've thought heaps about going there. I wouldn't mind lying down right now, and thinking about England. There are plenty of places I'd like to think about going. I'd like to go to the moon and back.

We're always on the go

Do we put too much on, and in our mind, at times when we should have an empty mind? Should there be special times when we shift everything from our mind, and clear it out? Should we be stripping? Can we strip our mind as well as our body? Can we be stripped of everything? Would this leave us out in the cold, or would it do the opposite? Would it be an 'out of body' experience?

Raindrops keep falling on my head

It's raining. It's raining hard outside my window. I'm looking at it and hearing it at the same time. This sort of rain makes me want to stay inside. It makes me want to curl up in bed to be warm and cosy. It makes me want to be comfortable, and be comforted. I want to take shelter. This would be in the minds of primitive man too. It's a primitive kind of feeling. What did primitive people do with themselves in hard unrelenting rain? Did they curl up together by the fireside? I guess this was the time for communing together. It's important. 'It's raining, it's pouring, and the old man is snoring. He bumped his head on the top of the bed, and couldn't wake up in the morning.' Was he dead? Rain, rain, go away, come again, another day.

I'm singing in the rain

Maybe they sang songs to entertain each other. They probably told stories. The wise man kept all the stories. He was the storyteller. He was charged with keeping all the stories safe. He had the job of keeping the very old stories alive and true. These are stories that get passed down from generation to generation. It was an important job to have, because he was the librarian, and the database for the whole tribe. He was the keeper of information, and of the wisdom. The wisdom is the spiritual element. This is the most important element of all. If the stories get lost, so does the wisdom. The stories are the advice, and the lessons. This is how wisdom was tort. Perhaps the stories were like the Torts that we have in our system of law today. The wise man was the teller of good stories and bad stories.

> **Tort:-** n. [< L. *torquere*, to twist] Law, a wrongful act (not involving a breach of contract) for which a civil action can be brought.

> When you realize how perfect everything is, you will tilt your head back and laugh at the sky. – Buddha

How wise was Buddha? He had the gift, didn't he? Look at all his wise words, and imagine how many people he helped. His words still help people today. These are people from all over the world. This is what you call far reaching preaching. Buddha had a gift for making everything sound so simple. Humans have a gift for making things sound so complicated. Is it simple, or difficult? It's whatever you want.

Was Buddha human?

Buddha rejoiced at the simple. He didn't want the complications. He wanted purity. He wanted the essence. I'm the essence. I'm Vanilla. I'm an extract. I got extracted like a tooth, just in the nick of time. I was delivered from difficulty at a complicated time. My job is to make everything smell sweet. If I smell something bad, I mask the smell with my sweetness. This is the balance I've chosen for myself. I always stop to smell the roses now.

Santa's wonderfully fat

Buddha was fat. There's nothing wrong with being fat, as long as it doesn't get in the way of your purpose. Buddha found his purpose. I found a purpose for fat. I've got fat. Some of my fat bits are cuddly and soft. I like the feel of these bits myself.

It's cake

This is what happens when you enjoy cake. You get a bit round in the middle. Fat isn't unattractive. Fat can be extremely attractive. Can extremely skinny, be attractive? Apparently it can, because you only have to look at some of our models in popular magazines. All of us are beautiful. That's what makes us beautiful. It's the differences. If we were all of the same proportion, we'd all look the same, and no one would stand out. Nobody would represent beauty. Behold, we are all so perfect. Our brains are being brainwashed to judge and compare.

Do you measure the ingredients when you make a cake?

I wonder if Buddha ever judged anyone by their looks. Would he care who was fat, and who was skinny? He'd accept whatever is. He'd look for the ingredients. He'd look for the essence.

He wouldn't start comparing how much more he weighs, than the other person, or how much less. Buddha would look for the balance. He was a yin and yang sort of a bloke. He would be looking inside as well as outside. He would be just measuring the balance.

This was his measuring stick

He didn't hit anyone with it, unless they asked for it. Have you ever asked for it? I have. I'm now getting it. He got it too. Everyone gets hit over the head with the measuring stick. Sometimes we learn from it, and sometimes we go back and ask for more. Sometimes, we just don't see it coming. I know people that have asked for it. They've been asking for it for a while. They'll get what's coming to them. Buddha liked fairness. He was fair dinkum about it. I'm fair dinkum too!

Back to Buddha and his rotundity

> **Rotund:-** adj. [L. *rotundus*] 1. plump or stout; 2. full-toned, sonorous [a rotund voice] –rotun'dity n.

He was the wise man. He was the enlightened one. He didn't need to dash around and cause his heart to be overworked. His body didn't have to do too much. His purpose was different to that of the rice picker. We all have our own purpose in life, and these purposes will require different body shapes.

I've totally rediscovered cake

If you're a chef, you're indulging in the delights of sumptuous foods. It's an art. You eat and rejoice, and you create joy for others. You're an artist. When you become too fat to enjoy creating your art, you know you must eat less. We need our bodies for our purpose. We need them for the purpose we want them for. It's not for anybody else's purpose. They have their own purpose. Stick to your own purpose, and if your body likes it, you'll know you're on the right path.

My body likes the look of cake

We need only listen to what our bodies are saying. Our bodies talk. Our bodies can communicate with us if we become aware. It's simple. Buddha just sat. He didn't have to do what other people wanted. He knew he could do what he wanted. He was doing what he was supposed to do. If we weren't supposed to get fat, we wouldn't. Fatness exists, so that skinny exists. If skinny didn't exist, we'd all be fat. Are most people of medium weight? Is this the middle ground? Buddha was fat, he was an extreme. What did he balance it with? Did he wise up?

Fat chance

What is fat, anyway? Fat is love. Do you know why? Love is our food. Some people don't like food as much as others, but we all need it, just like love. It's about overindulging in something we love. Is overindulging, just compensating?

Buddha loved to eat. Buddha did all the things he loved to do. He was full of love. When we get a hug from a skinny person, how much different is it, from getting a cuddle from a great big fat person. I know. You can feel the love. The spirit of indulgence is obvious.

Quick, she's sinking

I think I've just dived into some quicksand here, because I'm now thinking of the morbidly obese, and the anorexic. These are illnesses. This is the quicksand. This is when you've lost your purpose completely. This is when you can't see what your purpose is anymore, because you've gone to extremes. You can be rescued from quicksand, but it takes a long time to get out of. It'll keep trying to drag you down, each time you try to get out of it. It's heavy shit. It's usually happened for a reason. You either weren't looking where you were going, or you didn't care where you were going, and fell right into it. It's a trap, see. If we can find the strength to get out of the quicksand, we can find the strength to do anything.

The thing about quicksand

It's a danger to the rescuer. Sometimes the rescuer is doing all the work, and they can get stuck in the quicksand too. The rescuer can sometimes be the actual catalyst for your quicksand adventure. Many people want to be a rescuer. They think it's their purpose. They think they'll get the praise they need, from being a rescuer. They always want to appear as the rescuer. They just go around looking for people to rescue. When they can't find anyone, they'll push the closest one to them, right into it. They tell you to 'put your right foot in, put your right foot out, put your right foot in, and shake it all about.' They say this quicksand is just what you need, because quicksand is good for you, and they know best. They tell you that everyone else thinks you should try the quicksand too. They can be clever talkers. They talk up the quicksand. You start to believe them over yourself. So, you nearly fall for it. The only reason you don't fall for it on this occasion, is because you have a memory of it. You have a memory of being rescued from quicksand once before. You realize that you were talked into getting in the quicksand then. You got in, but all you wanted to do once you were in, was to get out. Subconsciously, you still feel like you have some of that quicksand stuck to you. Who pushed you in?

A mental change is in order

In my experience, and I'm not a psychologist, I believe the morbidly obese are starving and the anorexic are so full, they can't fit another thing in. I believe there are two different problems to contend with, but it really comes down to worth. One has too little worth attached, and one has way too much worth attached. They are both extreme positions to be in, and they need a balanced position to right themselves. The outside influences are the culprits of these systemic diseases.

Who talked you in?

You shouldn't have been talked into getting into the quicksand in the first place. Why were you talked into it? Why? Because the quicksand was the only place to put you, while that person was hiding the evidence. Fuck, this is what you call running off at the metaphor. It's run away a bit here, but I've been in that fucking quicksand. Someone pushed me right into it. I wasn't morbidly obese or anorexic, I was told I was nuts. The quicksand was the nut house. I shouldn't call it that, because as far as I could see, there were no nuts there. 'Nuts' is a frame of mind. Nuts is about who framed who. Who's framing all the nuts? There were no nuts in hospital. They were all perfectly normal except for the effects of the drugs that were being fed to them. These were people that had people problems, you fucking morons! The problems are usually other people. Some people are other people's problems.

I could work it out by the other people

I remember seeing the visitors arriving and I was fascinated, because they weren't rescuers. They didn't rescue the moment for any of those patients. That was the moment I figured out what was wrong with them. I could see those problems walking right in the door of the hospital, and right back out again when visiting time was over. That's where the problems lay. I had some visitors too, but I didn't see the problems. I should have been self-examining, instead of trying to examine other patients' problems.

No visitors please!

Have you worked me out yet? You're in *The Worker in Me* so you should know me by now. No, you shouldn't! You should be able to work me out, but you'll have to read *The Knowing in Me* to really know. Then you'll be able to make out the whole picture, but only if you get *The Maker in Me*, and read how, and who, made it happen. I'm dobbing!

She's not much of a looker

How do you speed up a sale? You make it cheap. You make it look cheap. You make it sound cheap, and you treat it cheap. Houses are cheap, but people are expensive. I'm not cheap. I'm just a little bird tweeting – cheap, cheap, cheap!

I don't mind if my Hoorah goes cheap, because it's not me. It's already been cheapened by what's gone on in it. It wasn't cheapened by me. This Hoorah cost $830,000 in 2005. It cost another $30,000 just for the stamp duty. People like to buy things cheap, but I must like to buy expensive. I've always paid through the nose for things. I've paid too much for everything. This house is just one of those things. It's been an expensive house to live in. It's been an expensive lesson. It's been at my expense.

I'm part of the bargain

How do you know when something is going cheap? You know, because it looks poor. It looks like it's uncared for, and unloved. Its packaging isn't perfect, and it's covered in dust. It looks like it's been left on the shelf too long. It's got a cheap old sign advertising it for sale. The agent doesn't even care for it. It's a good strategy for the agent to use. I'm impressed with his technique. He must be really thinking strategically about this sale.

I'm having a hand in it

I'll put my right hand in. I'll put my right hand out. I'll put my right hand in, and I'll shake it all about. I'll do the hokey pokey, and I'll turn around, and that's what it's all about.

Getting into the right position

Nobody will see the hand I'll play. It's magical. It's subtle. I'm as subtle as a king cobra in a bathtub. They won't have a leg to stand on. They'll be cut off at the knees, and be sending a prayer off from that position. I send off prayers from this position all the time. I don't have to get into this position, but I can if I want to.

It's not a good act to follow

A magistrate wants to act in my story. I hope she's a good actor. I wonder if she's as good an actor as me. Will she care how much my Hoorah sells for? Why would she? She won't be getting the proceeds, will she? She'll be just going through the process, and proceeding in the matter. It's a great power to have, this discretionary power. I won't have any power because I've been discredited.

> **Discredit:-** vt. 1. to disgrace; 2. to cast doubt on; 3. to reject as untrue –n. 1. something that causes disgrace; 2. disgrace; 3. loss of belief, doubt.

Help Me!

I have blisters on my fingers,
And pain right down my back.
I know that I have deadlines,
And I can't help feeling slack

It's hard when time's against you,
And you have no time to spell.
You're writing for your life,
And the kids want you to sell.

They won't get all the timing,
And conditions aren't yet right.
It's all about the special terms,
And the writing of our plight.

I'll push on with my pen now,
It's all I know to do.
When love comes knocking on the door,
I'll know that time, is due.

I'll have my cue to jump the gun,
And I'll sharpen up my sword.
It's a fight of words and fairness.
Too late for that accord.

If it's blood they want, no way.
If it's equity, it's nil.
If it's to cover up their dirty deeds,
Then they'll have to foot the bill.

I've been writing for my life now,
And I know it all needs tweaks.
Locked in my inner sanctum,
Away from sticky beaks.

Best to hold, until the last,
When it's as plain as day,
That what took place back in the past
Had just been kept at bay.

By Ms T.L. Bayonet.

On Determination
"As long as you have an iron will you can turn misfortune into advantage." In the words of Nelson Mandela.

On Misfortunes
"There are few misfortunes in this world that you cannot turn into a personal triumph, if you have the iron will and the necessary skill."

> **Bayonet:-** n. [< Fr. *Bayonne*, in France] a detachable blade put on a rifle muzzle for hand-to-hand fighting.

In the words of an admirer of Nelson
In other words, I've found my will and my words. I even found his words. I've found the reason for my reading, and the reason for my thinking. I've found the reason for me. I found the reasoning, and now I'm giving you the reasons. This isn't work and no play.

> **Battlement:-** n. [< OFr. *batailler*, fortify] a low wall, as on top of a tower, with open spaces for shooting.

"I've stayed around and played around this old town tonight, summers almost gone now…" I can never remember the words to songs. This is an old song, but I think it's about moving on.

Moving day
It's the pits! It doesn't matter how organized you are, it's just a chaotic day. It's not what you call pleasant, even though you might be excited about the move. Moving day is a great day, if you're so keen on moving, that you don't give a shit what happens, as long as you're out of the old place and into the new.

How good is moving day, when you get out of the old place with little more than your clothes and books, but you haven't another place to go to?

Am I getting too far ahead of myself? Will I have somewhere to go? I'll only have some place to go if I just go. If I'm on the go, have I moved? Is it a move for the better? Will I be on the move for a while? Should we have a home base, a headquarters, or a safety house, just in case? I'm not sure what's in case. What would be the case, for 'in case'? Is it the safety net I'm looking for? Do I need a safety net to break my fall, in case I fall off the tightrope? I'll no longer be on the tightrope. I'll be on the trapeze. I'll be swinging backwards and forwards.

Packing up

This is the easy bit. Packing the boxes and going through all your treasured ornaments, and throwing out what you don't want anymore. Actually, this is the hard bit. It's the parting with things that you don't want anymore, that's hard. They've been with you for a long time, but you sure as hell don't want to take them to the new house. They just won't go. You're going to better things, better surroundings, and everything needs to be updated. Do you update for a newer model? You could be getting rid of the old, in order to make room for the new.

Updating to an older model

I'm doing the opposite. I'm getting rid of all my new and expensive modern stuff, for old and second-hand stuff, and I can't wait. I want your old stuff. Maybe not yours, particularly, but someone's old stuff, but it could be yours. Not just anyone's old stuff. I want the stuff that I feel has a good energy with it. Does your old stuff have a good quality energy attached to it? I want old quality stuff.

Is old stuff of good quality?

It must be, if it's still around. It's more durable. It has more life in it, because it's been expertly crafted and made to last. It's been made by hand. It's been thought about, and contemplated. This is what 'crafted' is. It's a special quality.

> **Craft:-** n. [OE. *craeft*, strength] 1. a special skill or art; 2. an occupation requiring this; 3. the members of a skilled trade; 4. guile; 5. Pl. craft, a boat, ship, or aircraft –vt. to make with skill.

Everything that I have now, is less. It means nothing. It's been wasted. It got shit on, and I can't get the shit stains out. People shouldn't shit in their own nest. Every little thing, for which I'd worked so hard, was spat on. Everything I was, and did, was spat on from a great height.

The height of spitting

He spat from a higher position. For spit to land on me, it had to have come from somewhere above. Spit lands where it falls, or where it's been propelled. I'm spitting chips about this spitting. I hate spitting. I think it's one of the most disgusting habits in human beings.

> **Spit:-** n. [OE. *spitu*] 1. a thin, pointed rod on which meat is roasted over a fire; 2. a narrow point of land extending into a body of water –vt. spit'ted, spit'ting to impale, as on a spit –spit'ter.

I'm a late spitter

I didn't spit my dummy out until I was three-and-a-half years old. I had a dummy, and I remember having it. I loved it. Sometimes it's referred to as a pacifier, or a comforter. Mine was a dummy. Why is it called a dummy? The General didn't have a dummy. I don't know if Sweetness did, but I'd bet my last dummy that she needed one.

It's easy to give a baby a dummy. It shuts them up for a while. It shuts them up for longer, when you put honey on it. This is the memory that honey invokes in me. It's soothing. Mine was the hardest to get rid of, I was told. I've been told that when I was little, I just couldn't be parted from it. I hung on to that dummy for dear life. It was my babyhood. I must have wanted to stay a baby. I didn't want to grow up.

Taking a dummy from a baby

Parting a child from his dummy is easy, because you can just take it away. It's not easy though. I know how hard it is, to take something from a young child, that they aren't ready to give up yet. What makes mothers do this? I know what made me do it. I felt pressure from other people. I felt their pressure on my son. My son was already under pressure. He went to long day-care full time, when he was only two years old. This is sad, me having to tell you this. The sad part was for him. That was also the sad part for me. I want to forgive myself for this crime, because I've always regretted it. It was pain and suffering endured by a small infant, who was not ready to part with his mummy yet. If I'm honest, I wasn't ready to part with him. I was a dummy.

My daughter was at school, so we'd already been parted at the right time. She never needed a dummy, because she had her mummy.

Is it a dummy mummy, matter?

Do we leave a scar? What makes mothers go back to work earlier than mothers should? I'm thinking about the child's welfare here, and the special job of a mother. This special job doesn't get valued anymore. The only way this job is valued, is through the children who grow up to be healthy young adults.

This is where value is

You must wait a long time for it. It shows up in what they do, and who they are. I guess this is an apology that I owe my son. I can't see any scars on my son, but they may be hidden. They may rise up one day, when he least expects it.

I can sense the scars in me. I feel the guilt, and remember the pain of day-care assistants wrestling my screaming son off me in the mornings, before I went to work. I remember sitting in my parked car trying to compose myself after this emotional event, before entering the office for another emotional event. An early morning sales meeting was always an emotional event.

You can't talk about the events of the morning

It's not something you talk about in a male-dominated industry. You can't gain much sympathy from men. Men don't understand being a mother. They don't understand the true pain of motherhood. It goes on and on, and it will always be there. It's more than a job. It's a personal vocation. It's also a gift. It's a gift to be grateful for, and to cherish. It's the most rewarding job you'll ever do. Men don't get the gift of motherhood, because it's a woman's gift. It was Eve's gift.

Take the pressure off receiving a gift

Women are under pressure. I was under pressure. I also pressured myself. This is what pressure is like. If there's enough pressure, you finally give in to it. There's pressure to make money, pressure to succeed, and pressure to be the same as someone else, or different. There's pressure to measure up.

Do we always follow what our mothers did? Is this the example we all look to, for guidance? Is this the way? Who do we look up to? To whom do we look, for our model of motherhood?

What happens if our mothers aren't that great a model? Do we try to do the opposite sometimes? I didn't do all the same things. I did some things differently, but I was led to believe that she was the greatest model of all time. What did this make me?

A different model altogether

I can see the differences as plain as day. I see the differences in my kids. I was a different mother. I was making some of it up as I went along. What was made-up, happened to be the best bits.

I was an interested mum. I was interested in my kids. I felt for them. I still feel for them. I feel that they've had their world shattered over the last twelve months. Nothing looks the same. I see the pain in them both, and I feel it for them, and from them. It's palpable. It's all mixed up, because there's too many losses mixed up in it. It's hard to look at the big picture, because there's too much to look at all at once. I feel to blame, but it's not my blame. I'm not to blame. They know this, but they want to blame something. I'm the closest thing they've got. You can talk about it, but it doesn't always go far enough.

I'm doing something about it

I'm doing it now. I'm doing something instead of nothing. I'm doing something for myself. I want restitution. I want fairness, not just for myself, but for them too. I am, and will always be their mum. This time I'm doing something quite different. I'm not making up. I want to set them a good example and show the truth of the matter. I want to set my example, not someone else's. I don't want to copy anybody else.

Say it, don't spray it

I'm just going to have a spit. It won't be saliva, but it will be from the mouth. I could spit the dummy. I could use the preceding definition of spit, and roast someone on it. I'd like to land a spit on them that they'll never forget for as long as they live.

Long live 'My Spit'

Is spitting nasty words at someone, just like spitting in their face? There's nothing more degrading than to have someone spit right in your face, is there? Can you imagine how debased you'd feel, to have someone's spit hurled from their mouth, to be splattered across your face? The action of them disgracing you like this, with their poisonous venom, is enough to shrink you to less than nothing. Less than nothing is a minus, but it's more than a minus, it's a vacuum. It's a going backwards fast. It's a tunnel. It's a long, dark tunnel, with white noise inside it. This is all you can hear. White fucking noise! I heard it! Is white noise a metaphor?

Spit:- vt. spit or spat, spit'ting [OE. *spittan*] to eject from the mouth; 2. to throw (out) or emit explosively −vt. 1. to eject saliva from the mouth; 2. to make an explosive hissing noise, as an angry cat; 3. to sputter, as frying fat; 4. to rain very lightly −n. 1. the act of spitting; 2. saliva; 3. a saliva-like secretion of certain insects; 4. [Colloq.] the perfect likeness, as of a person: in spit and image −spit chips [Aust. Slang] to be very angry −spit it out 1. to speak with venom; 2. to divulge some information without more delay.

I'll spit it out

Is spitting a metaphor? I'll answer this one. I've used 'spitting' as a metaphor. It wasn't what happened, literally. Literally what happened was something much worse. To tell you the truth, it hurts so much, that I'm just not ready to tell it yet.

You'll try to imagine what it was that upset me so much, but you'll never get it, because you aren't me. You don't know where I've come from, and who I am. You don't know, and can't know, what my pain felt like. I can't tell you what it felt like, because I can't tell you in audible words. I can tell you in numbers, but numbers don't count. Words are going to count for me, but just the written ones.

The written word is louder

Truth can hurt, more than lies can. I stayed for the truth that night. I wanted lies, but I made myself see the truth. It was like jumping off a steep cliff, and hoping I don't hurt myself. This one horrifying night, I just made myself find out what was down the cliff. I finally found the courage to open my eyes. Obviously, the cliff is another metaphor. Is it obvious? Have I spat it out?

It was a trip

I've tripped myself up here. I don't want to talk about it. I keep trying, but there's just too much to tell. Metaphor is in my way.

It's something I hide behind, but some metaphor is almost too much for me. It would be too much for you, too. Watch out for metaphor, it can be very telling.

I'm emotional

Can metaphor have more emotion attached to it, than the real story? What does metaphor tell us? It tells us in code, doesn't it? Is it a simple code, or a hard code? It's an ancient code.

> **Code:-** n. [L. *codex*, wooden tablet] 1. a system of secret writing in which letters, figures, etc. are given certain meanings; 2. a set of signals for sending messages, as by telegraph, flags, etc.; 3. a body of laws arranged systematically; 4. any set of principles –vt. cod'ed, cod'-ing, to put in the form or symbols of a code –cod'er n.

Breaking the code

I'm reading the Koran. It's a book about God. Did you know? You wouldn't know that from *The Knowing*, because I didn't know it then. I'm working on it now. I'll tell you what I've found out so far.

Muhammad

Once upon a time, there was this dude they called Muhammad, and he was born a bloody long time ago. It was about the year AD 570. Now A.D. means, in the year of the Lord, so it's kind of a Christian era. Anyway, that's what was 'in' at the time.

So, Muhammad got lucky and married a rich widow named Khadija. She was a bit of a cougar, because she was some years older than young Muhammad when they married. Now Muhammad had had a pretty rough childhood. His dad died before he was born, and his mum died when he was six. He ended up with his pop, and then his uncle.

Anyway, like the Bible which belongs to the Christians, the Koran (Qur'an) is the sacred book of the Muslims. The Koran is the word from God, to the Muslims. They got their own book too.

The Koran is a bit different, because it's written in Arabic, but it's still the word of God. You see, God speaks all languages. You can take your pick of the languages, but they'll all talk you into the same thing. They all lead to the same place. God is multilingual. He knows all languages, because he developed language. He gave it to humans as a gift. He must have wanted to make everyone different, because he could have just made the one language for us all.

If we all had to share the same word from God, would it be as special?

Anyway, God has many workers that help him do all this work he's planned. He needs to employ workers, because he's the busiest man in the universe. So, God decided he'd get in touch with the Archangel Gabriel, to go and tell Muhammad that he can have a job as a prophet.

Muhammad can't believe his luck, because these archangels don't just appear out of thin air. Muhammad feels incredibly humbled by it all, and agrees wholeheartedly to do the job the best that he can. He's got no idea what a prophet does, and the Archangel Gabriel (who I think is a bloke), tells him not to worry, and that he'll be his supervisor for the duration. The tricky part for Muhammad though, is that nobody else could see the Archangel Gabriel. Muhammad knows he might be in for a bit of fast talking. He did feel confident about explaining though, because he'd been given 'the gift of the gab'.

Now, I'll stop here, because there's a really cool similarity that helps to support my theory that our soul, or spirit, is where our poetry comes from.

The Arabs call their spirit, or soul, 'Jinn'. Have you ever heard of the Jinn? I've heard of getting on the gin, but Muhammad wasn't a drinker.

Gin:- [< L. *juniperus*, juniper] a spirit distilled from grain and flavoured with juniper berries.

Gin:- n. [< OFr. *Engine*, engine] 1. a snare or trap 2. a machine in which a vertical shaft is turned to drive a horizontal beam in a

> circle 3. same as, COTTON GIN -vt. ginned, gin'ning 1. to catch in a trap; 2. to remove seeds from (cotton) with a gin -gin'ner n.
>
> **Gin:-** n. [< Abor.] [Aust. Derog. Slang] an Aboriginal woman.

Incidentally, before Muhammad's promotion to prophet, he'd been getting into some monotheistic meditation. Basically, 'monotheism' means believing in one God. It doesn't mean just their God, or only our God, or all the Gods. It just means 'The God'. Hymn!

You see, it's just that this 'One God' gets around so much that none of us can quite believe he's the same person. He does millions of things at once. He's a bit like Santa Claus. He's a logistics nightmare to try and work out. I'm referring to God as a person, because it's said that man was made in his image. Mind you, I'm still seeking an answer as to whom women were made in the image of.

Anyway, just like Buddha, Muhammad got into a bit of meditation. I call it consouling, so maybe I'm on a new path altogether.

So just like all the prophets in history, Muhammad's preaching came from revelations. The revelations came from the Archangel Gabriel, and the Archangel 'Gab', came directly from God.

> **Revelation:-** n. 1. a revealing; 2. something disclosed, especially when it comes as a great surprise; 3. Theol. God's revealing of himself to man -[R-] the last book of the New Testament (in full, The Revelation of Saint John the Divine): also Revelations.

Are you still with me? My revelation is coming up.

The story continued...

Muhammad is preaching away, but he hasn't been as successful at getting new recruits, as he was hoping. He's realizing that this prophet gig's harder than it looks. He reckons it's time to move his new mates to a better place, and low and behold, he gets offered another job.

You see there's this place where his wife grew up, and it has a couple of warring communities. It's like a big neighbourhood dispute, and both these mobs decide they want Muhammad as their Hakam.

A Hakam is a wise man who acts as a mediator to stop all the fighting, and help settle all their squabbling. Muhammad gets the nod from Gabriel, and decides it's a good idea. He moves his little congregation to Medina, and they get a few more stragglers along the way.

Basically, Muhammad's looking for wider exposure for his job as a prophet. He's become very busy, because he's now got two jobs, an archangel in his ear, and a cougar for a wife. He sees it as a step up though, because he'd been having a few economic problems trying to feed the converts back in the old place.

Now, not everyone was happy with this influx of Muslims. Muhammad had some opposition from the competition. The Meccans weren't all that keen, though he did gain some support when he changed the *qibla*.

The *qibla* is like a directional sign, and it pointed to Jerusalem, but they all agreed they wanted to face Mecca instead. There were Jewish people living in Mecca, and around these parts, and they followed a different path. There were paths going every which way, but God must have been building a new one just for the Muslims. It's always a bit frustrating, when there's building works in progress.

Luckily for Muhammad, there was a clash of caravans at about this same time, and the Meccans won. It was a good sign, and Muhammad got a good rap for it. When the clashes continued, the Jewish communities were moved on, and Muhammad converted the rest. Not everyone, but all the Arabs anyway.

Well this is as far as I've got, but basically Muhammad had the job of converting the unconverted to Islam.

Suras are the chapters in the Koran, and these are just like revelations. All but one Sura, starts with "In the name of God, the merciful, the compassionate". I guess it's a bit like the Christian "In the name of the father, and of the son, and of the holy spirit". There's a mystery to it though. It's a mystical code. In 29 of the 114 suras, there are mystical numbers that follow. These are the numbers to try on your next lotto form. Numbers: 2, 3, 29, 30, 31, and 32. Now this is uncanny because whenever I pick numbers 31 or 30 in a Keno game, they always come up.

What's more there are some very old and interesting texts somewhere, that describe Muhammad's experiences during a revelation. One of Muhammad's wives (I told you he was busy) saw him in a spasm, and sweating profusely. Now this sounds a lot like a Kundalini awakening, which is Hindu, I think. It's all much of a muchness, really.

It was just a story to wake you up

It's hard for me to learn everything that I want to, because history is so massive. There are millions upon millions of stories, and you just haven't got time for them all. I think most of the stories repeat themselves. I think all the stories are much the same. God makes the stories, and makes them all original, but there's a common theme. Once you have the theme, you can guess where God's going with it. They're all there to show us the way. There are so many ways to follow God. God is the answer to all our problems. You can't lose your way with God. He just comes and finds you again. You must remember to yell out though, if you're seeking wisdom. Don't forget to ask for him by name. God, I mean. There's only one God, but he probably has stacks of names. Just know that he's there, and he'll send you what you need.

What you need, can be different to what you want

Now this isn't always what you'll be looking for, because most often we don't know what we need. We're blinded by the forest of trees that we're lost in. We can't see the wood for the trees.

He'll always send something that'll show us that we'll only ever need him. He wants us to learn, so he'll often send us a lesson to do. It's worth getting tested. Most times, we can only learn through life lessons. This gives us the wisdom that we need. God gives us wisdom if we seek it.

I want to digress for a moment, because I've got something on my mind. It's been niggling away at me for a little while, and I think it could be a revelation.

> **Jinn:-** n., pl. of JINNI: popularly regarded as a singular, with the pl, jinns.
>
> **Jinni:-** n., pl. jinn [< Ar.] Moslem Legend, a supernatural being that can take human or animal form.
>
> **Genie:-** n. [Fr. *Genie*] same as JINNI.

Are you ready? Sit down for a moment. Yes, definitely brace yourself. My dictionary's like the Bible and the Koran. I knew it. It's my special book. It all translates. I must be a genius.

Am I genius?

I can't take the credit. I'm going to give the credit to the Goddess Lisatrace. She's with me right now. She's patting me on the back, but telling me not to get too excited. I might be good at words, but I'm still shit at math.

> **Genius:-** n., pl. ge'niuses for 1.2.3; genii for 4. [L., guardian spirit] 1. a) great mental and inventive ability b) a person having this c) popularly, any person with a very high intelligence quotient; 2. a great natural ability or strong inclination (for); 3. particular spirit of a nation, place, age, etc.; 4 a) [often G-] the guardian spirit of a person considered as having strong influence over another.

There's something coming through, isn't there?

We've all got a spirit. Is it more than we think it is? Was Muhammad's Jinn, the Archangel Gabriel?

Should we swallow our spit?

I hope you're still improving your skills deciphering metaphor, because that's Lisa for you. She loves metaphor. You may want to read the second book within this book, which is the metaphorical book. You get two books for the price of one, but you'll have to work for it. This is *The Worker in Me*. This is Lisa and me. Are you with me? Let us move onward and inward…

Am I a spitting image?

Some people insist on spitting, because they don't want to swallow it. Some people say it's like eating an oyster. Do you chew the oyster first, or just swallow it? To be truthful, I feel like spitting the oyster straight back out these days.

Oysters aren't my delicacy anymore. They're not my transport. I'm not transported by an oyster in the way that I used to be. I don't want to be transported by oysters anymore, because it only goes one way. It goes back to my past. It was an old pastime. It's past the time now, and it's past its use by date. It's an expired pastime.

I think I'll find a new delicacy. I need less expensive taste. I feel I could swallow my own, home grown delicacies. Do you swallow? Do you savour a taste?

Always accept a taste

A taste can be an acquired taste, did you know? Kids don't usually like oysters, but often, and as they mature into adulthood, they can acquire this taste. This is the amazing thing about taste. A taste can be terrible on your first go, but on the second go, it can be tasty.

There are ways to eat different foods and good places to eat them. There are better places for eating certain foods. These are special foods, and they need to be eaten in special places, for them to be as tasty as they can be. The timing should be considered when tasting these delicate, and very special tastes.

What haven't you tasted yet?

What does it mean to spit? Why do we do it? We spit, because we don't want to swallow. It tastes foul in our mouths, so we reason that it'll have a bad effect in our tummies. Our mouths are disgusted and repulsed. Our mouths are rejecting for more reasons than just the taste. Sometimes it's got nothing to do with the taste, just the thought.

Thoughts can upset our taste. Thoughts of where the food came from, how old it is, how it was prepared, and our past experiences of them, can interfere with our natural sensations. Our taste can be disrupted and influenced by other forces. Are the forces necessary and relevant? Have you been forced to dislike the taste of something? Has someone put thoughts in your head, so that when you think of it, you hate the very thought of it? Why do some people hate the thought of eating oysters? Have their minds been tightly shut against even tasting them? Do we close our minds, because of how others feel about something?

Who put a bad taste in your mouth?

I've eaten some weird things before, but I don't mind trying new things. I've eaten kangaroo and crocodile. I've eaten rabbit, snake, and quail. I've eaten duck eggs, snails, and frog's legs. I've eaten goat, and wild boar. I've loved eating frogs in Vietnam, and I'm a great fan of their lotus root salad. There are so many things I want to try before I die.

Discriminating tastes

People of the world eat different things. Aborigines eat goanna, snake, and witchetty grubs. I've always wanted to try a grub, but I wouldn't like to eat it while it's alive. I don't think I've ever eaten something that's alive, but I might have without knowing it.

Are we alive to it?

Some things we'll eat because we're hungry, and some things we'll eat because they just taste really nice. Some things are better for us, than others. Some things are advertised to us. When this happens, and we're bombarded with advertised foods, we think of these foods automatically when we're hungry. Our hunger makes us think a food thought, and advertising campaigns make us automatically think of their foods.

Some foods are designed to make us want to eat more. These are foods with special chemicals in them. They have added salt and sugar. They basically have added taste. The taste is there, and it sends a false signal to our bodies, that we should keep eating them. Even after our bodies have had a thoroughly hard time digesting the food, our bodies still want to go back for more, at a later date.

Don't make a date of it

It's like cake. I love eating cake. It makes me feel good when I eat it. It's sweet. It's not good for me. I shouldn't eat it all the time. When I eat too much of it, I feel a bit sick. Cake tastes better in moderation. Moderation is the key to food. When you eat foods in moderation, you need to have many, many foods to choose from. If you have only a few foods to choose from, you aren't eating in moderation.

Some Unrecognized Factors in Medicine.

This is a book edited by H. Tudor Edmunds and Associates. The people concerned with writing this book are Laurence J. Bendit, Phoebe D. Bedit; H. Tudor Edmunds, Adelaide Gardner, and M. Beddow Bayly. These are people with great wisdom.

"There are two classes of disease – bodily and mental. Each arises from the other. Neither is perceived to exist without the other. Of a truth, mental disorders arise from physical ones, and likewise physical disorders arise from mental ones. *Mahabharata*: Santi parva, xvi, 8–9."

It's a Quest book published with The Theosophical Publishing House, Wheaton, Ill., U.S.A., Madras, India/ London, England.

This has been a quest for me. I can understand how a mental condition, can have an effect on the physical condition. I did have trouble with vice versa. I'll use myself as the example, because I'm the guinea pig in all my books. I'm a scientist that experiments on self. Most well-known scientists have done this. It's the best way to work out.

Just another workout for my brain

I'm still in dispute about what the *Mahabharata* said. I deduce that if we didn't have a head, we wouldn't have a body. This doesn't prove anything. It's vice versa again.

When I've had a broken heart, I feel the pain in my heart. It feels like it's broken. It's real physical pain, and it effects my breathing. It probably effects my nervous system too. I imagine there's probably a lot of blood rushing to that area at the time of the pain. Anyway, a lot of my body is affected with a broken heart. The pain can spread down to the stomach causing a tight, gripping feeling.

Feeling the pain in your heart

I know my heart can't be broken, not literally, because it's still doing what it needs to do. It's pumping blood around my body. I'm still breathing. I have a pulse. My pulse is showing a raised blood pressure, so it's not pumping normally, at the even pace it's used to. This is what causes my breathing to be uneven. This can lead to less oxygen to the brain. So basically, my broken heart and the pain I'm experiencing in that region, is having an effect on all my regions. It goes deeper than that.

All my organs have been affected by the pain, because my bones are now getting a different blood make up, and my kidneys and liver are getting less oxygen too. My nervous system has alerted the rest of my body to the changes, and everything is copping the effects. My immune system is suffering under the extra workload, and it's now become susceptible to other organisms.

We have free-flowing organisms throughout our bodies to help them function properly. They're balanced by the workings of our body. When the body has a malfunction, it spreads to everything else, and the balance is lost. All the balance within our bodies goes out the window. Our bodies have become weak and can now be attacked. Our natural protections have been disrupted.

It's sick

With abnormal amounts of oxygen going to the brain through my bloodstream, my brain is now off-kilter, and it causes a series of thoughts. It's not normal thinking, it's erratic, like my heartbeat. The thoughts are worrying thoughts, because I'm thinking about how my body feels.

Am I having a heart attack?

I've become aware that my mind and body are not in sync. It's a bit of a worry, because I've lost control, not only of my body, but my mind as well. I'm anxious about what's happening to me. It's all blowing out of proportion. My temperature has risen, and I start to sweat. My tummy is in turmoil. I feel weak, and not in control of my world. My world is no longer stable. I'm anxious, and I'm trembling. I observe the tremor in my hands. I'm frightened I could lose control over the whole system now. I could lose my shit.

What's a shock to the system? Something sudden and traumatic. Death and disaster. Pain and loss. Anything can bring it on. All our systems are different.

Was the attack on my heart, just in my mind?

What has the power over the whole unit? My mind will, won't it? It's the most powerful force in the whole body. If I believe that my mind can overpower itself, then I'm empowered. If I don't believe in my own mind's power, I'm not empowered. I'd have to wait for another mind to rescue me. Now this leads me to my next conflict. Where did my broken heart originate? It came from outside my body. It came from another body. The only way in, was through my mind. That's the only door to my heart.

I've slipped

What if I fell over by accident and hurt myself? That would come from an outside obstacle, which would directly hurt my physical body. I'm just blaming, because it wasn't the outside obstacle that caused the fall.

It was my accident

The ground didn't jump up and trip me. I put my foot where it shouldn't have gone. My mind did it. It was my mind's fault. It's in charge of giving out the signals to the rest of my body. Why does my mind get a shock? Is it shocked because it didn't know it was going to happen? How did it happen?

It was my mind's fault

I'm in two minds about this. Was it physical, or mindful? It was mind. It was mindlessness. I didn't have my mind on the right things, did I? I took my mind elsewhere, and it was diverted. It must have been concentrating deeply, because we manage to do most things on automatic.

Who slipped me something?

We aren't aware of every step we take when we walk down the street. We don't notice how our arms are moving, because we're just moving automatically. What's doing all the work, when we're on automatic? It's a miracle, isn't it? It's the ghost in the machine. Is it the Jinn? Do we all have the Jinn, or was it the gin, that made me slip?

It was all in the mind

What's in our minds? Have we all got double standards? Have we two minds? What is the ghost? Is it the Holy Ghost? Is it the Spirit? Have we ever considered that having an accident isn't always an accident?

One false slip

When I hurt myself as a child, particularly when I'd been doing the wrong thing, adults would tell me that the fairies did it. They'd say, "Well you shouldn't have been climbing up there, and the fairies did that to you for being naughty". Apparently, the fairies were teaching me the lesson.

There's so much unexplained phenomena, that we just ignore most of it. Perhaps we should look more closely. What could the unexplained, be explaining? Where are we tripped up? What have you tripped on?

I have my reasons

Who is behind the phenomena? Who is behind the unexplainable? When you can't find a reason for it happening, where's the reason gone? Do we make up reasons for it happening? Does it make us feel better, when we do? What's better, to have a reason or not to have a reason? I like to have a reason. A reason is an understanding. Do you understand where I'm going?

Everything happens for a reason. It's up to us to reason why. Why aren't you reasoning? Is it too hard a puzzle for you? I've been puzzled, but I'm working it all out now. This is *The Worker in Me*.

I spat on it first

So I sold it! All the furniture, that is. I got a thousand dollars, for what cost me around eight thousand. I gave away a lot of it for free. I just wanted it all out. I wanted it out of my sight. Less is more. Less is less though, because now I eat on the floor, and have no TV. I have no place to entertain anyone, unless it's in my bedroom or my inner sanctum.

I know how to use my hands

I have no washing machine, but I know how to wash by hand. Hands came before washing machines. My hands are my tools.

They're a good tool for the job I'm doing. They're always handy when I need them. I'm aware of how handy they are for doing certain things. I'm aware of what they do now, that they didn't do before. My hands are learning to apply themselves. I'm aware of the results of their handiwork.

My hands have the energy

I like my environment better now that it's all gone. I'm trying to think about beginnings and not endings. I want to be surrounded in good energy. I want my happy energy. I have my sculptures on display and this makes me happy. This is all I want to display from now on. I want to display me.

The dream of getting back to basics

Everything I put in my new home, will be added to. I'll add the added value. I'll add my energy to everything. I'll choose second-hand energy and improve it with my energy. I've always loved old things. I'm old fashioned. I want to add my energy to it, and my touch of class. I want to give old and unwanted stuff a new lease on life. I want to touch it up and revamp it. I want to improvise. I want to play it by ear. I want to use all my senses to create a great vibe. I want to vamp up things, restore and repair. Just like me. Not like her. Vamp!

vamp:- noun

1. the portion of a shoe or boot upper that covers the instep and toes.
2. something patched up or pieced together.
3. jazz. an accompaniment, usually improvised, consisting of a succession of simple chords.
   verb (used with object)
4. to furnish with a vamp, especially to repair (a shoe or boot) with a new vamp.
5. to patch up; repair.
6. to give (something) a new appearance by adding a patch or piece.

7. to concoct or invent (often followed by up): He vamped up a few ugly rumours to discredit his enemies
8. jazz. to improvise (an accompaniment or the like).

Vamp noun
1. a seductive woman who uses her sensuality to exploit men.
   verb (used with object)
2. to use feminine charms upon; seduce.
   verb (used without object)
3. to act as a vamp.
   Origin: 1905–10; short for vampire

Is fair legal?

Our legal system in Australia isn't set up for equality between couples. It's not fair in love and war. Under our laws, the only fair way of being a couple is as follows:

- Always fall in love with someone that earns the same income as you, and will do so, for the duration of the relationship.
- Always fall in love with a virgin. This is so there's no chance of inheriting any undeclared offspring.
- Both must be the adulterer, just to keep it fair.
- Always have an even number of children, and never an odd number, because they must be divisible by two. You cannot cut children in half in this country. That's a mistake. You can do this under The Family Law Act. A child's life can be separated into two homes, equally. This is fair and just, between the loving couple. A child is a tool, so neither party should have the entire benefit of the tool. It just wouldn't be fair.
- Always have an even number of children, just in case he goes with her, and she goes with him, because the remainder child will over balance the scales.

- Always do the same job as each other, and work at the same rate, and with the same energy.
- Never stay home and look after the kids. When you lose this sort of time in the work force, you're behind in work experience, career advancement, superannuation etc., and you'll never catch up.
- The job of child care must be done by an outsider who is paid a weekly wage, so that it can be split down the middle between the couple. Keep all the receipts.
- It's probably fairer to both parties to never have kids at all. What happens if the kids prefer to spend more time with one parent than the other? There's also the pain and suffering of childbirth that needs to be considered as a contribution. Is it?
- Never do any unpaid work, including housework, cooking, washing, home maintenance, etc. It's fairer to pay an outsider a weekly wage and split it again. Keep the receipts.
- Never share the same last name. The woman must never have his Sir name because she's a Madam and not a Sir. You may not want to share the same name when you've given up sharing, and it will cost money to have the name changed. This is an added cost, and it's just not fair that she must pay for it.
- Never contribute more than your partner to any superannuation, life insurance, savings accounts, or any other future security schemes.
- Never purchase anything for yourself exclusively. It must always benefit you both. Always get two of everything.
- Always be qualified for exactly the same things. Example: driver's license, boat license, real estate license. These fees must be divided equally. If one has a degree, the other should too, because a degree must

be paid for, and it will pay for itself in the long run, after the relationship's run out. It's future job security, and must be considered.
- Always consume the same food, alcohol, cigarettes, and make sure it's the same quality.
- Always use the same utilities, electricity, phone, internet, water, gas and pay TV.
- Don't pay into a health fund, because you just can't be fair about health. Just don't, for Christ's sake, get sick. If one of you gets sick, it isn't fair.
- Don't pay car insurance, because the excess is in excess, and there's always only one driver driving when an accident occurs.
- Always go to the same places as each other, and with each other, whether it's to the beach, picnics, restaurants or holidays. This is so neither spends more than the other. Don't enjoy the outing more than the other.
- Always use the same amount of fuel as each other, and drive the same type of car.

The list goes on, but the gist of it is, that the law is unfair if you've done the lion's share. Love is not fair. How can you work out what's fair? It's never quite fair. Someone will always come off second best. The question is by how much? Sometimes, it's the lot. Sometimes, it's even a minus.

What are the penalties for the Lion?

We're penalized time and time again as individuals, when we're married. Even when we're not married, we'll be penalized. When we're a pair, it's not fair. When we're one, we can be equal. Once we're in a formal relationship with another, it's stacked against us. We may not see it in the beginning, but we'll sure as hell see it at the end.

The End!

Where are my benefits of hindsight?

Some people are clever when it comes to the above system. They know the system. They have a special formula, and are very good at finding all the loopholes in the law, or just in the system they've created. I've found no loopholes, nor am I a player when it comes to the 'system'. I was played like a fiddle. I've always done more than my fair share. I've done the unfair share.

It's left a bad taste in my mouth

I've gone off on a rant here, and I've lost the precise nature of the subject entirely. I'm feeling in a bit of a mood. I'm purging what I've always thought, but never expressed. It was bound to come up, bubbling forth, frothing and boiling, like molten lava burning my tongue, and hopefully providing me with the relief that I shall soon have.

This is cathartic writing

This is the best therapy anyone can have, without paying for it. Those last three words are significant. I may yet pay for it!

You can't just speak about these things in public. You'll be shut down so fast, your head will spin. Not only would you be resented by men, you'll also be resented by women. We don't want to know, do we? We don't want to calculate. I didn't calculate, because I didn't want to know the answer. The answer has come as a bit of a shock.

People don't want to accept the truth about what's fair in a marriage. It hurts. Do we all have this sort of stuff lurking in our psyches? Are we wretched in our suffering? Are we suffering in our inequality? Are we living in an illusion? I shall resume…

- Copped the responsibility of book work, tax, and administration for a spouse's lousy paying business

because he didn't know how to do it, and I was wary of receiving a surprise tax bill at tax time.
- Copped the flak for spouse's drink-driving charges, both personally and professionally, at a time when it caused extreme shame to our whole family and to another family, who lost family members in a drink-driving accident.
- Copped the flak in the same way as above, with more alcoholic antics. This was at the expense of my hard-earned reputation.
- Pretended spouse was father of the year and sang his praises to excess, at my own expense.
- Forgave and nursed him, loved, praised, and protected him, at the expense of myself and the kids.
- Created a 'Father of the Year' and 'Husband of the Year' reputation for him, and for his kids, so that nobody was aware of his true inadequacies and nature.
- Constantly propped him up, so that he could feel good about himself.
- Forgave him everything, excused everything, justified everything, hid everything, because he was, and continues to be a 'self-defined victim'.
- TO SAVE HIM!
- OR WAS IT TO SAVE MYSELF?

I SHOULD HAVE KICKED HIM FROM HERE TO KINGDOM COME, a long time ago.

The law has responded as follows:-

- He doesn't pay any penalty for committing adultery under the Marriage Act of 1961.
- He doesn't pay any penalty for his being an alcoholic, and making no attempt to rehabilitate himself, for himself, and by himself.

- He doesn't pay any penalty for what his life as an alcoholic, has done to his family.
- He doesn't pay any penalty for the betrayal and subsequent heartbreak to me, for committing adultery with an old friend, and busting up his best mate's marriage.
- He doesn't pay any penalty for his secret affairs with others in the community, including his wife's so-called friends.
- He doesn't pay any penalty for his affair with the witness of our matrimony, who was a close family member, work colleague, and confidante, and for the damage this has done to his children.
- He doesn't pay any compensation for the loss of his kids' entire family, due to the divisive and despicable nature of his behaviour, which started all this in the first place.
- He doesn't pay any penalty for pretending by phone to have committed suicide. This charade was performed no less than two weeks after my mother died in this same way.
- He doesn't pay any penalty for perjuring himself on Affidavits submitted to the courts.
- He's not required to pay child support, because he earns so much less than me, nor does he have to pay any school fees.
- He's not required to care and pay for the dog, because he can't afford to rent a house with a yard on his earnings.
- He's not required to care for the kids, because they're old enough and wise enough now, to know he's not capable, and that he has no desire to. The charade is over.
- He's not required to continue a relationship with the kids as their father.

- He's not required to care for, or maintain, the large house that he'll claim 100% of in the property settlement.
- He won't be seen to be the scoundrel he is, because he's such a compulsive liar, and is a clever manipulator. He's a self-defined victim, which means he's an expert in making people feel sorry for him, at the expense of others.
- He's never seen as the scoundrel, even though he's made application to the courts for the entire proceeds of the property settlement with the help of a barrister bankrolled by my family, because of the other family matter which they deny.
- He's not required to pay for private school fees, excursions, uniforms, and educational expenses, phone credit, etc.
- He doesn't have to emotionally support his two kids and listen to their dramas, fix their problems, or console them on the distressing nature of the death of their grandmother.
- He's not required to manage and attend to his half share of a thriving business, and take responsibility for once, because he had the most stupid wife in the history of the universe.
- He's not required to maintain, pay mooring/marina fees, insurance etc., for the thirty foot cruiser, because he can't afford the fuel to run it on his earnings, and because it looks crap now that she's stopped looking after it, because she was too busy looking after the whole fucking lot.
- He doesn't even pay for his own car insurance, because his car is owned by the business, run by his stupid wife. The stupid wife was protecting an asset (the business) from risk of an accident by him being uninsured. He couldn't afford it anyway.

- He doesn't have any knowledge of how much he earned, because his stupid wife always made him look better on paper to ensure his ego was not shattered. She increased his wage with business earnings, in order to protect his ego.
- He was never required to pay his own tax. I always found the money. He never knew where. He never ever knew how much the tax was.
- He was never aware of how big the mortgage was, or what the repayments were. He didn't know how much we owed, or how little.
- He never knew how much our holidays cost, or what bills we had, because he never bloody saw them.
- He never ever wanted to know about bills. He was just never interested in taking any responsibility.
- He was too weak to be given this sort of information – it might have worried him, or made him feel less, because it was way more than he could afford.
- He was not good at handyman jobs, so I'd have to pay for tradesman or handymen to come to the house for basic maintenance jobs. He was tired. He had worked all week. Plus, it was better for all, if he didn't touch anything. Things that he'd touched turned to shit.
- He was a failure at maintaining our two investment properties – upsetting the tenants etc. – so again handymen had to be paid to do the jobs required. His wife was forced to sell them, due to his complete lack of interest on his part.
- He was not required to know what money came in, and what money went out. He had a credit card that did the trick no matter what bottle-shop he went to. He did what he wanted, and spent what he did. He didn't mind about anything, and paid it no mind, because his stupid, hard-faced bitch of a wife took care of everything including him.

- He didn't have to cook the evening meal, even though he was home earlier than me. I always brought home the bacon, and then cooked it.
- He doesn't get penalized for five years of no earnings, because even though I wrote this down for the magistrate, she didn't take any notice of it. He lied about everything, and the magistrate believed his affidavits and dismissed mine.

'All's fair in love and war'

So far, we haven't had the war. Oh, we've had his war, but not mine yet. My war is just starting. I'll be waging a war, because I've worked hard for it.

Keep it mean, and keep it keen!

This book isn't finished. It won't be finished until the last Hoorah is sold.

This is what was going to happen, before I got mad:

1. I was left with the business because he knew nothing about it. It was said to be valuable, but it couldn't be sold at the value it was valued at. I wonder if it could have ever really been sold, without me in it. It's gone now, the business. The company is left. The Magistrate says it's worth $311,000, but the rent roll was sold for $11,000 instead of the $260,000 it was valued at. The $300,000 is missing in action. The Magistrate doesn't want to know about any action that caused the action. My actions were justified!
2. I'll get nothing. I'd say, when all is said and done, $0,000 is my share for all my hard work and loyalty.

He's getting the lump sum without having to do the work. It's interesting to note how someone working in the auto repair industry, could have accumulated that sort of dosh. Are car vampers usually this cashed up? Are they really this eligible?

He got my packet. He got my pay packet. This is why I'm having my own spray. All of the above, is fair and just, under the Family Law Act.

THANK YOU LAW!

Whole-us Bowl-us (his words)

I bequeath to my former spouse, the whole dream. I don't want that dream anymore. It's a nightmare!

My car's gone. I might keep the kids for a while, because they might have to keep me. I'll be getting the valuables. The valuables are my beautiful kids.

He won't get the valuables

How fortunate I am, to have such a great business partner. He has made the decision to close the business and have it wound up. Happy ten years in business honey! Since when have you played the role of Director? Has anyone ever seen you? Are there witnesses to your entrepreneurial skills? Were you qualified to make this decision? Did you consider liaising with me on this matter?

You would have been very interested in what I had to tell you. You decided to trust the staff, over the Licensee. Or did you trust another Licensee? Bad License! Who else have you trusted more than me? You entrusted everything to me, but you didn't trust me? How could that be? Do you trust what your kids say? Do you trust your own instincts? You must distrust me very strongly, to turn against your own instincts. I know who you trusted.

Entrepreneur

A person who organizes, operates, and assumes the risk for a business venture.

[French, from Old French, from *entreprendre*, to undertake; see enterprise.]

Adj. 1. entrepreneurial – of or relating to an entrepreneur; "entrepreneurial risks"
2. entrepreneurial – willing to take risks in order to make a profit
enterprising – marked by imagination, initiative, and readiness to undertake new projects; "an enterprising foreign policy"; "an enterprising young man likely to go far"

Wow, I'm impressed. You made your first decision as a Director.

He made a decision!

Have our real estate business wound up. Cleaned up, and swept away. Disposed of quickly, no matter what it costs to do so. Why didn't he just open the doors again? Was there pressure coming from somewhere? Were there allegations made? Why didn't he sell the rent roll for the $260,000 it was valued at? What an astute businessman he is. What a catch!

True or false?

Are you falsely being accused, or am I falsely being accused? Is there a third party that needs to do some explaining? If so, would they be the party directing you in your most recent directorship? You should have first conferred with your business partner. Can you fake it and make it? Are you an entrepreneur? Do you even have an imagination? Do you take the initiative? Do you long for new projects to undertake? Are you likely to go far? I thought so too. You're a person who organizes, operates, and assumes the risk for a business venture.

So I signed it all over to you in a Deed of Agreement.

'Deed' from Wikipedia

A deed is any legal instrument in writing which passes, or affirms or confirms something which passes, an interest, right, or property and that is signed, attested, delivered, and in some jurisdictions sealed. A deed, also known as an instrument in solemn form, is the most formal type of private instrument requiring not only the maker of the deed (grantor, transferor) but also attesting witnesses as signatories. A deed has therefore a greater presumption of validity and is less rebuttable than an instrument under hand, i.e., signed by the party to the deed only, or an instrument under seal. A deed can be unilateral or bilateral. Deeds include conveyances, commissions, licenses, patents, diplomas, and conditionally powers of attorney if executed as deeds. The deed is the modern descendant of the medieval charter, and delivery is thought to symbolically replace the ancient ceremony of livery of seisin.

The use of attesting witnesses has replaced to a large extent the former use of seals to create a higher degree of formalism; this explains the traditional formula signed, sealed and delivered and why agreements under seal are also called contracts by deed. Where the use of seals continues, deeds are nothing more than a special type of instrument under seal, hence the name specialty for a contract under seal. Specialties differ from a simple contract, i.e., a contract under hand, in that they are enforceable without consideration (i.e. gratuitous), in some jurisdictions have a liability limitation period of double that of a simple contract, and allow for a third party beneficiary to enforce an undertaking in the deed, thereby overcoming the doctrine of privity. Specialties, as a form of contract, are bilateral and can therefore be distinguished from covenants, which, being also under seal, are unilateral promises.

At common law, to be valid and enforceable, a deed must fulfil several requirements:
- It must state on its face it is a deed, using wording like "This Deed..." or "executed as a deed".
- It must indicate that the instrument itself conveys some privilege or thing to someone. This is indicated by using the word hereby or the phrase by these presents in the clause indicating the gift.
- The grantor must have the legal ability to grant the thing or privilege, and the grantee must have the legal capacity to receive it.

- It must be executed by the grantor in presence of the prescribed number of witnesses, known as instrumentary witnesses (this is known as being in solemn form).
- In some jurisdictions, a seal must be affixed to it. Originally, affixing seals made persons parties to the deed and signatures were optional, but most jurisdictions made seals outdated, and now the signatures of the grantor and witnesses are primary.
- It must be delivered to (delivery) and accepted by the grantee (acceptance).
- It should be, but not necessarily, properly acknowledged before a competent officer, most often a registrar (deeds office, deeds registry) or notary public.[3]

Indeed I did

The only thing I didn't do was have my signature witnessed. This is where I hit a brick wall. The first agreement between us was witnessed, and the witness did the deed. What's the point in having a witness?

To have a witness, or not to have a witness – that is the question

A deed is a word with two meanings, depending on what word you put in front of it. It can be a good deed. That's me! Or it can be a dirty deed. That's you!

There are many deeds in this here book. They are not yet Deeds of Agreement. There are always two or more parties to a Deed. An exception to the rule is the kind of deed that I will do.

I have less, but I've learned the lesson

When you have less, you make sure that you look after it, because that's all you have, and it becomes more valuable for its lessness. What I do have, is more of myself. It's way more valuable.

Less isn't more! It's more or less the same thing. It's nothing. Do I make less sense than him? I wish I had one cent for every word I've written. This would calculate to roughly $1,946.15 per book. Do words pay? What are words worth?

What were the words 'I do' worth?

I stand here with my hat in my hand. Could anyone spare a cent? One cent folks, that's all I ask. Give a poor beggar a go. You won't notice it. Have mercy on my poor beaten soul. Drop a cent per word into the hat. I'll be most grateful. Each and every one of you, could put your money where your sympathy is. Words aren't cheap you know. Words have been very expensive for me. Would you like to get me off the streets, and put me back into the life to which I'd earned my right to?

STOP!

Erase that last paragraph. Shit, I don't want to work for it this time. I just want to write for my dear soul. Not die for it. I don't want to beg for the listing, suck up, or flatter you. I don't want to win you over, or compete for the business. I'm over it. I don't want to ingratiate myself, give you the same old patter, or hoodwink you out of your hard-earned cash.

How can I get you to throw some money my way, without me having to ask for it? Is there a way? Is there a campaign I can wage? I could launch a crusade. Could it be the crusade to get even? Do you want me even, or odd? Could you make it happen? Could you make anything happen? Can you make a happening? Are you sympathetic to my cause?

A virtual loss of words to explain it

This is like virtual reality. It's for a good cause. It's the good cause. It's the good cause for the bad effect. I've spilled my guts and my brains out in front of you all. You've taken what you wanted, and left what you don't. You've messed around in the spillage of my life. That was overly generous of me, don't you think? Where's my pride?

Proudly sponsored by...

You can't have pride when something like this happens to you. There's no pride in having nothing. I left my pride way back in *The Maker*. It got left back on the first page of that book. It was my first. I left my pride in the first sentence of that first page. I left it in the hands of someone. I left it with Lisa. Lisa has my pride. She's looking after it for me, while I've been writing these three books. This is the Trinity she wanted me to write. I've just about done it. This means my pride will be back with me soon. I'll take back my pride and build it back up again. It needs building up, because it's shrunk. It's extremely small these days, because I haven't been looking after it. It just gets in the way of things. It trips me up all the time. I work better with my pride out of the way. My pride was taking opportunity away from me. It was holding me back. It's been a big obstacle in my life.

Pride is arrogance

I haven't given myself a chance to be arrogant. There's nothing to be arrogant about. I'm rid of pride and arrogance. I've watched what can happen when you get rid of pride. The arrogance goes too.

Are they arrogant?

It's good, because it's all still happening, but I'm not doing it. It's getting done for me. Other people have more pride than me. Pride makes you do stupid things. Pride makes you stop doing good things. Pride gets in the way of knowing yourself. That's why Lisa took it away. I see myself now without pride. It's good. Do you see the real me, or do you have too much pride for a second look at the story?

Art collectors

It's shady with leaves. Shady deals have been done, and dusted away. I've turned over a new leaf. I saw what was under the last ones.

Another Shady character in the ranks

The painting of the leaves was what I gave him. That's what I wanted him to do on that beautiful morning, as we enjoyed a celebration breakfast. I wanted him to turn over a new leaf. But he left us. He left us in the lurch, and he lurched off the premises undetected. "Sweep up all the dead leaves at the property." The old chap didn't manage to leave everything behind. Don't put it all behind you, because you'll need to have money behind you for any new venture.

Joint Venture Agreements

Don't venture into one of these. Do you remember Adventure Land? I think it closed when I was about ten years old. I got to go there on a school excursion once. They had a replica of the Flintstones' House. That's all I can recall, and the fact that I almost got left behind. I've been left behind in this whole sorry adventure. It's been a misadventure. Sorry. I'm venting once again. Other people have had an adventure in, and with, my story.

A seven-day adventure

They're a nice crowd. They don't work on the Sabbath. They like crystals. They eat breakfast cereal. They have a good Joint Venture Agreement. They're venting their Joints of Agreement together. They're bonded by joining. Agreed? Do we have an accord? According to them, is according to a God awful Adventure. God is a good mate of mine! I think they've got the wrong bloke. Fair crack of the whip! You might want to jump ship. It might be giving you the pip. Is it a good trip? Joined by the hip? Is it for people with a chip? What about getting the snip? Did I let slip? I'm letting rip. I'll give you a tip, if you take a dip without a drip. Get a grip! It's no Love and Friend Ship. I've got a lip. Pay me for lip service. Just throw me a cent per person. I'm a good charity, and I've been a giver to yours. You help the refugees.

I'm only having a lend of you!

You'll get the money back. I promise. I'm good for it! Just think. Thinking is good. You could raise me $1,946.15 for one book. I don't mind if you pass the book around. It's a whopping big amount for my valuable words of wisdom, but I'm only asking for one cent per word. That's my commission. I don't expect you to do it single handed. Help spread the word, and help raise the funds, so that I can publish my other books. Could you possibly understand how much it has cost me, to get my words out?

Your own book, with you in it

Help! I'm single-handed typing. I have a broken nail right through the middle of my finger. I'm banged up and abroad. I'm a banged-up broad. Bandaged Mother Bear Day! Pain and suffering. Must slow speed to fifteen words a minute, not the ninety words as minute I'm usually travelling at.

I'm nailed

Must, must, must. I must improve my bust. Need room to grow. I need time to grow the nail, before I can be healed. Then I'll claw my way back.

Pay it Back!

This was a great movie, wasn't it? Do you want to see if it works? If everyone who reads my books contributes one dollar per page, I'll see to it that your charity of choice gets a profit share. For every person you tell about this little joint venture, I give you my solemn promise that I'll donate the profit to **Adra...as in Abricadabra.**

> Abricadabra, Abrica Do,
> Of all the charities, I've given to.
> Abricadabra, Abrica Be,

it's time to give charity, back to me.
Abricadabra,   Abrica More,
let's let Karma open the door.
Abricadabra,   Abrica Show,
you'll get your wish, if you read *The Know*.
Abricadabra,   Abrica Say,
there's also *The Maker in Me*, to play.
I'm magic, 'C'! It's just for a Charity.

Pretend It's e-Bay

Internet banking is the way,
Take a chance, and start to pay.
Don't be a loser, and lose a day,
Add your dollar on the charity tray.
If you have a friend that wants to play,
I have no qualms, they can, and they may.
We'll add it all up, and then we shall pray,
For a world that's not, so dark and grey,
Okay?

By Ms T.L. Charitable

Participation is the key

Add it to your Facebook page, and that will spread the wealth further. Make a difference if you can. Be the person you want to be, it's just humanity. If you use it, you won't lose it. Let's make gossip work for good, and not evil. It's easy. This is The Worker in You. Can you work for me? Can you work for 'The Worker in Me'? It could be contagious. People could contract it. Buy into it. Words going around and paying off. Would you be prepared to make a worthy cause go viral, for the greater good? Are you just? Are you justice? Are you my just desserts?

My new painting

This is my new painting. I want to be an artist. I want to be a real artist this time, not a bullshit artist. No faking. The dream must be true for me.

Time to rehash the story

Mull it up a bit. Mix it, and chop it, and whatever else they do with it. I don't know. It's no good for you in the long run. It's no good for you, if you rely on it to run.

Before, or after, the big race

Don't be reliant on it for running. Your running costs will spiral. You'll feel like you're running on empty. Your time will run out. Like sands through the hour glass, these are the days of our lives.

I only tried it about ten times. Ten times, is not trying it. It's using it. I used it. I didn't need to use it, because it wasn't my thing. I only took part when I had a few too many drinks, and I didn't do this very often. I was just out of it. I was no longer in it. It just put me out. Out cold! It's cold and alone. Not together. Not altogether fun.

What's the use?

The above isn't entirely the truth. This is what I'm trying to get at, with my self-examination. I'm trying not to leave gaps. The gaps are usually the answer to the reason why.

This is me, coming back to edit my book properly at the last hour. I'm putting in the bits I've left out. I didn't leave them out of the original draft on purpose. I just hadn't thought it all out properly. I didn't look for the reason why.

I've been doing some re-examining of the facts, and I want to be as factual as possible, about what I put in. I don't want you pulling it apart later. It's almost later, now. I'm just a day away from submitting the final manuscript, and it's a significant day in my life.

I remember the day

Today is the day of my divorce. It's the 28th of August, 2012. It happens in a day. It happens without you even being in court for the day. I could have been there, but it was just stamping day. I thought I'd share this day with you, because I have nobody to share it with. I'm alone, but I'm still stamping.

Have I left anything out?

Courts leave things out all the time, but I'm in my own court now and it's now, or never. If there is something I've left out, then I've put it somewhere else. I could have put it in any one of my books. Those books are to come. It will all come out in the end.

Back to rehashing

I have a fair idea on why I used it those ten or so times. Those times were as a mature adult, but it wasn't that mature of me at that time. I regret it now as I look at it, and look back on it. I'm feeling some shame about it. I've had time to think about what marijuana means to me. It means a memory. The drug was a means to another time.

I think it was to get back

You see I first enjoyed using it when I was young and carefree. I was carefree as a nineteen-year-old, because I was away from home. I was free. I was kind of free, because I was with my ex. We weren't married, but we were enjoying ourselves as young couples do at that age. We were exploring new places in our travelling Kombi van show. That show was a working holiday which lasted two years. During the show, we made firm friends with another young couple who shared some experiences with us. They aren't together anymore either. I remember I had one marvellous experience which I'll always remember, but perhaps never have again. Of course, I'll never have it again!

The experience is just a memory

I remember being at a secluded waterhole. It was up north and deep in the tropics. It was just us, frolicking in the waterfalls, and enjoying the serenity of such a natural and most beautiful environment. There were lazy overhanging trees blocking the sun's rays, and we smoked up the joint in a mellow yellow moment. I looked up, while floating weightlessly on the surface of the water.

I really can't describe it

This pristine water grotto was on a scale of beauty you can't begin to imagine. I was beside myself. I was out of it, as far as I was in it. I was in amongst it, and part of it. I had that experience, when you become one with everything. You just feel part of it all. It was supernatural. I loved that feeling. What a feeling it was!

Was it the joint, or the joint?

I guess I just always wanted that feeling back again. Whenever someone passed a joint around, I thought of that experience, and longed for it to happen again. The whole experience was awesome.

Find yourself the right sort of joint

I got it back! I got it without using it. I get it now all the time when I'm in nature. I'm going to get it now, when the kids read this. I've never told them. I suppose it's time to tell them. I was just exploring nature, and what it had to offer. I didn't realize it was on offer naturally. I didn't know I could get that feeling for free. I didn't need a joint to open my eyes. I just needed to open my eyes to the joint.

Alone fun, or alone un-fun

I think he did more than I ever knew about. I thought he wasn't keen on it either, until just recently, when I took the time to scrutinize the past more fully. There was one little clue. It occurred to me, that he'd been the purveyor of these fine goods. What I mean to say, is that whenever someone suggested it at a party or gathering, it was him that had the contact. I remember it surprised me at the time, but at the time I was not sober enough to realize the soberness of it. I was surprised at the various vendors who had supplied him, but more surprised at why they all knew each other. It was perplexing. Not then, but now. He was a dope anyway. I found it really easily on the net…

http://www.sigmaaldrich.com
3-Hydroxytyramine hydrobromide
161136 - 99%
DOWNLOAD MSDS (PDF)
Synonym: 3,4-Dihydroxyphenethylamine hydrobromide, Dopamine hydrobromide
Price and Availability

SKU-Pack Size	Availability	Price (AUD)	Quantity
161136-10G	Ships on 15.11.11 – FROM	89.78	0

Bulk orders?

ADD TO CART

The New 2012 – 2014 Aldrich Handbook!

Your resource for the widest selection of innovative chemistry and materials science products, with chemical structures, literature references, and chemical and physical data in its traditional print format and now as an iPad® App.

Request your copy or download the iPad app today.

It is what it is. I would like to clear my name in the aforementioned story, but basically it was just a short story. I was careful about what I did in the presence of certain people. I would only ever indulge in the presence of a select few, and mainly just two. It was a rare occurrence. I had a name to uphold.

All smoked out

At this time, I'm being smoked out like a fox in a hole. I cannot pay the telephone bill, the water, electricity, or the council rates. They've all come in, and are now resting on my shelf, with all the others. I look at the cup half full. My glass of water is full, so all is well. I'm sitting at my desk typing. I've just eaten a meal which I didn't cook, nor pay for. I'm a healthy sixty-two kilos, even though I'm still eating cake almost every day. I bought a slice of cake today for $1.25. It's a joy to be alive. Let us all eat cake!

How much is a cut?

This next part was supposed to be at the beginning, so this book's a bit out of order. I wrote it before writing *The Knowing in Me*. I had all three on the go at once. It's easy to get confused. I won't confuse you any further, only to tell you that this next bit is really out of order.

It won't matter, because I'm always out of order these days. I don't know what Orders I'm supposed to be obeying. I could cut and paste it, but I just don't feel like sorting it all out. I like collages.

Let's get physical

I'm a healthy sixty-two kilos even though I'm still eating cake every day. I haven't been for a decent walk for weeks now. I've been working out in private. I'm happy. My finished book *The Maker in Me* is printed, bound, and resting on my desk. There's just sufficient food in the pantry and fridge. We have a new house guest, who is good and easy company. He's girl wonder's main company. We're all happy, and living as normally as we can, under the circumstances. We are a cynosure, and this is good. It's bad of course, but it's quite good as well. The cup is half full.

I'm still halfway on the sand, and halfway in the water, but not able to move quite yet. I'm feeling more movement will be possible soon. I sense the tide is almost on the turn. I've had a card and an email which gives me hope for a turn of the tide.

It's tidal

When waters slow up in the middle of the channel, then for a short interval, barely an intake of breath, they just stop.

It's tide

They completely stop midstream. Just a lull, a mixing of currents, and we're at the turn. It's the point at which there's a questioning of a body of water, as to which way it now wants to flow. There's only one way. It's had all it can of going downstream, and feels the urge for change. The force is behind it.

A change of direction

It's the precipice of change. It's propelled along in its turn by the natural forces of the universe. This is true nature at its most powerful. You cannot stop a tide. You can't stop nature. Once the current has decided direction, the ripples are sent out like the scouts from the cavalry. What report will they bring back for their leaders? That the tide has changed. Is she on her way in, or on her way out? Am I on my way in, or on my way out?

From Wikipedia.

Baden-Powell's gravestone bears no cross or other religious symbol. Rather, in addition to the Boy Scout and Girl Guide Badges, it bears a circle with a dot in the centre, the trail sign for "Going home" / "I have gone home"

Where are my Scouts?

Have they come to my rescue? Are they rescuers, or are they just survivors themselves? Should they rescue themselves first? Who will help rescue the scouts now? I promise to be their fearless leader and show them how to live fully, under Scout Law.

Chalk It Up To Experience

Was your fundraising a fizzle,
Until that sausage sizzle?
Did you make a bit of cash,
At the other person's bash?

Did you get some good P.R.,
For the one that will go far?
And did you sing their praise?
Of the one that's in a daze?

It's a crazy, hazy, maze!

By Ms T.L. Scout Meister.

From Wikipedia

Meister has been borrowed into English slang, where it is used in compound nouns. A person referred to as 'Meister' is one who has extensive theoretical knowledge and practical skills in his profession, business, or some other kind of work or activity. For example, a 'puzzle-meister' would be someone highly skilled at solving puzzles. These neologisms sometimes have a sarcastic intent (for example, 'stubble-meister' for someone with a short, neat beard or 'crier-meister' for someone who often cries).

Thanks Wikipedia the information Meister.

The Poet-meister in Me

Goodness me, I'm hardly an Edgar Allan Poe, with his haunting poem, 'The Raven'. I shall endeavour to write you a personal version of his version, much later in this book. You must first enlighten yourselves as to the mastery of this great poet.

Find your own

For anyone that doesn't/hasn't looked up my favourite writers, you'll have to make do with nursery rhymes. Do me a favour though, just Google it. For me. Remember, everyone's a writer at heart. Some of my favourite writers wrote nursery rhymes. This is no nursery rhyme, but the insult was from the nursery.

Dear Mrs Bucket

With what can we filla
When she's the Vanilla?
With what can we giva
When she's all a shiva?
There's a hole in her inner
And she's got so much thinner
With what can we patcha
And how can we catcha?

By Ms T.L. She'll fix it.

Roll the projections:

A bouquet isn't necessary. This is who I was accused of being. This was my crime. He said I was like that Mrs Bucket, from the TV show. I really wasn't that showy. I care nothing for snobbery or labels. I don't know an expensive brand name, from the Now. 'Now' is a good brand name. I lived in this brand name. It's a K-Mart brand name. Don't brand me with a name that I'm not. Where did you get this brand name from? Who did you get this brand name from? This was him turning things around on to me.

Or, was it her?

I asked what was wrong. I tried to get to the bottom of what was going on. He just used lame insults to lame me. It was a lame attempt, but I took it to heart. I looked inside my heart for the answers, but for the life of me, I couldn't understand where this lame attack on my sensibilities was coming from.

I used to love this show. I thought it was hilarious. I don't think it's funny anymore, and I won't ever watch it again. This show is a send up. I'm sending it off because it doesn't belong with me.

> Dear Bland,
> With what shall I fix it?
> Dear Bland, dear Bland.
> With what shall I fix it?
> Dear Bland, with WHAT?!

I'm in a quandary as to what to do with these books I've written. My books may not be for everyone, and yet they are everyone. My books are written for the public. I know the public. I dealt with the public.

Some things for me to consider are timing, direction, and diction. Actually, that's all.

Timing

The timing is everything, and everything is in the timing. Are you timing this? It's about time. What a campaign that was, hey? 'It's Time.' It was a great time. It was another timed win. They won, time and again. Some talented timekeepers were on show and watching the show with me. Some names escape me, but the people underneath them don't. We had a fun time. They were the keepers of time.

Keeping time to the music

A step back in time, to better times. His time was up. It's time it all came out into the open. I'm taking some time out. It takes time to publish a book. It takes quite some time, in fact. It's at times like these we need Minties. It's Mauritius time. I think that's how you spell it. I'm hopeless with some names. It's a good name though. It's at times like these, that we need a good bedtime gem to pick up, and take our mind away from the humdrum of daily toil. When will it be time? Is it a time to be wary?

No name dropping

I've dropped a couple of hints that I've written it. It should be just enough to get tongues wagging, but I have a bit of a situation. I have no money to publish it. I don't believe that it's good enough for a publisher to want to publish it, until the timing is better. The publisher won't know how many names are in it. It's a big cast of names. It should get a name first. I'm saving up some nasty names, for *The Teacher in Me*. The Teacher will deal with them, when the time's right.

Why not start the way I always start?

High exposure for this northern exposure

Marketing and advertising that just entices. Less is just that little bit more. I'll leave just enough crumbs along the trail to get the phones ringing. From there, I'll have an opportunity to properly describe the benefits and features. What am I featuring? What is the feature movie? The features will be the creatures.

A creature feature

I'm going to be lifting these creatures out of the deep. Creatures from the deep, like the dark. Deep, dark pressure, keeps them way down there in the depths. They want others to feel their pressure at these depths. Don't go down into the deep with these dark creatures. Stay up in the light.

Direction

It needs every direction. North, South, East, and West. I need to be directed. I'll wait for my direction. I know they're coming. I'll listen for the cues. I'll be at ones and twos. I might wear my new shoes. This is the direction I'm waiting for. I need a direction before there's detection. I just need a section. One act, and act one.

Diction

This is where I'm a bit Off. My diction isn't perfect. I run Off at the mouth. It's perfect for me, but it's not perfect for others. I'm not good at dictation either. I couldn't be a dictator? This could be rude to the lucky publisher.

> **Diction:-** n. [< L. *dicere*, say] 1. manner of expression in words; 2. enunciation.

I don't speak as I write. That's a good thing. I write as I think. I have great enunciation when I'm thinking. You should hear it, I sound great. I can use all manner of styles, when I'm thinking, and I like my style. I like it, when I'm thinking. I don't know if I can speak in the same way. My diction is fast, because I'm a fast talker. I'm too fast. (Not that fast!)

I have so much to say. I get by, because I have my dictionary. Slow talkers have better diction. I've slowed right up now. I'm slowing down my thinking. I think I'm stalling. I must be stalling for time. Not back to timing again. It's always timing with me. I'm so impatient. Bring me on, for heaven's sake! 'Bring it on.' 'Come on down.' Is this how you were thinking?

Don't ever, ever, ask the universe to 'Bring it on'!

I don't like to say this anymore. It's tempting fate. I've had a fair bit of fate, of late. I'll have no fate left, at this rate. Fate isn't my mate. It puts me in a state, and I run out the gate. When fate arrives, it's way too late. This is what I hate. Fate is what's on my plate. I've had a crate of fate. There's been a bit of a spate, of late. It could be innate. It might be a trait. I don't like to wait, so I guess that's my fate. I don't really hesitate. I try to slow down, and masticate. Is it time to macerate? What's on my plate? Is fate, my date? Can someone facilitate? I don't want a Magistrate, and I don't want to mediate. What could emanate? I need to contemplate. I may need to dictate. Will that sate? Will it implicate? Calculate? At what rate?

I need to hydrate. I may need to legislate. It's not like I want to populate, or postulate. I'm prostrate, for a post-date. I need a mandate. Am I a candidate? Will it activate? I want a mate. I want it to be great. Will this be my fate? Or is it too late? I don't want any effete fate. I've had it!

Being a visionary

That's the very point of advertising. To get them to ring and ask questions. Put less in the ad, so that more information is requested. If you offer too much, you've missed out on a connection to a purchaser. You can miss out on the opportunity of discussing the sale item, in great detail. You may have just the house, but it hasn't appeared in the ad that day. You may have the house that will suit them down to a 'T', but you're due to list it for sale next week, or the week after. You can hook them on that, but you can't reveal where that house is. Revealing where the house is, before you've listed it, is asking to be shafted. A purchaser won't wait. A purchaser will just knock on their door, and make the deal without you. Fair go!

Information is gold, so don't give it away

Ads must create the contact. They must inspire the phone call. Selling real estate isn't just about the now. It's also about the future.

Advertising on the internet

I believe it can make it easier for a buyer, because he can do some online homework first. The buyer can be justifying price, comparing, watching, and waiting for new stock to appear. It's about watching for a bargain, before it gets snapped up. It's also good for real estate agents, because it looks like they're doing a lot more advertising, when they're not. It looks like they provide high exposure for their clients, when they don't. They just expose to their clients their sites.

The internet is homework

I hated doing homework. Home was for play. I hated coming home from school and sitting down to do more work when I'd already done it at school. I wanted to take my shoes and socks off, and fly out into the street on my bike. I wanted to go to the park, or play out in the street with neighbourhood kids. I didn't do much homework. My homework all made its way back to me in another form. It was all about forms and homes.

Is it in their language?

We get the idea that the World Wide Web is global. We shouldn't get the idea that our property we've put up for sale, has too. Our property's profile may be accessible all around the world, but that's only if the person accessing, knows how to access your suburb. They may never have heard of your suburb.

Consider a popular real estate site, and how you'd search for properties in your area. Luckily you already know where you live. You know the name of your perfect little suburb. You may even know your postcode, and this would help in widening your search to all the suburbs with the same postcode as you.

If a prospective purchaser from down south, or up north, doesn't know, or hasn't heard of your beautiful little patch of heaven, they'll never find your property. If it doesn't occur to a purchaser to type your suburb name in, it doesn't occur. He'll not see your property. He'll not know it exists. He'll not know where to look for it. He'll not know you exist. He won't know your agent exists. The only way most purchasers know, is if they're already familiar with the area, or if they were tempted by an advertisement in a local real estate magazine or newspaper. When your agent tells you how many hits you've had on your house from the internet ad, this is just the other agents doing their homework. (They're looking for who to hit next.)

Don't be deceived by all the websites your agent subscribes to. They all work in the same way. You cannot search a region or a waterway. It's not that clever yet. Maybe I just gave someone an idea. I've tried to do that on several occasions.

Double-entendre:- n. [Fr. (now obs.), double meaning] a word or phrase with two meanings, esp. when one of them is risqué or indecorous.

I've just had another idea. I could put a place on the map with my books. This is what books can do. They can put places in faces. I wonder how many people would check out the place looking for the trace, of the book's home base. Have I made the place a disgrace? Watch this space. You could join in the chase, and find my home base, whatever the case. You won't see my face, but you'd see who'd joined the chase. It's an intricate piece of lace, put in place by a race, from a very small place. It's a small, small place, to be hit in the head with a mace. That was my face, what copped the mace!

Just The Place

Hail Manner, full of Grace.
The Lord is still Parking,
And finding his space.
Halcyon days were all over the place.

Give us The Cut,
Of a bird-shaped spot.
And find a bloke, by the name of Scott.
Blessed is he, that don't like to Gamble,
And find the past, that was had in Campbell.

It's not too hard, I'm not in Mensa.
Another plot got owned in Spencer.
In Griffith was a cedar wood.
So much power, where it stood.

Wavering Waverley, was close behind,
A better view, you'd never find.
And a turnover in, a graveyard of sales,
Was the sad storied street, by the name of Vales.

Give us this place,
and our daily fish,
And serve it with sorry,
When you find street Macquarie.

By Ms T.L. Street-scape-goat.

Mace:- n. [< OFr. *Masse*] 1. hist. a heavy, spiked club; 2. a staff used as a symbol of authority by certain officials, esp. as carried before the Speaker of the House of Commons.

Mace:- n. [< L. *maker*, a fragrant resin] a spice made from the dried outer covering of the nutmeg.

Nutmeg's a poison

Either way, you can't advertise property properly, without using all mediums of media. Mediums like newspapers, real estate magazines, window displays, and (a favourite of mine) word of mouth, are the best sources for attracting buyers.

Words from the horse's mouth

Word of mouth advertising is the grape vine. This is the ball breaker of all advertising. Using your word, and your mouth, is the best advertising campaign out there. I know this for a fact.

Is the internet a medium, for word of mouth advertising? Is it 'thought to button' advertising? The internet is an instant audience when you've made the necessary connections. The internet can provide the platform to get your message across. Not all messages get the go ahead.

A free consultation

Open your mouth wide, and say "ahhhh". Hello down there. There's an echo. I can hear my voice coming back to me. I can hear lots of words coming back to me. It's an echo alright. This is what I've been waiting for. I've only given them a taste. I've given a place a taste. I don't know if they like it, because it's coming straight back up again. It's being regurgitated and spat out. I think they've just eaten too much other garbage. There was nothing wrong with the words I fed them. My words were wholesome and nutritious words. They must have been mixing their words, with some contaminated and unclean ones.

Word poisoning

Okay, you can close your mouth now. I know what the problem is. You've got word poisoning! Someone's given you word poisoning with their words. You shouldn't eat poisoned words in future. Don't just swallow anything. Check first. Check it first, to see how it smells. If it smells a bit off, don't go near it. This will stop you getting sick in the future. No fee for today - it's on the house.

Or I should say, The Hoorah? Can one thing lead to a big thing? Can one small bite of a rotten oyster make you so sick, that you feel like you're dying? This isn't quite the analogy I wanted, but you really should consider what some small stories can do to another story. It can turn into a steamroller. Do you know what a steamroller can do, when it's out of control?

Steamroller:- n. 1. a heavy, steam-driven roller used in road building; 2. crushing power or relentless force –vt., vi. to crush, override, or force as (with) a steamroller –adj. relentlessly overpowering.

I never liked steamrollers. They were a mint from the oldies, and they burnt the hell out of your mouth. They weren't for kids. They were too hot for kids to handle.

Have a mint to freshen your breath

Do you know what happens to a fire when you add more fuel to it? Add more. Now add some acid. Have you got any other nasty chemicals to put on it? Have you got any oil? That's flammable! Now picture everything I've worked for, and put it in the fire. Everything I owned, is in there. Gee, the fires burning nicely now. Did you set fire to it?

No?

Did you throw anything in it? Did you warm yourself by it? Did you get excited by the tall flames? Did you try to keep it burning? Were you asking around, to see if anyone had any more fuel? Did you find some of your own, to add to it? It's a pretty big fire, and it looks a bit dangerous now. Did you try to put it out?

What happened to my fire fighters?

What happens when a fire gets out of control? You can't control it, can you? Do you run for cover, and get out of the way? Do you stay around, and help put it out? Are you worried about getting burnt by it? Is self-preservation, your first priority? Could someone be hurt by a fire of this nature? Would you help them? Would you try to rescue? What if you knew the person in it? How brave were you? It's too late now, I'm gone. Finished!

Just put the fucking fire out!

Find out who started it in the first place, and be careful next time. This could happen to you one day. Consider the lyrics of the Billy Joel song 'We didn't start the fire'. It's a good song to listen to. I guess it's about who takes responsibility.

Hold that thought

It's a conspiracy that the real estate industry is such a conspiracy. Agents don't like talking to each other. Agents can't trust one another. They just can't. They can't trust themselves.

They know what they do, so they know what other agents do. They're all looking for the best deal. They know their own kind. They don't like their own kind, because they don't like seeing themselves. They're deceivers. They see deception in their counterparts. They know deception, because they're good at it. They know it, when they see it in others. They don't like what they see. They don't want to be reminded of who they are, and what they do. They can pretend to be friends with another agent, but they'll never trust the friend.

David Hustle-off

I had first-hand experience with this. It's a shame. It's a shame that agents can shaft one another, even when they purport to have a friendship. You can't have real estate friendships. You'll just get shafted.

> **Shaft:-** n. [OE. *sceaft*] 1. a) an arrow or spear b) its long stem; 2. a missile or something like a missile [shafts of light, wit, etc.]; 3. a long, slender part or object; specif., a) the stem of a feather b) the main, usually cylindrical, part between the ends of a column c) a handle, as on some tools d) either of the two poles between which an animal is harnessed to a vehicle e) a bar transmitting motion to a mechanical part, as of an engine; 4. a long, narrow opening sunk into the earth [a mine shaft]; 5. a vertical opening through the floors of a building, as for a lift; 6. a conduit for air.

I learned it the hard way

This was one of the first words I learned when I started work in real estate. Unfortunately, it wasn't a good word to start with, because I was on the wrong end of it. I didn't quite get the meaning of the word, until much later in my career. I think it's a rude word. Some people use it in a rude way. It can mean another thing. I know now, that when I said, "I just got shafted", it could have meant I'd just got shagged. I'd already bandied this word about in mixed company, before I knew what I was actually saying. It's a harsh way for a lady to talk, but then it's a harsh job for a lady to have.

I got shafted plenty of times. Sometimes I got a little bit shafted, and sometimes I got big time shafted. Either way, it hurt when it happened. It wasn't enjoyable, whatsoever. It was money down the tube.

Was I a good shaft?

I've just had the biggest shaft of my life. This shaft that I'm talking about is massive. Think of Cher's music video clip, when she's sitting on the missile with the navy watching on.

I guess it's a fitting end to my career really. I think it's kind of poetic. If this is karma, I must have given as good as I got. Did I ever send a missile your way?

Getting shafted

It's the same with the word 'shagged'. They just don't sound like rude words, do they? I'm a shag on a rock now. Have you ever felt like a shag on a rock?

> **Shag:-** n. [OE. *sceacga*] 1. a heavy, rough nap, as on some woollen cloth; 2. any disordered, tangled mass; 3. course, shredded tobacco; 4. a cormorant –like a shag on a rock [aust. Colloq.] abandoned and alone.

It's hard core

I can sometimes be a bit naïve. To be honest, I think I'm a lot naïve. My dictionary's a bit naïve too. There are many words that I know, that it doesn't know. Even some of the words it does know, it doesn't know enough about. I know more than it knows about some words, because I can test them out, and my dictionary can't. I can feel words. I've felt many words. I haven't chosen all the words that I've felt, but some of them I have. Some words that I choose, feel good and some feel bad. It's good to feel both, because it's the balance.

I'm not full of words

I know that there's a lot more to words than just reading them in a dictionary. I know there's a lot more attached to a word. I like to thoroughly examine some words. I now have the time to get involved with words that I haven't experienced before. Some I have, but only to the degree that the dictionary knows them. I think I'm earning my degree by words. I think when you're studying, the practical learning is as important as the theory. I've practically studied my words. I like studying words.

Consider the word 'words'. Take the last letter and put it at the front. Suddenly, you have a weapon of words. You have a sword. I'm a double-edged sword sometimes. I'm wielding my sword wherever I go. I'm welding a few swords as I go. This is my war on words. That's *The Maker in Me*.

Did she vanish?

Have I been hiding? Have I been hiding behind my books all my life? Have I had these books in me, all the while, waiting to bring me out of hiding? I was in hiding before. I was always in hiding. I was copping a hiding. My soul was hiding from all those hidings. I'm out now. I've come out. This is an understatement. It should be an understood statement. I've come out fully and totally. No hiding now. Never again will I hide my head in a book for oblivion. This should have been a sign for me. It's an open book sign. I'd never truly opened.

My backbone's connected

I won't have to escape from me anymore. I like me, especially now that I see me in my books. I see the real me and you will too. I've brought the inside to the outside. Outside has changed. I've changed on both sides. I'm both sides of the coin. I've got a head and a tail now. I'm at odds and at evens. This shouldn't strike you as odd, because I'm now getting even.

I'm luckier now than I've ever been, because it doesn't matter how I land. I'm going to land in the middle. I'm always a winner if I have a bet each way. I'm not a better. I don't bet. I'm the better for it.

On target

Do you want to know something funny? Pam Ayres says in her DVD entitled *'Word Perfect'*, that one should always put the funniest bit at the end for a lasting effect. I think that's true, because everyone remembers the last bit. Everyone loves to laugh last.

Are you still waiting for the funny bit? Guess who left this Pam Ayres DVD all wrapped up as a Christmas present, on my doorstep for me? I'll try to be Word Perfect as I spell it out to you:

> It was the vain and villainous, vandalizing varmint, who is vapidly venal, and a vaudeville vampire. She's the venomous villain not venial, and a Venus Fly Trap for the victims of vitriol. She's a veteran of vivacious verbalism, with a version of a vicious vernacular, of my volcanic story.

> It's been a vindictive, vile, and vigorous violation, of all that is veritable, and virtuous. With a viper's voltage, and a volatile voice, she's voracious for that vinegar from the vine.

> She continues to vouch for her vulgar veracity, like a ventriloquist ventures in venting a veneer. It's not valid, but valuable, for her vestal venetians, to hide the vengeance so vast, and vivified.

> I've virtually voiced my voluminous vocabulary, and vomited voluntarily of my own volition, a vexatious but viable victory.

> I visualize Vol-au-vent's visiting vices, and my vibrant vicinity has all the vibes of a verily venerating, valediction. This venue is the vital venture, of a vocation veiled in a vehicle vehement of my vested interest, and a veto of a vulpine virus.

I'm vying for vindication, and I view my versatility with vertigo.

How did you go with 'V'?

Y?

This is the score, I'm looking for.

V is for vertebra

> **Vertebra:-** [L. < *vertere*, to turn] any of the single bones of the spinal column.

A vertebra is a backbone. I'm hoping I have a very strong backbone. I've got a bad feeling that I'm going to need it. I have a book about backbones. It's a textbook that was owned in 1967 by a Mr or Miss R. Woods. I can't spell it all out, but it sounds like an Indian Christian name, but it might not have been Christian. The book is called *The Invertebrata*. It's by the late L.A. Borradaile & F.A. Potts with chapters by L.E.S. Eastham, Professor of Zoology in the University of Sheffield and J.T. Saunders, fellow of Christ's College, Cambridge. This is the fourth edition, and it's been revised by G.A. Kerkut, a lecturer at the University of Southampton, a sometime fellow of Pembroke College, Cambridge, 1961. This is a book that was published before my time. It's a large hard covered book, with that important looking binding, and gold lettering. It's over 800 pages long, and I'm sure to learn something from it. Does a book like this get read from cover to cover? Would a student just look up certain chapters for specific answers?

A book has a spine

I don't have this sort of an education. I left high school at year ten. I didn't have the spine for it then. I dropped out of the education system, but I didn't drop out of learning.

I'm not going to compare myself with the people that wrote and researched for that book, nor am I going to compare myself with the people that have studied it. What I am going to do, is compare myself to a sixth grader. I might well have left primary school at year six instead of year ten. This would have meant I'd have a lesser education than I have now. So now that I've got that out of the way, I'm feeling much smarter. It's just a fair comparison.

Are you smart?

Are you smarter than a sixth grader? I am. I'm smart. We're all as smart as we want to be. We can always be smarter, but we could always be less smart than we are. Have you ever asked yourself the question as to smartness? Are you bright? Does bright define smart?

> **Bright:-** adj. [OE. *bryht*] 1. shining with light that is radiated or reflected, full of light; 2. clear or brilliant in colour or sound; 3. lively; cheerful; 4. mentally quick; 5. a) full of happiness or hope b) favourable; 6. splendid; illustrious –adv. in a bright manner – bright'ly adv. –bright'ness n.

I feel that this could be a definition that describes me. I could fit into this definition with a bit of imagination. I could easily justify myself by this definition. I only lack an amount of knowledge. I lack certain knowledge. I have different knowledge, to that of the writers of the aforementioned book.

Seeing it clearly as I walk

We've clearly walked in different shoes. My shoes have gone a different way to their shoes. I've picked up knowledge along the way, and some knowledge I've set out to acquire on purpose. What's the purpose of your knowledge? Do you have a purpose for all your knowledge? Are you using it for the right purposes? This is where I get rapped over the knuckles with the ruler. I've been using what I have, for an unworthy purpose. I've been unworthy of this knowledge, but I now want to be worthy of it. I want to do something worthy with it. It's worth a lot to me, to use it wisely.

Did you choose your knowledge?

I didn't get to choose a lot of my knowledge. Knowledge has a way of choosing me. I have chosen to acquire some knowledge for myself. I set out to learn what I wanted to know. Do we all have the freedom to do this?

I once considered reading a whole set of encyclopedias, and thought it would be the most marvellous thing to do, if one had the time. I wonder how much I would have learned, and whether it would have been of much benefit to me in my life's path. Would I have been wasting my time?

The dumb broad's way

This would have been a pretty broad way to learn, and possibly I'd have had problems taking it all in. I would've taken some of it in, but only the things of which I was interested. Some of it would have gone in one ear, and out the other. What goes in, and what goes out? Do we decide, or is it decided for us? I can't decide.

Being fed through an intravenous drip

Can you force feed knowledge? Do you remember the knowledge that you were forced fed? I know people tried to force feed me knowledge. This is the knowledge that's now almost beyond my reach. It's a vague knowledge, compared to the knowledge I chose, and devoured greedily. I've always been hungry for knowledge, but only certain kinds, and through certain mediums. I might have unorthodox methods of finding knowledge, but nevertheless I learn many things. I learn all the time. I'm learning from the privacy of my inner sanctum. I don't have to go much further than this, for the knowledge I'm acquiring now.

What I don't know, won't hurt me

I've just learnt how much I don't know about backbones.

> **Invertebrate:-** adj. 1. having no backbone, or spinal column 2. of invertebrates –n. any animal without a backbone.

I'm humbled by my lack of knowledge. I'm humbled by my lack of education, but I'm not lacking without it. It's in a book. I have the book. I have easy access to knowledge. Some of you may have easier access than I do, because you may be connected to the internet. Knowledge can be just buttons away. Knowledge is also free. Libraries are free. You can order any knowledge you want from a library. I'll have to order up some specific knowledge for a specific problem. I'll have to visit the library, because this spineless book isn't going to help me much after all. It has no backbone. I need to go to the library before going to the doctor. I want to find out what the doctor knows.

My internet doctor

I used to be one of those internet doctors, and I'd look up my own medical problems. I thought I was expert in diagnosing my own symptoms, but my doctors were probably annoyed by it. If I were a qualified doctor, I would be annoyed at me too.

There's a message in the knowledge that you seek

I think everyone has the right to their own knowledge. Everyone has the right to search for their own knowledge. Knowledge is for everyone. One must be knowledgeable about one's self. I don't want to put myself in the hands of someone I don't really know. The doctor I'm going to see next week, isn't a doctor I know. I've never met him/her before. I don't know that either. I don't even know if the doctor is a man or a woman.

I didn't get a choice really. There isn't much of a choice these days. Given the choice, I would have chosen a woman. It's a woman's problem. It's not a manly problem. It's not my back, I'm worried about. It's my front. It must be my front back. I'll make no bones about it, and just tell you the problem. I probably don't know you from a bar of soap either, so it's much of a muchness.

I was put off by people

I've had to put off something I shouldn't have had to put off. I chose to put off something important. I've put off dealing with a health issue, and now it's become an issue. There are two issues now. Both issues have been an issue, but now I've noticed a couple of extra issues that have formed in my armpits. It's the pits! I've now discovered lumps under each armpit. I don't see this as a good sign. I see it as an ominous sign.

Ominous:- adj. [L. *ominosus*] of or serving as an evil omen; threatening –om'inously adv.

I didn't deal with this issue when it started, because that's when it all started. This issue raised its ugly head in the same week that I found out about my ex-husband's ugly deed. This issue has been put on the back burner, because of other pressing issues. They just kept pressing down on me every time I came up for air. I couldn't get enough air to deal with all these issues. I just couldn't cope with it all at once.

Spare a thought

I haven't had a spare moment to spare. Now I'm going spare, because I now haven't got a penny to spare for medical expenses. I used to spare no expense when it came to health. We had good health cover, and now I'm not covered. I'm exposed. I'm out in the cold, and I'm feeling cold from all the exposure. I'm hoping I won't have to be disposed of.

It doesn't mean I'm disposable

I can't worry about something that I can't yet do anything about. It's no use worrying about something I don't know anything about. That's why I'm going to find out about myself.

What do you propose?

Should I have not disclosed? Is this of such a personal nature, that you feel I've imposed? Is writing this in my book, a tad disclosed? Why, have you supposed? What have you supposed? Do you wish it had stayed undisclosed? It's okay though, I'm quite composed. I'm not home and hosed, and it's not open and closed. Do you think I want your sympathy? I do.

I want someone's sympathy. I haven't got much on offer. I've told my two kids, but I didn't completely disclose. Should I be more responsible and not tell anyone? Is this the response you want? Is this the more comfortable repose? I should have responded earlier. I should have responded to this health problem, but I was too busy defending myself. I was clearly indisposed because of the people that had imposed. This is what I'm doing now, I'm imposing. It's just evening up an old score.

Settling an old score

This is why I was so keen on looking for my backbone. I need to strengthen my backbone, before seeing the doctor. Your backbone is your resolve. My backbone is so important to my body, because it's the main structure and support. Some matters are a trifle unsettling.

I've settled on faith, because I've turned a corner

I have a cornerstone that I wear on my body, and I have much faith in it. It's a Talisman.

> **Talisman:-** n., pl. -mans [< MGr. *telesma*, a consecrated object] a ring, stone, etc. bearing engraved figures supposed to bring good luck or to have magic power –tal'isman'ic adj.

I've just learnt something. I just looked up what the abbreviation 'MGr' stands for, and it's Middle Greek. It sounds better already.

I have this Talisman for good luck, and to remind me of things that I sometimes forget. It holds me together, when some things try to pull me apart. It hangs around my neck on a gold chain, and when I get caught up, I hold it in my hand religiously.

It's a gold filigree heart with rubies around it. There are two small diamonds, but there's a symbol which is hidden from everyone else but me. There's a letter from the alphabet embedded within my Talisman. This letter stands for three very important words, for me. They're my very special words. There are three, because they're a trinity. I'm a Trinitarian.

> **Trinitarian:-** adj. of or believing in the Trinity –n. one who believes in the Trinity.
>
> **Trinity:-** n., pl. –ties [< L. *trinus*, triple] 1. a unit formed of three persons or things 2. [T-] Christian Theol. the union of the three divine persons (Father, Son, and Holy Spirit), in one Godhead.

I bet you can guess what letter it is. It's not seen as the right way up, or upside down. Its angle is sideways. It's positioned half way. It's neither upright, nor is it downright. I see it as the middle ground. This is the balance. It's not B, and it's not M for middle. It's an A. I got an 'A' going sideways.

The trinity of words

The three words that my 'A' stands for are sacred to me, and I'm not telling you what they are. They shall stay sacred. They were given to me in secret. I use them for myself. They wouldn't be any good to you, because you're not me. You might have your own words. I won't know what your words are, because I'm not you. We all have our own words. Words can be extremely valuable.

Would you want words, or numbers?

A very valuable word

> **Ace:-** n. [< L. *as*, unit] 1. a playing card, domino, etc. with one spot; 2. a serve, as in tennis, that one's opponent is unable to return; 3. golf, a hole in one; 4. a combat pilot who has destroyed many enemy aircraft; 5. [Colloq.] an expert –adj. [Colloq.] first-rate; expert –ace up one's sleeve, a hidden and powerful advantage –within an ace of, on the verge of; very close to.

It's a good word, isn't it? 'Ace' isn't just a card, it's a gifted word.

A very informative word

> **Answer:-** n. [< OE. *and-*, against + *swerian*, swear] 1. a reply to a question, letter, etc.; 2. any retaliation; 3. a solution to a problem

–vi. 1. to reply in words, by an action, etc.; 2. to respond (to); 3. to be sufficient; 4. to be responsible (to a person for an action, etc.); 5. to correspond (to) –vt. 1. to reply to in some way; 2. to respond to the signal of (a telephone, etc.); 3. to comply with; serve; 4. to refute (an accusation, etc.); 5. to suit –answer back [Colloq.] to reply rudely or impertinently.

It's a good word, isn't it? 'Answer' isn't just a word, it's the last word.

A comforting word

Always:- adv. [see ALL & WAY] 1. in every instance; 2. all the time; 3. if need be.

It's a good word, isn't it? 'Always', isn't just a sometimes word, it's a constant.

Divine words

This is my trinity. You might be able to see how these three words represent a lot more in my life, than what the definitions have quoted. My words are my life. The first is an inspiration, the second is the tool, and the third is the security. These are the only words I need. I recognize the importance of these three words in my life and future. I'll always have something up my sleeve with the first letter of the alphabet.

Alpha:- n. 1. the first letter of the Greek alphabet (A, a); 2. the beginning of anything.

Alpha and Omega:- 1. the first and last letters of the Greek alphabet; 2. the beginning and the end.

Alphabet:- n. [Gr. alpha + beta] 1. the letters of a language, arranged in a traditional order; 2. a system of signs to indicate letters.

I'm at the beginning. I'm beginning a new life, so it's apt.

Apt:- (apt) adj. [< L. *aptus*, pp of *apere*, to fasten] 1. appropriate, fitting; 2. tending or inclined, likely; 3. quick to learn –apt'ly adv. –apt'ness n.

How apt are you? Are you, as apt as me? Will I be able to come up with an apt ending to my story? I ponder this, in the middle of my open house inspection. People have wandered in, and people have wandered out. What are they wondering? How do they figure out, if this Hoorah would be apt for their needs?

Do people have a criterion apt for buying a house?

Criterion:- n., pl. –ia, -ions [< Gr. *krites*, judge] a standard, rule, or test by which something can be judged.

Should real estate agents listen to the criterion of prospective purchasers, before taking them to inspect property? Is the criterion reliable? Are people reliable? People think they know what they want, but often they don't. Some people end up buying the complete opposite to what they think they need. Criterion is just a guide. It's the basics.

Is your emotion apt for telling you what to buy?

When emotion comes into the picture, criterion takes a back seat. Emotion is stronger than criterion. Does price form part of the criterion? Price is always at the top of the list, but when emotion plays a part, it can get shoved down to the bottom.

Are some people attracted to price, more than by a criterion? Some people are. When this happens, it is in fact, an emotion. It's not a beneficial emotion, because it might be a greedy emotion. Greed isn't an attractive emotion. Have you ever seen this emotion in people? I've seen this emotion more than any other emotion, when I was a real estate agent. It was the most common emotion of all. It wasn't common among common people, but it was very common among the most common people real estate agents deal with. This doesn't mean that these people are in fact buyers of real estate, nor does it mean they end up with a deal. They're mostly just opportunists wanting to buy someone else's bad luck.

Opportunists are vultures

Bad luck is cheap, did you know? Bad luck is the cheapest thing you can buy. Who wants to buy someone else's bad luck? Do they think that someone else's bad luck is their good luck? I'm not having a moan, I'm just thinking about it. I think my bad luck will be somebody's good luck, and I'm just hoping some people will sniff it out and be attracted to it. I think this might be the best way for me, because I have some other bad luck to deal with now. It's going to be extremely bad luck if I don't have any money to deal with it.

Who will listen to me?

I wish I were a man sometimes. I think men listen to men, more than they listen to women. I think many men see the man as being superior to the woman. I see this in couples. I'm not one of a couple anymore, and I don't get a say. I've had my say, and it's beneficial for the agent and me. That's two against one. Why doesn't he listen to the woman's side, and not just the man's? Who's the man of the house?

Who will listen to the woman?

How would this scenario work, if it was two women in a break-up, and the home was being sold? Which woman would the agent listen to? Would he look for the alpha? How would he ascertain who the alpha is?

Would it be the one with more knowledge? Would it be the larger, and more powerful bodied one? What about the wiser one? Is this where the alpha value is?

How do you ascertain the wiser one of the two, no matter which two? Can you see wise? Can you hear it? Can you know it? Can only the wise recognize wise? Is length wise, lengthwise? Is this a real question? You can bet your shorts, it is. It's a short question. It's about sizing something up. It's a position. I think I just got all my questions answered all at once.

What's my position?

Has the agent been told of my position? There are lots of assumptions I could make. There's more assumptions for him to make, but only if he doesn't have to assume. Someone may have saved him the trouble. Do we all have the disease?

Do we have assumption of the brain?

Is it like consumption? 'Consumption' is an old word to describe a disease that clogs up the respiratory system? 'Assumption of the brain' could be a more modern disease which clogs up the mind. Are we clogged with assumptions? Are we clogging ourselves with assumptions, when we don't have to? What would happen if we didn't make assumptions? Would we fall apart? Assumptions don't keep us together. They hold us apart. They hold us down, and they hold us in one position. It might not be the correct position.

We can make guesses. These are different to assumptions. Guess what? I'm not going to say what you think I'm going to say. You may have guessed wrong.

> **Guess:-** vt., vi. [prob. < MDu. *gessen*] 1. to form a judgment or estimate of (something) without actual knowledge; surmise; 2. to judge correctly by doing this; 3. [U.S.] to think or suppose -n. 1. a guessing; 2. something guessed, surmise –guess'er n.

Let's play a guessing game. I have something that I didn't have before. What do I possess, that nobody knows I possess? Could you guess what I possess? What's now in my possession, which was out of my reach before? I've done all the guesswork for you.

> **Guesswork:-** n. 1. the act of guessing; 2. a judgment, result, etc. arrived at by guessing.

How bad can we be sometimes, with our guesswork? Is our guesswork up to speed? Guessing can be a bit hit and miss, can't it? That's why we measure. We use tools to help us make the right guesses. Is your guess right? How will you know if your guess was correct? The only way you can know, is to ask me. When you give me the correct answer, and it's just been a guess, I can make a fool out of you, and make you guess again. I can tell you your first guess was wrong, and tell you to guess again. Guessing isn't foolproof. This is how I could keep you guessing.

Is it still a guess, when we use tools? Math isn't guessing, is it? It either calculates accurately, or it doesn't. It's black or white. It doesn't have a middle ground. There's no grey matter with math. That's why I can't do it. The answer will be either right, wrong, or half way right, and half way wrong. This halfway point doesn't count, does it? I'm not being counted.

The answers are here

I have something else to help me guess. It doesn't help me guess, it just gives me the answers. I used to do this with primary school math. I remember looking in the back of the book for the answers. It was a Mental Arithmetic Booklet. It was easier just to copy the answers out directly from the back of the book. They were already written out for you. Why go to the trouble of working out all the problems, when the problems have already been worked out already? This is what I have. I have an answer book. I have a book with the answers written in it. You don't have to work them out. They've already been worked out. Regrettably, you can't just look up a particular answer. You must read the whole book. This book will only give me the answers to the questions I need to have answered. It won't always give me the answers to what I want answered. Those are the answers I must work out for myself.

The truth that's never revealed

Some truths never see the light of day. This is a fact. Some truth, just never gets a mention. Assumptions and guesswork take over, and the truth never surfaces.

We can assume, or guess, that a crime was committed by someone we know. We'll cut a connection with them, based on these assumptions being the truth. We can be so sure of our assumptions, or guesses, that we don't even look for the truth. The truth can be told, but only when we create the opportunity for it. Sometimes creating opportunity for truth, can be harder than making the assumptions. It puts us in the dark, when we want only to see the light. We want someone to put some light on it.

Switch it on yourself

Listening to someone else's assumptions can sometimes sound like the truth, and there's no more guessing needed. It can be all wrapped up as the truth, so it looks like the truth. Assumptions can look very much like the truth, but can be the opposite.

Some assumptions we make can have an effect on our emotions. When this occurs it's harder to find the difference between what we assume to be the truth, and what the truth of the matter is. We protect our emotions, because we find it hard to expose ourselves to pain. This is the pain of being right, or wrong.

Are we frightened of the truth, when we assume the worst? Or is it vice versa? Would we prefer to assume the best of a situation, when it looks quite the reverse? Is second guessing, that hard? Do we always have to be right the first time?

1. Shouldn't we be assuming the best of each other first?

2. Why would we want to assume the worst of each other first?

What about number 3? Is it both? Should we be open-minded and wait for the truth, truthfully? Should the third question, just be a question mark until you've hit your mark with the question?

3. Shouldn't we be open-minded and wait for the truth, truthfully?

4. Why not ask the person in question for the truth?

There's heaps of ways to find the truth. It's already inside you. If you don't know the truth, you may know the untruth. Weigh it up truthfully. Is it any of your business in the first place?

Measure your shoes

Who gets in first? Have you ever put yourself in someone else's shoes? It's not that easy, because the shoe size may be different. Just for this exercise, I want you to try to put yourself in someone else's shoes. The shoes I want you to put yourself in, are the shoes of someone you know, who's offended you. This is a person you're not so keen to associate with now.

You're not getting my shoes!

Don't try putting on my shoes, because I don't want you even trying my shoes on. They're for me only. They're off-limits to anyone else. The only person that can put my shoes on, is me. I know my shoes better than anyone. I'm the only one that knows where they've been. I've been the only one wearing them. They've just about worn me out, because they've done a lot of footwork. I don't want you to do all this footwork, because it would be way too hard for you. It's too hard for anyone but me.

Shoe envy

My shoes are what I've been given. This is my lot in life. Whatever has come my way, I've dealt with to the best of my ability. I've dealt with it, using what I know. I've only had my knowledge to help me, and my personal experience. This is what I've had to base my choices on. I've done the best I could under the circumstances I found myself in. I haven't wanted to accept it all, but sometimes we must accept what comes to us. Maybe I had it coming to me. Maybe it was a lesson. Whatever the case, I've accepted this role I've had to play, and I've played it to the best of my knowledge, and my ability. I've played it the very best way I know how, under the circumstances. I've played it for me, which means that I've also played it with others in mind. The others in mind, were who I was sparing. What I must accept now, is my shoes. I can't walk in another's shoes. I can't possibly walk in yours. I can try, but I won't succeed. You can't be in two pairs at once.

Back to the exercise

Put both your feet together. Stand to attention like you own those shoes. Now proceed to walk in a straight line. You have this offending person's shoes on now. How do you feel? Do you like being in this person's shoes? Are you imagining you are them? Do it. Imagine you are that offensive person. Do you like yourself? Do you like where their shoes are going to take you? Would you want to know how it really feels? This is the end of the exercise.

You don't want to wear that person's shoes, do you? They feel horrible to walk in, don't they? They aren't a good fit. You feel uncomfortable, and your emotions have been affected. Your perspective will be affected by your emotions.

Some people do

Nobody really wants to be someone else. You don't even really know that someone else. You can't walk like that person, even if you are wearing their shoes. They aren't as good as your shoes after all. Staying in your own shoes feels more comfortable. Your shoes are your own security system. You will always feel more secure in your own shoes.

Author-enticity

I don't want to be someone else, and I wouldn't wish on any one of you, the hardships that I've had to endure, because they've been very hard for me. They may not have been as hard for you, because you've only just stepped into them. You may have faced much harder things in your life, of a different nature. You may have felt much less. For me, it's different. I'm just me. I've had what I've had, and I've done what I've done. I've said what I've said, and been what I've been. It's only going to go one way, for me. It will only go my way.

Baby's first shoes

The word 'shoe' is one of the first words we learn when we're a toddler. I don't know why that is, but it's true. It's right up there next to the word 'dad' or 'dog'. Why 'shoe'? Is it because we see that it's our very own? We don't say jumper, or pants, because they aren't as interesting to a toddler as a shoe.

Once upon a time, man never wore shoes. I wonder what the first words of a toddler would have been in those days. I bet it was food, or nose, or something. I don't know about this. I'm thinking of a shoe, and the definition is a typical definition derived from Old English.

I know what a shoe consists of, and it's truly enlightening.

A shoe is made up of the following:-

- Tongue
- Heel
- Sole
- Upper
- Instep
- Toe

Heel:- n. [OE. *hela*] 1. the back part of the foot, under the ankle; 2. that part of a stocking, etc. which covers the heel; 3. the built-up part of a shoe, supporting the heel; 4. anything like the heel in location, shape, or function, as the end of a loaf; 5. [Colloq.] a cad -vt. 1. to furnish with a heel; 2. to touch or move as with the heel -at heel just behind -cool one's heels [Colloq.] to be kept waiting -down at heel 1. with the heels of one's shoes worn down; 2. shabby; seedy -kick up one's heels, to have fun -on (or upon) the heels of, close behind -take to one's heels, to run away: also, show a clean pair of heels - turn on one's heel, to turn around abruptly.

Heel:- vi. [OE. *hieldan*] to lean to one side; list -vt. to make (a ship) list -n. the act or extent of heeling.

I know you get sick of the dictionary playing a starring role, but it's important, because it's got something to say about the shoe. I thought the definition would have included the call to a dog. We tell a dog to heel. Are we telling the dog to stop?

Tongue:- n. [OE. *tunge*] 1. the movable muscular structure in the mouth: it is used in eating, tasting, and (in man) speaking; 2. an animal's tongue used as food; 3. a) speech b) a manner of speaking [a glib tongue]; 4. a language or dialect; 5. something like a tongue in shape, position, or use; specif., a) the flap under the laces of a shoe b) the clapper of a bell c) a narrow strip of land extending into a sea, river, etc. d) a long, narrow flame -vt. tongued, tongu'ing 1. to touch, lick, etc. with the tongue; 2. Music. to play by tonguing: see TONGUING -find one's tongue, to recover the ability to talk, as aftershock -hold one's tongue, to keep from speaking -on everyone's tongue in one's cheek, ironically; humorously.

Hold your tongue, I'm not finished yet!

Instep:- n. 1. the upper part of the arch of the foot, between the ankle and the toes; 2. the part of a shoe or stocking covering this.

Upper:- adj. 1. higher in place or position; 2. farther north or inland; 3. [U-] Geol. later: used of a division of a period -n. the part of a shoe above the sole -on one's uppers [Colloq.] in need; poor.

This is a contradictory definition – it's both lower and upper, and it's in the middle. Would you consider being upper, as being lower? Is farther north or inland, taking the upper hand?

Toe:- n. [OE. *ta*] a) any of the digits of the foot b) the forepart of the foot c) that part of a shoe, sock, etc. which covers the toes; 2. anything like a toe in location, shape, or function -vt. toed, toe'ing, to touch, kick, etc. with the toes -on one's toes [Colloq.]

alert -step (or tread) on someone's toes, to offend someone, esp. by intruding on his rights -toe the line (or mark) to follow orders, etc. strictly -turn up one's toes [Slang] to die.

I'm pointing it out for you

Do we use our toes? The only thing I can think of that I do with my toes, other than paint them with nail polish, is to point them. We point our toes when we dance. We use our toes in the way that we use our fingers, in that we point. We don't need our toes for much else, because our fingers do all the work for us. We don't need to climb trees like primitive man, so our toes aren't as useful any longer. Once upon a time our toes would have been what held us to the tree, while our hands were carrying, or doing something else. This makes me wonder about something.

What a man

Would primitive man have used both hands evenly? Would primitive man have been right handed, or left handed? Would he have been ambidextrous? I'm going to have to search out the meaning to this, at a later date.

Ambi:- [L. < *ambo*, both] a combining form meaning both.

Ambidextrous:- adj. [< L. *AMBI-* + *dexter*, right hand] 1. able to use both hands with equal ease; 2. deceitful -am'bidexter'ity n.

I'm a bit concerned with this definition. Why would it be deceitful to be ambidextrous?

Dexterity:- n. [see prec.] skill in using one's hands, body, or mind.

Dexterous:- adj. having or showing skill in the use of the hands, body, or mind: also dex'trous -dex'ter-ously adv.

Why is it deceitful? Being ambidextrous would be balanced, wouldn't it? One hand wouldn't be any stronger than the other hand. I'm confessing here, because I am in fact right handed. I'm not deceitful.

It is said that right handed people always water ski with their right foot forward. This is where I beg to differ. I am a left foot forward skier. I must have a strong side, and a weak side. I must try and balance this out in future.

I like to arch right back on my ski

Is an arch a part of a shoe, or just the foot? It didn't say anything about either, when I looked it up. I have arches in my feet. They're quite high arches. I'm not flat-footed. My feet get sore in flat shoes. I need shoes with a raised heel. I can't wear flat shoes for any length of time, because my feet hurt. My feet feel more comfortable in a heel. I like a heel.

Stay with me, I beg you. We're about to go all the way.

Arch:- n. [< L. *arcus*, arch] 1. a curved structure that supports the weight of material over an open space, as in a doorway, etc.; 2. the form of an arch; 3. anything shaped like an arch –vt., vi. 1. to form (into) and arch; 2. to span with or as an arch.

Arch:- adj. [<ff.] 1. main; chief; 2. gaily mischievous; pert –arch'ly adv. –arch'ness n.

Arch:- [< Gr. *archos*, ruler] a prefix meaning main, chief [archbishop, arch-duke].

Arch:- 1. archaic; 2. architecture.

The arches in my feet might represent strength. They have supported much weight in the past.

Why would I have an arch in my foot, as opposed to someone that has a flat foot with no arch? Am I more evolved?

It is said that people who can wiggle their ears are not as evolved as people who can't. This skill was inherent in primitive man, or ape, depending on whether you believe Darwin. I guess primitive man must have needed this skill for hunting and protecting himself. What else could be a throwback from primitive times, but can be seen in modern day man? What about very hairy men? What about people who have very long toes that look a bit like fingers? What's the difference between a more primitive man, and an evolved, and more modern man?

> **Primitive:-** adj. [< L. *primus*, first] 1. of the earliest times, original; 2. crude, simple, etc.; 3. primary, basic –n. 1. a primitive person or thing; 2. an artist or a work of art characterized by lack of formal training.

Now we're getting somewhere. If a work of art can be characterized by lack of training, then that means our soul must be primitive. It's wild and primitive. It's in all its natural glory with no training. This would be authentic art, wouldn't it? I think I'm looking for a work of art, but maybe I'm just looking for art.

> **Art:-** n. [< L. *ars, artis*, art] 1. human creativity; 2. skill; 3. any specific skill or its application; 4. any craft or profession, or its principles; 5. a making of things that have form and beauty; 6. any branch of creative work, esp. painting, sculpture, etc.; 7. products of creative work; 8. a branch of learning; specif., [pl.] the liberal arts as distinguished from the sciences; 9. cunning; 10. trick; wile: usually used in pl.
>
> **Art:-** archaic second pers. Sing., pres. Indic., of BE: used with thou.
>
> **Art:-** 1. article 2. artificial.
>
> **Artificial:-** adj. [see ARTIFICE] 1. made by human work or art, not natural; 2. simulated [artificial teeth]; 3. affected [an artificial smile] –ar'tifi'cial'ity n. ar'tifi'cially adv.

Is art artificial? I thought my dictionary said it was primitive and natural. Can some art be artificial, and some art be real? Can we know the difference? I want to know the difference, and I want to know the truth.

> **Natural:-** adj. [< L. *naturalis*, by birth] 1. of or arising from nature; 2. produced or existing in nature, not artificial; 3. innate, inborn [natural abilities]; 4. based on instinctive moral feeling [natural rights]; 5. true to nature, lifelike 6. normal [a natural outcome];

The Worker in Me | 369

> 7. customarily expected [a natural courtesy]; 8. free from affectation; 9. a) illegitimate b) not adoptive; 10. Music. neither sharpened nor flattened –n. 1. A person who is naturally expert 2. [Colloq.] a sure success; 3. a yellowish-grey colour; 4. Music a) the sign (?) cancelling a preceding sharp or flat: in full, natural sign b) the note affected: in full, natural note; 5. an idiot –nat'uralness n.

I protest. This dictionary is being a bit contradictory tonight. If true art is primitive and natural, then why is it artificial too? Can art be both artificial art, and natural art? Wouldn't all our art be natural? We are humans after all. We are natural beings. Everything we do is natural, isn't it? Man has evolved. We have evolved, compared to primitive man. We must still be natural, because we're nature. What could we possibly do, that isn't natural? Everything we do must be natural for our time. We don't live in old times, because the natural progression of time has taken us to new times. Naturally, that's time for you. It just keeps moving forward. If it went backward, would it be natural? It would have to be. It would be a natural phenomenon. Nothing that humans do is unnatural. Naturally, everything happens for a reason. What about what we've done to the planet? Is it natural? Captain Planet would know the answer.

> **Planet:-** n. [< Gr. *planan*, wander] any heavenly body revolving about a star, as the earth does about the sun, and shining by light reflected from the star: the major planets, in their order from the sun, are Mercury, Venus, Earth, Mars, Jupiter, Saturn, Uranus, Neptune, and Pluto –plan'etary adj.

Dear Captain Planet,

What are your thoughts on this natural phenomenon?

"God blessed them and said to them, 'Be fruitful and increase in number; fill the earth and subdue it. Rule over the fish of the sea and the birds of the air and over every living creature that moves on the ground.'

Then God said, "I give you every seed-bearing plant on the face of the whole earth and every tree that has fruit with seed in it. They will be yours for food.

And to all the beasts of the earth and all the birds of the air and all the creatures that move on the ground – everything that has the breath of life in it – I give every green plant for food." And it was so.

God saw all that he had made, and it was very good. And there was evening, and there was morning – the sixth day.

I'm at sixes and sevens about this bit at the beginning of the Bible. I've got a bad feeling about what we were supposed to be eating and ruling. I'm pretty sure there's a big difference between eating and ruling. 'Subdue' is to tame, isn't it? To subdue something, would be to rule it, I would say. Would it have meant destroy?

> **Subdue:-** vt. -dued', -du'ing [< L. *subducere*, remove] 1. to win control of, conquer; 2. to overcome, as by training, control; 3. to make less intense, diminish, soften -subdued' adj.

I've really got to learn to stay on track, because I've just travelled light years away from where I was.

How did I wander so far from my subject?

> **Subject:-** n. [< L. *sub-*, under + *jacere*, to throw] 1. something dealt with in discussion, study, painting, etc., theme; 2. a branch of learning; 3. Gram. the noun, noun phrase, or noun substitute in a sentence about which something is said; 4. one undergoing a treatment, experiment, etc.; 5. a person under the authority of another; esp., a person who owes allegiance to a ruler; 6. a main theme of a musical composition; 7. a cause; reason -adj. 1. under the authority or control of, or owing allegiance to, another; 2. having a tendency (to) [subject to fits]; 3. liable to receive [subject to censure]; 4. contingent upon [subject to his approval -vt. 1. to cause to undergo something; 2. to make liable or vulnerable [to subject one to contempt]; 3. to bring under the authority or control of -subjec'tion n.

I'm never very far away from a subject these days

I'm subject to being thrown from what I've been talking about, to another altogether different subject. This is a diversionary tactic, for when I get too close to the source itself. It's all subject to approval. I'm just a vulnerable subject, subjected to this and that. What about what I've subjected you to? Are you my subject? Are you my subjects for a new subject?

A high-ranking subject

I'm still perplexed, because I can't understand why I have such high arches in my feet. I must have been born to wear high heels. I must have been born to wear shoes. I must have been meant for gorgeous high heel shoes, and I've never known it until now.

In the east, women's feet are bound from when they're very young. This is done, in order for them to walk in a dainty fashion. It's believed to be a feminine affectation. I could be a throwback from some eastern culture.

Why do people who come from the west look different from people who come from the east? We're opposites, aren't we? Who looks more primitive? Who looks more refined? Which of us, is more evolved? Have we got more hair on our bodies in the west? Don't worry, I'm just writing as I'm thinking. I just wish we could look more closely at our opposites, so we may balance ourselves more fully. We're sure to learn something.

> **Sole:-** n. [< L. *solum*, a base] 1. the bottom surface of the foot; 2. the part of a shoe, etc. corresponding to this; 3. the bottom surface of various objects -vt. soled, sol'ing, to furnish (a shoe, etc.) with a sole.
>
> **Sole:-** adj. [< L. *solus*] 1. without another; single, one and only; 2. not shared, exclusive [sole rights].
>
> **Sole:-** n. [< L. *solea*, sole of a shoe: from its shape] any of certain sea flatfishes, highly valued as food.

This is the best sort of fish to eat, isn't it? It's a plate fish. It fits on the plate. It's a most odd looking fish though. I can never understand why its face is just on one side. It's a one-sided fish. It's not two-faced, is it? When it swims at the bottom, which I know it does, which way up is it facing? Is it looking down, or up? If my son were here, he'd be able to tell me this straight away.

He's an expert on fish. He doesn't say there's plenty more fish in the sea, because he's worried about how many fish are being left in the sea. He's always been concerned for marine life. He's interested in aquaculture right now. He has great dreams for his life. I don't know if there's plenty more fish in the sea, or not. You see, I'm not a fish. I can't be caught. People put nets out for me, but I don't swim into them. I'm not that easy to catch. I always look up.

A bottom dweller

A sole is at the bottom. It's the bottom surface, and I guess that's why this fish is named as it is. We're all soles really, and we exist on our own, exclusively. Should we exist only above the surface, or always below the surface? Midway could be a good place to start our journey.

It's our soles

We have sole rights to ourselves. We are shaped just like a shoe for a comfortable fit. If we're uncomfortable, we may have the wrong shoes on.

Some people can be seen to be completely comfortable in their own skin. I've known such people. They're the people who are happy within themselves. Peace and contentment emanate. They look to be satisfied with where they are, and what they're doing. They are calm in a storm. All the while the storm rages around them, and they're calm and in control of their emotions. They don't seek further strife, nor do they seek to further the strife. They remain detached. You can't ruffle their feathers, and they won't be flustered by others. These are wise people. They seek an easy resolution to problems, and understand time.

Every dog has its day

Time is often a resolution in itself. To do nothing, is sometimes the best resolution of all. To understand the power of time, we must understand when time is important, and when time is unimportant.

Some of us have time worked out to the hour, every day. We've worked time out for the weekend ahead, and the week after that. In these weeks, we'll have to make more time. We don't have to make more time, but we invariably think we do, and we will. We add things to our time, which has already been taken up with other things. When we do this, we feel like we're in two places at once. While we can't physically be in two places at once, we continue to do so in our minds. Our minds are continually racing time. When our minds can't compete with time, we end up in turmoil. Our minds can't decide where they want to be, at any one time. They try to be everywhere at once. They can't prioritize without another priority jumping the queue.

> **Queue:-** n. [Fr. < L. *cauda*, tail] 1. a line, as of persons waiting to be served; 2. a pigtail –vi. queued, queu'ing, to form in a line (often with up).

It's hard to get a proper queue going inside your mind. You need to control a queue. First you need to take responsibility for it. It's your queue, so you don't want any pushing and shoving, and you don't want any unfairness going on. You don't want cheating and confrontation. You want a peaceful queue. Queues are fraught with problems because they involve patience. You must be patient in a queue. This is the only way to success. Standing in a queue can be frustrating, but only if you allow it to be.

Frustrate:- vt. –trat'ed, -trat'ing [< L. *frustra*, in vain] 1. to cause to have no effect; nullify 2. to keep from an objective or from gratifying certain desires –frustra'tion n.

Get back in line

Emotions will always want to take over the queue. If you meditate in a queue, time flies while you're having fun. Throw the clock out of the window. Throw it out of the mind. The only think you can do in a queue, is think. This is valuable time. You should be grateful for this solemn thinking time. Hopefully you've been gifted solo thinking time.

Don't be a queue jumper

Just like our bodies, our minds can't be in two places at once either. This is not mindfulness. It's not using our mind properly, and it's not the best way to use your mind. The mind doesn't like it, and it will show you this, by affecting your physical body. Your mind is a tool and it needs to be used correctly for best results. If your mind is working on two or more things at once, it won't work anywhere near as well as when it's working exclusively on one problem at a time.

Keeping a healthy mind

We humans, have the amazing ability to become aware of how our minds work. We can sit at rest, and listen to the thoughts coming and going, in our minds. We can hear our intellect putting its two cents worth in, and we can become aware of the whole workings of it. Are we working it? Being aware of how we think, and listening to our mind and its thinking patterns, is the way to peace and contentment. By becoming aware, we're just slowing down the machinery.

Through greater awareness, we can see how silly our minds can be, and how we go about putting them in a tizz. We've whirled them around too many times, and they become dizzy. It's not the mind's fault that it keeps getting things wrong, because we're constantly confusing it with so many issues at once. We bombard the mind, because we think it can handle anything. We think it will cope with whatever we throw into it. We think we must think of everything. We have expectations of ourselves which can be unreasonable. We even go out looking for more things for the mind to cope with. This is habit, because we're just in the habit of having so much on our minds. When our minds start to empty, we just go and find more problems to put in it. They're often not our problems, but they'll do, to keep our minds working overtime. Do we pay our minds for all the work we make them do?

Who pays any mind?

Our minds get tired, just like our bodies. When our bodies get tired, they start acting up and hurting. Our bodies will give us hints that they aren't happy doing all this extra work. Our minds are different, but they still give us the hint that they're over-functioning, and not being given enough time to function properly. Our minds want to do the best job for us, but they need to have the best conditions for the best possible results.

The first few times you start to heal your mind by emptying it, you won't like the feeling. The feeling will be different to what you're used to. This is like most everything that we try, that happens to be the opposite of what's usual. It's not the feeling we're used to, and we're not sure how it's done, or how we should feel. We have no experience with which to compare it. We only have our frantic mind to compare with this new calm and composed mind. Our mind will try to play tricks, because it's suddenly been made redundant, and it doesn't know what to do with itself. It will search frantically for something to keep it occupied, because this is a different job to what it's been used to. It doesn't slow down so easily. It just needs practice at slowing down, and then you'll see how beneficial it can really be, when it's not overworked.

A mind-blowing job

It's hard starting a new job. It's change. It's just about getting the hang of new things, and how they work. It's becoming aware of the differences, and different systems used. The new systems can seem better than the old systems, but they do take some learning. In the long term, it's better to learn the new system, because it's often the more efficient way.

Habitual minds

Our minds are addicts. You can become aware of the addictions of your mind, by becoming aware of what it does. Becoming aware of how your mind works, is the most important skill you can ever learn. Why do we have this skill? Many people aren't aware that we have this skill inherent in us. Now that you know you do, what will you do with this wonderful new-found knowledge? Both these questions are the most relevant to your life. The relevance is to do with your happiness. This is what we all aspire to, but only when we're unhappy. When we're happy, we don't look for happiness, because we're already in it. Our mind, that is. Happiness is in our mind.

A shoe is made up of the following:-

- Tongue
- Heel
- Sole
- Upper
- Instep
- Toe

Now that we've come full circle, and what a circle it's been, we can change the statement to read:

A shoe is made for the following:-

The tongue is purely to protect you from the laces that will tie up your shoe. It will always act as insulation from the gaping holes left by those laces. If you talk the talk, you can walk the walk.

The heel is the back of the shoe, and this is what you show to others, as you walk on ahead and leave them behind. It will always protect you from heeling under unwanted pressure. Being down in the heel is a clear sign of this outside pressure.

The sole is your protection from what's below. It will make your shoe more comfortable to walk on. It will insulate, and keep you suspended from the rough paths. Only you can feel what your sole does for you, because there are no other feet the same as yours. It carries the weight solely. When you have a hole in your sole, you need to stop until you've repaired it.

The upper is what keeps you in your shoes, and it's often the shiniest part of the shoe. The uppers stop you getting above yourself, and from going too far north. The uppers will keep your foot grounded.

The instep is to do with the chief part of the shoe. The chief is the arch. The arch is the height your shoe will go. The instep is at the front of the arch, and is what you place upon the pedals. A shoe needs to be in step with what, and where, you're pedalling. When we use our instep, we're using it after the heel has touched down. We push on with the instep as we walk. It must be in step with our heel, so that we can walk properly.

The toe is the front of the shoe, and it's strong. It's the leader of your shoe's path, and can kick obstacles out of the way. This is the part of the shoe that sticks out the furthest, and for this reason it will be stepped on from time to time, but it will point you in the right direction, and score you some goals.

Thank God for our shoes

I didn't use laces. I didn't use laces in my lengthy diatribe, because I don't like the word. They're the ties that bind us. They're a pain in the arse to undo, and to do up. They can be a lot of extra work. You'll be bending to reach your laces. As you get older, it gets harder, and all the blood rushes to your head. That's blood pressure for you.

Would this be good for your brain?

Is this a good yoga move? Is it good for an excess of blood to rush to one organ of your body? Could it be a healing exercise? I'm leaning towards this idea as a good idea. When we incur an injury, it becomes inflamed and hot. It can sometimes swell up, and it hurts and bleeds. All this happens, because of the healing nature of our bodies. This is what an injury does. It draws blood.

What's in our blood?

Our bodies are mostly self-healing. Half the time we don't even know we have something in our bodies that needs healing. It just does it on the quiet. We can sometimes feel a bit tired or run down, and need extra sleep. Extra sleep is important for healing bodies. We're asleep to most of our healing. We don't even know what's healing most of the time.

Don't lace your shoes up too tight

It's important that we don't cut off circulation. This circulation of the blood will keep our entire bodies healthy. It needs to circulate, for us to live. We need to get enough exercise and eat well, for our blood to be well. Walking is a great exercise for both body and mind. When circulation is bad, our bodies can develop ulcers and skin complaints. Our skin relies on blood, because of the many vessels it maintains. Skin is important, because it keeps us together.

It's not good to have leaks in your body, because bodily fluids will be lost. This isn't good, because then our bodies will work harder to produce more fluids like blood and saline to replace what's gone missing. It's all about fluids. Make sure you drink enough fluid.

Massage is an ancient remedy

Old people suffer from ulcerated skin. I know it's hard sometimes, for old people to do exercise, especially when they gave up too early. I wonder if massage could help with circulating the blood of old people who are no longer mobile.

Massage is an ancient form of healing. Massage encourages blood flow. This can be demonstrated by rubbing a patch of skin on your arm for a few minutes, especially if you rub it rapidly. You can try other parts of your body, and get the same result. You've probably seen a similar demonstration, or taken part in such a demonstration before, with good results. Anyway, I was talking about laces, and laces can cut off circulation. Be careful of laces. My rant on laces has just been laced with a dash of medicine. Old people need good medicine too.

Are your shoe laces too tight?

I remember learning to tie my laces when I was a youngster, and it wasn't easy. I think it's something that you're just good at, or something you're knot.

I don't get how some people tie all those different knots. I've seen all those nautical knots, people seem so competent with.

> **Lace:-** n. [< L. *laqueus*, noose] 1. a string, etc. used to draw together and fasten the parts of a shoe, corset, etc.; 2. an openwork fabric of linen, silk, etc., woven in ornamental designs -vt. laced, lac'ing 1. to fasten with a lace; 2. to weave together; intertwine; 3. to ornament with lace; 4. to thrash, beat; 5. to add a dash of brandy, etc. to -vit. 1. to be fastened with a lace; 2. to attach (with into).

I get knotted up

I can tie knots. I can tie the most wonderful knots that go on, and on, and on. You would never have seen a knot like mine. I never see knots like mine. Some people don't have any imagination. My knots are pure artistry. My knots are dependable. They're very creative knots. They're very strong knots, and very resilient. They often get preserved, because they can't be undone. They can take so long to undo, that the rope just gets cut, and my knots are left for prosperity. This is what knives and scissors are for. They're for chopping off the knot and letting the rope run free. There will always be knots that we can't undo. There's always a simple way of getting rid of a knot. Don't get knotted up over it, and just use the scissors.

Scizzor Sisters

What a great invention. Who invented the scissors? I haven't got the internet, so I can't answer this straight up, but I bet it was a really important invention in its heyday. It's an important tool. It's such an important tool, that not only does it get used in industrial trades, but it also gets used in every household today. We are quite lost without a pair of scissors.

I like their sound

I like the sound of those old seamstress's scissors. They make that cool sound as they cut through the material along the length of a wooden work bench. They sound so efficient. My grandmother was a seamstress. She wasn't professionally qualified. She never worked in a formal sense, but she worked hard doing what she was talented at.

She made many of her own clothes, and they were very fashionable. She used to like going window shopping. This is an oxymoron, I think. I've never been a window shopper. I either go to buy, or I don't go. This is changed now. I can't buy, so I just go in for a look. I have the time to look now. Looking is learning. I didn't know this before. Now I look and learn. This is *The Looker in Me*. It's a book I'm writing. You'd be surprised at what you can find, when you look.

I don't have to look very far

I'm still looking for my subjects. There's a lot of looking to be done. I won't be looking local. I'm going further afield to look. I won't stop looking behind my back, though. Looking back is as important as looking forward. I'll be looking both ways, as I cross the threshold. I'll want to know where my parameters are, so that I don't get blocked. I don't want to be blocked in, or run over. I don't want you to come across me in the street. I don't want to be knocked down by oncoming traffic.

> **Traffic:-** n. [< L. *trans*, across + It. *ficcare*, bring] 1. a) the movement or number of cars in a street, pedestrians along a pavement, etc. b) the cars, pedestrians, etc.; 2. trade, sometimes a wrong or illegal kind [traffic in drugs]; 3. dealings or business (with someone); 4. the amount of business done in a given period – adj. of traffic or its regulation –vi. traf'ficked, traf'ficking 1. to carry on traffic (in something); 2. to have dealings (with someone) –traf'ficker n.

I've had the odd bit of traffic here of late. I see it come to the door, and I hear the dog barking. I peer through the peep hole, and they don't know I'm looking. I look and consider the type of traffic it is. I must be very careful of traffic, because I don't want to get run over again. My doors are locked now, and I'm more vigilant than I was.

Behind closed doors

When people come to my door, do they expect me to open it? Do they want me to, or just expect me to? I know the answer to this. I don't mind if they know I'm at home, because the house looks like somebody's at home. It shows all the signs that someone's inside.

Peep holes are a good invention and so are scissors. Leonardo De Vinci invented them. (This is what you call a quick peep.) You can see them, but they can't see you. You can see their body language, and assess their attitude. You can watch them head back to their car in frustration. You can watch as they peer out from their car window, watching to see if you'll appear from behind the curtains. What if I did? I probably should do that in future, because that would be more of an honest answer. I won't answer the door, but I'll answer them from behind the curtains.

What is it about Mona Lisa's smile? It knows something, but it's never going to tell you. I know that smile, and I know what's hiding. It's what she knows, that everyone else doesn't. Mona Lisa has the enigmatic smile.

The lie detector in me

What makes someone so determined to see you, when they've never cared much before? They've been given the message, but still, they don't take the message. There's a secret message in it. Are they worried the secret will come to light? Are they trying to assess if the secret has come to light, or is likely to come to light? Are they just worried their secret may have caused someone else's light to fail, and are watching the failures adding up? Are they worried about a final failure? Would they be worried that their secret may cause a final failure? Are they worried about their conscience if they fail to find out, and set it to rights? Is their conscience playing havoc with them, and playing out worst case scenarios? How much could your conscience handle? How big a secret could your conscience deal with? Did Mona Lisa have a conscience? I'm talking about an oil painting, aren't I? The one I'm talking about isn't much of an oil painting. She's a fake. She's also a snake, but she's a walker. Spot the mistake. She's a copy of her own past. She's a regular Mills & Boon story of betrayal.

Are there some conscientious objectors?

The way to a good conscience, isn't through manipulation and control. This won't be enough for a conscience to be satisfied. To satisfy a conscience, one must own up to a wrong doing, and confess it. Confessing is putting it to rights. No, it isn't. Apologizing is.

Being honest with self

Accepting responsibility for poor choices and acknowledging our errors, is apologizing to self. That's just on the surface. The surface doesn't go far enough. There may be another, who deserves a verbal apology. We need to say sorry to the person that was hurt by our error. Who is hurt the most? Is it ourselves, or the person we trampled on? It's a two-way street, and both streets are of the same length. One street takes you in one direction, and the other street takes you in another. We are free to take any direction.

What street are you in now?

Have we gone far enough for our conscience? Can we explain why we were in error? Have we considered where, and why, we went wrong? Who do we blame for our errors? Who knows of our errors?

Should an apology include a reason?

Who apologizes these days? Who confesses? Who accepts responsibility for being a shit head?

The shit heads cleaned me up

All the shit in my life wouldn't have been cleaned up, if it wasn't for a bunch of shit heads. I'm grateful to the shit heads that did this to my life, but I'm not letting them know that just yet. I want them to get a feel for it first. I want them to feel like shit heads. I want them to acknowledge their own shitty deeds, done with their own shitty heads. The only way to get rid of a shitty head is to offload the shit first. Relieve your head of the shit, and you'll feel much better. But that's not enough of an apology.

What's the liability of an apology?

What about a letter of apology? Are these good to write? Would the person writing the apology feel they can trust the person they're apologizing to, with their apology in writing? Does the apologizer deserve to have the trust of the victim? Are they worried about what the victim will do with their written apology? Do they want their letter of apology bandied around, and shown to everybody? Do they think they'll end up in more shit? Should the shit be fair? If you've put someone in the shit, should you be prepared to step into a bit of shit yourself? Do you need a taste of your own medicine, before you can fully understand the shit you've caused?

What was I liable for?

What if you already know of the medicine that you've so liberally dosed someone with? This is the shit I don't understand. Why would a person deliberately inflict a pain on somebody, that they've already had inflicted on themselves in the past? They already know what it feels like, and they didn't like it one little bit. They then inflict it on a friend. I think this is where I beg to differ.

They haven't quite got the true feeling, because their pain hadn't been inflicted by a friend. It's a real step up, isn't it? Now I get it. I was never a friend. I must have just thought I was, and there must have been more going on beneath the surface that I wasn't aware of. Perhaps she didn't like me after all. Why? Why would you pretend to? Why would you feel the need to? Why pretend? Was it good for your conscience to pretend?

I'll look it up

Have you ever been pulled down a peg or two? Have you ever been knocked off your high horse by someone? Have you ever had the rug swiped out from underneath you? It's a leveller. People do this to level you out. They do it to take you down from wherever they think you are. They may think that you're higher than them, or in a better position. They may not like looking up at you, and want to see you on a lower level. When they're on a higher level than you, they can look down on you. Is looking down, better than looking up? How does it make them feel? Does it make them feel better?

Don't look down

I'd rather look up than down. You learn more from looking up. When you look up, you can aspire to something better. We look up to people we admire. We don't look down to people we admire. What are we doing when we look down to people? We're feeling sorry for them. We all look down to some people, because there will always be some people down on that level.

Everyone can look up for a change

It doesn't mean they have to stay on that level. They can move up. I like to see people moving up. I like to show them the foot holds for their rise. I like to see people rising to that next level. It's growth. I worry about people staying on the one level, and not wanting to rise to another. I've always been ambitious. I've been ambitious for myself, as well as for others. I could have gone up further, if it wasn't for the others, but I'm not blaming them, I'm blaming me. I should have untied my laces.

I'm getting up the others

I got laced up, and tied myself in some knots I couldn't undo. I've cut the knots out now, and I'm ambitious once again. I'm going up. I'm going up a notch. Going up a notch can be painstakingly hard. It's just one notch at a time for me. What are notches for?

The Ravens of a Poor Bitch.

That poor sad bitch, she'd had it bad,
When she lost her best mate Red.
It took a lot of guts and stuffing,
To try to fix up, what was dead.
    Did the poor bitch know the score?

   Would she have heard of nothing more?
That poor sad bitch, she went to ground,
But with so much ground to cover,
She ends up in that place insane,
Put inside by the unknown lover.
  Did the poor bitch read the score?
    She couldn't read no more.
Now things get put away like that.
They were things that aren't so nice.
He would've spilt the beans, the lot,
So detoxed, rehabbed, and locked up twice.
  Could the poor bitch feel the score?
    She couldn't feel no more.
The poor bitch copped the blame and shame,
But 'twas another, as had dunnit.
She almost lost her business place,
When the devil tried to run it.
  The poor bitch tried to score.
    This is what she'd worked hard for.
The devil was amongst the cover,
And living like the hallowed saint.
The devil, the related lover,
A different picture was in paint.
  The poor bitch didn't know that hidden score.
    She didn't see through the bedroom door.
Five years gone with the devil entrenched.
The poor bitch sees an angel benched.
A seeking, sneaking, plagues her past,
As a spell is broken, of a wicked cast.
  The poor bitch was searching for the score.
    She dared not look behind that door.
Well life grows dark, when evil's close.
And it was lurking there.
When things aren't fixed along the way,
Truth reveals a hidden snare.

> The poor bitch was due to score.
>> What had she been working for?
>
> He walked right in that trap with her,
> And drank too much, it's true.
> Of devils, there are many near,
> Old friends can run you through.
>> The poor bitch, she gets under-scored.
>>> For betrayal means, there's no accord.
>
> The poor bitch had been led astray.
> Her only crime, her best illusion.
> She'd worked so hard to paint it all.
> A painting spoiled, but not delusion.
>> The poor bitch had expected more.
>>> But he just went on, to score and score.
>
> She kicks him out, beside herself.
> It's doubly bad, and he just don't quit.
> She's got lumps, and clinic tests,
> Mammograms, biopsies and scary shit.
>> The poor bitch scored a lump in each.
>>> "Leave me alone!" she did beseech.
>
> There's no time off, it's back to work.
> It's a sorry tale in telling.
> It's time to sort it right throughout,
> And find what he was selling.
>> The poor bitch, she didn't score that well.
>>> The joint, she did not want to sell.
>
> The poor bruised bitch, she wants the truth.
> She wants to know it all.
> Her thinking, checking, finding,
> And the cards just start to fall.
>> The poor bitch, her eyes were never poor.
>>> She knows just what she's looking for.
>
> A few pages through the calendar,
> And the next offender's off.
> Her mother ups and chucks it in.

Why say it was her cough?
    The bitch, she never was that smitten.
        This was a score, which was under-written.
The poor bitch, she's in extra shock,
And the ex gets all pie-eyed.
He wants to get some sympathy,
And makes out, he just died!
    The poor bitch was made to feel, the double of that guilt,
        But finally finds the truth behind, all that he had built.
She takes apart her painting now,
And has a better look.
She sees the writing on the wall,
And sees what she mistook.
    The poor bitch adds it up, the entire music score.
        She looks around and sees it all, and wonders who
        she'd played it for.
Meanwhile, behind the office doors,
There's a private meeting going down.
She's pushed towards that place once more,
And she's headed for that laced-up gown.
    The poor bitch didn't see this score.
        Her kids deceived, and many more.
It's clever, is the devil when,
It's too close an exposure.
Infiltration was the key,
Before the big disclosure.
    The poor bitch, she can't see the score.
        And it's right behind her office door.
See, isolation, is the key,
She uses madness, as the play.
Of this, she's had some practice.
This madness job, is the devil's way.
    The poor bitch, she's not to know.
        She wonders whether she should go.
The poor bitch is surrounded now,

And the devils with her doc.
The doctors been manipulated,
And she thinks it's just for shock.
> The poor bitch says enough, and no more!
>> She's sane right through to her inner core.
And this is where the story's hard,
For a label can be wrong.
It said that she had the bi-polar bear,
But 'twas the devil's devilish con.
> The bitch was never a polar bear, nor was she ill before '06'.
>> 'Twas just a post-traumatic affair, with just a rest to fix.
She figured it out, when the kids let on,
About those bad old meetings.
She had to face what she must do,
And make those formal greetings.
> The poor bitch looks at the score, and sees a hell of a game.
>> She wants it done and sorted out, and the devil to take the blame.
She sacks the devil for all her lies,
She smells the guilt, and found it true.
It all adds up, and it's not surreal.
What can one do, when one can't sue?
> The poor bitch has the scoreboard tally.
>> She's strong, and knows that she must rally.
It causes a stir of the utmost height.
The family's lost its grip.
The Matriarch, just dead a month,
And the poor bitch, was joined, at the hip.
> The poor bitch just lost and entire score.
>> In that family, she is no more.
The devil is a clever dame.
It's frightening, but it's true.
The poor bitch wonders, how on earth,

She can make good things anew.
>   The poor bitch tries to score, from the inside of her office door.
> >   She rallies troops and fires up, and gives it just one more.

It's expansion, and redemption,
And trying to survive.
She knows just what she's doing.
She has that inner drive.
>   The poor bitch tries to score some more, but takes a little break.
> >   To work from home, and grieve and such, it's been so much to take.

This was the greatest folly for,
The Devil came back in.
Infiltrating everywhere.
The Devil wants to win.
>   The poor bitch, she had her staff in place, and everything was fine.
> >   Then every little thing she did, got seen to be a sign.

She knew that things didn't smell so good.
The community looked on, knowing.
Was something written on her wall?
What was the devil sowing?
>   The poor bitch, she couldn't fight it, the devil was so tricky smart.
> >   A devil gets much practice when, she's a devilishly tricky tart.

A label is, as labels do.
They make your reputation.
It's harder still, when it's in print,
At the doctor's consultation.
>   The poor bitch, they had the proof, with a medical opinion fated.
> >   Of her records, she just thought, that her privacy was rated.

The story goes, and it's on the nose,
With poor bitch home and working.
There are things that go a-missing,
But it's only more shit, lurking.
> The poor bitch knows, she knows the score, she's seen it on the wall.
>> And just so she can beat them, she'll have to make them fall.

It's finished now, it got wound up,
And all the people tainted.
The office gone, her job, her work,
And with truth, she's well acquainted.
> The poor bitch knows, she was on track, but changing a direction.
>> Her life is hers, to be and do, and did not need correction.

A devil's ire, has the phones a going.
The Mental Health, ring like a treat.
The police, they come to and fro,
And she bunkers down, but must retreat.
> The poor bitch was nearly scheduled out.
>> The kids are mad, and fit to clout.

There's not a corner, left in sight.
All her people, known so well.
Nobody left to trust her side,
When the devil's around to tell.
> The poor bitch has no-one much these days, except her two big babies.
>> Her credibility slandered well, and there isn't any maybe's.

It got much worse before the end,
And the courts got a fair old cracking.
Her daughter takes no rap at all,
For her mother's dreadful sacking.
> The poor bitch did avoid the court, to avoid a scheduled trap.

> She did not go. She'd had enough, and didn't give a crap.

And now the court's in charge,
And she hasn't got a say.
She never really did, you know,
The bitch just had to pay.

> The boor bitch hasn't told you all, because there's more in play.
>> But "better the devil you know" is a stupid thing to say.

And here she is with more at stake.
The house is up for sale.
She doesn't have a cent.
And it's a sorry little tale.

> The poor bitch has a problem, another one, it's so.
>> She has more lumps just showing up, and hasn't any dough.

This is me, and I'm poor bitch,
And I would hate to be this lady.
I can't deny it's me, alright.
My life's looking pretty shady.

> The poor sad bitch she has some light, and she'll always make it catch.
>> She needs to score a turn real soon, to fire up, and take the match.

By Ms T.L. No Match.

This is my personal version as promised, of 'The Raven' which was written by the famous, and most audacious Edgar Allen Poe. My version is by no means on par, or anywhere near it, for skill and beauty. The true story, however, would have been admired, I feel sure, by Poe. He had a fascination for the human mind in all its darkness. This is what I'm supposing, that we may have had in common, Poe and I - not the dark mind, but just the fascination for it. If it weren't for this fact, the poor bitch would have fallen in a heap. Thanks Ed.

Studies of a psychopath

This story of mine has left me without an ounce of credibility. It's put me in an unsafe position. I've been placed in a vulnerable position as to my personal safety. When you've had a false label attached to you, and slanderous false accusations made against your character and state of mind, it's demoralizing. I have become unbelievable. Anything I say, has become questionable. I've lost all credibility, and I feel unarmed.

> **Demoralize:-** vt. -ized, -iz'ing 1. to lower the morale of; 2. to throw into confusion –demor'aliza'tion n. –demor'aliz'er n.

This doesn't seem to be a strong enough word, or maybe it's just the definition that's weak. It's definitely thrown me into confusion, because I can't think of a better word, or a better way of defining how I feel.

I can explain

My actions and reactions have not been explained by me. They've been explained away by others. I've been explained away. I didn't get explained away, in the way I did last time. Last time I got explained away to a mental hospital. This time they didn't succeed.

Would you like a piece of the pie?

Just thinking about it now, makes me think of another story that you'll have heard. It's about a little boy. He was a shepherd. He didn't have to do much, but he did have to watch those boring sheep all day, every day. His job was to make sure the sheep didn't wander off. His job was to protect the sheep from being attacked by wolves. Little boys on their own all day, tend to get up to mischief if they aren't kept well occupied and supervised.

That little boy wanted some excitement. He waited every day for a wolf to appear, but there were no wolves to be seen. He might have thought his job was a bit mundane and not very praiseworthy. He wasn't gaining any respect from anyone. The only way he could gain some respect, was to show how good he was at looking after the sheep. He decided he'd pretend that there was a wolf, and cried out to the townsfolk as follows:-

"Help, a wolf, a wolf! There's a wolf attacking the sheep. Come quickly!"

The townsfolk ran to the scene, a high paddock some way away, only to find the sheep grazing peacefully. They asked the boy where the wolf was, and the boy replied that it must have gone back into the forest. The townsfolk went back to what they were doing, but only after telling the boy that he was doing a good job, and to keep up the good work.

The boy was chuffed. He'd had his bit of excitement for the day, and he'd also enjoyed some praise. He'd got a fair bit of attention out of this little caper. He was a child, so he didn't see how his reputation could be damaged by telling falsehoods. He thought it would improve his status, rather than lower it.

The next day the boy decided to repeat the scenario again. The same thing happened, but the townsfolk thought it a bit mysterious that the wolf could not be seen a second time.

On the third day, the boy continued with this new and more interesting part to his job. The townsfolk came, but they were a bit annoyed. They still couldn't see any wolf. They inspected the sheep, and the sheep were all grazing peacefully. They were starting to catch on to this little boy's antics, and wondered if it was a scam of some sort. They let their irritation show, in order to let the child know that their time was too important to be wasted running up to the paddock each day for no reason.

On the fourth day, the boy was considering whether to pull another fast one. He was a bit wary about it, because he knew the townspeople were becoming upset with him, and he didn't want that kind of attention. He only liked the good attention.

As he sat watching the sheep on this fourth day, out of the forest stalked a giant black and grey, ferocious looking wolf, with fangs dripping with drool, and eyes bright with hunger. The boy was terrified. He yelled at the wolf, but to no avail, as the wolf was eyeing off a lamb. The boy called out to the townspeople and ran down the hill yelling at the top of his lungs.

"Come quick, a wolf is at my sheep. Quickly, come quickly, it's huge. It's going to get my new lamb. Come as quick as you can, the wolf has come!"

The townspeople ignored him and shooed him away. They took no notice, even while the child was jumping up and down, and obviously distraught. The townspeople were imagining the sheep grazing peacefully. They had guessed the same plot was about to unfold. They'd already seen this story. They'd seen it three times already. People tend to get tired of the same story over, and over, again. They already know what's in it.

I hope you get my side of the story

Can you read more into some stories, the more times that you read them? This is such a story. All the townspeople needed to do, was to distinguish the true story from the fictional story. There are ways to do this. You have to be able to see the difference. What difference would it have made? It would have been the difference of two sheep and one lamb.

Have we got the moral wrong in this story? How many morals are there?

Was it the boy's fault? I want you to look further than the surface. There are many incorrect answers on the surface. If we look deeper, we can try to understand the reason the boy was faking in the first place? Why all the faking?

How many lessons are there in this story?

The boy obviously learnt a lesson. He's learnt that his credibility is now in tatters, and he can't be trusted one way or the other.

The reason the boy told the lies in the first place, was because of his lack of credibility. He told lies to get credibility. Credibility isn't built in this way. Credibility comes from inside, before it can be seen on the outside. It has to be worked hard for.

Will this mistake cost him his credibility the next time the wolf comes? The townsfolk may never trust this boy again. The boy probably got the sack. Did the townsfolk stop to wonder why this sorry tale happened in the first place? Could the child have just wanted some attention? Did the child want special attention? What kind of attention does the child crave? Not the sort of attention the kid got at the end.

There are so many stories to tell

Another possible scenario might be that the boy did in fact achieve the credibility he wanted, because the wolf did indeed show up. The townsfolk may have been left feeling guilty for not believing the boy, on those earlier occasions. The townsfolk may have been feeling guilty for their impatience and distrust of the boy.

Is this where we're all up to?

They may now believe that the wolf was in fact there, each time the boy called. In this scenario, the boy has achieved the credibility that he wanted purely through lying.

Who felt the loss of the three sheep the most?

Did the boy feel guilty? The boy may well lay the blame on the townsfolk. He has every right to blame, and the townsfolk may be making it easy for him by wearing that shame. The boy could have just had his first lesson in righteousness. His remorse may be absent, because the townspeople have taken it on board for him.

An external locus of control

People learn things from experience. They don't always learn what's obvious to learn. Their learning can be habitual learning. They may be learning nothing new at all, especially if they don't truly think about it. Looking below the surface is true learning. Just considering what appears on the surface, is not enough learning. It's only half-arsed learning.

Do we always blame the wolf?

The wolf will come back, won't he? He's just had a successful feed on three sheep. He's only doing what's natural for a wolf to do. Nobody came to scare him off. He's learned a lesson too. There's more where they came from. He's coming back, whether the boy has credibility back, or not.

To attain some credibility, should we discredit another? Should we lie about a situation, to gain credibility? What lengths will people go to, to gain credibility? Did the boy take away the wolf's credibility?

Does this story take away the credibility of the storyteller?

I'm a wolf. I'm coming back. Am I wearing the sheep's clothing? Where did I get the sheep's clothing from? I used to be a sheep. Are there any other sheep out there?

Nuisance calls

If I were attacked, and rang the police for help, would they believe me? They've been called too many times, and with too much information offered. I've offered little information. Most of the information the police have about me, is from other people. Whose information will tip the scales? How much information is on offer, and what sort of information is it?

If shepherds come to my door, and I've had them here before, (and they don't bring shepherd's pie), will I ring the police? Can I trust the police to trust that I'm sane? Will I be credible? Will anything I say, be credible?

I can tell when people are assessing me. It's easy to pick up on, when it's being done continuously. It's easy to learn how to tell, when you've had plenty of practice. It's an awful practice to get used to. This is what you call, truly being aware of yourself. What you do, and what you say, can be held against you. I even started to hold myself against me. I had my doubts.

House arrest

My house is my sanctuary, but nobody knows what I do all day in here. I've been here for months, keeping to myself. I don't get seen out very often. It's rare for me to go anywhere. Am I insane? The house is almost empty, because I had to sell the furniture so that I could feed myself. My job status is nil, because I'm apparently being investigated for fraud. I've read this in a letter, so I don't know if it's true or not. I don't believe everything I hear or read these days. I know I'm not a fraud. I know what I've done, and what I haven't done. Everything I've done, and continue to do, is for a purpose. It's self-preservation.

Preserving the truth

I'm just doing what I want to do. I'm writing. I have a purpose. If it doesn't work out, it's not the end of the world. I'll just have to find another purpose. It will be on purpose. It just has to work out, because this is *The Worker in Me*. This is how I work now.

At the least

I'll have at least tried. It's better to have lost in love, than to have never lost at all. That's not how it goes, is it? I like it better. There's no difference really. It's better to have loved and lost, than to have never loved at all. It's better to have never loved, than to have never lost a love. I'm talking about my books. I'm not making any sense. I don't make much sense sometimes, because a sense is just a sense, and it's not a purpose. I hope my purpose makes sense to some people. I hope all this makes sense to me one day. I hope I can make sense of what happened to me. My purpose was presented to me. I accepted it.

Do I make any sense?

I don't make a lot of sense to people, living here in this big empty house on my own. They must think I'm sedated.

Sedate:- adj. [< L. *sedare*, to settle] calm or composed; decorous.

Decorous:- adj. [L. *decorus*, becoming] having or showing decorum.

Decorum:- n. [L.: see prec.] 1. whatever is suitable or proper 2. propriety in behaviour, speech, etc.

It just happens to be what I'm doing. Half the time, I don't know what I'm doing, like now. I'm doing the opposite of what I would have done a year ago. I'm trying to do things differently, so the same thing doesn't happen again. I'm reacting differently, in order to get a different reaction. I'm certainly getting that. I'm getting no reaction. People are keeping their reactions to themselves.

I'm desperate for a reaction

I've written away to the ex, to ask for some money. I've asked for $2,000 from our joint account. I've said it's for medical expenses which it is, but it's also for food. This is medical too. I have to eat, or I'll die. That was a bit melodramatic, but it's true.

Show me your meat

I'm having trouble with protein. It's expensive. Eggs have been the main way to go for me, but I also bought six frankfurts for 95 cents. I'm not sure what sort of protein is in frankfurts, but there must be something. I also buy a sausage roll or a pie from time to time. I've never had this problem with meat before. I thought nothing of bringing home eye fillet to throw on the BBQ midweek. I'd give my right eye for some fillet steak at the moment. I thought nothing of a leg of lamb, and couldn't have told you what the price of it was. I still can't, because I can't bear to look at what I can't now buy.

It's illuminating

It's more than illuminating, it's downright fucking humbling. I guess I have a touch of anger. You just read about it. Did you get a sense of it? I shouldn't be this poor, should I? I'm still driving around in my Mazda 6, so I don't look poor. I'm not allowed to sell it, because it'll be taken from me soon enough, in the winding up of the business.

I'm not supposed to sell anything, but he is. I've got a few Medicare receipts that I'm holding on to for a rainy day, but it's raining now. I've also got a couple of rings left, that I might be able to scrape another $150 for at the pawn brokers.

Self-destructive behaviour

Are you wondering if I'm still smoking? I've just got to now, don't I?! (That was anger too.) I would surely die if I had no smokes. Why no sympathy? You righteous non-smokers! I know you lot. You're perfect, aren't you? I don't want to be like you. I'd rather die right now, where I'm sitting. I know your kind. I've had it up to here, with your self-righteous attitudes.

Smoking is legal, so it must be moral. You non-smokers think your God's gift, don't you? You're wrong! One of God's gifts to me was tobacco. Judge him. Now look who's being self-righteous. Self-righteousness stinks. I don't give a shit what you think. I just give a shit what I think. Where are my smokes? Ah, that's better. I was getting a bit edgy. Sorry for the outburst.

I'm going up in smoke

I'm just wondering if there were any famous holy people who smoked. I shall research this when I get back on the internet someday. You could look it up for me now. I bet there was. Anyway, Walter Murdoch smoked a pipe, and so did Montaigne. I'm just doing what my mentors did. They set the example.

Dealing contraband

Smokes have become more important to me than ever now. They're my luxury item. My daughter's a pet, she's supplying me. It's contraband, isn't it? She knows I'm okay, as long as I've always got a smoke handy. She doesn't smoke. She used to, when she was going through a rough patch, but she doesn't now. This is a good sign that things are going better for her. I wonder how many smokes I've smoked while writing these books. My books have been supported by my smokes. They're the sponsors of my books. You might be supporting my habit by buying my books. You may be enabling an addict. Are you enabling my addiction? I may be enabling yours.

> **Enable:-** to make able; provide with means, opportunity, power, etc. (to do something).

Just to get this into perspective, I have recently witnessed a drug deal going down outside my window. It was very interesting, and I had time to observe how it all works. I watched the cash get sorted out, and I profiled the two people getting fixed. That's what they called it, anyway. I watched as he got stuck into some sweet lollies like there was no tomorrow. I watched the agitation, and the mobile phone calls. I think they may have been on something harder than tobacco.

From the looks of them, and the car they were driving, and given that they were also getting stuck into some Bourbon and Cokes, I'm guessing their income was from Centrelink. These were my observations, but I don't know if it's true. It could be an entirely different story.

The entirely different story

This lovely couple are tireless charity workers, hence the old worn-out car piled high with bags for the poor. They clearly supported The Salvation Army depots, from the manner of dress worn. The Bourbon and Cokes were for celebrating their achievement of raising much needed money for the disadvantaged family up the back. The lollies were an added treat, because the chap had just given up smoking, and they were taking the edge off his nicotine cravings.

They were clearly disadvantaged themselves, but they didn't see it that way. They felt that there were people worse off than themselves, who needed their help. They drove off with their cans in their laps, because they had to get to the next disadvantaged family, fast.

The poor and the needy, are always their first priority. The reason they had so much cash, was because they had raised it through their nightly fundraising pursuits. They liked to see the funds being spread generously around to the other unfortunates in the community.

My report

I got the story. I'm a good reporter. Hard facts are what I'm into. The hard facts of the matter can be hard to stomach. I felt sorry for these people. I really didn't know the hard facts. The hard facts are below the surface. I wasn't able to see the hard facts from my window. I'd have to know something of their past, to make any sort of judgment. Once I had all the past information, I bet I wouldn't stand in judgment. I won't have walked in their shoes. You can't judge what you don't know. Why make a judgment anyway? All I want to do, is learn something from it. I want understanding.

Is Centrelink an enabler?

Centrelink would not enable me. I wouldn't let Centrelink enable me. I am able. I'd have to say I'm disabled and labelled. I'm not going to enable the label. I'm able to take care of myself.

I have enabled Centrelink. All the years of work and the tax I've paid, has enabled Centrelink to help the disadvantaged. I'm disadvantaged, but Centrelink didn't do it, did it? How much tax have I paid? How much tax am I being charged? I just got another tax bill, but I can't pay it yet. I might send it on to Centrelink, and they might be able to pay it for me.

He enabled me to stay

I wouldn't really do this, because I've always paid my own way. I'm getting paid in a way. My boy wonder is getting an allowance for his youth, so I don't have to pay. He's away. He lives away from me now. I won't have a house soon, and I just don't get paid like I used to. Don't worry. He'll no doubt pay his way, when he starts work. There's plenty of time for him to pay his way. He'll make plenty of hay, by the time he's had his day. I made plenty of hay in my day. I enabled myself to pay for my hay.

Did I enable this story?

Are you an enabler? It's not the good enabler, I'm referring to. It's the bad enabler. I'm referring to an enabler who enables bad behaviour in another. You probably don't like the behaviour, but you probably aren't aware that you're the one enabling it.

Dear Nanna and Grandpa

I'm considering grandparents. This comes to mind, because I used to see a lot of hard working grandparents. I used to see exhausted grandparents. Often, I saw great grandparents in roles they shouldn't still be in. What is the job description of a grandparent? I think we need to look at this philosophically.

Job Description of a Grandparent/Great grandparent

A new day…

- Thank the Lord for another day;
- Feel your whole body is in working order, before getting out of bed;
- Thank the Lord for small miracles;
- Put your teeth in;
- Get up and go to the toilet;
- Look out the window and assess the weather;

- Go and make a cuppa;
- Sit down, you've done enough already;

…and age.

This is a bit much, isn't it? I've got you in your dotage. I must be talking about great-grandparents. I'll try again.

Is this any kind of a day?

- Get up with the alarm, or you'll be late;
- Get the bed made, and throw down some breakfast;
- Put a load of washing on before you go;
- Grab your trackies and get dressed;
- Take that leftover stew from the fridge and put it in a bag to take with you;
- Let the dog out;
- What's the time? Get cracking;
- Get in the car and pick up those few things from the shop that your daughter requested;
- Arrive at your daughter's place, and watch her fly out the door to work. She looks immaculate;
- Greet the grandkids with your hands full, and let them jump all over you, because they're just happy to see you;
- You have three here, but others are spread out all around the place. You have other responsibilities in other suburbs;
- You get straight to work, and get breakfast ready for the grandkids. They make a mess;
- One's got a foul nappy, so you change it, and wonder why your daughter didn't do it; You don't have to wonder for long;
- You wipe the vegemite out of the middle child's hair, and tell the eldest to clean her teeth;
- The dog's eating the leftover toast and honey off the floor, so you put the dog outside;
- You look at the time, and know you've got to get one to school;

- The baby's crying, and you pick him up and put him in the high chair. The baby's eighteen months old;
- You get a look at the eldest child's head as she's bent over cleaning her teeth, and you go and put your glasses on;
- Yep, it's nits, and you don't know whether to take her to school now, or not. You glance at the baby who now has snot running down his nose, with his fist rubbing in it, so you make a decision that school is the best place for nits;
- The middle grandkid's a bugger, and has ripped up the eldest grandkid's drawing from the fridge. She's making a song and dance about it;
- You tell her to go and put her uniform on, and she says it's in the wash;
- You make your way to the laundry in trepidation, and look for the uniform. It's there in the dryer, thank God! You throw it on the ironing board for a quick press;
- You've forgotten the baby, who's now screaming the place down, and you're now paranoid about what the neighbours are thinking;
- You pick the baby up, and realize you'd buggered up the disposable nappy, and it's falling off; Your glasses are knocked from your head by a flailing baby hand, and you've got to iron the uniform;
- You do a quick job, while the baby crawls through all the unwashed clothes at your feet;
- You look around at the disarray, and feel sorry for your daughter;
- Okay, so you dress the middle child in odd clothes, because you can't find anything decent. It's all in the ironing basket that can't even be seen, under the monstrous pile of crinkled clothing;
- Shoes are not where they should be, and you can't find enough to go around. You throw on any old

thing, as long as it has a matching other. "Get your shoes", you trill at the eldest, because you can feel your stress level is rising to great heights;
- You get all three kids in your little car, and the middle kid promptly kicks off the shoes you so hurriedly tied the laces for;
- You've forgotten the baby seat. Back to the house with the baby in your arms, as you search everywhere for where your daughter's left it. You search the garage and finally see it amongst a hell of a mess of sports equipment, and boating gear. It's a nightmare. The garage is packed with stuff. Expensive stuff. It's lying around forgotten;
- You lug the car seat out under one arm and strap it in the car, with baby still on your hip. Your hip is aching;
- The other two are fighting;
- You drive to the school and walk the child in through the gates, as instructed by your daughter. "She always likes to walk in the gate with you, and the teachers insist on it now";
- You're looking exhausted as you make eye contact with others, the same age as you, doing the same job as you. You have empathy by the bucket load, for all your reflections;
- You head home. No you don't! You head back to your daughter's unholy mess. Her large and disorganized home, with the in-ground swimming pool, the spa in the pergola, and the boat in the carport. She has the big screen TV, and all the other paraphernalia with speakers set up throughout the ducted, airconditioned house. He has the hot-rod, and his Harley, and they do very well for themselves. They go to Bali every year, and leave you with the kids. They spend up big, because they're both on good money. They have important jobs to do;

- You take the baby in, and you simply have to bathe him, because he just stinks and you're noticing what looks like cradle cap on his scalp. You grimace with distaste. The other one's raced inside, and no you didn't lock the door when you left the house earlier;
- He's now squirting you with a water pistol;
- You yell at him, but you don't want to, and you feel bad for doing it. You turn the TV on;
- "I want this show, I want that show" is all you can hear as you pack the dishwasher, and clean up bits of last night's dinner and the morning's breakfast;
- You open some blinds and windows, and then wish you hadn't, because you just got a glance at the backyard, and know you'll have to talk your husband into coming around with the lawnmower. He doesn't mind helping out with a bit of gardening, as long as the kids keep out of his way;
- You consider how busy your daughter is, and the important jobs that her and her husband do, and know they work so hard. You're feeling a tad guilty for the venomous thoughts that come and go through your rebellious mind;
- You know there's a frown in place on your forehead, but you know that this is the first thing that turns up when you visit your daughter's household;
- You feel bad again, because your daughter just hasn't got anyone else she can trust with her precious kids. This is what she tells everyone. "I wouldn't trust anyone but Mum with my kids";
- You throw a load of washing on;
- You run the bath for the baby, and just as you have him undressed and ready, the phone rings. You answer the phone with the child on your hip, and you're hoping you wiped his bum well when you changed his nappy earlier;

- As you're trying to get off the phone from the phone company, you see the streak of vegemite smudged across your thigh, and realize that your reflections would have picked up on it when you were back at the school. It isn't a good look. It's not a good reflection;
- You bathe the baby, while your middle grandchild races a matchbox car up and over your back, and through your hair;
- You yell again, and he runs off. You dry the baby off and wonder at the silence, and think of the unlocked door;

Sorry I can't even get to morning tea time, because I'm exhausted just typing all this out. I'm going! I'm not enabling this. This is pathetic. It's not my responsibility. Is it yours? Is this a bad reflection? This was just three hours in the life of a grandparent. I bet you know a grandparent like this one. I feel sorry for her. No I don't!

Life. Be in it

Is this the life for a grandparent? Have you got déjà vu? If you're a grandparent, and you're doing something similar, you need your head read. For your information, déjà vu means something different.

> Déjà vu:- [Fr., already seen] 1. Psychol. the illusion that one has previously experienced something actually new to one; 2. anything which is unoriginal: said esp. of the arts.

Been there, done that

If you're a grandparent, you've already done this bit. Your bits are done, you duffer! You've completed the parenting role, and you're through to the next level. Your daughter and son-in-law have to go through this level, before they go to the next level. They'll fail if they cheat, and let you do this level for them. You're not them. They're not you. While you're busy feeling so sorry for them, who's feeling sorry for you? You're an enabler. Your job should be as follows:-

Wake up

Only see the grandkids when you want to (special occasions), and only with a pleasant time in mind. Don't spend too long with them, because they'll become irritating. Grandparents should have a lovely relationship with their grandkids, so keep it short and happy. Grandkids will only love a grandparent who they remember as being happy to be around. The relationship can be just love and happiness. Nothing more than this is required. No baggage. That means no nappies and shit. No baggage means to know baggage when you see it.

Be a good memory

Grandparents can be great memories for kids. Everyone wants to remember their grandparents fondly. Don't stuff it up for the grandkids, and don't stuff it up for yourself. Say 'no'. Fill your days with social outings, and with better reflections, or join a club. Do some volunteer work and start some hobbies. Learn to do what you've always wanted to learn to do. Take a course.

Make the transition to grandparent wisely

This is the time of your life, that you've waited your whole life for. This is your free time. It's your time to be free, and this means carefree. Take the van and piss off for a while. You have no timetable. You're not obligated to family. They're just family, and they have their own family now. They're people that you love, but love isn't baggage. Don't take them on your trip as baggage. Don't be their baggage either.

Too much grandparent to be special

You're not being loved by your daughter. You're not being loved by your grandkids. You're being taken advantage of. You're not the special grandparent you want to be, because they see too much of you. And you're seen as the hired help. You don't want quantity time. You want quality time.

Your daughter had you as a parent, and she doesn't need you like she once did. She's now a parent. Your daughter is not more important than you. Her time is not more valuable than yours. They have their own family now, and with that comes responsibility. It's their responsibility. Who said it was your responsibility? Did you spawn the kids? You spawned your daughter, but she's no longer a kid.

You're no longer the immediate family
Sorry to have to break it to you, but you shouldn't be 'immediate' any more. Your family has grown up and left. If they haven't left yet, and they're over the age of twenty-five, you're in real trouble. It's your trouble, so you'll have to fix it. The trouble is how you've made it no trouble. Make it trouble. It's a troubling situation. It will cause you more and more trouble, in the long run.

Enable your wonderful life
Do you remember taking your first child on his first day of school? Remember how he didn't want you to leave, and he wanted to go back home with you? He was kicking and screaming, demanding to go home, and you left him there. You had to, because the child needed to go to school. This is what all kids do at a certain age, and it's just a part of growing up. Tell your twenty-five-year-old child to grow up and leave.

Done and dusted
I was just thinking of my own kids then, but they've both gone. They've had to find another nest for us all. They've flown off and found their own home. I have a seventeen year old son, and twenty-year-old daughter. I won't have the sort of trouble some parents seem to have with their young. I sure as hell, can't wait to see my grand kids though. I'll so enjoy them. They'll be the apple of my eye. They'll be a gift, and not my job. I don't want another job, but I do want the joy. My kids are pure joy to me. That's pure!

Cross it off

Don't make a rod for your own back. This can mean... don't make a cross for yourself to carry. Grand kids don't want to be a rod or a cross, for you to bear.

Get paid to do a job

If you're the aforementioned grandparent, go and get yourself a job. You'll earn great money, and you can pay someone to clean your house and mow your lawn. You'll get respect, and your services will be respected. You can get your nails done, and enjoy the theatre once a month. There's more to life than being a grandparent, but there can be less to life in being a grandparent if you don't do it right.

No more driving

It's your choice, not theirs. You are the grandparent, so you must decide what you do. They're the parents, so they must decide what they do. It's their choice, because they're now the parents, not you. You take the back seat now. You're no longer in control. Being a grandparent isn't a job.

Finished...

If we get too many more grandparents doing more than their job, it could become a stereotype, and grandparents everywhere may think they have to conform to it. This is how cultures are started. Don't put pressure on your own kind. Don't be a reflection. It's hard enough having to do parenting once, without having to do it a second time, with somebody else's kids. If that sort of Grand parenting takes off, grandparents will have nothing to look forward to. This is how it spreads to great-grandparents. Imagine having to try and do it a third time. Grand kids shouldn't be a burden.

Grand, isn't always that grand

In primitive cultures the elderly are revered for their wisdom. They have skills to teach the young ones, but they also have wisdom to convey. They have authority over certain things, because they have experience. They're respected. They also have special privileges, because they've earned them. They are the wise ones.

Wise up!

The older you get, the more say you should have. Is this a wise statement? Do you think there's some truth in it? At about what age, can I expect to have my say? I say, I say, I say. Why did the punk cross the road? To spew on the chook! Boom, boom! I don't think this joke is lame enough yet. How long do I have to wait, and how will I know when I'm old? Is the quality of your joke, a good indication? Should you measure the generation gap by a joke? How big is the gap of a generation?

Don't over generate

Has this been measured before? I could be onto something here. How do you measure a generation? I don't have to measure the generation, just the gap between. Measuring the gap between my generation, and my kid's generation is a bit harder, because I'm biased. Is it really a gap? Is it a black hole? I can't measure myself. I guess it's a comparison of some sort, but what would I compare?

Don't generalize them

Some people criticize the modern generation, and make comparisons to their own generation. Generations can't be measured. How can you measure a generation that grew up in a different era? One generation simply can't have the same conditions as another. What they do and say, will be different. Who created the modern generation? Who is responsible for the next generation? It's a line of dominoes. Who decides who wins? The generation that wins, is the generation that survives.

Be generous to the next generation

I must admit, I'm glad I'm not part of one of the earlier generations. I'm glad I didn't live in a generation from back in the early 1900s. And now that I think about it, I wouldn't want to be part of any other generation but my own. It's all I really know. I'm more informed about my generation, than any other generation. I get my generation.

> **Generation:-** n. 1. the producing of offspring; 2. production; 3. a single stage in the succession of descent; 4. the average period (c. 30 years) between the birth of successive generations; 5. all the people born at about the same time.
>
> **Generation gap:-** the difference in outlook, resulting in lack of understanding, between people of different generations.

You can't judge another generation. You haven't got the same perspective as them. You'll most certainly have a different viewing point. 'The Gap' isn't a good viewing point.

From my viewing point, I see great things in the modern generation. I'm talking about my kids' generation. I'm not talking about my kids specifically, but I've had opportunity to observe their friends. I see and hear young people all the time. I live at the beach, so young people flock to this area.

They don't have to accept what our generation tells them

I think their generation is a more accepting generation. I can see the good in this new generation. I recognize the bad in my own. Is it just progress? Progress isn't always good progress, but some of it is. Has their generation been taught to accept people who are different?

I say this, thinking of minority groups. I think that when generations progress, they just become more adaptable to new things. I think my generation, has a responsibility push them along, and not hold them back. We've got to allow them to make their own judgments, based on what they've learned, not what we've learned. We need to let them come up with their own ideals for themselves, so that their generation can be a better generation.

This is pointed. It's pointed at the younger generation. What's been generated?

Can you degenerate a generation?

It's good for the new generation to reflect on where the last generations have gone wrong. It's important for them to see where our mistakes lie. The new generation will no doubt see the mistakes of past generations, and try to fix the mistakes in theirs. Each new generation must look back to see what was wrong with the last generation, so they can make a difference in theirs. This is what generational change is. There's so much more to it, and it shouldn't be a blame game. It should be a learning game. We have much to learn about ourselves, by the following generations.

> **Degenerate:-** adj. [< L. *de-*, from + *genus*, race] having sunk below a former or normal condition, etc.; deteriorated –n. a degenerate person, esp. one who is morally depraved –vi. –at'ed, -at'ing, to lose former normal or higher qualities –degen'eracy n. –degen'erately adv. –degen'erative adj.

Progress doesn't stop with the new generation. We must progress too. Progressive societies are enlightened societies. Modern societies need to be modern. Modern is new. Old fashioned is old. What is the middle ground? Is this my generation? This is where I feel I am. I don't feel old, and I don't feel young. I just feel in between. My body shows signs of ageing, and I'll have to wear that. My mind is old-fashioned sometimes, but I try to be open-minded about new things now, and I try to keep up to date with what's important. It's in *The Knowing* – what's important, and what isn't, and that seems to be the most important bit.

Read *The Knowing in Me*, to know

I read quite recently in my local paper, of a new drug that can help a smoker's lungs to self-repair. This is a new drug which is still being researched and tested, but it's great news for smokers. I was happy to hear about this, and so were my lungs.

RPA – Restoring people's average

I was ecstatic the night I saw the lung transplant on RPA. I love modern medicine. It's incredible what cures we have now, compared to my grandparent's day. Can everyone afford it? This is what I want to know. Are all these modern cures available to everybody? Is the Hippocratic Oath being adhered to? We want a fair society, don't we? Freedom for all, and fairness for all, is a democratic society, isn't it?

Are we truly democratic, when it comes to health? Who's out of line? I mean, who doesn't have to wait? I think I'll be in a line soon. I hope my wait, isn't too late. How long do others wait?

Restore the balance

I saw a woman wait too long recently. She was in the right place, because she was in the emergency waiting room of a public hospital. I'm warning you, that I'm about to let loose an emotional rant here, because I can feel it building in me as I write.

She stood at the counter for what must have been twenty minutes, at least. Nobody came to attend her. By the time she got someone's attention, she could hardly speak. She explained that her tongue had swollen up after eating something. They told her to sit down and wait, and I saw her leave.

Where do you go in an emergency?

It was after midnight. I wondered where she went. I thought she should have gone out into the street and called an ambulance. Why couldn't the nurse have listened to her properly, and made her more comfortable? This woman looked to be about sixty and she was alone. Where can someone go when they need help? Maybe she did call an ambulance. At least the ambulance attendants would have been able to help her in case she stopped breathing.

Restoring our pride and prejudice

While I was at the hospital, my son and I were taken into triage and asked to wait. While we were there, we were privy to many personal conversations between the medical staff and the patients. They were conversations about the likelihood of pregnancy, antidepressants, and bowel movements. There was more, but I won't embarrass you with it. These were young patients sitting in consulting rooms with the doors ajar. They were suffering already. They were spoken to, in a robotic voice, with no feel for their dignity or sensibilities. I was embarrassed to be hearing such personal information about sick and vulnerable people.

Who am I to judge?

When we're sick, we're at our most vulnerable. We are, at our most sensitive at these times. Is anyone sensitive to other peoples' sensitivities anymore? We have all these privacy laws, but there's no privacy. I wonder why a consulting room has a door.

A consulting room needs a door, doesn't it? The door is for closing. A door is for privacy. There was holly around this door, and this should answer the door for that insensitive Doctor.

I'm done

Do you know why there are so many people in hospital waiting rooms now? It's because they have an emergency. You don't have to pay a $60 consultation fee at a public hospital.

What's emerged…

Doctor's surgeries aren't open till late nowadays, and doctors don't make house calls like they once did. You have to wait a long time for an appointment to see a doctor in a surgery, and often it can take days. How do people get doctor's certificates for a sick day now? Is having no money for medical expenses, an emergency?

Is a doctor's certificate a pass?
You wake up with stomach cramps and you know you're sick. You call work, and tell them you won't be in. They say, "No worries, just bring a Doctors certificate when you come back to work".

You ring the doctor, knowing that you ate something last night that didn't agree with you, and that it will soon pass. You're too sick to go into work, but not really sick enough to go to the doctor. The doctor will just tell you, "It will pass". He won't have to prescribe you anything, because you've just contracted a bug, and you're in for a bout of gastro. The last thing you want to do, when you have a bout of gastro, is to go out anywhere.

Paying for a sick day
You ring the surgery, and you can't get an appointment for another three days. You ring around, and you're not having much luck getting in anywhere. You give up. What's going to happen? Will you get paid your sick pay? Will the boss believe that you were sick? Will he insist he needs a doctor's certificate before he'll pay up? Will he trust you were sick?

Pass it to him
Instead of taking the doctors certificate, get a specimen jar, and 'shit through the eye of a needle' into it. Screw the cap back on, and take it to work with you. Give it to your boss. I bet he pays you for it. It's sure to pass muster.

When employees are treated like liars, thieves, and slobs, from the outset, how will they act? If you don't respect your employees, they won't respect you. It's just trust.

Did I respect my employees? I've sat here for a long time. I've sat here wracking my brain, trying to think of anything that I've said or done, that was disrespectful treatment. I'm still here, because I don't want to give any bullshit. I want to be truthful, and if I think of something that I've done, that was a sign of disrespect, I'll confess it. I don't mind confessing. It's not easy being a boss.

I've never asked to sight a doctor's certificate

I've got to have done it, haven't I? Ten years in business is a long time, but I haven't had many employees in that time. I rarely had to replace staff. I even had staff come back. I've had staff wanting to come back, after they'd handed in their resignation. I'm still waiting for the answer to arrive in my head, but I've got nothing. I'll wait now, because if something pops into my head later, I promise I'll air it. I want to learn by it. I want to learn something about it all.

How did I gain their respect?

Is flying your staff interstate, and taking them out to a popular theatre restaurant that evening, a good Christmas party? What about paying for all the entertainment on both days of the weekend, and for the four-star accommodation? Is this better than having a few drinks and crackers in the office on Christmas Eve? What does it mean?

I paid for it

I know what it means now. It means I was an idiot. I've been an idiot in lots of ways. Many people treated me like an idiot. People take advantage of idiots. I've learned this the hard way. I'm no longer an idiot.

Insular and small

Is this a good heading? Do you want to come under this heading? Do small communities come under this umbrella? Does it keep the rain off them? How do you make a small, insular and shallow community, into a big broad minded and deep community? Which community would you choose? It's the big and small of it, that you're having the trouble with, isn't it? Do you prefer small? Are you small? Are you hiding?

Is community work a protest? What is it for? Is it altruistic? What is the motivation? I guess there are many motivations, but I don't think they're all altruistic. I must ask myself the question.

What was my motivation?

It was for approval, and to repay a debt to the community. It was to incur the debt of a community. As I continued, it became an obligation. Once I'd got involved in it, I started to enjoy it, and it became pleasurable. I enjoyed the people I was in contact with, and I felt that I was helping to connect a community of people. Were they like-minded people?

I liked the feel of a community coming together for a common cause. I had too many causes to be there. I wished I'd just had one cause, and just the good cause. I wished that my community work could help people. There were people in the community that needed help. I tried to get them involved in the community work, but some members of a community can be off-putting. It's a shame you can't just put them off. They can be a real put-off sometimes.

> **Altruism:-** n. [< L. *alter*, another] unselfish concern for the welfare of others - al'truist n. -al'truis'tic adj.

The fairest of them all

I knew someone who was altruistic. I think he was just motivated by altruism. He wasn't particularly a protester, but he got things done slowly, and methodically, and to the best of his ability. He always went the extra mile, and was the quiet achiever. He's a great example of a community leader, and a truly authentic person. He was open-minded and accepting, and these are great qualities to have. Often these qualities aren't appreciated by others, but they were appreciated and admired by me. He was a positive person, and was positive he was on the right track. I'm positive about this. He made me feel positive about people, and about myself. I hope he stays positive around all that negativity.

Why is it so?

Why isn't it possible for committees and community groups to stay positive? Why can't everyone just get along? Is it because their motivations are different? Are their aims conflicting? Should everyone be agreeable to the aim of the group, before being part of it? Is it competition and power, that's in play?

I've observed these problems, and I'm resigned to the fact, that some things just shouldn't get mixed up, in what should be altruistic endeavours.

I should never have got involved

I wanted to be involved, but without the baggage that I was holding on to. What's the answer to peaceful community groups? Is it peaceful people? You get more bees with honey. This isn't always true, because I've seen wasps flock to honey when it's too sweet. Wasps can give you an unholy sting.

Why does niceness, sometimes get seen as weakness? It's not, it's strength and power. To be nice, when facing the enemy is empowerment. It's strength of character. It's also a win, for the good side.

To continue to be nice in the face of opposition, is strength of purpose. It's courage. I think we can get mixed up with what courage is, and isn't. There's a song that comes to mind, and I think it's an old protest song from the 60s. 'We Shall Not Be Moved'. It's about inner resolve. It's about standing your ground in a peaceful way, but not budging an inch. It's about not being swayed from your purpose by others. I've learned this from the fairest of them all. He was born with wit. He was born intuit.

A paltry protest

I have a little protest going. I have lots of protests going. My old protests are going, and I've got new protesting to do. I'm a protester for fairness. This is just the middle ground I'm standing on, and it's a great place to view both sides.

> **Paltry:-** adj. -trier, -triest [prob.< LowG. *Palte*, rag] worthless; trifling; petty -pal'triness n.

This old man, he played four. He played knick-knack on my door, with a knick-knack, paddy wack, give a dog a bone, this old man came rolling home. Old Mother Hubbard went to her cupboard to get her poor dog a bone. When she got there, the cupboard was bare, and so the poor dog had none. What can you read from this? How much is that doggy in the window. Woof! Woof! The one with the waggly tail? Woof! Woof! How much is that doggy in the window? Wolf, wolf. I do hope that doggy's for sale. How can I keep the Wolf from my door?

I can't do the dog!

The little dog laughed to see such fun, and the dish ran away with the spoon. I can't feed the dog. The dog wants dog food and kibble. I never wanted the dog in the first place. We'd had dogs in the past, and I didn't want to take on the responsibility again. He wanted a dog, and so did the kids.

We'd been in this Hoorah less than twelve months, when we had a home invasion. This is how I got talked into getting the dog. When the police came, they advised getting a dog to warn off unwanted intruders. I like the dog. It warns me of unwanted intruders. I need the dog. I need the dog for company. A dog isn't much company, but it's the sort of company I want in my life lately. I haven't lost any credibility with her. She doesn't judge me.

A dog of a judge

She'll be judging me soon, if I don't feed her. I hate asking the kids for money. They've barely got enough for themselves.

Hi ho, hi ho, it's off to work – I won't go!

I hear a voice, and I don't know whether it's emanating from your head or mine. It says, "Go and get a job!"

I know I could get a job if I wanted to. I know how to sell myself to an employer. I have qualifications I can rely on, to get me a decent job. This makes me want to cry as I'm writing it. I feel weak and weepy, and I know I just can't do a job. I don't want to, and I'm afraid to. I can't do it, because I'm scared. I'm scared people will figure out who I am, and I don't want anyone knowing who I am, or what's happened to me. I don't want anyone to know my story. I can't bear the thought of being judged by another, single, person!

I'm the accused

I guess in a way, and I can't believe I'm about to say it, but I've lost my confidence. I simply can't do people. I can't do people any more. I don't want to know any more people. I've known too many people. I don't think I've lost confidence in myself, but I've most definitely lost confidence in people. That's sad!

Freaked out about what I know

I'm a freak! Who freaked me out? I haven't told the kids this, but I think they understand. I don't think they want me to put up with people either. They don't want me interrogated. I've had enough interrogations to last me a lifetime. I've had person to person, and phone interrogations. I've had plenty of terror.

I was interror-gated

I was interrogated by the police, the night I came home. The kids were glad to see me, and I was glad to see them. We didn't talk about what happened. I kept it to myself. I haven't told a soul. I didn't tell the police what happened either. I was a missing person. I was missing in action. It wasn't that good a story, but it was indeed a story. It's a story I haven't told, for a very good reason. It's locked up inside me for the time being. It's safe.

The kids would freak!

I received a funny gift from my kids for Christmas. We didn't have much money for gift giving, so we had funny presents. My kids gave me a red studded dog collar with a pendant attached. The pedant is engraved at the front, with the following:-

>Hi,
>My name is
>(My Name)

On the back is as follows:-

>If found, please
>Return her to
>Her children who
>Love her very
>Much.

I've never had a dog collar before, and I can understand how some people would find it offensive, but I love this dog collar. I guess they collared me for running away. That's what dogs do sometimes. They just dig themselves a hole under a fence, and slip out undetected. What makes a dog want to escape? You're missing the point entirely. I'm not a dog. I'm not a bitch!

I'm a bird. Not a jailbird. I'm not a raving lunatic. I can rave on, but I'm not a lunatic. There was method to my madness.

Lunatic:- adj. [< L. *luna*, moon] 1. [Rare] a) insane b) of or for insane persons.

Lunatic asylum:- [Rare] a mental hospital.

Lunatic fringe:- the minority considered fanatical in any political, social, or other movement.

I have a fringe

The dictionary's telling me it's rare, but I've known plenty of lunatics. My grandmother, it is said, used to scream this at her husband. "You bloody lunatic!" she'd say in exasperation. I shouldn't put this insult in quotes, because I never heard her say it. He was dead before I was born. He apparently spent time in lunatic asylums. I would love to know the reason for this. I don't want to know all of this, but I do want to know why. I just want to know the reason why he went. Did someone else make him see reason?

Did anyone look for the reason?

I want the deep answer to this, not the surface one. On the surface, I'm told it was depression, and it was recurring depression. I want to know what had caused it. What was buried way down underneath? I want the whole story, but I've only got bits. I think I might have the right bits.

I might have to ask the lunatic fringe. I think the lunatic fringe had more of a political punch, than she ever let on. I've been told bits, but bits need to go together to form a picture.

> **Bit:-** n. [< OE. *bite*, a bite] 1. the metal mouthpiece on a bridle, used for controlling the horse; 2. anything that curbs or controls; 3. a drilling or boring tool for use in a brace, etc. -vt. bit'-ted, bit'ting, to put a bit into the mouth of (a horse) -take the bit between one's teeth, to be beyond control.
>
> **Bit:-** n. [< OE. *bita*, a piece] 1. a) a small piece or quantity b) a limited degree [a bit bored] c) a short time; 2. [U.S. Colloq.] 12 ½ cents; 3. a small part, as in a play -adj. very small [a bit role] -bit by bit, little by little -do one's bit, to do one's share.
>
> **Bit:-** n. [b(inary)(digit)] Computers, a unit of information representing the physical state of a system having one of two values, such as, on or off.
>
> **Bitch:-** n. [< OE. *bicce*] 1. the female of the dog, wolf, etc.; 2. [Derog.] a bad-tempered, malicious, woman 3. [Slang] anything unpleasant -vi. [Slang] to complain -bitch'iness n. -bitch'y adj.

Why have I kept going straight to the next word in the dictionary? I haven't used up all my bits yet. I've got more bits to go. I'm just doing my bit for justice. Every little bit counts. You'll find the bit that adds up all these bits. I'm not running low on bits yet. I've saved up enough bits to last me a lifetime.

Bits just keep coming to light. When I shine the light, I just find more bits I didn't see before.

Be careful changing light bulbs

It's kind of like dropping a light bulb. You have these thin slithers of glass, splinters lighter than a feather, and hard to see. You have to get right up close, to see them. You must be careful to pick up every piece methodically. They're incredibly sharp, and can slice your skin easily, and without you even feeling it. The only way you know you've been wounded, is when you see the blood. You must make sure to pull these tiny bits out. You don't want them getting embedded in your skin. If a bit does get embedded, you'll be aware of it, but probably won't be able to see it. Like a splinter, you can always tell that there's still a bit in there.

> **Embed:-** vt. -bed'ded, -bed'ding 1. to fix firmly in a surrounding mass; 2. to fix in the mind, etc.

Can things like this get caught up in our system, and travel around our body? I've heard said that they can, and I remember something like this happening to me once. I could never explain it, and I wouldn't mind knowing more about it. Have you ever heard anything like it?

The human body is extraordinary. Can this be so, when it is so ordinary, amongst so many human bodies? If you put human bodies beside every living body, I think you'll find that it is indeed quite extraordinary. It's more than ordinary, next to an animal's body. Animal's bodies aren't ordinary either.

Think of the bluebottle for instance. Do you know anything about bluebottles? I've had the biology of bluebottles explained to me by my son, and I'm not an expert, so I don't know the scientific name. I've just tried to look it up in my book *The Invertebrata* but this really isn't my line of work. I don't have access to the information I need, to work out its scientific name. The dictionary doesn't know it either.

Bluebottle:- n. 1. a large blowfly with a steel-blue abdomen; 2. [Aust.] a small marine animal with a blue sac, and one long threadlike tentacle, inflicting a painful sting; 3. [Old Slang] a policeman.

My dictionary tends to be a bit sexist, and refers to men, way more than women. Perhaps it's just being a gentleman. Have you ever been stung by a bluebottle? I have.

Blue collar:- adj. designating or of industrial workers, esp. the semiskilled and unskilled.

Yep! Stung again.

Blue pointer:- a large Australian shark, having a blue back and pointed snout.

Scrap the one above, because it has a backbone.

Blue:- adj. [< OFr. *bleu*] 1. having the colour of the clear sky; 2. having a blue tinge through cold or anger: said of the skin; 3. sad and depressing; 4. [Colloq.] indecent –n. 1. the colour of the clear sky; 2. any blue pigment or dye; 3. anything coloured blue; 4. a supporter of the British Conservative party; 5. a) a sportsman who has represented his university, esp. at Oxford or Cambridge b) the badge awarded to him; 6. [pl.] [Colloq.] a depressed, unhappy feeling; 7. [pl., also with sing. V.] Negro folk music, or the jazz evolved from it, with slow tempo and melancholy words; 8. [Aust. Slang] an argument or fight; 9. [Aust. Slang] a summons; 10. [Aust. Slang] a mistake; 11. [B-] [Aust. Colloq.] a nickname for a person with red hair –vt., vi. blued, blu'ing or blue'ing, to make or become blue –once in a blue moon, very seldom –out of the blue, as if from the sky; unexpected –blue'-ness n.

I didn't expect it

It's a mistake, isn't it? Did I get stung? Yep. This one stung more than the others. This one still stings, even now. It stings, because I can't get those invisible barbs out. They're still in there. Every now and then, they just erupt and ooze out more poison, and it stings all over again.

Blue heeler:- [Aust.] a dog with dark speckled markings, used for herding cattle.

I used to respect it

Are Blue Heelers loyal dogs? Are they just loyal to whoever feeds them? Is it about what you feed them, or how much of it? Can dogs read? Can dogs read between the lines? Can dogs read signs? A blue heeler is just a sheep dog. Is a blue heeler sheepish?

It was bloody yarra to drive home that night

I wasn't annoyed about not getting called last night. It happened at around 11.00 pm, I believe. He was on his own, in the pitch-black night. It was a long and winding, lonely bush road. The road was wet and slippery, and not lit up at all. It was stormy weather outside as he listened to his music and drove towards home. He tried to slow down before the bend, but the car skidded as he took the turn, and he lost control.

Was it within his control?

Did the car lose control, or did he lose control of the car? Can you lose control of your car? I've lost control of my car before. It kind of takes over, and reacts to the conditions. The conditions were bad last night, and once the car hit the edges, it lost it. It was totalled. Right up against a tree. The air bags inflated. He didn't really have control.

The control is in place now

Every time he gets in a car, he thinks about the accident. The accident keeps flashing back through his mind, over, and over, again. He's still in shock. He's suffering from trauma, and he's tired and fatigued. He has some minor lacerations, bruises, and sore ribs. He's lucky. I'm lucky, and his sister's lucky. All three of us are very lucky. We're lucky we all still have each other. We're lucky we can tell the story.

He's lost the control of his car

He's grieving the loss of his car. It's understandable. The car represented more than just a car. The car was his escape and his compensation. The car was what he identified with, when all the drama was happening in our lives. That car represented his safety, security, and independence. He loved the status of that car. It transported him. Not just literally, or metaphorically, but psychologically. The car gave him his rights as a person. He felt it gave him some control over a situation he had no control over. That car gave him the joy he'd lost.

Sometimes there's no substitute

He only had it insured for third party, so it's gone. It's gone to the wreckers, and it's probably now worth the cost of the tow. It should have been insured for more. Why don't we have hindsight? He was worried about how much it was costing. So was I. Things cost money. Hindsight wouldn't have mattered. This is what he's learning. It's been a very big learning curve. Last night was a very good learning curve. It was a good and bad curve. He got taken off his path. It's set him back a bit now. Hindsight is expensive, because it's a valuable lesson.

His first port of call in a storm

He called his big sister first. She came with her boyfriend in the middle of the night, and went to her baby brother. They love each other fiercely. She cried when she saw him and his car wreck. All three of them hugged each other in the pouring rain in the middle of the night, at the side of that dark and treacherous road.

She took him home, made him a cup of tea, and put him to bed. She rang me this morning and broke the news. I guess they didn't want to worry me last night. They just got it sorted out by themselves, together. I couldn't have done much more anyway. I couldn't have done a better job of it myself. I'd already done my job with my pair. They'll always have each other to fall back on.

Bonds. James Bond

This is an important bond for them to have. They've always had this bond. It's unbreakable. It's well known amongst their peers, and it's been forged with both happiness, and sadness. It works both ways, for them both. It's a bond that's respected by their respectable others. I mean her boyfriend, and his girlfriend, respectively.

I respect their bond. It's a bond separate from me. It's a bond that I encouraged when they were littlies. It's a bond that's grown and matured. It's incredibly strong. I can't get between it, because it's too powerful for me. It stands behind me, and props me up when I need it. Our word is our bond.

He's out of the car

I've seen the car. It's a mess. I'm sad. I see the car without him in it. I see what that car had meant. That car was a good car, and I bonded with it too. We bonded when I took that long trip up to Far North Queensland and back. I'd bonded with that car. That car meant escape to me. It was the escape car. That car had journeyed through our crisis with us.

Can you judge a person, by the damage?

I'm not sad for the car. I'm just sad for him, because his sadness is infectious. He feels ashamed, but he shouldn't. I don't judge him, because my judgment means nothing. I too, had a car accident at about his age. I remember it all too well.

Can you judge the damage, by a person?

He's judged himself. He's been judged. I told him it was an accident. It's just poor judgment. It wasn't intentional, and it's something that we can all learn from.

Judgments we make about road conditions, can only be learned through our own experiences. Judging road conditions, distance, traffic and such, are only judgments we can make more accurately through experience. Only once we've experienced what can happen, can we know to be aware of it the next time we're in a similar situation.

I caused some damage

I wrote my car off, when I was not much older than him. It was a Datsun 180B, with a black vinyl top. I still remember the sudden impact, the sound, and the silence afterwards. I wasn't on a lonely bush road in the middle of the night. I didn't have the situation and circumstances in my life that my son's had in his life, over the last twelve months. He's learning that security is a myth, and that he has less control in life than he thinks.

We don't always bring these things on ourselves. We don't always attract them by poor choices or behaviour. Sometimes we can be doing all the right things, and disaster just strikes out of the blue. I don't know what the situation was, because only he knows that. I know that he knows something more now. It's his lesson, and I'm grateful it was a lesson he can learn from, and not a lesson he couldn't go on to learn from. In my view, he's gone forwards and not backwards.

The best lessons are the hardest lessons

Young people need lessons. You can't always teach them everything, because they must experience things for themselves. That's life. Some lessons are out of my hands. I can't wrap him up in cotton wool, but I'd like to. I'd love to be able to insulate my kids from all the crap that life throws at them, but they wouldn't grow up healthy if I did. Growth is important. Growth is spiritual.

He's grown overnight. I can see it plainly. He's stranded now with no transport. He doesn't want to go anywhere. He wants to stay home. He needs to recover his equilibrium. I know he'll be doing lots of thinking today. I'm doing a bit of thinking myself. I'm thinking of a way to fix things as usual, but I can barely fix things for myself now. I'm only just managing as it is. You can't always replace what's lost.

Getting value for money

It's a rainy day, so I've been to Medicare with the receipts I've been saving, and I've got some cash. It's not much, but I wanted to cheer my son up. Does money cheer you up? I think money can cheer you up. Money can help you to feel better, depending on what it's used for. I think just having $55 in your pocket, when you only had $15 makes you feel better than you did. Forty dollars doesn't go far these days, but it goes further now than it used to. It goes way further. Money is precious now, and more valuable than it's ever been to all three of us. Its value has been keenly felt. We've never felt its value so poignantly before. The value of life has become poignant too. His life, her life, and my life, have become poignant.

What is a hard question?

This is a hard question. Should I replace the car? When, or if, I get any money from the last Hoorah, should I fork out for another car? I bought him the X-Trail and it cost $11,000. It sounds like a big expense, but it was an important expense at the time. His father had made a poor choice at his son's expense. He continues to make poor choices at his son's expense. I've just answered this hard question, and it wasn't that hard after all. Fuck the expense!!!

The money is nothing, compared to what joy a car can bring to a suffering seventeen-year-old boy, going through his HSC, and all the other shit in his life. You can't measure something in terms of money all the time. If you've got the ability to help in some way, you just help. I think if I can get a car for him, I'll move heaven and earth to do it. It's for a good purpose. It's just compassion. It feels good to express compassion.

Money well spent

If my son had been driving a car like the one his father gave his daughter when she got her license, he'd be dead right now. My son simply wouldn't have survived. The money or the box?

Virtually happening, as we speak

Every day, life is full of topics. We have many of these topics in common. These are the topics of life. These are the very topics that can ruin our lives, or improve them. My topics are serious topics and funny topics, but they're honest topics.

I went to the bank today. I thought I was home and hosed. I asked how I could access $20,000 from the home loan. Our mortgage payments are in advance, thanks to me. I asked her if I could have it in cash, because I don't have a bank account, but she said that wasn't possible, and it would take a couple of days to process anyway. We decided the best way, was for me to open an account now, and the money could be deposited into it. I thought all was going well, and then the bank teller realized that she'd have to have the authorization of the other mortgagor.

What was I banking on?

I'd remembered doing every scrap of banking without him in the past. I never needed him, unless it was for the initial Mortgage papers. I know I've never required him before, so there must be something I'm missing.

Different people tell you different things

I'm not missing anything. I've rung the bank tonight, and they tell me that I don't need his authorization to access this money. I just need to ring them again on the day of collection, so that they can prearrange it with the branch, before I get there to pick it up. I can collect it in cash. As I'm writing this, I'm hoping I'm not putting the mockers on myself. I don't want to seem cocky, but it sounds like I might be in the money again.

I think I'll hold my breath for the moment. I wish I could go tomorrow, but it's a public holiday. It's Australia Day.

The Australia Day label

This is a topic that brings up some unwanted emotion in me. Australia Day seems to have some bad connotations attached to it now days. It seems to have been taken over by a sub-culture, and I think it will be forever changed in the minds of most Australians. Australian icons such as the Australian flag, and the Great Southern Cross, have been bruised and battered in Australia, by what I hope stays a minority group.

I wish we were minus this minority group. I think there's one of these minority groups in every suburb. The particular suburb with the worst reputation for this minority group, is a suburb now labelled and tainted, by what took place some years ago now. It will be forever in our memories, after watching people being chased and beaten by drunken brawlers and louts. These were sick people, with sick attitudes, and little in the way of brains. They were not thinkers, they were reactors. They were activists for unworthy and selfish ends. If only they could think. The whole suburb needs to think. "The Shire" needs to have a good think.

> **Activism:-** n. the policy of taking direct action, esp. for political or social ends. –ac'tivist adj., n.

I saw the footage of this bullying behaviour, and I was terrified. I was terrified for our society. If so many people could be attracted to an unfortunate rally as this, what could happen to our Australia?

It's not my judgment, just my thoughts

These were people whom I think, haven't thought individually. They've only seen and thought on the surface. I think they probably think so highly of themselves, that they don't think they have to think. They're short-sighted. They can only see themselves, and they can't see past that.

It was a demonstration of the dark insecurities lurking down deep in some people. They came to the surface. It demonstrated what can happen when a crowd becomes identified with one another.

> "Many social psychologists explain these acts, in terms of deindividuation, in which one loses one's sense of individuality and personal responsibility. In collective settings, people 'blend' into the crowd, achieving a sense of anonymity that causes them to assume less responsibility for their actions (Diener, 1980)"

This is from *Psychology* (3rd Ed.) eds G. Neil Martin, Neil R. Carlson & William Buskit.

I like to think, that this is just what happened with the majority of people, on that day. They lost their identities.

I want to know how strong their identities were, because I think this has a lot to do with it. Do they really know who they are? Is this the person they want to be?

Reinventing an identity

There's a certain culture that exists in this suburb, and similar suburbs. It's a culture that Australians have identified with for many years. I have identified with it, because I love the surf too. I don't have to be 'it'. I don't have to look like 'it'. Is it 'it' or 'in'? Is it about being 'in' the crowd? Why would you so desperately want to be 'in' the 'the' crowd? Is 'it' childish?

Don't be in the wrong crowd

Groups of children behave irresponsibly when they're all together. One follows the other, and so on. They lose their sense of responsibility. They can lose their sense of judgment as to the degree of mischief, when more children join the mischief making, but only if they forget themselves. Can your mischief get diluted with more people involved?

Am I a behaviourist?

Can bad behaviour be diluted, within a group of bad behaviourists? This is a poorly worded question and it's ambiguous, but I think it could fit into another topic. It's probably a more interesting topic. It's probably a topic some behaviourists are discussing right now.

Distracting the crowd

I'm not a psychologist, but I am an avid reader. I'm not just an avid reader of books. I read the scene, and the profiles. I put myself in the scene with everything I know. Then I think about it. I then sometimes read about it. I'm just reading other people's thoughts. I'm often using other people's studies and research, to back up my own theories. I love Google Scholar, but I'm not as connected as I used to be. I used to love having access to scholarly information. Lay people like me, need to be able to access this information, because we form part of society. Lay people like to think too.

I'm not going to include all the definitions that my dictionary has for 'lay'. I've got a good lay. My lay comes from Greece.

> **Lay:-** adj. [< Gr. *laos*, the people] 1. of the laity, as distinguished from the clergy; 2. not belonging to a given profession.

Lay doesn't mean lay about, but I do lay about a bit. I'm laying about today, reading this and that. I'm laying about, just thinking and observing. I'm thinking all the time about what's behind what I've observed. What's on observation, is not always a good observation of the situation. In some situations, people know they're being observed, and your observations of them, can be the very reason for the distortion of what you've observed. Don't be observed observing, if you want a true observation. I don't lie about much.

> **Layabout:-** n. [Colloq.] a lazy idler or loafer.

I probably look like a layabout, but I'm a scholar. I'm learning. I'm teaching myself. I'm a strict teacher sometimes. I'm dedicated to teaching myself as much as possible. I can't take all the credit, because I'm teaching with other people's work. I'm using their work to teach me what I don't know. This is what most teachers do. Many teachers already know what they're teaching, and they just teach by rote. Are they still teaching themselves? Does a teacher continue to learn? We'll learn about this, I've no doubt, in *The Teacher in Me*. I might even learn something. Can you teach and old teacher new teaching? Does a teacher already know it all?

I'm getting degrees

I've said this before, but I want you to know that I'm learning by degrees. I already have degrees of knowledge. I'm not stuck up about a degree. A degree can be the degree of time that you learn for. Is it about the degree of work you do? Shouldn't it be, the degree of knowledge that you have acquired? What degree of knowledge is remembered? Don't degree holders go off with their degrees, and then rely on books for information, to a certain degree?

I'm an autodidact

Will I have any credibility without a degree? Would a degree give me any credibility? If I could have any degree I wanted, I'd want a degree for thinking. You couldn't go wrong, because it wouldn't matter what you were thinking. You could think of good things, and bad things. You could think the right things, and the wrong things. A degree in thinking would cover the lot. It wouldn't matter what sort of thinking you did, so long as you could do it all. Would any thinking be censored? Nope. Can you break any rules by thinking? Yep. Thinking is thinking, but it does take time. It takes a lot of time up.

The Thinker in Me

'The Thinker' is a famous statue sculpted by a Frenchman by the name of Auguste Rodin. It cuts a solitary figure. I've never liked this statue. I must confess, I've only thought about why, just now. I've been repelled by this statue of a lone man, because of his somewhat closed-off sort of pose. It's not an open pose, or a flamboyant pose. He doesn't even look that composed. He's all sharp angles. I think he looks a bit troubled. He looks within, so he doesn't look like he wants company. If you read his body language, you can see he doesn't want to have a conversation with anyone. His body is warding off any unwelcome intruders from his solitary thinking world. He's way inside himself, and he's locked away from what's happening outside himself. He's deep in thought. It's a place we could all do with visiting more often.

Discover the hidden depths

Deep thought is a troubling place to go. You only travel there when you're desperate to know what the answers are. You brave the deep, for the new and unknown. There's not too many that venture down there. Not many people want to travel all the way, and there's so much just waiting to be discovered. It can get dark, and you can't always see where you're going. You need to have your eyes open wide, just like the fish from the very deep, deep. It's a whole new world.

Open wider please

Owls have big eyes. This is so they can see well at night. They're nocturnal. Nocturnal animals are awake at night, and this is when they're most active. An owl is said to be wise, and I think it's to do with the eyes. Is it to do with the dark?

> **Nocturnal:-** n. adj. [< L. *nox*, night] 1. of or happening in the night; 2. active during the night.

I've been an extrovert. I've carried on my life as an extrovert, but I've always secretly been an introvert. Does this make sense? Can it make sense? I've swapped, haven't I? I've become introverted, but I'm pretty sure I'm an extrovert privately. This is private. This book is private. I've been keeping it in the dark. I'm writing it to myself. I'm keeping it to myself, and keeping myself to myself. This is a lie. Sometimes bits slip out. I don't mean to be deceiving, but I want to keep you in the dark about some subjects close to my heart.

> **Nocturne:-** n. [Fr.] 1. a painting of a night scene; 2. a romantic, dreamy musical composition.

Trust the French to come up with a word like this. What sort of a scene would I paint for myself? I could try to Frenchify myself.

> **Frenchify:-** vt., vi. –fied, -fy'-ing, to make or become French or like the French.

Extra! Extra! Read all about it! Introvert turns extrovert, turns introvert, turns extrovert! Can it be averted? Will she revert? Will she revert to her former self? That's an overt statement. She's not perverted. Be on the alert for her covert, revert. Don't assert she's overt, she'll divert. She's inert for some dirt. Will she wear a shirt, and convert? That's pert! She won't spurt all the hurt. That's curt.

I'm amusing myself. I'm amused by myself. I'm amused at myself. I'm a muse. I'm my own muse. I love this word - it's inspiring.

> **Muse:-** n. [< Gr. *mousa*] 1. Gr. Myth. any of the nine goddesses who presided over literature, arts, and sciences; 2. [m-] the spirit regarded as inspiring a poet or artist.

> **Muse:-** vi. mused, mus'ing [< OFr. *Muser*, loiter] to meditate –vt. to think or say meditatively.

It's right up my alley, isn't it? Are you amused? I think my dictionary is my muse too, because it amuses me. When I think of the word 'muse', I usually think of an artist's beautiful study. I think of the beautiful siren reclining in a sensual pose for her lover, the artist.

I think love is the greatest muse of all time. I think if you have love, you can be inspired to create great things. Love can motivate you to great heights of passion. Art is passion, and love is art. Love is art, isn't it?

Love is at the art of 'it'

Are we supposed to be creating something great, when we make love? Is it a passionate performance? Is it a private performance for our lover? Do they inspire us to love with great passion? Here she goes again, crapping on about love again. Why? You do the thinking. You figure it out.

Am I just amusing myself?

How many muses should one have?

I have a muse right outside my window. This muse inspires a passion in me, but it's a negative kind of passion. It's fierce and encompassing, because it's my angry passion. It inspires anger now, where it used to inspire sympathy. I think I've outgrown the sympathy.

I watch him angrily mowing and clearing up the garden rubbish, and I see it as a form of justice. I'm feeling a bit smug, and a little satisfaction creeps over me. These are new feelings for me. It's about time he did something around here.

He was angry at the dog, but it's not the dog's fault. He was obviously angry at me, when he discovered his record albums in the 'Fuck Off Pile', because I watched him shuffle the soggy mess out to his car. Why would he think I would want to care for his stupid record albums, after he'd demonstrated how much he cared for me? Why would I care what happened to his shit, when he can't even give a shit about his kids? He shat on everything I cared about, so this tiny bit of justice is in some small way, rather satisfying, but it's not nearly enough to balance the scales? Cleaning up a bit of garden refuse in the rain, doesn't cut ice. I don't think it goes anywhere near enough, to evening up the score. I'd like to be compensated in some way, because I feel I'm worth a scrap more than some scraps.

Getting rid of the scraps

The kids haven't had a scrap from him, and they deserve more than that. They didn't deserve any of this. When you hurt and damage a relationship, shouldn't you compensate in some way for the damages incurred?

He always wants the same thing

He just wanted their sympathy. Why would he deserve their sympathy? He wasn't being very sympathetic last night at 12.30 am. Why did he feel it necessary to be texting nasty messages to his daughter at that time of night? She'd been up the night before looking after her brother, when he should have been taking care of his son. A son should expect to have his father around, when he's just had his first car accident.

I'm taking a quick run through *My Brilliant Career* by Miles Franklin. I notice that back in the early 1900s, there was such a thing as suing someone for judicial separation. I have more than enough grounds for this, but we don't live as fairly now, as they did then. Are there any grounds whatsoever, for me to lay a charge for damages incurred?

The common currency

Sweetness is on the prowl again too. She's also ringing for sympathy. She was using sympathy to manipulate. She rings my daughter to tell her, that her great-great aunt is ill and dying. She would be, because she's in her nineties.

I realize by this news, that I've already grieved the loss of family members. I've grieved for the loss of relatives. They weren't much of a loss, because they weren't important relationships. We can kid ourselves about how special some of our relationships are. I know what special relationships feel like now. I know what good relationships are, and what bad ones are. I now know the difference. I can tell the difference.

I bear no relation

Family relationships can be just obligatory relationships. We just happen to be related. It doesn't mean that we necessarily relate. It doesn't mean that we want to relate, or have to relate. I don't want to relate to people I don't relate well to. It's a waste of time. What can come of it? They don't relate to me either. I've let them off the hook. I've released them from any obligation. That's how evolved I'm getting. It's liberating. I've liberated them, and I hope they're grateful. They don't have to be concerned with any of my shit. It's my shit. The good shit and the bad shit, is all mine, and I can damn well do what I please with it. I hope they stay out of my shit from now on.

A foreign legion of lesions

My hopes have been dashed. I'm crushed. I've just been to the bank to collect my $20,000 and I haven't passed Go. I can't collect. He put a stop on the loan account, not two months ago. I haven't had a reply to my letter asking for $2,000, either. How much are two solid breast lesions worth? An ultrasound won't cost me anything, so I'll turn up for that, but I'm now a little worried about what's going to show up.

I can't show up

I can't go to the specialist without any money. You need money for health. There's a horrible message that's coming through to me. After being with this bloke for thirty years, and bearing two beautiful children to him, he can't cough up $2,000. I invested thirty years with him. It's a bad return. Do you just cut your losses, or do you fight back? I've got no money to fight with. You need fighting money. A fighting fund is what I need. I'm a cause. I'm a good cause. I always funded him. Where are my dividends for all these years? I reinvested them back into a bad fund, didn't I?

He apparently has authority to put a stop on the account, so that two signatures are now required. The bank's been informed of the situation, without my authority. Why haven't I got authority to remove his authority? Aren't we both as powerful an authority, as each other?

Reverse of authority

I don't want sympathy money. I just want the money. I've never had his sympathy, and I realize that now. The selfish prick! How much sympathy could he milk from my family, if he had a solid lesion in his left ball-sack? I would no more hold money back from him, under any such circumstances, because my sympathy for him was never ending. How could he hate me that much? Is it over the money? Is this his gripe? He could be taking $20,000 too. We could each have $20,000, to tide us over until the Hoorah sells. Is my life worth more than $20,000? What's life worth?

This is panic! I'm not in the moment. I'm not in the Now. I'm not grounded, centred, or present. I'm not being mindful. I'm mad! Insanely angry!

Is it worth a court appearance?

In three days, I could represent myself at court. I could try to make a stand. I'm invited to appear, but nobody will be expecting me to. Should a court have jurisdiction over me? I've never been in trouble with the law. I could have taken plenty of people for a row in my life, but I always cut my losses. It seemed a heavy price to pay, for a commission or two. I've never done it, have I? I've never had this experience before. Should I be experiencing it for some reason? It's not something I want to experience. I'm not a protagonist. I like to remain in the background. I'm not good at speaking in public.

> **Protagonist:-** n. [< gr. *protos*, first + *agonists*, actor] 1. the main character in a drama, novel, or story; 2. a person playing a leading or active part.

I guess I really have been the main character in a story. I've been the main character in the marriage. The trouble is – my character's been assassinated.

Assassinate:- 1. to murder (esp. a politically important person) 2. to ruin (a reputation, etc.), as by slander – assas'sina'tion n.

I just don't know what to do. I don't want legal aid. I don't want anyone's aid, because I have my own aid tied up in the Hoorah. I should be allowed access to my aid.

I've decided I might draw up an Affidavit. I might even set straight in my Affidavit, what was false in his Affidavits. Will they take any notice? Will they care? They won't give a shit, will they? I don't want to stand up for nothing. I don't want my stand to mean nothing. I don't want to mean nothing anymore. What I might do, is play it half way. I might submit my Affidavit to the court, but not myself. I'll only present in person to lodge my Affidavit. I'll just copy the format from their format, except for the lies.

Written on the 1st of February in the year two thousand and twelve and probably posted the next day, because it's raining.

To the dearest three people,

In my life, who live in the cosy little cottage known as The Toy House,

At Number 6

In the state of New South Wales and in

The Post Code ****, which isn't the same as mine now.

I write this letter because I never can say the words that I want to say, in person. I feel the words passionately, but it's hard enough to feel them, without trying to say them, and not cry.

These aren't the tears of sadness that I write about now, but the tears of gratefulness that I feel. The feelings throw up the words on paper, that I want to say to all three of you, because I now think of you as the three Amigos.

Three is my lucky number these days, because I've spoken of the trinity in my books. I first heard the word 'Trinity' in Hermione's play, and I thought it was divine. I don't know why I think of mathematics when I think of you three now, but you three have been the suppliers of the numbers that I've been relying on lately.

What I do know, and remember from mathematics, is Pythagoras' Theorem.

> **Pythagoras' theorem:-** [< Pythagoras] the theorem that the square on the hypotenuse of a right-angled triangle is equal to the sum of the squares on the other two sides.

I'm proud to see that each side of your triangle is equal now with each other. I can see the respect of the three sides, and the bond that has formed between you all. What I can feel in your home, is a good and happy energy. I see and feel the love radiating in your house, and have witnessed the compassion and respect you have for each other as individuals. It feels like a special home for you three. You've all done such a great job of making it a home under difficult circumstances. You've created something important. You've created something for yourself, and you've created something for me to come to when I need to. I feel welcome and cared for, when I come to your home.

For me, this is a wondrous place to be, because I've never been the cared for before. I have only ever known the opposite.

What you create now, and for however long you three are together, will be memories. These are the memories of being young, and I know they'll be treasured memories for you, when you get as old as me. I'm not that old, but the memories I have of being your age, are poignant.

A triangle can be odd, but it can also be even.

> **Treble:-** adj. [< L. *triples*, triple] 1. threefold; triple; 2. the highest part in musical harmony, soprano; 2. a high-pitched voice or sound; 3. treble the amount, size, etc –vt., vi. –bled, -bling, to make or become threefold.

You all have my deepest respect, and have a perfect score as far as I'm concerned. You are three incredible people whom I have the greatest love for. I used to have double, but now I have triple.

When I was three, I was always given the triangle to play. I now hear your triangle playing great music so don't let other people criticize it. It's your triangle, and you three made it.

This isn't really what I wanted to say, but sometimes music is better than words.

You three are my music.

Love Mum

They want a fighter

They want me to go to court and fight. The three Amigos want me to take him out. They don't realize that justice isn't that easy, when you don't have a barrister. He has a barrister. He'll have to incur more costs now, won't he? I don't know whether he'll be wasting money or not, but I know whose money it is, and most of the time he's wasted it anyway. I won't be there to find out, but I guess I can look forward to some more Orders from Her Majesty. She, most generously, keeps me in the loop.

God Save the Queen

Her Majesty was rather prompt with her hearing date, because I only lodged the documents on Monday, and the hearing has been set for the following Monday. She must believe in the urgency of the situation. The other side won't have much time to prepare, because they were only posting the sealed documents to me today, and I probably won't receive them until Friday, or possibly Monday. As soon as I can, I must serve them on his solicitors. We'll have to wait and see how prompt the mail is. We'll have to wait and see how prompt I am. How prompt will we all be, for an impromptu hearing?

Impromptu:- adj., adv. [< in prompt, in readiness] without preparation; spontaneous –n. an impromptu speech, etc.

Impromptu happens all the time to me. What prompts impromptu? I had a call from boy wonder's teacher today, and I'm wondering what prompted it. I think I know, and I think it was unnecessary. I'm not a person who likes to take people to court. I think he felt he may be held responsible in some way. What way? I told him that my boy wonder is an adult, and as such, was responsible for his own wellbeing on the night of the BBQ dinner. A person old enough to legally drive around in their own car at night, is no longer a child. A person who learned to drive by clocking up the 120 hours' experience, before sitting for the driving test, knows how to drive. I did most of these 120 hours with him, but we didn't practice along that road, in the middle of a dark and rainy night. Maybe I should take responsibility.

I blame bad luck

It was an accident for Christ's sake! Any person could have had an accident on that road, and I'm told the treacherous conditions on that road, are well known by the locals. Accidents are accidents, because you don't mean them to happen. He wouldn't have wanted to smash his car. He adored that car. He didn't mean it to happen.

Who meant it to happen?

Was it meant to have happened? Was it meant to be? Was there meaning to it? I think there was meaning to it. I think there's meaning to all accidents. I could have meant well, and told him he couldn't drive that night. A well-meaning lecture in his ear before he went out that night, might have done the trick, but he's moved out of home. That it happened after leaving the house of the teacher, was pure coincidence, wasn't it? The teacher in question, just happened to be the father of the friend whose party it was. The teacher isn't in question. My son could have stayed the night and slept in his car, if he'd had a mind to. He didn't have a mind to. He's so much more mindful now than he used to be.

My son is a man

I hate to admit it, because it got taken out of my hands, but he's had to grow up quick. He's an adult, because he's had to be. His father pushed him to adulthood, because his father is still a child. His father is the only one ever wanting to be babied.

For services rendered

He didn't deal with any accounts. He left all that to me, until one memorable day, when he decided to change his mobile phone provider. I thought he'd found a better deal. I was surprised that he was actively dealing with something of a business nature. I thought some phone company had talked him into a better deal, and I thought it was wonderful that he was taking an interest at all.

You see, I kept all accounts in one bundle. I always bundled everything up together with the business, as an easy way of accounting for services rendered. He no longer wanted me accounting for this particular service anymore. He wanted to get serviced elsewhere.

Why hide this post?

One afternoon he rang our innocent son, who had just got home from school, and directed him to retrieve his personal mobile phone bill from the letterbox, and deposit it into his bedside drawer. My son did as he was told without question.

Sharing his duplicity with his son

Why involve an innocent party in his dirty deeds? Who deceives a son, into deceiving his mother, for the benefit of his father? My son didn't know he was a co-conspirator. My son confessed his deed, after the fact. He didn't know the facts of the matter then, but he does now.

Is this worth posting?

How prompt is our Cobb & Co service these days? It's not that prompt these days, is it? Is it just me noticing this? Who else has noticed? Have our postie's become busier? I thought with email and such, the postie's would have less to do, and more time to deliver on time. They still battle it out every day in rain, hail, or shine. What other occupations battle it out every day, wind, hail or shine? Coppers do, and so do real estate agents. Yep, they do! I did.

It's the service that always runs on time

It doesn't matter whether it's 40 degrees in the shade, or the other direction in the sun, but we're out there. We don't want to be there, but the buyers and sellers do. I've been drenched to the bone, and had to come back to the office to dry out in the air conditioning, shivering through to my bones. I should have boned up, and asked the boss if I could go home to change, but that's another bone of contention.

It's more than rain, hail, or shine

What are the conditions of a real estate agent? All the conditions you can think of. Your car must be in good condition, and this is one of the conditions. Your body must be in good condition, because you can be on your feet all day. You can be tramping through bush acreages, and trotting down a wobbly wharf, trying not to get your heels caught between the planks. You can be a food supply for a plague of fleas, and I just don't see how they make their way into your underwear as they do. You can be wrestling with jammed roller doors, and undoing corroded padlocks. You'll be upstairs and downstairs, and under the stairs. You can be on dangerous ground. You can be standing on verandahs that are rotting away, and on decking that's defective. You can be dealing with people you just don't know, and can find yourself in an empty house with a menacing moronic maniac. You can be trapped in your car with characters not unlike the infamous Snowtown sicko's. Holy smokes, you don't know the blokes! You'll traverse your way through a drug house or two, or through galleries of poster girls nude. You'll be privy to what's kept in unhidden places, like sawn-off shotguns, and a cannabis plant or two. You'll see dirty underwear hanging around, and the medicines people are on. You'll observe dirty dishes, and week-old food, and band aids, and tampons, and poo. Dog poo! You'll see lots of animals uncared for, or petted, and menagerie's just like a zoo. There's cats and rats, and tortoises, and snakes, and birds fly free. You'll smell it, and the smell will eventually go, but the scene just never will. I've seen some scenes. I never made a scene, but I'm creating a scene for you now. It's not a pretty scene, but there were some occasionally. These are the terms of the conditions.

That letter back there was impromptu

I've added it in here under impromptu, because I like impromptu sometimes, but only when I can write it, not when I stand up live. I hide behind my writing. I sent that letter because I wanted to post something to their letterbox. It was an extra contact, and I happened to have some stamps left. A postage stamp costs just 60 cents, but I'm unaware if they can be cashed back in or not.

Contact for me is hard, because I only have a limited amount of credit. I ration my credit on my mobile, and ration my petrol in my car. Everything is rationed now, even my time. I have just over two weeks left of electricity and gas. I'll try to get a further extension, if I can. If I can't, then I'll have to leave. I might have to write a good letter with some powerful words. I have a lot of powerful words now, because powerful things are happening. Powerfully emotional, I mean.

The Power of my Ocean

The ocean this afternoon was so powerfully moving. It was undoubtedly and literally, wholly poetic to me.

The rain had stopped, but there was a light drizzle still drifting in the air and swirling around me. The sea was swollen and turbulent, and I couldn't distinguish the salt spray from the squally feather-light mist, as I walked with my head nestled down into my hoody.

I was heaving alongside it, as I marched ahead with my hair whipping out at my face and neck. The parallels of nature had us merging rhythmically to a haunting and hypnotic dirge.

It was just the dark way of it this afternoon. It was the opposite of my lovable place of shimmery, shiny sun, and bubbly surf.

The beach was littered with brine-soaked debris, and the cold shoreline was ravaged by the surging torrents of sweeping sea water. The dog, energized by atmospheric pressure, galloped mindlessly through the strong headwinds. The mountainous waves smashing against black walls of rock with their roaring mad intensity, was the energy I felt reaching right through to my inner core.

Where do these waves rise up from? Voluminous troughs and molten white water, was all I could see from the lighthouse steps. Show me some light. "Show me the light" was the scream within me.

It was the white noise inside my head and outside, deafening, but cleansing too. I stood. I stood it. I stood it down.

The ocean was rising and willing its monstrous strength at me. I was raging back. My insides were churning, and the drama was in action. Big wave reactions. The two natural rivals. The internal rival was against the external, in a battle of high tidal performance.

I could smell its unfriendly odour as I stood my wet sandy ground. It was emitting that hard, strong salt smell, and not the sweet tang of it, but the hard storm of it. I stormed right back as it tried to claim me, this fractured, frightening, afternoon. It lit me up.

My internal ocean was keen on matching it for both velocity and temper. We were matching tempests, and the wind united us in our wild soulful rantings.

I was lifted and invigorated by this nature in me. It was just her nature taking it all out on the outside of me too. This was our nature this afternoon on that grey and misty beach.

We were lit up by our natures. The whites of my eyes matched the whites of its waves, as the salty suds cascaded down the sides of our rock faces.

Have you been there?

Were you with me? Was I able to take you there? I wanted to, because I wanted you to know me alone. I wanted you to be alone on that beach with me, as I wrote this. I wanted you to be moved along that beach, by the nature of what I wrote. Is it in your nature to be moved by such a scene? It's more than a scene, isn't it?

You cannot tame her nature

This is what nature does for me. It affects me. Its effects, cause me. It's my cause and my muse, and it's my nature. She's got to be female, hasn't she?

My real mother

Take a walk on a bush track, preferably near the seaside if you can, and use all your senses at once. Stop still in the middle of the bush and use each one. Stay in it for as long as you can. Restore your nature. See, and hear, every bit of nature. Go when nature is raging. Protect yourself with a raincoat and the right gear, and be in it. Your nature. Be in it!

This could be our new Life campaign. 'Be in it today, and live more of your nature.' This is good community awareness. Celebrate our nature. Celebrate your nature, in nature, as part of nature. I'd be great in advertising, wouldn't I? I'm selling nature.

Selling myself

We've got to start selling it to each other, because they're selling it off. Our country's nature is being sold off. I've seen it! I've seen the dirty big holes they're drilling all over the place. When I say a dirty big hole, I mean acres of a hole. Acres and acres of dirty great holes, are being dug up all over our country. Queensland's being dug up, without you even aware of it.

I'm fractured by this

Do you know what hydro-fracturing is? You can take a guess. Hydro is water, and fracture is to break. This is what I'm most afraid of. Our water is going to be broken. Broken water is no good. You can't fix it. Hydro-fracturing (and I'm no mining engineer), is great pipes drilled down into the earth (hundreds of metres down), until they reach the shale. This is so far down, that it goes beyond the underground water table, or basin. High pressure water mixed with highly toxic chemicals, are pushed way down deep, until it hits the shale and fractures it. This is what releases the gas. What else do you think it releases? Have Australians been made aware of the effects of this type of gas seam drilling? Check out some of the effects they've experienced in the US. This is being kept quiet.

Just quietly, we're the driest in the world

We are the driest continent in the world. Water is precious. We rely on underground water supplies in this country. It's what our poor farmers rely on, and it's what our regional population rely on. Our population is going to need to rely on it. Our country's water is pure gold. Stop all the mining. Mining is not self-sustaining. Mining is ravaging the land and polluting it. Once it's poisoned, it's dead. It can't be revived.

I don't know much about this line of work, because I'm just an ex-legal secretary, ex-real estate agent, ex-wife, and I've been ex-communicated.

Let's communicate on this one

This matter hasn't been communicated properly either. Have the people of Australia lost communication with big business? Have we lost our rights to our nature? Communication about nature is vital, because communing with nature is second nature. We are 'the great outdoors' people. We're known for our great outdoors. There needs to be some doors opened. Stop locking the doors on us. They're our outdoors.

I hope to open some doors

Bring it all out into the light, so we can have a good look at what you're doing. Don't be so private with our public space. I don't care if you own it, or lease it. It's not yours to do what you like with. It's all connected, you idiots. Land is one. It's one mass. That's why it's called mass destruction. Don't destruct our mass.

I haven't been to Mass

I don't go to Mass. The last few times I was in a church, was for funerals. I don't like church. It's not for me. My church is my nature. When I'm in nature, I'm in church. This is where I feel spiritual. That's why I wrote that spiritual piece of writing, about the poetry of the ocean. It was my spirit talking to nature. We were in church together. We are nature. We are part of her. We are like the animals.

Where's our animal nature?

How cool is it, when we see a ringtail possum in the wild? We've all seen them, if we live here in Australia. It's a given. It's a gift! What else have you seen in the wild? Straight away, you can run off a dozen animals that you've had the privilege to observe in their natural habitat, and now you're boasting about it.

One day we might not have as much to boast about

Is there nothing better than seeing our wildlife in their natural habitats? Isn't this what makes us feel Australian? Our nature and wildlife, are our great identity. Who doesn't think our kangaroo isn't the most exquisite creature on two legs?

God made Australia and had some fun, didn't he? He made a whole host of soft and cuddly toys for us. He put a lot of imagination into it. He gave us the echidna and the emu. He gave us the ferocious koala bear and the platypus. These creatures aren't found anywhere else on earth. Where on earth did he come up with the ideas?

Take the kangaroo for example. It can fight with its two legs, while balancing on its tail. What a spine! What balance! The emu has two long legs to balance its big body on, and it can't fly. It can run the pants of a kangaroo though.

The Tasmanian tiger couldn't run very fast, and it just ran out. We ran out of these in 1936. In 1798, when the first platypus specimen was sent to England, many zoologists believed it to be a hoax. They thought it was made up of different animals and sewn together. They thought it had a duck's bill, an otter's body, and a beaver's tail. God got a bit crafty, and blended some together. I'm not a zoologist, but I have an interest in animals. I think we can learn a lot from animals.

If we could talk to the animals, squawk with the animals, jump and squeak and stalk with the animals. Be a Doctor Do-more and don't Do-little. Doing a little on this subject is doing more than you would have done. Less is more.

Big mining companies aren't our identity

I suspect we've lost our resourcefulness in Australia. We think being resourceful is selling all our resources. This isn't being resourceful, it's being stupid. What happened to all our food production and manufacturing? I think we're totally unbalanced in this country. Someone hasn't balanced it out properly. You can't just balance the books, and say that it all balances. There are other factors that need to be considered. Money isn't everything. Let's get the balance right. I'm not saying "No" to all mining, but there's always a middle ground.

Don't use what's sacred

Let them go right to the centre, and use that ground, but only on the grounds that it's not sacred ground. What ground isn't sacred? It's all bloody sacred, so let's start worshipping the ground we walk on, every bloody bit of it.

Let's unite and reinvent the unions

I believe in the union. I believe in the power of a union. I believe in a certain kind of union. I believe power and money can be as valuable as each other, when it comes to battle. Power and money, are not a good union. Our unions are no longer good unions.

An old-fashioned union

I believe in the power of the voice against the power of money, because somewhere along the line, money runs out. What does money pay for? It can pay for a hearing. One voice without any money, can't be heard. It's a pip squeak. What about when you add so many pip squeaks that the squeaking becomes so loud, you can't hear anything for the noise? I'm a pip squeak, and I don't want to be turned down.

> **Pip:-** n. [< PIPPIN] a small seed, as of an apple.
>
> **Pip:-** n. [< ?] 1. any of the spots on playing cards, dice, etc.; 2. the emblem worn by certain officers in the army indicating their rank.
>
> **Pip:-** n. [< L. *pituita*, phlegm] 1. a contagious disease of fowl; 2. [Slang] a bad temper or depression [he gives me the pip].
>
> **Pip:-** vt. pipped, pip'ping [< ?] [Colloq.] 1. to wound, esp. with a gun; 2. to defeat someone, esp. when their victory seemed certain [to pip at the post].
>
> **Pip:-** n. [echoic] a high-pitched sound, of which a sequence (the pips) acts as a time signal, esp. on the radio.

I've given my dictionary the pip

My dictionary has the shits with me. It thinks I should be using the English language correctly, and it hates the way I contrive a definition. It's trying to tell me that I don't have a definite definition, and some things aren't worth defining. It reckons 'pip squeak' is one word and that it holds the definition already, if I've a mind to look it up properly.

I don't have a mind

I think a pip squeak is worth defining, and I think it should be two words. Both words have a better definition, from where I'm coming from. Anyway, if my dictionary had listed all the words in the first place, I wouldn't have to contrive a way to define. I found 'pipsqueak', but I don't like it!

> **Pipsqueak:-** n. [< PEEP + SQUEAK] [Colloq.] a person, etc. regarded as small or insignificant.

This shouldn't be a word. There shouldn't be a word for this definition. I think my dictionary's lacking. It's lacking imagination, and it's not keen on the colloquial. I think I've been quite definitive with my contrived meanings. I think it should just stop its squealing, and let me write my book in the way that I want. It's creative writing!

Psst!

A dictionary can teach you only so much. Just because it's taught me its words, doesn't mean it has control over me. I like to be creative, and my dictionary can't teach me that. Creativity comes from the soul.

> **Definitive:-** 1. decisive; conclusive; 2. most nearly complete and accurate; 3. serving to define –defin'it'ively. Adv.

I'm getting my ruler out

It's an argument. We've been building up to this for a while. I've felt the tension mounting, and I knew it would come to this at some point. I'm getting a bit above myself. That's what my dictionary's telling me. I don't think I'm going to use my dictionary in *The Teacher in Me*. I've decided! I'm going to promote the Thesaurus. I can't be told when I can, and when I can't. I'm sick of rules. Who says that I have to play by the rules? I'm taking away all the rules in *The Teacher in Me*. I've seen too many rules, and I'll be the one using the ruler this time!

Squeak:- vi. [echoic] to make or utter a short, sharp, high-pitched sound or cry –vt. to utter with a squeak –n. a short, shrill sound or cry –narrow (or close) squeak [Colloq.] a narrow escape –squeak through (or by, etc) [Colloq.] to barely manage to succeed, survive, etc. –squeak'er n. –squeak'ily adv. –squeak'y adj.

Pip squeak

A pip squeak is much more than I thought. It's a survivor. It's got more than I thought behind it. It starts as a tiny seed, and becomes an emblem of official rank. It has a fowl temper, but can win at the finish, even when the odds are stacked against it. The phlegm is probably what makes it squeak, and it always squeaks in, at the end.

    A pip squeak is not what it sounds, is it? I'm a pip squeak, but I'm not how I sound. I wrote to Her Majesty, and she got the following mail from me a couple of days ago:-

IN THE FEDERAL MAGISTRATES COURT OF AUSTRALIA
REGISTRY:

| File number: |
| Court Location: NSW |
| Court Date |
| Court Time |

BLANK
Applicant

BLAND
Respondent

AFFIDAVIT

Name of deponent: Blank

Date: 30/01/2012

I, Blank, of The Hoorah in the state of New South Wales, make oath and say/affirm:

I am the Applicant Wife and I refer to the Orders made on the 11th October 2011, and on 21 December 2011, No. (P) NXXXXX2011.

1. I refer to the Court Orders of 21.12.2011 and advise that the balance of my AXED Superannuation Fund is $82,996.01 as at the statement dated 09/01/2012.

2. I have recently sold furniture from the property at The Hoorah in order to cover basic living expenses. The balance of the furniture and effects from the aforementioned property, have been given to my children as agreed to by the court on a previous occasion, when my daughter Girl Wonder sought her own legal aid counsel and lodged an Affidavit on 17/11/2011. I will continue to reside in the marital Hoorah until the property is sold.

THE BUSINESS

3. I have never embezzled any moneys from the company accounts of Jerry Holdings Pty Limited (trading as Blank Jerry Real Estate), nor has it ever been my intention to do so.
4. My reasons for closing both the general and trust accounts of the business, was for security purposes, and to ensure my own legal protection.
5. Bland did not earn income in the years 2001 – 2006. Bland has never been involved in the business, in any capacity, other than for minor maintenance or sign erections, in the entire 10 years that the business was operating. He has no sales or property management experience, and has never had anything to do with running the business at any time. He has never shown any interest in the business and rarely visited the office at Forks.
6. On 24/01/12 the Nissan X-Trail belonging to my son Shark Boy and registered in his name, was destroyed and written off in a car accident, and can no longer be included in the asset pool. The Proton, also referred to in the Affidavit of Bland of 02/10/2011, belongs to my daughter Girl Wonder and as such, is registered in her name. The car that her father Bland had bought for Girl Wonder for $1000 was unsafe and un-roadworthy. It was sold for $500.

LEGAL REPRESENTATION

7. I have no legal representation due to a conflict of trust with my former solicitor, Two Dopey People Lawyers of Yrong. It has been alleged in Affidavit of Bland, dated 30/09/2011, clause 35, that information regarding my health and mental capacity had been traded between my former solicitor, and his solicitors, Bird. Bird.

Lies & Associates, without my knowledge. I have no evidence to prove where this false information about my health, has originated from, however I have become aware of a conflict of interest between myself and Two Dopey Lawyers, due to the fact that they also acted as lawyers for my family (of whom I am now estranged), in a probate matter for the estate of my late mother, deceased 01/04/2011.

8. I refer to clause 38, of Bland's Affidavit of 30/09/2011 and negate that any such Power of Attorney was enforced, nor was there any intention by me, to have it enforced. It was only ever my intention to protect myself against involuntary incarceration, which was being pursued, and continues to be pursued by people known to me.

THE CHILDREN

9. I refer to clause 40, of Bland's Affidavit of 30/09/2011 and negate that my son Shark Boy has not left school, nor has he any intention of doing so, until he has completed his HSC this year. Shark Boy holds the position of Vice Captain at The Fisho's Catholic College and has an outstanding record of impeccable behaviour.

10. My daughter, Girl Wonder is aged 20 and as such, makes her own decisions as to her work and study. She is currently employed full time, and currently resides together with her brother.

THE PROPERTY

11. I refer to the Affidavit of Bland dated 30/09/2011 filed on 04/10/2011 and can advise that false allegations have been made throughout this document. I deny these accusations and claims, and can advise that to date, I have had no consultation with The Department of Balanced

Swapping, nor have I had any involvement with either the winding up of the business, or the proposed sale of The Hoorah.

12. I draw your attention to clause 14, of Bland's Affidavit dated 30/09/2011, with regard to the said property valuation of The Hoorah of $700,000. I have today consulted with the selling agent Mr Audi, of Aldi Estate Agency, Handy, appointed to auction the property on 18 February, 2012 by Bland. Mr Audi has advised me, that Bland indicated he would accept a price of between $800,000 and $900,000. Mr Audi advised me on 29/01/2012 that based on current market conditions and current feedback from prospective buyers, that the best price likely to be achieved at auction would be around $700,000 however this has not been the price range given to prospective buyers. The price guide being quoted to prospective buyers, on the instructions of Bland, is between $800,000 and $900,000.

13. Since early January 2011 and from the time of the marriage separation, I've had a serious and ongoing medical condition. I am under the care of specialist Dr Breast Surgeon. I currently have both breasts affected by solid lesions, and it is at her urgent recommendation, that I don't delay this matter any further. It has been a distressing twelve months for me both personally, and professionally, and I now find myself with no private health cover, no income, no family support, and no money left to pay for any of my immediate living expenses or health expenses. I am in possession of the Mazda 6 which is registered under Jerry Holdings Pty Limited, and understand that this car cannot be sold as it may form part of the asset funds needed to wind up the business.

14. I seek that this most Honourable Court makes the Orders sought in my Application.

Sworn/Affirmed by BLANK   )
the deponent at   )
On day of January, 2012   )

....
Before Me:

....
Signature of Witness
Full name of witness:
Qualification of witness:

Psst!

This is what I asked her Majesty for, and I hope it works. It looks like a solicitor drew these documents up, but I drafted them. I reckon mine are way more articulate than his, because mine don't have spelling mistakes. Go back and take a gander at his Affidavit and Application. I think it should be in the first quarter of your book. You're my Legal Eagle, so I want you to choose the best ones. I admit, I did copy his format, but I couldn't possibly have handed in the sort of rubbish he handed in to Her Majesty. What do you think my chances are? I reckon I've got a 50/50 chance, don't you? Let's see how Lady Justice sees it. I don't want any favours, so I don't know in whose favour she'll rule. There's probably a rule of thumb.

> **Rule of thumb:-** a rule, method, etc. based on experience or practice rather than on scientific knowledge.

I don't think she can use this rule with this matter, because it's not about the thumb. It's about the wedding finger. What's the 'rule of wedding finger'?

> **Rule:-** n. [< L. *regere*, lead straight] 1. a) an authoritative regulation for conduct, procedure, etc. b) an established practice that serves as a guide [rules of grammar]; 2. government; reign; 3. customary course of events; 4. a custom; 5. a ruler; 6. printing, a thin strip of metal as high as type, used to print lines; 7. a set of regulations in a religious order; 8. Law. a decision, order, etc. made by a judge in regard to a specific question -vit. Ruled, rul'ing 1. to govern; 2. to have an influence over, guide; 3. to determine; 4. to mark (lines) on (paper etc.) as with a ruler; 5. to keep under control -vi. 1. to govern; 2. to prevail; 3. to issue a formal decree -as a rule, usually -rule out 1. to leave out from consideration; 2. to make impossible; prevent -rule the roost, to be in control.

> **Wedding:-** n. [OE. *weddung*] 1. the act or ceremony of getting married, or the festivities that go with it; 2. a marriage anniversary.

Finger:- n. [OE. 1. any of the five parts at the end of the hand, esp. any of these other than the thumb; 2. the part of a glove covering a finger; 3. anything like a finger in shape or use; 4. an approximate measurement based on the breadth of a finger -vt. 1. to touch with the fingers; 2. to play (an instrument) by using the fingers -get (or pull) one's finger out [Colloq.] to begin or speed up activity -put one's finger on, to ascertain exactly -twist (or wrap) around one's little finger, to have complete control or influence over.

Rule of wedding finger

This isn't really a rule, is it? I thought it was. My head drops, and I sigh after saying this. I said it aloud. I said it in front of a lot of people. I said it in front of a registered celebrant, and in front of my parents and his. I thought that was the rule. We exchanged wedding rings. I got one, and he got one. He never wore his. I wore mine from that day forward. I thought that was the rule. I always obeyed the rules. I never bent these ones, not ever.

We signed on the dotted line in the presence of witnesses

I'm staring at the above heading. I don't know what to make of it. I don't feel inclined to make anything of it. I don't feel it's needed. I don't feel these rules are needed. Why do we obey all the rules when we get married? We register the Marriage Certificate and pay a celebrant to perform the rights. I want my money back. Who enforces these rules? What are the penalties for breaking them? I want a divorce. I want to be divorced from this stupid rule breaking system. I'm going to divorce myself from it. I'll make him pay for it, since he was the one who broke the rules. It really wasn't a hard rule to obey.

> **Divorce:-** Hang on, 'before we go any further, do you love me, will you love me forever, will you need me, will you never leave me, will you make me so happy for the rest of my life, will you take me away,

will you make me your wife. I want to know right now, before we go any further, do you love me...'

"Meatloaf for dinner, Darl?"

I slept on it. We both did. We slept on it nine years before we did it. We did it for nine years before I agreed to it. He wanted to do it, but I was reluctant.

We had this album, and it used to come out at parties and at different times in our lives. We danced to it, and sang at the top of our voices, all the words to that song. They were our songs from our era.

Was he praying for the end of time? No. During the time of his affair, we were still having our affair. We continued to go out overnight on our cruiser. This is a strange state of affairs.

I went to the look out

He was acting weird. He'd started to pay more attention to how he looked. He started changing. He changed his look. He wanted new clothes, so we went off shopping and bought him modern clothes. He wanted my help. I helped him look. I wondered why he was suddenly interested in looking his best. He'd never been interested before. He'd lost weight and he looked good. He looked too good. He was overly, and abnormally happy, that day. We held hands as he all but skipped along beside me, visiting one shop after another. He was in high spirits as he shared his new-found happiness with me, but then it changed...

I stood looking out over it all

I noticed the way he looked at me. It wasn't the kind of look I was used to. It's weird looking back now. I should have looked more closely at everything he was doing. There are always signs that someone's having an affair. I'll list them for you, just in case you think there might be something going on behind your back. On second thoughts, maybe I won't, because it could give you a hell of a shock, if you recognize the signs. To sum it up, if you suspect something is going on, it is. Why else would you suspect? Why suspect, if nothing's suspect? If it's a bit suspect, suspect the worst. The worst part is coming. This is your part. You'll have to prove your part. You'll have to turn suspicion into evidence. They don't always leave room for this part. They cover this part up. Your part is the hardest part. This is the last part you take.

If you have reason to suspect, you have reason

Don't ask them and expect to get a truthful answer. Truthful hasn't played a part so far, so why would it play a part at all? You must find the truth yourself. It's a hell of a journey. Be prepared. Be prepared for the worst, because it's one of the worst things that can happen to you. It will feel worse than terrible. Your closest person, and your cherished long-term partner, has betrayed you. They want someone else, more than you. For a while they're having both at the same time, and now they compare. You're not comparing well, because he'll be justifying his deceitful behaviour to himself. He knows exactly what he's doing. On the one hand it feels good, but on the other hand, it feels bad. He's playing two hands.

He's telling his lover on the side, how much better she is than you. He's comparing her body with your body. He's making love to her, and then he's coming home to pretend to love you. He's pretending, just in case you're suspecting. You're the bit on the side now. You're just the side dish. You used to be the full course, but now you've been pushed to the side.

I'd never have suspected him

I know so much about him. I know so much more than she could ever suspect. I know, because I've been with him since I was fourteen. I've known him since he was a sixteen-year-old boy. We grew up together. We have history. It's big! It feels like a lifetime. I didn't know him at all. I didn't know he'd done this before. I didn't know there was a history of affairs. I didn't know he was screwing me on the side every now and then.

We made history together

He stole that from my life. He gave it, and then took it back off me. Who has he given it to? He didn't give it to her, because she went back to her happy little marriage to play happy families. We aren't a happy family any more. We used to be, to the best of my ability. He didn't have the ability without me. He has no ability now. He only has his availability. He's now available. I wonder what he's waiting for. He's probably waiting for someone like me to come along and fix everything for him. It's going to be a very difficult search. I don't think too many people will do what I did.

An historical three months

From what I can gather, he had at least three months in that affair. He had plenty of time to consider what he was doing. Three months is a long time to consider. It's a long time to think. He would have been enjoying his time, or why put all that time into it. You couldn't avoid thinking about it for three months. He knew damn well what he was doing. He was having his cake and eating it too.

I should have been given an option

He had more than enough time to consider his options. Did he think he had options? He'd had options before, but he never went the whole way. They were just one-night options, and whenever-he-could, options. I wasn't aware of these options until after I found out about the three-month option. Did he ever give me an option? What would my options have been? I'd have liked to have been given the first option. I should have been given an option first. We didn't have an Option Agreement, we had a Matrimonial Agreement.

Is this an option?

I've made application for an option. This seems to be my only option. I hope that my appearing in court on Monday is optional. I haven't got any option, because I've got no money for this option. I won't be there. If I had a guarantee that I'd be granted access to my money, I'd go, but there aren't any guarantees in life. There's only one guarantee, and that's death. I'm guaranteed to die one day.

**IN THE FEDERAL MAGISTRATES
COURT OF AUSTRALIA
REGISTRY:**

File Number:	
Court	
Location:	
Court Date	
Court Time	

BLANK
Applicant
BLAND
Respondent

APPLICATION IN A CASE

This application is made by (name): Blank Blank Blank

Court date

....

(for) Registrar

Date:

Filed by: Blank

Prepared by: Blank

Address: The Hoorah

Phone: Not applicable.

Orders sought (state precisely each order sought)
1. That the parties do all acts and execute all documents necessary to sell at auction the property known as The Hoorah on 18 February, 2012 with a reserve to be set at $700,000. If the property fails to sell at auction, then a

list price of $700,000 be marketed, and any offer above $650,000 to be accepted by the parties registered as proprietors, on the Certificate of Title Volume Folio Identifier No: 15/4/758779.

2. That an amount of $50,000 forming part of the proceeds of the sale of the property, be held in the trust account of solicitors Grovel More Sevens' Legal, (the Applicant's solicitors) pending the completion of the winding up of the business, and to be used to cover any debts, and amounts incurred, in the course of the winding up of the business (Jerry Holdings Pty Limited, trading as) Blank Real Estate.
3. Once all costs have been paid in relation to the winding up of the business, the balance of the $50,000 to be divided equally between the parties being the said (Applicant) and (Respondent) hereto.
4. That the balance of the proceeds from the sale of the matrimonial home at The Hoorah, be divided equally between the said parties being the said (Applicant) and (Respondent) hereto, once all mortgages secured against the property have been discharged, debts and expenses pertaining to the property, including agent's fees, legal fees, and council rates have been paid.
5. That the Applicant Wife and the Respondent Husband make no claims against each other's superannuation funds.
6. That a sum of $10,000 be paid by Bland (father) as a first, and final payment of child support for the last twelve months, for his son Shark Boy, cared for by the Respondent Wife and to be made payable to the Respondent Wife, for expenses incurred.
7. That the motor vehicles owned by the business and registered under the name of Jerry Holdings Pty Limited, being Mazda 6 in possession of the Respondent Wife, and the Mitsubishi Triton, in possession of the Applicant

Husband, stay in their possession respectively, and be transferred and registered into their separate names.

8. That the court make urgent orders for the Applicant Husband to authorize Dragon Bank to release the amount of $20,000 to the Applicant Wife, from the line of credit facility, which is available immediately from the Portfolio Loan account 065 441 907, for the purposes set out and supported by the Applicant Wife's Affidavit.

Affidavit/s (Provide details of the affidavit(s) supporting this application)

This application is supported by an affidavit made by BLANK, 30th January, 2012 and filed in the Court on 30th January 2012 in support of the Application in a Case of Blank.

Signature of person applying or lawyer

....
Signed by (print name)   Blank
Date: 30/01/2012

Form approved by the Chief Federal Magistrate pursuant to Subrule 2.04(1A) for the purpose of Subrule 4.08(1)

This is no bull

Do you want to know how to turn sadness into blind rage? I see red. I see a blood red rag. I'm the bull. I want vengeance!

I went and visited my son tonight. I'm on empty. The orange light is on the whole way. No petrol. I went there and cried. I got the comfort, but then my son texted his father and asked him if he was intending to authorize the bank to issue me with some money out of the re-draw facility. He has the letters from my doctors. The... (Forget it, it's just more profanities.)

> **Profane:-** adj. [< L. *pro-*, before (i.e., outside) + *fanum*, temple] 1. showing disrespect or contempt for sacred things; 2. not connected with religion; secular –vt. –faned', -fan'ing 1. to treat (sacred things) with disrespect or contempt; 2. to put to a base or improper use –profane'-ness n.

This isn't me, it's him. It's also the slimy agent. The text message said that the bank accounts are frozen, and that I'm holding up the sale of the house by smoking in it, and making it hard for the agent. He said that I walked out and left everything for him to do, and that I should ask my father for help. Oh, and the first bit was a question to my son about why he'd been contacted now all of a sudden, when there was no response to his earlier instruction to seek assistance from his grandfather. Oh, and he also wants the outboard-motor back!

Such a message turned sadness and despair, into an infernal, internal, rage. It's 11.30 pm and I can't go to sleep in this state.

> **Infernal:-** adj. [see INFERIOR] 1. of hell; 2. hellish, fiendish; 3. [Colloq.] hateful, outrageous.

Spontaneous Internal Combustion

This is what I will die of. Have you ever experienced such an inferno inside you, that you simply don't know what you'll do next? The agent should know better than to get involved in something he knows nothing about. He seems to be telling tales about my habits as if I'm a tenant breaching lease conditions.

This is my home. I am an owner. I can smoke inside if I want to. People keep their animals inside their homes for Christ's sake. It's not for Christ's sake that they do it, but they just do it. I'm smoking in the house for Christ's sake buddy! Put that in your pipe and smoke it!

Did he just slip up?

That slimy agent used my private ensuite on the day of the auction, and left the toilet seat up. He doesn't take off his shoes when he enters the Hoorah, and he lies. He even admits to his lies. He couldn't lie straight in bed. Does he have any idea of the volatile nature of marital feuds?

He will!

I've made that the heading, because he needs to learn a lesson. It won't be me dishing it out, because I'll be throwing it at him. I think the agent is lying to both of us. He wants to be sweetness in the middle. He's gotten himself into the middle of something that he shouldn't have. Why? Because he thinks he's fucking clever. When people are emotional, they can be quite dangerous. This is what he needs to be aware of. You can't mix business with pleasure. He's getting pleasure from this matter, and that's why he's getting involved.

But I'm dangerous. I'm so dangerous right now, that I'm glad I'm alone.

The creation of evil

I'm evil at this moment, and this time I'm going to let it have its own way. It was never my way, but I'm tempted to let it have its way. Evil needs a force. The force is anger. Vile anger is the force inside me. I feel like tearing this house up. I feel like shredding the curtains, and putting a sledgehammer through the granite bench top. I want to smash every window in the house, and that's just for starters. This isn't me. This was never me. Who are they crucifying? Me! Who are they attacking and persecuting? Me. What did I do?

I was the doormat

The doormat is dirty! I'm so fucking dirty about what's gone on, and I want to put some dirt where it belongs.

There will always be dirt that you can't see, but it's there. This is the dirt that may never surface, because it's so dirty. This sort of dirt does untold damage. The dirt is in the detail. The agent hasn't considered where all the dirt lies. It lies with another agent occasionally.

I'm livid

> Livid:- adj. [< L. *lividus*] 1. discoloured by a bruise, black-and-blue; 2. grayish – blue, lead-coloured; [livid with rage] 3. [Colloq.] furious.

They ain't seen nothin' yet!

I watched an old movie with boy wonder earlier tonight. It was to take our minds off our anger. It didn't quite do that, but it did show me my moment. It showed me where I am.

"I'm going to go the distance."

Rocky went the distance with Apollo Creed. He hung in there, battered and bloody, through sheer bloody mindedness. This is my mind now. I'm in a fight. It hasn't started yet, but I'm in training. I'm running up those steps, and I'm going the distance. I'm silently beating my chest. This is my creed.

> Creed:- n. [< L. *credo*, I believe] 1. a statement of religious belief, esp. as accepted by a church; 2. any statement of belief, opinions, etc.

It's the bell of the ring

I'm already in the ring. I keep getting tired, so I keep getting back out. I'm back in the ring for the full round. I want another bout. It's the heavyweight championship. I'm a heavy. It's just another round about. In a round-about kind of way, I think I'm winning. The agent isn't winning. He has a winning smile, but he's a flop. He's got a very floppy package. His advertising just doesn't stand up.

A smoke break

There's some trivial information printed on my cigarette packet about the causes of death in Australia. Obviously, it's a Health Authority warning, but I don't think I'm taking the information in the right way.

>Causes of Death in Australia.
>   Alcohol – 2,831
>   Motor Vehicle Accidents – 1,731
>   Illegal Drugs – 863
>   Murders – 203
>None of these would be the way I'd like to go.
>   Tobacco – 19,019
>It seems I'm not the only one who feels this way.

How will you go?

We're all going to go. If we don't go by way of any of the above paths, there are plenty more paths to take us. We'll be taken down a path to our death. We can't stop driving cars, and we can't help being murdered. Alcohol could mean that other people get hurt along the way. Illegal drugs would be a way, if you can't see any other way, and you've already lost your way. Tobacco is clearly the most popular way to go. I'd pick tobacco any old day. These cigarettes are as good as a holiday, and they're made in Singapore. There's a little bit of fancy writing that says 'Easy Taste, Sunny Times'. Singapore is a lovely place for a holiday. I'll bet they're a lot cheaper to buy over there. This money from cigarettes is revenue. I'm keeping the country going. I'm also supporting an industry of workers in Singapore. It's all about how you look at the big picture.

The people picture

Peoples' pictures have become so small, because they don't think.

I know of a bloke who was out in his garden just smelling his roses, and was stung on the leg by a wasp. He had an allergic reaction and died right there on the spot. I can tell you about the people I knew that died. I'll tell you how they died, and spare a moment to consider whether these deaths could have been avoided.

Heart attack, stomach rupture, drowning, car accident, unexplained medical issue, bowel cancer, lung cancer, kidney disease, suicide, cot death, overdose, old age, brain tumour, Leukaemia, broken heart.

Sudden death

I know of many deaths, and some people know about their own impending death, before they die. Some people know how they'll die, and some don't. Some people will have a hand in their own deaths. Some people die when they're infants, and some die in the womb. Some people die after one hundred years of life. Some people take themselves off to war and die. Some people seem like they're dead, when they're still alive.

I'll take my path, and you can take yours

What if we all had a destiny, and we've already been given our ways to die. This would put a different slant on smoking. It would put a whole new slant on living. Is avoiding death all about the will power? Who has all the will power? How do we know? How do we not know? It's theory. It's not knowledge. It's just my theory, and I'm sticking to it.

What are we hereafter?

"Many men go fishing all of their lives without knowing that it is not fish they are after." – Henry David Thoreau.

I'm fishing. I don't know the answers. Neither do fishermen. It's blind luck. You never know if you'll catch one or not, but you keep going fishing anyway. You try your luck.

I've been pushing my luck. I don't know what I'll die of. If I die next year in a car accident, I'll be glad I never gave up smoking. What do you think you'll die of? Have you got a hunch? I have. I have a hunch, because I've eliminated much of the risk already. You won't know what this means, and it's best that you don't.

The exhibition

I'm going to be an exhibitionist. I'm going to hold an art exhibition. I'm going to hold it here in The Hoorah. My lounge room is going to look like an art gallery. I have art. I've created art, and I'm proud of my pieces. They're pieces of me, and all of these pieces are in my story. They've all come from my story. I have names for all my pieces. They're pieces of the puzzle. They all tell a story. I've almost finished my most recent sculpture, and it's called 'Orifice'.

>**Orifice:-** n. [< L. *os*, mouth + *facere*, make] an opening or mouth, as of a cavity.

Who's talking through their arse?

I don't know how to describe it to you, but it's damn interesting. It's burnt orange in colour, with yellow and mustard-coloured cracks and orifices. There are crevices, and holes, and ravines. There's one angle where it looks somewhat obscene. I know this is how it looks, because of the expressions on people's faces when they've examined it. I turn this side to the wall now.

I also have a half-finished amphibious creature. It has five flipper-like legs and a long tail. It has a strange looking head, and it's all smooth and slimy looking. I think I'll paint it a dark olive green, but maybe not. It's just not finished somehow.

>**Amphibious:-** adj [< Gr. *amph:-*, AMPHI-*bios*, life] 1. that can live or operate both on land and in water; 2. of or for military operation involving the landing of troops from seaborne transports.

I think I'm an amphibious creature. I love water. I love it. I love drinking it, washing in it, swimming in it, and relaxing in it. I love looking at it. I love washing my hands. I suppose I love it, because I've never been fussed with dirty hands.

I hate it when they're sticky, or I've been patting the dog. I used to wash my hands after shaking peoples' hands. I always knew when they needed to be washed. I could sense it. I used to shake a lot of hands once. It was my way. I liked shaking hands. I think it's a nice thing to do.

It's personal

Hands are personal. Our hands handle personal things. We scratch our heads, touch food, bite our nails, pick our noses, cough into them, scratch inside our ears, pick a scab, scratch a mosquito bite, wipe our arses, and touch other people. I look under my nails now, and see a brown discolouration. It's only clay under there, and it won't come off. It's stuck to the glue on my false nails. If they were my real nails, I could get all the stains off. I've never had stained fingers from smoking. I remember my grandfather did. Have you ever noticed hands? Hands tell a story. Hands have character.

I remember my son's hands when he was a toddler, and it brings a smile to my face just thinking about it. They were pudgy. He was chubby and squashy when he was a little tyke. His knuckles were just dimples.

My daughter's hands are quite small. They're dainty. She had trouble learning to play the organ when she was a child, because her fingers just couldn't reach the right keys. They are still small. They're smaller than mine.

Little hands make light work

My hands are bigger than hers. My hands have character. They've seen a lot of work. They haven't been cared for. They're much better cared for these days, and it shows. They've seen a fair bit of sun, and water, and I've never worn gloves for washing up, or gardening. They aren't particularly soft, my hands. They never have been. They've never been sweaty, just dry. I look at them and see the freckles and age spots. I see the wrinkles and the large veins sticking up. They've been good strong hands. They've always worked so hard for me, both at home and at work. My hands do what I want them to do now. I write, type, and now I create art too. They are brilliant hands, and I don't know what I'd do without them. Thanks for giving me a hand or two.

Let's have a show of hands

Hands are sensitive. They're intimate. It's all in the way you use them. Even just touching someone else's hand in a certain way, and at a certain time, can be exquisite. I used to like holding hands. I used to hold my ex-husband's hand every night as we walked the dog. We always used to hold hands. Sometimes it was nice, but sometimes it was forced. It was sometimes forced upon me, when I didn't feel like holding hands. It sometimes felt like a restriction or a lead. It could sometimes feel like a rope tied to me, especially when in certain company, or on certain occasions. It was done for effect. It was done, when I couldn't resist. The reason I couldn't resist was because I would have been seen to be making a scene. I hate a scene. I hate a show. He liked this kind of a show. It made him look good, and me look bad. He was provocative. He could provoke this sort of a scene easily. I hate an exhibition. An exhibition is for show. It's showing off. It's putting on a show for everybody. Were we putting on a show for each other?

What's on show?

I think all married couples do this. I think everyone does it. My ex would try to be affectionate towards me in company sometimes. He wouldn't bother so much when we were on our own. Sometimes I resisted, and showed my irritation, and it was noticed. That's why he did it. He wanted me to be irritated. He wanted people to notice my irritation. It labelled me. It labelled me hard. It labelled him a softie, and people would feel sorry for him. This was his aim.

There are times and places for intimate affection. Was it 'effection', or 'affection'? 'Affection' is feeling, and 'effection' isn't even a word, but it's effective as an effect. You can tell the difference easily if it's affecting you. You can't! I didn't quite get it. Not really. It was stealthily done.

Private is where the truth lies

I think I'm private with my affections. I'm private, because it's personal to me. I can be extremely affectionate in private. It's a show of my most personal feelings. It's my true feelings. It shouldn't be false, because it's meant to be real. I'm less private these days. I want to show my true feelings more. I don't hide them these days. I think it's because I feel them more keenly now. I've never held back on affection for my kids, not ever. Neither have they, for me.

His affections lied elsewhere

It's never been the same with him. If it was him, it was always an affectation. It was brought about by alcohol. Alcohol can be very affectionate. Some people prefer the affection of alcohol. They just love a drink.

Feeling too much is the problem

I have a bird on my verandah. It was being attacked by Indian Myna birds, and I heard the thump when it hit the sliding glass door. It's just sitting there trying to regain its senses. I put some water on the tiles for it. It looks like a honey eater of some sort, because it has a long beak. This is what I am. I'm a honey eater, and I'm trying to regain my senses. I've flown into a glass sliding door. I couldn't see it. I lived an illusion. The bird knows there's an invisible wall there now. I'm seeing clearly now too. I'm not looking through it, I'm looking at it. I've been knocked conscious.

It was the glass sliding door, not the glass ceiling

He said I couldn't see it, Blank did. This is a Blank from the past. He's passed now. I remember before he died, he said I wasn't even aware that the glass ceiling existed. "You just see right through it," he said. Why could he see it, and not me? He was younger than me, and he was a bloke. I never thought much about what he said to me all those years ago, until this moment. It's come up out of nowhere just now. It was a past experience. It's something sad from the past. It's odd how I hear the voices from nowhere, when I'm somewhere. Who's there? He lived for his girls.

He was a voice. He was a loud voice at the end. The end was the hammer. He worked it. The job, I mean. He worked too hard and long in the job. He had an accident just doing what he always did. It was out of the blue. It was too early.

Just an offering

I think I've made a bread basket. I've made it with lace. I've made it with mum's lace table cloth. It was a beautiful tablecloth, and the lace work was hand done. It had some holes in it. Lace has holes, but these are my holes. I'm wondering whether I should be feeling guilty about cutting into it. I know she cherished it. I don't cherish it, but I appreciate it, because it's provided me with what I need now. It's just something I can use to make something else. Wondering isn't feeling.

This is what I'm doing now

I've used two pack resin. You mix it together. I hope I got the measurements right. I guessed it. It doesn't matter if it doesn't work, because I can always go back and fix it later. Some mistakes can be fixed later. Some mistakes can't.

Sometimes you can spill something on your clothing, and no matter what you do, the stain can't be removed. You can't hide it, but you can try. You can dye the whole garment another colour. This can cover up the stain, but the garment isn't the same as it once was. You just don't like it as much. Sometimes it's just better to throw the garment away, and cut your losses. Cutting your losses is saying goodbye. You always remember the garment, but only the way it used to be.

A garment is disposable

> **Garment:-** n. [see GARNISH] 1. any article of clothing; 2. a covering –vt. to clothe.

Is clothing a garnish?

> **Garnish:-** vt. [< OFr. *Garner*, furnish] 1. to decorate, trim; 2. to decorate (food) with something that adds colour or flavour –n. a decoration, esp. something used to garnish food, as parsley.

My hands are sticky. I've got the resin all over them, and I've tried to wash it off. Nail polish remover is expensive. It's Acetone.

Acetone is caustic

I've got a stain on me that I can't remove. I didn't put it there, and it wasn't an accident. If my stain was made big enough, nobody could notice where the other stain was. This is how she got rid of her stain. She tried to take away her own stain, by making a stain on me, that people would take notice of. If all the attention was on my stain, her stain couldn't attract any attention. I'm out of the picture now. She's in the picture. The picture looks a bit crooked without me in it. It might get straightened out soon. I don't know how soon, but there may be a different slant to the picture.

Vengeance is victory

I've just got to go the distance. I've got to last the distance. I don't know how long it will take, or how battered I'll be, but I want vengeance. I want revenge. I want the balance. I want justice, and I want fairness. I want my say. It's a big say. "I say, I say, I say, why did the chicken cross the road?" It was in the chicken joke.

The chicken jokes have been around for a long time, haven't they? They have heaps of different punchlines, just like me.

No joke, I'm not a chicken

This is what could happen. The chicken could walk. Is the chicken scared of being the joke? I've been the joke up till now. I didn't cross the road. I stayed put. I stood my ground, stain and all. Did she think I would be moved along? Did she think I would try to remove the stain? Did she think I was going to just piss off, never to be heard from again? Once, I would have. Once upon a time, I would have let the other side win, and have put it all this behind me. I would have put my head in the sand, swept it all under the rug, and never bring it to light. This was my way. It was the only way I could feel good about myself. I used to think it was the 'good' thing to do. I thought it was the noble thing to do. It's not the 'good' thing to do for myself, just the 'good' thing to do for others. Others have done well enough out of me, and it's time I got some wellness out of others.

Taking possession

Are my books haunting? Who would they haunt? Are people haunted by what happened to me?

Haunting:- adj. often recurring to the mind.

I know they're haunting a lot of people, and they haven't even been read yet.

Have you ever haunted? How do you know? Have you ever wanted to haunt somebody? I'm haunting somebody. I want to haunt everybody. Forks is haunted. Forks is in the *Twilight* series, and it's a place with vampires. The Forks I'm talking about isn't the same, but it is the same.

Same, same, but different

These vampires in Forks don't all want blood. They don't want my blood. Some do, but not all. The ones that want my blood, just want to see blood. They don't care whose blood. Some just want dirt. They don't care whose dirt. They'll have to pay for the dirt. I've dug it all up and put it on paper, and nobody helped me. A few people watched me do it, and they encouraged me to keep digging. These few people have read a little of me, but mostly I've been the reader. I've read only what I've wanted to. I've read extracts. Just snippets have been read.

Just the sweeteners

Forks is an old haunt of mine. I haunt the place. I don't haunt in person now. Other people are doing my haunting for me. I'm very grateful. Less is more. The less said about me, the better. Just a subtle remark or a throwaway comment, is enough of a sweetener. This is true haunting. It means they won't have much to go on, but they'll be looking for more. They'll probably want more to go on with.

It's growing dark. Soon Forks will be in complete darkness. I'll come back when it's dark. I'll present myself in the cover of darkness. Someone will be very dark about it.

On with the show!

So, without further adieu, I say hello.

> **Adieu:-** interj., n., pl. *adieus', adieux'* [Fr.] goodbye.

I want to make a last request. If my books, or if only one book gets published, I want my name in the hall of fame. I want very little fame. I just want my story to be acknowledged by the folks in Forks. I want Forks to be acknowledged for my story.

This little town I call Forks has its own community website which attracts minimal community traffic. It has all kinds of information, and I used to admire it for its content. News and events are posted on it, the history of the area, and there's a directory of local businesses. My business used to be on it. I want all my business on it now. I'd like to have an extract of my book on it, after I've been given a green light.

Do you always have to wait for the green light? I want it up in lights. I want it to light up the whole of Forks. My Guy Forks has been in the dark for too long.

> **Guy:-** [< Guy Fawkes] 1. [Colloq.] any person, esp. a man or boy; 2. an effigy of Guy Fawkes; 3. a person dressed oddly –vt. to make fun of.

When the lights are out...

If there was clearly nobody coming in any direction, could you just proceed? It's breaking the law, isn't it? If the traffic lights are broken, what do you do? You proceed with caution. This is a cautionary tale. I'm taking every precaution, just in case. I'm shoring up the competition. I'm filling the gaps. Some gaps are hard to fill, and you can get your hands a bit dirty. My hands are dirty. I can't get the resin off them. My friend's hands are dirty. She's been dirtying her hands at my place each week. I bet some people are dirty about that. I hope the dirt doesn't stick.

Am I intentionally leading someone up the garden path?

I'm trying to look at worst case scenario. Worst case scenario is that her credibility could be at risk. Risk is about credibility. If the plan fails, our credibility has been lost. It's lost, only until it's found again, and then it's success. Success ensures credibility. I'm just ensuring success. It's a good intention.

Is possession a success?

Is success getting people to want to read my book, or is it having my book/s published? I need both. I need more. I need them to buy it. I need them to buy what I'm selling them. It's no good getting published, if nobody buys my book. Is buying, buying what I'm saying? Will they buy it?

A market haunted, or a haunt marketed?

This sort of marketing takes a while. It's not marketing, it's haunting. I'm a ghost. I'm the ghost in the machine. This is a term that was first coined by Rene Descartes. "Descartes was a French philosopher and mathematician, and he argued that mind and brain are made of different substances and governed by different laws. The brain, he claimed, was a physical, material thing, existing in space and obeying the laws of physics. The mind (or the soul, as Descartes called it) was immaterial, a thinking thing that did not take up space or obey physical laws. Thoughts, he argued, were governed by the rules of reasoning, judgment, and desires, not by the physical laws of cause and effect. Human beings consisted of this duality, this marriage of immaterial mind and material brain."

This is an excerpt. It's also an extract. It's from *The Brain That Changes Itself* by Norman Doidge M.D. This book is made up of stories of personal triumph from the frontiers of brain science. Basically, it's about the discoveries of neuroplasticity. I've learned from it. I've learned that the power of my imagination is almost as powerful as learning how to do something. My brain can, by imagining, learn how to do something, before learning how to do something. This isn't that great a discovery, is it? I thought we all knew this already. This is the power of visualization. If we use our mind by practicing a powerful visualization, it can manifest in real life. This has happened. It's happened to me plenty of times. The mind is a portal to everything we desire.

This is worth marketing

Our minds are powerful, and they can be dangerous in the wrong hands. Our own visualizations are best. This is too big a subject for me, but I have a lot to say about it. I'm not an M.D., and I'm not a neuroscientist. I am however, a thinker. I have a brain. I have a brain just like the M.D. I have an imagination, and I have a mind of my own. It goes seeking. It seeks information. It seeks the information I need. It finds the answers, and finds the questions.

My mind also likes to rest. It tells me when to rest. It stops comprehending. It struggles. It tells me to take a break, or that I don't need this bit of information. It's just not interested. If it's not interested, it won't learn that bit. It strikes. It strikes 12 midnight. The ball is over. I have one more book to read, and then it's back to the library with my six borrowed books. I hit the jackpot, because so far, all five were a success.

Successful books

There's something to be learned from every book you pick up and read. You can even learn something about the author. There's an author behind every book. A book can have a life. Not all books are going to be for us. Books are for seekers. Books are for seekers of knowledge. All books give us something. Some books give us oblivion. Some give us escape. Some give us sex and romance. Some give us skills and know-how. Some give us a history of the past, or an idea of the future. And some give us the inspiration we're looking for.

What are you seeking? You know what you tend to look for in a book, so you must be able to answer the question. The answer will be telling you something. It's an important question. Be wary. Be aware. Are you picking up self-help books, spiritual books, or wellness books? This is a sure sign of things to come.

I picked up, where he left off

I've just painted the stairwell banister and my hands are covered in paint. It took me twenty or so minutes, because it was just undercoat. I think it's all I have. It was a shitty paintbrush too. There's paint on the carpet and on the tiles. It's on my dress, because I'm angry. I'm angry on my daughter's behalf. She texted the agent on my behalf, and received this in reply:

> "Hermione, I've got no time for games or getting involved in anything other than the sale. Everybody wants this sold so if you want to help, we need to get the presentation of the property up to standard i.e. fix the hole in the wall, perhaps paint the rail – anything to enhance. If there is a problem, talk to your parents."

I've fixed the hole in the wall, with PVA glue. I didn't have any gyprock. This is what I do, I fix things!

I want to say so much about this agent, but Hermione said it. She said, "Keep out of our parent's feud". She said, "If you keep adding fuel to the fire, it could become dangerous".

He's been playing with fire. I'm the wrong fire to fight. I can't be put out, but I can be inflamed. My inferno has found its mark. It's an indelible mark now.

Can you get paint out of carpet?

I'm not a painter, but I know real estate. My ex was the painter. He had a painting business for a couple of years. It was a liability. I couldn't manage two businesses at once, and run a family at the same time. I did however attempt it. Some things are too much, even for me. I do know how to paint though, but I don't like painting houses. It's boring. The end result is nice, but it's finicky kind of work, and it's not my thing. I used to pay people to paint at The Hoorah. All these expenses were paid for by my business. You can write off a lot of maintenance this way, but I always paid for it.

Maintaining his ego was costly

I had to write off my ex as a maintenance man, because it was too much like hard work. It was a battle, and I could never see the use in it when I could just pay someone to come and do it. It just wasn't worth all the gratitude and praise. I had little energy left to organize him to do a job, and help him to do it. I had nothing left over for all the carrying on it would cost me. It was always such a mammoth effort. I don't know why there was always so much 'hoo ha' about a job. Other blokes don't go on about it like this, do they? Where is a quiet achiever when you need one? You just pay them in quiet, don't you?

I did it my way, on the quiet

I was a quiet achiever. I was too quiet. That's what left me in some of this mess. I've made a mess to get out of a mess. The stairwell masterpiece will get a hearing. I want it to. The agent won't be able to help himself. He'll have to tell the master of The Hoorah. A big fuss will ensue, but they might send a painter in to rectify my handiwork. This is what the agent wanted. He wanted a house painter to take over the lot.

What's done is done!

I didn't renovate this house. It was already done up. I decorated it. I bought the furniture and had the curtains hung. I collected the ornaments, chose the pots and arranged everything to look modern and up-to-date. I did everything. It was my taste. It was my creation. It was my idea. It was my mind at work. It was my money. I did the thinking. I did the planning. I did the number crunching. I always crunched the numbers. He didn't seem to care much, one way or the other.

When it came to the crunch, I fixed it

I've been crunching some numbers, and I think I deserve a payout. I've just arrived at an idea that I'm surprised his solicitors haven't suggested, or maybe they have. It was my solicitor's suggestion to me early in the piece. He said I should borrow the lot, and pay him out. It was an awful lot of money. I tried, but I couldn't borrow it. The bank wasn't keen, even though I'd have the business and the house as security. As I said, it was a huge amount of money. I don't think the house let it down, I think the business did. How good an asset is a business?

What bad business?

Banks don't like securing against businesses. They're a bad risk. It was a bad risk. Is a ten-year-old business a bad risk, or was I? This is what the broker was hearing. He was listening to people. Somebody was telling him about a certain Risk Analysis. Certain people were in his ear, and he wasn't keeping my affairs private.

The Broker was Keen, until the mustard gas

I'd been snookered again. I never liked him. He was a sleaze. That's why sweetness liked him. She was a sleaze too. I don't know why I trusted him to be private, because he'd never been private before. He was a friend of a friend, who is no longer my friend. I know who my friends are, and I hope I keep her. I hope they don't get to her too. I know they will, but I think they'll be barking up the wrong tree. She's a rare and beautiful tree. We both love trees. We have a lot in common. That's all friends are, really. They're just people that you enjoy being with. She doesn't discriminate. I think she was sent to me for a reason. I think our paths have crossed just at the right time.

Is a quick payout on the cards?

Should I negotiate a payout? It would have to be low, otherwise he couldn't repay it. How much would a bank lend him, with an income of $700 per week? I might start a ball rolling. I might push the envelope. I might push some buttons. It would certainly push his buttons, and then his solicitor would get to push more buttons. Would a $100,000 payout to me, push his buttons? I wouldn't tell the kids about my proposition, because I don't know if he'll go for it. I'm just seeing if he will. I bet he'll try to negotiate a lower amount. This will make me feel low. If they make me feel low, I'll forfeit the game. It's not like it costs me anything to find out. It will cost a stamp, but I could always drop the letter in. I'd drop it to his solicitor, and she'll be delighted. She'd get to charge some extra money. It's a hidden charge, receiving mail on behalf of a client.

Stayfree for agents

What's the alternative? The alternative is to stay in the ring. I'll keep getting clobbered, but at least I get a few punches in of my own. I'm bound to cop one for the staircase. I can fix it, but I'll wait till the agent gets a gander at it. I want to see his reaction, but I won't be here. I'll leave the key. Is this a bad idea?

He wanted to take someone through the house this evening at 7.00 pm. I said no, but I would be here at 7.30 pm. He declined. He declined for the sake of thirty minutes. It didn't take me thirty minutes to work out why. He wants to call the shots. He didn't make the call, his underling did. He's too much of a big shot to make a call. He likes to call all the shots, but I don't mind taking a few shots myself.

Are you a good loser?

I wonder if you're critical of my behaviour. I think that if you are indeed critical, you may be just like I was. You could be on the losing end of a deal. You might lose well, like I used to. I was a really good loser. I thought it was fair to lose gracefully. Can you win gracefully? You can win a good fight gracefully. You can't be a victim if you win. Winning for me, is different to winning for him. I know how he'll do it. I think if he accepts the deal, he'll offer the kids some money. If he thinks they'll reject his money and him, he's an even better victim. He's no victim, he's a manipulator. He'll use ill-gotten gains as his tool, when the gains have been made at my expense.

They'd be grateful

If he was concerned about the kids, he'd have offered some money already. That hasn't happened. There hasn't been one cent from him since we split up. You offer what you have now. He has a job and I don't. I offer everything I have now. I offer my personal support and love every day. These are valuable. They're far more valuable to my kids, than money. I've seen this. I've felt it, and known it. I wasn't too sure about it in the beginning. I wondered about it. I wondered how valuable I'd be to them, without any money to support them with. I don't have to wonder now. They're my special wonders. They've supported what's most valuable to them. I'm a person of high value. I'm not valuable, just because I happen to be their mother. I'm valued as a person. They like me.

I'll get the valuables after all

My son sat with me the other night, here at The Hoorah. We just talked for three hours non-stop. Every subject gets talked about. We talk about anything and everything. We talk on all levels. He's on the level and so am I. We have intellectual conversations that range from literature to science, and philosophy to love. We talk about knowledge. We talk about what we do know, don't know, and can't know. We talk about what we want to know. He's a visionary. I know this. He thinks. He has a great thinking mind. I love his mind, but sometimes I'm out of my depth. He knows a great deal more than me about some things. I wasn't as good a thinker at his age, as he is. His brain is in perfect working order. He teaches me a lot. He shows me his textbooks, and explains the science to me. I don't get all of it, but I get the gist of it. The gist of it is, he's a reference for me. He's a good reference point for any information I lack. That's what knowledge is. It's just information. Some information goes in one ear and out the other. Some of it gets stuck inside. This is the stuff I use. It gets saved up sometimes, and comes out much later when I need it. I don't look for it, because it just arrives out of the blue. We don't know what information will get stored, and what won't. This happens without us knowing. We aren't aware of this storage system. I've stored so much. I only know this since I've started writing. Some of this info has been stored for so long, I'd forgotten I still had it there.

I've turned some corners

Memories have come from the deepest darkest corners. I sometimes want them to stay there. I resist the urge to keep them buried. Now I just let them out. They sometimes disturb me. I'm disturbed by some of them. Why? If they're disturbing, they must have pain attached to them. Why? They must have been painful times. It can be painful looking back. It can be painful looking forward. I can always get to safety. Safety is now. It's the here and now.

I'm writing and I'm thinking. I'm focused and concentrating. I'm watching my hand write, and I'm conscious of being unconscious to it. I don't think about it, I just do. My hand knows what to do. Is it the pen that knows what to do? I'm not even aware of making the words on the page. Both my hand and my pen are working together, and my eyes watch on. The pace is fast, and there's a tiny voice in my head and it's automatic. Most of the time I'm on automatic. I'm an automatic writer. How? Is it experience? Does the ghost in the machine take over? Is it our spirit? Is it something divine? Am I just a watcher? Am I just a spectator?

Who's to know?

When I automatically pick up a cigarette and light it, I don't know that I've done it. I haven't been aware that I did it. Who is smoking? Who wanted a smoke? It must be the automatic me. Sometimes I realize what's happened, and I'm annoyed at myself. I realize I really didn't feel like having a smoke, and so I put it out. This is strange. It's a strange kettle of fish. Would a habit make you do this? Is that the answer? How much could you do, out of habit? Who is your habit?

I've got fish

My son brought me some fish. It was left over. It was left over from his hospitality class. It's on Monday nights, and the students get to cook for a community group. They make a special dinner, and raise funds for the school. It's an enterprising idea. The students don't get paid, but they learn. We got fish. I like fish. It's healthy. It's brain food. My son loves fish. He adores fish. He simply adores Salmon. I think it's a good memory for him.

Salmon isn't at The Butcher's

I think this love of salmon comes from an experience we had. It was a great experience. It was an experience of a lifetime. It seems a lifetime ago. We ate a lot of salmon in Canada and Alaska. We saw those beautiful places. It was sublime. The scenery was breathtaking. It drove me to tears. It moved me to tears. I didn't understand why I was crying, but I do now. My soul was awakened. It was pristine beauty. It was nature. Nature can do this to me. It awakens me.

Did you do it yourself?

The stairwell stinks. It stinks of paint fumes. It's a bad job. It looks like a very poor DIY job. I've seen heaps of these kinds of jobs, in my old job. Investment properties often look like this. Some peoples' homes look like this. This was a slap happy job, so now my home looks like this. I felt happy, slapping it on. The paint is sprinkled over the carpet. I always said that some people have a flair for renovating and doing home makeovers, but some don't. I always said I was one of the ones that didn't, but could admire the talent of others. This is bullshit! I can do it, because it's not that hard. I just don't like to do it. It was easier to get someone else to do it. I was way too busy.

I'm doing it myself

I may never be able to pay for it again. I'll just have to make do. I'll make do with whatever I have, and whatever I end up with. I just made do tonight. I only had an old paintbrush, but I could have done a much better job if I'd wanted to. This is the story. This is the story of my life.

I made do with what I had. I did the best I could with what I had, and the circumstances I found myself in. I could have done a lot better. I could have had more, but I might have had less. More might have been less. Do you work as hard, if you have more? Some people work harder, but it's just because they think they're less.

All by myself

I want balance. I'm on the platform. I've just jumped off the trapeze. I've been swinging backwards and forwards for a while now. I'm looking down. I don't want to look up from this height, because I might get dizzy. I'm looking for a safe place to fall. I can see the net below. It's a long way down and I've been up high for a long time. I walked the tightrope and I didn't look down. I used the balancing beam. I made it across eventually, but now I've only one way to go. It's not the last leg of my journey, but the journey's getting easier. The net will save me, because it will catch me before I hit the ground. I'm looking for the middle. This is the safest part to land. I'll have to find the middle of the net. I can't jump. It's too high. Even though I know I'll be safe, I just can't jump. What's stopping me? My intellect says it's fine, but my nerves say no.

A battle royal

A battle of wills is in play. It's the fear. Fear is a strong opponent. I understand fear of the unknown, but what of the known? I'm fearful about the unknown. There will always be unknown factors. The net might break, or have a hole in it. It might not be constructed properly. It might be an illusion. It may not be there at all. I must trust it's there, to make the jump. It's there. If it's not there now, then it never was there, and never will be. It's under me. It's always there. It supports.

Ace, Answers, Always

I have it. It's around my neck. It's my luck. It's my lucky charm. I have charm. I can charm the pants off you. This is a funny statement. I've never used it on myself before. I've said it about others, but not about myself. I like the word. I like the word 'charming'.

Charming:- adj. attractive, fascinating; delightful.

You can't be charming all the time, can you? Do you think you can? Would you be able to pull it off? I can't pull it off. I can pull it off for a while, but I wouldn't want to do it all the time.

I know what I've written, because I've just read it back. I've read it back to front. Maybe I'd charm the pants on you. This is charming. This sort of talk is charming coming from a lady. How charming am I? You'll never know. You won't know everything. You can never know everything about a person. Sometimes they won't want you to know. This is good. It's a good card to have up your sleeve. I'm keeping it for a rainy day. I might keep it for *The Lover in Me*.

That's the net. I made it, and I'm safe. It wasn't that bad after all. I can't withdraw it. It's been written. It's out. I've been outed. It's out there alright. It's started, but it's only just getting going.

I'm still bouncing in the net, reeling more like it. Is this a subject under discussion? No. It's not written. It shall not be written. It shall not be written, until I'm ready. I've got this tune playing in my head, and I can't remember the words to it. 'Love grows where my Rosemary goes', or is it the other way around? Where does she go?

I'm cursed

My printer just shat itself. A spark flew off the power pack transformer thingy. I don't know where I am now. I don't know whether it's time to move out. The kids want me with them. There are reasons for staying here though. They're very good reasons. I don't need a stupid printer. Less is more.

I want to take the computer though. I have a laptop and they already have a computer, but I want what I'm used to. This is what's hard about moving out. Things are not your own, but they used to be. I'd be going back to furniture I got rid of. This would mean I'd be going backwards. I'm at ones and twos. I feel edgy and distracted. I have a feeling. It's just a feeling, but it's not a good one. I feel intuitive, but not as intuitive as I'd like. I feel like there's a storm brewing somewhere. I hope it's a storm in a teacup. I've just got this uneasy sense, that something is about to go down.

Is this all a storm in a teacup?

I don't react to storms in the same way as I used to. I used to be frightened of a storm. Now I'm just fascinated. I marvel at the beauty and power of nature. I wonder whose powerful nature I'll be enduring. I won't endure it. I'll just be fascinated by it. I might even be amused by it.

The power of speech is a wondrous thing. It's mightier than the sword. I want interest. I want to make the agent's job interesting. I don't want to make it hard, but just interesting enough to talk about.

Bamboozled was a talking point

I'm bamboozled. He has stated The Hoorah is not up to standard. He said it lacked presentation. It's clean, but I know it's not spotless.

Nothing's spotless. Nothing can be perfect. Not under the current circumstances. Spots appear all the time, but you just clean them up. There are some white spots on the carpet in the stairwell. I'm leaving them there. My ex is not spotless. He's covered in unholy stains. His stains can't be removed. They won't clean off. He thinks nobody can see his stains, because he's quite clever at hiding his stains.

It's Shakespearean

He reminds me of Macbeth. Once he'd murdered, he couldn't remove the stains from his hands. He always saw blood on them. It didn't matter how much he scrubbed them, he kept seeing red. I think he'd developed an OCD and compulsively washed them, but to no avail.

Nobody is completely spotless. Once you have spots, you have them for life. You've got to accept what spots have been left on you. Hopefully you can learn from your spots. A leopard can't change its spots. If you're a leopard, then you're a leopard. God created the leopard. He created the spots. Humans aren't born with any spots. We choose our spots. We have free will.

Spotting it out?

I've never painted anything in quite the manner that I painted the stairwell in, or the mood. I'm an artist. I like things to look nice. I like nice things. Presentation is all important to me. When I look at my home presented well, it makes me feel well. It's easy on the eye. I like things that are easy on the eye. I like things that draw my eyes. My eyes take on the form, and appreciate it. They appreciate beauty and passion. They also appreciate different. I think they appreciate originality. My eyes spy it, and my mind thinks about it. My soul is inspired by it. I know it when I see it, and I know it when I make it. I might make the stairwell truly original.

Appreciating true art

I've just taken another good look at it from the top of the stairs. It was painted with soul. You can tell. It has a lot of emotion showing through. It speaks to me. It's poetic and inspiring. It's quite a powerful statement. I'm leaving it as it is.

You can't improve on perfect

My two greatest masterpieces are hanging in that stairwell. It's apt. Large framed photos of my kids, when they were littlies, are hanging there. They're originals. They're authentic. They can't be improved. They are who they are, right now. I love my work. I'm grateful for that work. I worked on them, and they worked on me.

Going off the rails

I'll fix it. I'll fix the paint on the railing. I want the agent to see what he caused, with his effects. Once he's seen my masterpiece isn't up to standard, I'll bring it up to standard. I might even improve on standard. It will be useless, because it still won't make the house sell. People don't buy a house listed at offers over $790,000 because of the paintwork on a banister.

The banister was an effect. The previous owners left it with these effects, for a modern effect. Just because it didn't affect him in a good way, doesn't mean the effect wouldn't affect someone else in a good way. He's only seeing the picture from his perspective. He's nitpicking. He's not looking at the broader perspective. He lives in a housing estate near the Shopping Mall.

His perspective is out by a mile

His perspective's been predominantly about the house. He doesn't understand the perspective I have now. I see the sand, the rocks, and the ocean. I see the waves, the boats, and I feel the sea breeze. He's a dimwit. He's dull. His senses are dulled. He doesn't sense his own nature. If he did, he wouldn't like it. He hasn't got a nice nature. The Hoorah needs a natural purchaser. It needs someone with a sense for nature. Someone with a good nature, will buy it. It will be somebody that appreciates nature, not the house. A house is just a house, after all.

It's a beautiful house with a very modern bathroom. It has a sunken spa bath and dual hand basins. A house can be changed. It will be changed. When a house is lived in, it changes. Things wear out and need maintenance. This happens with an empty house too. There will always be maintenance. You don't have to maintain nature, do you? Will somebody take the ocean away? Will somebody stop the waves? A house isn't permanent like nature. Everything sells with the right price.

You must believe in the product

I don't think the agent believes in the product he's selling. He doesn't want to believe in the value of this position. By doing this, he devalues his own position. He'll have to take the de-valued position personally. Personally, his is less valuable. He shouldn't let his personal position, interfere with his professional position. By putting someone else's position higher than his own, his position is lowered. He can't do that, even though it's the true position. He wants me to be less, but he already knows I'm more. His mind is finding ways to make me less. His mind is irritated by me being more. He doesn't want to believe I'm more. He's measuring himself against me. He's comparing. I didn't compare myself, and I didn't make a judgment. I waited. I've gathered information. I've observed and stored information. I've only used his information, against him. I didn't like the information he gave me, so I used his information, and gave it back to him with my regards. He didn't like it either. He didn't mind dishing it up, but he didn't like it being dished back up to him. It was just the same meal. What's good for the goose, is good for the gander.

Why all the fairy tales?

Why is Mother Goose always the storyteller? It seems to be a recurring theme. It's like Mother Goose is the boss of fairy tales. Why Mother Goose? Why not Father Gander? There's some role playing going on. I need a new role. I need to work on the role I want to play. I've played a lot of different roles in my life. I know a role I haven't played. I haven't played the role of a lady. I have always been a lady, but I haven't always been treated like one. I want the lady in me to come out. I never had a 'coming out'. I never made my debut.

> **Debut:-** n. [Fr. < *debuter*, lead off] 1. the first appearance before the public, as of an actor; 2. the formal introduction of a girl into society.

I think it's a special occasion. It's old fashioned. It's kind of like a girl's first ball. There are boys, and they dance. It's a chance to dress up and show your best self to society.

I have a vague recollection that The General made her debut. I think she made her debut with the friend across the road, but I could be mistaken. They were Catholic.

Are we all disturbed in some way?

This question could be a little disturbing, depending on how you think about it. It will depend on your memory and your past experiences.

Does what we feel when we're kids, also feel good as an adult? Is this how and what, we're associating our occasions with? Are some pleasures triggered by a memory of past experiences? Norman Doidge M.D. thinks so. Me, I think so too. Abnormal input equals abnormal output. This is me, and it's my quote. It's most likely to have been quoted before me, by someone else. Did we both have the same experience?

What disturbs you about parts of your childhood? Be open to examination. Let me examine you. Let's play doctors and nurses. That's not what got played, is it? It was doctors and patients. I'm not a doctor. Are you a patient? Are you sick? What's your output? Output is the answer. Is your output normal, or abnormal? What's abnormal? Whose standards apply? Is there such a thing as normal? Is there such a thing as a normal childhood? Was it normal for kids to play doctors and nurses in your day, or was it forbidden?

How does it start?

It always starts with the examination, doesn't it? Is it a private examination? What did we learn? We learned about private places. We learned to keep the appointments private. Were we guilty of anything? Is it natural for kids to play this game, or do parents provide the doctor's kit for them to experiment with?

Forbidden parts

I was told once, that those massive anthills in the far north of the country are built to specification. What you can see on the upside, is the exact opposite to what you can't see on the down side. The positive picture of the anthill is a maze of channels throughout the dirt mound. The negative picture is under the ground.

Are humans built like this? Do humans build like this? Are ants predictable? If you could predict the inside of a person, could you predict the outside? Do you have to know what makes ants tick?

Why is it so?

It's for survival. It's the same thing. Survival is what makes humans tick. Once you've discovered what makes you tick, you can predict what your next move will be.

I'm a fitter and turner, granted

People decide to survive, or they don't. There are reasons why they do, and reasons why they don't. Is it survival of the fittest? I fit. I fit the mould to survive. I'm a survivor. I have survival techniques. I didn't have these ones before. These are new ones. The old ones weren't working that well. I'm praying for a come-back. No I'm not. I don't want to come back. I'm praying for a forward. I want a come-forward. A move forward is what I'm praying for. I'm praying for a window. I'll be watching for it. I'll be waiting for my window. I'll know it when I see it, and I'll jump at the opportunity it affords me. I can't afford much.

Windows are everywhere, but choose one that fits the purpose

My window of opportunity has been supported by my wonders. They've been wonderfully supportive. They've supported me emotionally, creatively, financially, nutritionally, and spiritually. It's good karma coming back at me. It was good karma coming my way, because I'd already sent it their way. I think good karma is bouncing back and forth between us. You can't calculate karma. It gets measured elsewhere. You can't time karma. Karma doesn't have a time schedule. Karma doesn't have the same rules as us mere mortals. Our rules are different. Our rules have been learned. Karma follows the laws of intention.

It follows good intention, and it follows bad intention

Things that look immoral are judged by us, measured by a set of rules and a formula adopted by society. Society is just society, and they aren't the ultimate rule makers. Rules can't fit every circumstance. The circumstances are the trouble with rules. We can't always change the circumstances. Does society take into consideration the range of circumstances? It could, if there weren't any rules.

Society:- n., pl. -ties [< L. *socius*, companion] 1. all people, collectively; 2. a group of persons regarded as forming a single community; 3. the system of living together in such a group; 4. companionship; 5. any organized group with work, interests, etc. in common; 6. a group of persons regarded as dominant class because of their wealth, birth, etc. adj. of or involving society (n.6) -soci'-etal adj.

Some people reject the laws of common society and form their own societies. They make their own rules up according to their own beliefs. Some are good societies, and some are not. The ones that aren't, may not be bad, but they may not be that good either. It depends on intention. If it's with good intention in mind, then it can't hurt others. That's not true, is it? Good intentions can hurt others. Sometimes others just need to be hurt, for the good intention to work.

Should we kill the infidels?

Infidelity is said to be immoral in our society. We judge infidelity without looking at the whole picture. We judge before knowing the underlying reasons, ramifications, and the facts of the matter. Often, we'll never know these. Some people will judge infidelity harshly, and others won't judge at all. They won't see it as such a serious matter. They've heard it all before, because it's quite common in our society these days. We read all about it in the gossip columns. The celebrities are on the cover of glossy magazines with their affairs out in the open. We feel sorry for the betrayed party, but it all looks like a big party from the photos. It all looks pretty good on paper. New partners, one-night stands. He's been seen with her, and she's been dining out with him. We're all dining out on it. We're entertained by all the fanfare. It's news!

It's a headline

What if it doesn't make the news at all? What if it's been swept under the rug, and the unfaithful party is forgiven by the faithful party? They go on with their lives and try to act normal, as if nothing untoward has happened. What's the underlying story? Where's the damage? Will history repeat itself if the lesson is not learned?

The story is…

We'll never know what ultimately caused the second story to unfold. We won't know karma when we see it. We could all be judging the second story, without knowing the first story. The first story stays hidden, and so does the first offender's offence.

There's always room for thought, and time to think. There's always a reason to consider the actions, and reactions of others, but we can't really know. How can we judge without knowing?

> **Infidel:-** n. [< L. *in-*, not + *fidelis*, faithful] 1. a person who does not believe in a particular, esp. the prevailing, religion; 2. a person who holds no religious belief –adj. 1. that is an infidel; 2. of infidels.

When a soldier comes home from the war boasting about how he shot down the enemy, do we judge him immoral? Some may see him as a hero. Other people may feel it's in bad taste to boast of the killing, and rather not be hearing about the detail.

The details are where the ugliness is

The soldier did the job he was ordered to do. He was paid to do it. He was defending a cause. He was a success, because he was awarded a medal for his efforts. It's a big picture, and one with much detail, if one cared to look closely. There's plenty of perspectives to take. He may have been drafted, in which case, he's been forced by a society into a situation he may not have ventured into of his own free will.

Do we really know what we're getting ourselves into?

He couldn't have known what he was venturing into. He's now being celebrated as a brave war hero and respected for his services to the cause. He may have saved his own comrades on the firing line. He may have helped to win a battle, and bring the war to a close. He may have done exactly what he was meant to do, and now he lives with the consequences.

He's still boasting

He's psychologically damaged, and boasting is his way of confessing what he's done. He may feel they were terrible deeds, but trying to put a positive slant on it. He has horrific memories. Visions of death and destruction haunt him. He's changed. He's not the same person he used to be. The devil is in the detail.

Do we make a career out of it?

He may have discovered that he likes killing people. He may do it again. He's been rewarded after all. The soldier lost his best mates out on that battlefield. He may feel he made restitution for their deaths. It may be the only way he knows how to express, or justify, his guilty conscience.

Do we believe in what we're doing?

Was he politically motivated? Did he feel that the deaths he'd caused, solved a problem? And now for the big question… Were his intentions good or bad? It's not black or white. Are we talking about his intentions, or other peoples' intentions? Both must be considered. One needs to consider oneself first, for this matter of karma.

Saving private questions

What were his intentions towards self, as he fired the fatal bullet at the body of the enemy soldier? Was it fired in self-defence? Was it to make his sergeant proud, and to gain his approval? Was it to get a medal? Was it just doing a job, and being paid for services provided? Was it for self-gratification? Did he want to cause pain? Did he want to inflict pain and suffering? Is he a psychopath?

What's more...

Did he think of the wives and families of the soldiers he killed? Did he hate the people he shot? Did he hate the society he was fighting against? What did he want to cause? Did he have an effect? Did he think about it at all? Are you thinking what I'm thinking?

Options can be hard to take up

A conscientious objector could have opted for jail. Many conscientious objectors shot themselves. They gave themselves injuries, to avoid battle. This is what I hope I would have done, but I'll never know. You can't know if you're not him. Would you want to be him? This is the sort of damage societies can do, if we don't consider our own rules first. Societies make rules, we obey them, and find ourselves in situations we're confused about. When we're confused, we need to think more deeply, until we're no longer confused. It can be a battle to justify it. It can be a lifetime's battle.

What's right, and what's wrong?

You must confer with yourself. You are your own society. This is the only society you'll have to live with for the rest of your life. We don't ask ourselves enough questions.

I don't always understand karma. I just know to be good to myself, and try not to hurt others while doing it. Trying not to hurt others, is the good intention. I don't want to hurt anyone by my actions, but I must stand up for myself too. Trying not to hurt others, at the expense of yourself and your own society, is not right either. It's a bad intention towards self. One must find the balance. It's the healthy balance I'm looking for. If I've confused the situation, forgive me. I'm still a little confused.

Defending the write career

I've been drafted. I didn't ask for this war. I didn't want to fight in it. I fight in self-defence, and for long-term self-preservation.

I don't want to hurt anyone. I haven't wanted to cause pain, however pain has been caused. It was never my intention to fight a war. I've lashed out in anger. My lashing out has been nowhere near the lashing I've had. I've copped a fair lashing. I've swallowed a lot, to be able to spit it out like this.

This was a private dispute

I can remember someone telling me years ago, that neighbourhood disputes in the old days, used to be settled with a quick biff to the nose, followed by a beer over the fence afterwards. This is a quick way to deal with anger. Was it really anger over a neighbourhood issue? Mates would sock each other in the mouth and then make up. They didn't discuss the issues. They didn't discuss what was on their minds in the first place. They just wanted to forget about it. They just used each other as a punching-bag to get rid of the negative energy that had backed up. A pressure cooker was exploding. All the negative energy dispersed in one blow. Did they resolve the underlying problem?

Is this saying what I think?

I never knew this about men. I didn't understand how important it was to let off steam regularly. I guess it's why a lot of men love to play sports. What are the other men doing? Coaches advise their players not to have sex before a big game. Rocky Balboa was advised the same thing. What can you do with all that stored up energy? How powerful is it? Is sex this powerful? Is sex this powerful for men? What sort of power does it hold for women? How much power does a woman hold? This is the great quandary that men and women find themselves in. I've been learning about this. I thought it was about time I found the answers to these significant questions. It never used to be that significant a question for me. I just never gave it much thought.

I'm fascinated by human nature

It's human nature, with two different natures communing. A man's nature is different to a woman's nature. Sometimes true natures are hard to find. They get buried under all the problems, and the business of life. Life isn't a business, it's nature. I'm going to answer the question about how much power a woman holds, because it seems I might have some power after all.

A woman has the power to make a man happy. This is a powerful statement, but it only exists in the moment. A woman has the power, but only while she holds onto it. When it's over, it's over. She's no longer powerful. The more regularly a woman holds it, the more powerful she becomes. This isn't totally accurate, because when she holds it too regularly, it's not significant. Power must build up first. This can take a couple of days, or even a week. Imagine how much power would build up in a month. Don't! That never happens. Men don't wait. They hold the power over themselves. They blow it! I think they need to. I think it's the way of their nature. I think it's natural. This is just my theory, because I'm not a man. I'm a woman, and we're different.

Don't mind my body

As human beings, we consist of both mind and body. You can look at these two parts separately, or you can look at them together. A man is more physical, and a woman is more mindful. It's mind over matter really. A man feels a physical need, because this is where he feels his energy build up. Both men and women have both. This is what both are for. A woman must be mentally stimulated before a man can be physically stimulated. Both mental and physical positions, can be shared. Once this happens, both needs are met. To get to a man's head, you must use his body. To get to a woman's body, he must use his head. How hard or simple, is this? It depends on whether you're a man or a woman.

How hard is simple?

Are we measuring up? It's not simple, if it's not hard. It's not hard, if it's too simple. Get it?

Where are our energies going?

What happens to a woman's energies? Are a woman's energies as powerful as a man's? Yes, but they don't blow it on mindless pursuits. It's not in our nature. It is in our nature, once nature has taken its course. There's a course to negotiate first. Mothers are nature, just like Mother-nature. We have a mothering nature, and that's where our energies get directed. You need a lot of energy being a mother.

What happens when our chicks fly the coop? We get all hot and bothered. We look desperately for ways to expend this energy. We sometimes forget that we aren't on duty anymore. This is when we discover the joys of mindless pursuits. One must have a time and a place for such pursuits. Sometimes we discover an easier way. It's good therapy. We use our mind to think up ways to find pleasure. We invest, because we've heard how good they are at providing optimum pleasure. We remember to put our toys away in a safe and secure place, because they're our very own personal possessions. They're our special treasures, so we hide them away from prying eyes. We're modern women in modern times, with modern devices.

What more could a woman want?

What happened to the man? She held too much, or too little power, and he went looking for another power point.

They both need a natural power supply

She's been busy loving herself sick, but she's missing something. She's missing a body. She's missing a mind. She's missing her opposite nature. This is the quandary of nature.

How powerful is Mother-nature?

Why is she in a quandary? She's lonely, cold, and empty. It's her mind. She can't take her mind off men. She imagines a man's body, and a man's powerful urges. She imagines the company of a man. She wants a man to mentally stimulate her. She wants a mate.

Does a man now have extra competition? Is he competing with her pleasurable pursuits? Is she competing with his pleasurable pursuits? The answers are the same. There's no substitute for Mother-nature, but a substitute can be an addition. It can be the added ingredient, just for extra spice.

Is it wrong to share my thoughts?

Is my theory morally wrong? Is it karma, all this holding on? Does it have the ring of truth? Is it ringing bells? Are they alarm bells? Don't be alarmed. We live in a modern society, and this is progress. It's a change, and a change is natural.

There's one more thing I want to say about men and women's opposing natures. Open your eyes. This is the mind's connection point. It's like the other power point. When you open your eyes, the power is turned on. It's the windows to your souls. Let your souls connect, and you'll light up entirely. You'll see one another in a different light.

Be mindful of the light

What's a rush? What's a trip? What's a buzz? What's a high? It's exhilarating! It's overwhelming. It's moving, and mostly indescribable. Is it an 'out of body' experience? Did you go somewhere? Was it uplifting? Was it euphoric? I'm not talking about sex. I'm talking about your mind. Was it mind-blowing? Have you had such a feeling? How do you get it? .

Surrender!

That's how you got it. You allowed yourself to be vulnerable to something. You fully opened up. You risked. You pulled down your protective walls, and went for it. You put aside your worries. You let go of inhibitions. Some people can do this easily, but some can't. It takes some practice. I've practised, and practised. Sometimes it hurts. It's scary and unknown. It's diving into the water with your eyes closed. It's can be, just opening your eyes. I've had to open mine. I've had to push the boundaries. I've pushed my boundaries out further. I've opened myself up, and it's total exposure. Opening, is letting in. Closing, is keeping out. I want in. I want to let stuff out, and let good stuff in. I've surrendered. I've surrendered my control. I'm no longer in control. Losing control is a fearful thing to do, but only if there's no net. I have a net. I can't see it, but I know it's there.

Always

Having faith that there is a net, is transcendence. It's not blind faith. I'm not blind anymore. I'm multisensory. I make sense. Are you on the scent?

It wasn't theory. It was practical. I'm practical. I like to check things for authenticity. I like to see proof. It's just how I am. I'm a sceptic, until I see reason. What's a reason? A reason is a formula. It's how we find the answer. It proves. Can a reason be proven? Yes, but only until a better reason comes along.

This is the history of knowledge

Old knowledge has changed. It's been used to find new knowledge. Was the original knowledge wrong? Not for then, but for now, yes. Knowledge changes with time. We just have new knowledge now, but one day it will be old knowledge. It won't be quite correct in a hundred years from now. But that's only if we're still seeking knowledge throughout the next hundred years. I'll probably be wrong by then. Knowledge will have evolved.

Fearing what you don't know

Does some knowledge just languish? Does some knowledge just stagnate and not get improved upon? What knowledge gets stuck? Which knowledge do we avoid? Why do we avoid thinking about specific subjects? Is it fear of what we may learn?

Have you ever feared certain knowledge? Would it change your whole outlook? Would it change your thinking? Are you afraid to change some of your thinking? Are you afraid of updating your knowledge? New knowledge can be hard to store. It can be hard to digest. It's hard to integrate with an already existing system. It can cause a disturbance in the system. It can make you feel uncomfortable. Some people resist new knowledge, when it's disturbing to their system. It leaves their whole system in disarray, when the new information arrives and the system then requires an overhaul.

I used to do this. I was choosing what knowledge to integrate with my system. I chose the easiest way. I thought I had a good enough system without looking to update it. It was a system with holes in it. There were gaps. I plugged the gaps with nice knowledge. It made digestion easier.

Keeping the system going

I've had a fair bit of indigestion over the last fourteen months. Disturbing knowledge isn't easy to stomach. I've integrated it, because this unwanted knowledge did get stored. It got stored in the 'unwanted knowledge' area. This is way up the back. I didn't want to store it, but I didn't have a choice. Once we know something, and once something has arrived into our system, it gets remembered. You can avoid remembering it. You can just block it by thinking about something else, or by changing it. I changed the look of it, and made and excuse for it. This changed the way it made me feel.

Bend and stretch

Our brains are plastic. This means they can be changed. Neuroplasticity is about the brain's ability to change and compensate. This is how blind people can develop their other senses more fully. Our brains adapt. They can relearn to do something in a completely different way. It's called compensating for a lack. Our mind and bodies can learn to adapt to the changed environment and conditions.

There's stacks to compensate for

We all compensate. We compensate when we're lacking in some area. When we can't compensate, we make allowances. We can make allowances for ourselves, by using other people. I compensated by bluffing. I was all bluff. No I wasn't! I did bluff a lot, though. I called their bluff. I'm a good bluffer. A bluffer is a pretender. I'm a good pretender. I learned how to pretend when I was a child.

I learnt from the best

Pretending games were learning games. We sometimes don't know when we're pretending, and when we're not. I got mixed up sometimes. My job was a game of pretending. Pretending is part of life. We pretend we're happy, when we're not. We pretend we're grateful, when we don't feel grateful. We even pretend to ourselves. We tell ourselves how happy we are. We tell ourselves how grateful we are for what we have, and that allows us to be happy in it. It's just pretend. Are we feeling it, or are we just saying it? I could pretend so well, and talk myself into a state. I could talk my feelings into it. Would it happen naturally, if we didn't tell ourselves?

I've forgotten how to let things come naturally. I think I pretend everything into life. Not everything, but some things. It's a habit. I've been pretending to be happy for a long, long, time. I've been putting on an act. It was a good act, because even I believed it. I'd been forcing. I didn't know I didn't have to force.

Are we all just great pretenders?

In the same way that I pretended nice things into my life, I've also pretended bad things out of it. I pretended I didn't have anger, frustration, sadness, resentment, and fear. These were my natural emotions. They were there for a reason. I shouldn't have reasoned them away. I should have used them to reason.

I already knew the reasons, and that's why I pretended them away.

Is it mental or physical?

This is how sick our brains can be. It's not the brain that's sick, is it? It's our minds. Our mind uses the brain as a tool. Our mind is not matter. It does matter though. Our mind is mystical. It's a force of its own. Our mind is the ghost in the brain machine. My mind was sick. No it was not! My thinking was dysfunctional. Who gave me dysfunctional thinking? Who taught me to function in this way?

Trust is only one side to it

It's not a word I like. The word 'trust' doesn't mean itself. It hasn't done what it's supposed to. It's me. I'm trustworthy, but I can't be trusted. I know this, because I can't trust myself either. I don't know what will happen next. Neither do you. I could die tomorrow, and anyone who trusted me, cannot trust me anymore. I could fall over accidentally, or cause a car crash. This is a lame way to explain what I want to say, and it's a bit weak to explain what I want to explain, but don't trust me.

Words you can trust

Have you ever said something automatically that you didn't mean to say? It's out, before you can pull it back in again. It's out of your mouth, before you realize you were even thinking it. You only realize you've said it, after you've said it. What about what we write down? Can we trust ourselves with what we write down? Can we trust ourselves in a situation of high emotion?

Was the trust under control?

Things happen that change us. The person you trusted implicitly, could change because of circumstances beyond their control. It may be from circumstances beyond everyone's control. Your understanding may not be up to speed, because you don't have the knowledge to consider the reasons why they're not in control. Imagine that! Are we still talking about trust? Trust is imperative for a healthy life, but so is distrust. People need to trust themselves, but know and be aware, that they can't always be trusted. It's just the way we're made. Trust is what keeps us relating to each other. We must trust. Trust, we must.

The trust wasn't a bust

I trust differently now. I trust only in the now. I know now, that then, can change it. I must find the courage to trust when trust doesn't really exist. This will leave me wide open, but it's honest. This is the same as surrender. What's the risk? It's the same, but different. The trust I used to believe in, just doesn't exist. I acknowledge the real risk now. I never saw it before. I never understood the risk. I never properly understood trust. Now I do. I still risk, but I risk just now. I may even risk a bit less. Less is more.

> **Serendipity:-** n. [< Per. Fairy tale, *The Three Princes of Serendip*] a seeming gift for making fortunate discoveries accidentally.

This looks like a sign to me. The Three Princes, have put fortune at my door in the form of a Magician. I hope he really is magic. I need some magic around here. What are the chances? What would the chances be, of finding a magician to be a flatmate? We might be flatmates. I've offered, and I'll know for sure soon. I've got a feeling I won't be so flat, and nor will he. What's the opposite of flat?

From my Thesaurus:

uneven, rough, rugged, broken, irregular, scabrous, hilly, rolling, slanting, sloping, vertical, upright, perpendicular, bubbly, effervescent, sparkling, fizzy, flavoursome, tasty, savoury, palatable.

These all sound better than flat, except for scabrous.

Scabrous:- adj. [< L. *scabere*, to scratch] 1. rough, scaly, scabby, etc.; 2. full of difficulties; 3. indecent, scandalous, etc.

He probably has a printer that works. He's an intellectual. We're both talkers. He'll be talked about, indecently. Will there be a scandal?

He'll be teaching me what he knows, and I can teach him what I know. Neither of us will really know if we're on the right track. We'll be trying to work each other out. This is what we do. We're both seekers of knowledge. Our brains will reconnect. We're both thinkers, but we think differently to each other. I'm a magician too. Magicians are illusionists. We're clever. We're far too clever by far. We are the type of people that consult an expert for help, and then help the expert. We're expert illusionists. We ask someone to work us out, and then work us out for them. They believe. We hide behind our expert illusions. We're strong and convincing. Our theories hold weight. We can hold our own, in expert company. We're quite practised at it.

My old mate from Uni

We call their bluff, but who are we bluffing? We know how to look credible. Can we see each other's cracks? I think we could both partake in some free therapy for the sake of old times. I'm going to be aware of what I project onto this magician. It may be the magical answers I've been looking for. I've never had a flatmate.

Hold on, what word am I using instead of 'flat'? What about 'irregular' mate? Nope. 'Broken' mate? No fear! 'Bubbly'? Not on your nelly. 'Slanting' mate, 'sloping' mate? No, he can't be these either. 'Hilly' and 'rolling' don't do it for me either. Does 'flavoursome', or 'tasty' mate, fit the bill? It might have to be 'scabrous'.

My scabrous mate

He's bound to like it, because it sounds like a pirate. He'll hate it!

I like upright. He's my 'upright' mate. He's downright upright. He's not flat, he's inspiring.

I'll have to curb my personality, if he does decide to move in. My personality can be overpowering. I was never one to beat around the bush. I cut to the chase. He's upright, and I'm upfront. He's in his third year of psychology. This is where I would have been, had I not given it a miss. I missed out, but I don't think I missed much.

We met as students in our first semester. A lot has happened since then, so there's a lot to catch up on. We've caught up because of a protest in the newspaper. He was protesting about the treatment he was receiving from real estate agents. He was protesting unhelpful real estate agents, and his lack of success in securing rental accommodation. I helped him out for old time's sake, and for heaven's sake.

Is this karma?

It smells a little like karma. We'll see.

I'm looking forward to seeing his books. I suspect he has a collection of great books, and I'll be showing him mine. I feel sure our brains will have a lot in common. We have common ground. We're fascinated by human nature. I hope we can talk philosophy, science, evolution, history, theology, neuroscience, feminism, and masculinism. Is this a word? I bet he starts making it one. What's in a word? A word can provide great insight, great feedback, and hopefully, enlightenment. Is 'honesty' a word?

Can oil and water be mixed?

Do you worry about oil? I do. I worry about using it, and I worry about disposing of it. Oil and water don't mix. I see the rain trying to wash it away, but where does it wash away to? Oil can't be got rid of, can it? It makes everything greasy. I never know how to dispose of unwanted oil. What's the best way for the environment? I know something about bio fuel, but not much. I know it exists. You can burn oil. Is this what we should be heating our homes with? What about old paint? I know there's a special way for it to be disposed of, but I can't say that I know what it is. I imagine a great industrial vat. All the old paint gets poured into it, and it's buried somewhere. Maybe there's a huge furnace, and the paint and paint tins are just thrown in to be burnt. Where does the polluted air go? Where does any waste, really go?

My oily relationship

Is this progress? I've progressed. I've got no oil. That's not true. I've none left to cook with – that's true. I moisturize with it. It's in my make-up, so I decorate with it. I paint with it. I eat it, because it's in margarine. It's already in lots of food I eat. It's in meat and bacon, but I don't eat that now.

> **Oil:-** n. [< Gr. *elaion*, (olive) oil] 1. any of various greasy, combustible, normally liquid substances obtained from animal, vegetable, and mineral sources: oils are not soluble in water; 2. same as PETROLEUM; 3. same as: a) OIL COLOUR b) OIL PAINTING; 4. [Aust Slang] fact or news [good oil, dinkum oil] –vt. 1. to lubricate or supply with oil; 2. to bribe [to oil someone's palm] –adj. of, from, or like oil, or having to do with the production of use of oil –oil the wheels, to make things go more smoothly –oil'- er n.

That's why we have oil. It's to make things go more smoothly. I agree with that, but it's a no, no, to pour down the kitchen sink. Is it the same with bath oil? I love to take a bath in scented bath oil, but then I have to let the plug out.

Is it a waste?

Oil is luxurious, but sea birds caught in black oil slicks, don't think so. Oil baths aren't good for birds, or sea life. Our thinking doesn't go far enough. We think about a new discovery or invention, but forget to think about the consequences. We stop thinking once we've had the bright idea. We just hope the bright idea makes money. Our thinking isn't as advanced as it should be. Can we be any further advanced in our thinking?

My thinking isn't advanced

How advanced are you?

Fish oil is oily. Where do the fish get their oil from? Fish oil is said to be good for the brain. Is oil for our brains? Is it to keep our brains running in perfect order? Is it to keep our brains running smoothly? It isn't fuel, is it? Oil is fuel. It's to fire up our minds. This is just more fuel for the fire.

Oil is a lubricator. Oil makes my clothesline winder work better. It's waterproof. It protects things from water. Water erodes things, and oil doesn't. Oil is a barrier.

The Great Barrier

Our bodies produce oil. It's produced from our hair, right down to our skin. Our bodies have oil and water. We need both to function. I'm making this up as I go along, because I don't know the actual science behind it. My essay on oil needs research. It needs better facts. Would my essay read as smoothly with facts and figures? Do you have to be an expert to write an essay on a specific subject? Can you just have an opinion, based on what you know? This is my humble opinion.

> **Essay:-** n. [< L. ex-, out of + agree, do] 1. a short, personal literary composition 2. an attempt –vt. to try; attempt.

I've written short essays throughout my books. Why? I'm just letting you know what's on my mind. I'm showing you how I think. I'm sharing it, because my mind is me. I read from my first book, and I can see how my writing has changed. I've just added oil to my writing so I can be freed up.

I've made the attempt, and I've attempted to get to the heart of the problem. What's at the heart? What's at the problem? Do I have the heart to tell you?

"I am the matter of my book." – Montaigne

They have their hearts in it

I can see two fishermen in the distance. They're standing on the rocks. I can hardly see them through the rain and the salt mist. White water surrounds them. It's a big swell. It's lousy weather, and it's cool. It's the 1st of March.

Are the two fishermen there because they must catch a fish? They want to fish so badly, that they risk the discomforts of nature. Is it for the fish, or their nature?

Nature is one of the greatest healers

Here comes another short essay. It's an attempt to get to the heart of the problem. Is it, 'a problem shared, is a problem solved'? Is it supposed to be, 'a problem shared is a problem halved'? Where is the other half? Is it a good intention? Should you offload your worries onto somebody else? What's the difference between offloading, and sharing? I think there's a difference. Sharing is a dual effort. As I see it, one person shares their problems with another, and that person shares his problems with them. It's a two-way communication. It's fair and balanced. It's fair play. It's better than just dropping a line in. It's better than just dropping off a load, and then leaving. Sharing is learning. It's understanding, and/or trying to understand. It's compassionate and loving. Often the same problems are shared, but they just look a bit different. We can learn a lot from other peoples' problems. We can learn a lot about ourselves, and the way we handle problems.

Do problems attract problems? I think they do. I think it's the common fishing ground. It's sometimes where we meet. You can have many problems in common. Problems of personality are often what we have, which comes from our experiences, forming our attitudes and opinions. This has a bearing on how we react to situations.

Changing personality with new experiences

This has changed for me. The rules have changed. I've changed the rules for myself. We can do this at any time we want, but we must become aware of the rules we make for ourselves. Are they good rules? Are they safety rules? Are there any others?

No. Rules get made for safety and security. That's the only reason for rules. Are they infallible? In other words, are they guaranteed? Is our safety guaranteed by rules? No. Rules are for conformity. They keep us in line. They keep us from going off the rails. What happens when we go off the rails?

We've overstepped our boundaries

Do we always get discovered? Can you step out of your boundaries without getting discovered? What's the risk of breaking the rules? The rule is, not to get caught. Is this risking your safety? Rules only claim to make you safer, but they can't guarantee your safety.

Getting caught out of bounds

You don't always get caught breaking rules. It's not guaranteed. We all break rules from time to time, and don't get caught. We don't think of this. We only think of the instances when we've been caught. This is what makes us wary of breaking rules. The other stuff gets forgotten. Sometimes it doesn't get forgotten. Sometimes it's a special memory. Do these special memories, inspire us to more rule breaking? Does your ego play a part in this charade? It's playing charades, isn't it? We think we can get away with it by not telling anyone. We think if nobody finds out, we've performed the ultimate charade. We are clever! This is the ego getting high. It gets high, because it thinks the personality is clever.

> **Charade:-** n. [Fr.] 1. [often pl.] a game in which a word to be guessed is acted syllable by syllable or as a whole; 2. a mockery, farce.

The ego wants more cleverness. It wants to show off. The personality has ventured outside the boundaries, and wants to show off what it's learned. Usually it's syllable by syllable. Sometimes it's acted out. The game of charades is played with a little too much expertise.

Breaking the rules, changes us

We don't conform as well in the same way. It's noticeable. Any small change is noted by people close to you. When you change, they are forced to change a little too. Your change causes an effect. They either want to change too, or they don't. The other person is perplexed, because they're still looking for the cause. What's caused the change in you? What, and where, is the cause for this sudden change? Something doesn't smell right. It doesn't look right. Something doesn't sound right. It's not the same, and it's going to have an effect. This goes backwards and forwards. There's a cause, and then an effect, and then the cause of another effect, and so on.

The person close to you has now been affected, and you're seeing and feeling a new effect. It's causing another effect in you. You don't like the effect it's having on that person, or the effects they cause you. You're seeing it and not liking it, because it means you've been affected by their new effects. You are now changing again. You must go with it somehow. The change is out of control. You can't go back. You can't turn back the clock. It's going too far forward, fast. It's fast forwarding. Change is in motion and it can't be stopped. It's fast and furious now.

Motion sickness

When does it eventually stop? This is an important question for me. It might be an even more important question for him. He won't arrive at an answer, not until he's come clean. I'll stop the motions, when everybody's owned up. That won't happen in a hurry. I've got plenty of time.

Who set the third wheel in motion?

He set me in motion. He should have thought about this more deeply, before he had his brilliant idea of breaking the rules. Some people don't think about the future, do they? They don't do any forward planning. People who seek change, must realize it's going to have an effect. It can sometimes have a lasting effect. It can affect many, many, people, in ways none of us could possibly suspect. But you could consider.

Good intentions are the intentions to change in a positive way. Don't take the negative way. Good intentions may mean being honest with yourself, and your close others. Being caught is not the bad intention. You didn't intend to be caught. You may have been breaking the rules, but you weren't intending to get caught breaking them. Is being caught, being caught between a good intention, and a bad intention? Do you deny any rule breaking, or do you confess to rule breaking?

What's breaking?

Which is the better intention? Which decision hurts another? You can deny, if you feel this is the good intention. It might be, if you cease your rule breaking, but has being caught hurt the other person? Yep. Damage has already been done. Already you've caused an effect. The effect is there, and you've caused it. What's the good intention from this point? Do you continue to cause the bad effect, or do you stop causing the effect? Either way, it's too late. Change has taken place, and you can't go back inside the boundaries. You've been seen outside the boundaries, and it will always be remembered. You can no longer be trusted to obey the rules.

You can't go back

Even if you deny breaking the rules, and promise never to break them again, it's been felt. The feelings are felt by the close other. It's a feeling. It even leaves them with a feeling, and you can't deny that. You don't like the feeling any more than they do. They feel it more though. They feel it so much more strongly than you do, because they didn't have a choice in this matter of change. You changed things by breaking the rules without giving notice. Giving notice is a better intention. It puts everyone in the picture. It's a true picture of who broke the rules.

What are your intentions?

This is what a father asks of their daughter's suitors. Fathers want to know about the young man's intentions. They want to be sure that there are good intentions towards their daughter. Fathers are protective of their daughter's feelings. That's the good intentions of the father. Some fathers have such good intentions. Are all fathers well-intentioned?

I felt the change in the air

Things change. Intentions change. Fathers change, mothers change, and husbands change. Wives change. It's not the same as it used to be. Things don't stay the same. People don't have the same intentions as they used to.

Friends change

Do we hurt people intentionally? No. Sometimes we do. Sometimes we defend our position, because our position is threatened. What's one-upmanship?

> **One-up:-** adj. [Colloq.] having an advantage (over another): often in, be one-up on – one'-up'manship' n.

Is it 'Advantage Server'?

Is it an advantage? Is serving, the advantage we think it is? The ball can be returned at the same velocity. What we serve to one side, can come back at us just as hard, if not harder. It depends on the type of hit, and the consequences of that hit.

The winner takes it all

Was the intention to win the game? Was the intention to win the game at any expense? Was it for one-upmanship? Do you put the other person down, to attain one-upmanship? Who gets one-downmanship? Is it their fault? Are they the man down? Have they been put down, for you to be put up? Will they put up with it?

Playing by the rules

When you break the rules, there's usually a consequence. When you breach a contract, there's usually a penalty. Is there a punishment? No. It's just cause and effect. It's just karma. It's spirit. It's a spirited come back.

Balls are involved

Can you break someone's spirit? What happens to your spirit, when it's been broken? We all know, because we've all felt it. It's not a nice feeling. It's raw and agonizing pain. Your spirit's been shattered, and you can't put it back together again in the same way. There are too many pieces, and some pieces are irretrievable now. They're lost. You refill these gaps the best you can, with anything you can find. You're just trying to survive. You get on with the healing process. A broken spirit needs time to heal. Sometimes we don't get given any time. Sometimes there's just no time, so you put something in its place, and it helps a bit. You're not as strong as you were, are you? You have weak spots. You protect those, because you know they're vulnerable.

I'm the big purple vase

I'm thinking of a vase. It's a vase that I've had for a while. It's made of glass, and it's a wonder I still have it. It wasn't originally gifted to me. It comes and goes. It keeps coming back to me. My wonders wanted it. For some reason, we still have it in our possession. It will appear later. It will appear out of the blue. Maybe it's more of a dark blue vase.

I can imagine breaking the spirit of a horse. I'm not a vase and I'm not a horse. I've got spirit though. I might be a spirit lamp.

> **Spiritualism:-** n. 1. the belief that the dead survive as spirits which can communicate with the living; 2. the philosophical doctrine that all reality is spiritual – spir'itualist n.

My spirit is unbreakable. It can't be broken. My personality was shattered, but not my spirit. Make of it what you will. Make of him what you will.

What willed me to slot in that definition? What's the meaning of it? Why mean? It was mean. His intentions were mean. He was mean spirited. HE WAS GIVEN OPPORTUNITY TO BREAK UP. OPPORTUNITY TO CONFESS. HE WAS CAUGHT, AND HE DENIED. HE THEN WENT ON TO DEMONIZE ME. HE TORTURED AND DAMAGED. HE ROBBED ME BLIND. He's blind, but I now see.

Let's play 'blind man's bluff'

Are there dark spirits and light spirits? Yep. We choose what spirit we do anything in. We choose our spirits. Sometimes we're in good spirits, and sometimes we're in bad spirits. What do we say in good spirits, and what do we say in bad spirits? We're free to choose, but it's an extremely important choice. What spirit are you in? What spirit is in you?

I have even more spirit now

I used to want to be in good spirits. I wanted to be in good spirits most of the time. I worked hard to do it. I worked hard with my thoughts. I don't work so hard now. I let nature have a hand in it. I do what comes naturally. I'm way more natural. Nature's a good healer. I let nature take its course. Nature is a force. It's a force we can't control. There are lots of forces we can't control. Sometimes we're forced. We're forced by forces outside our control. Does this make any sense? Is it one of our senses? Have I affected your senses? What sense am I affecting in you? Is it a sixth sense? Is it nonsensical?

There's over 230 'non' words in my dictionary. I bet there's heaps more now. Nonsmoker is there, nonpunishable, nonpredictable, nonparental, nonexempt, nondiplomatic, nonpaying, nonintuitive, nonsalable, nonthinking, nonattendance, and nonchargeable.

Nonmoral:- adj. not moral and not immoral.

I like the sound of this word. It fits the bill. I have a bill. I have a 'bill of rights' that needs paying. Do you know what that is? It's an invoice. Do you know what an invoice is? It's the opposite of one's out voice. My invoice tells me that I need my rights paid for. He took my rights away without paying. This is not a right, it's a wrong.

I've paid for this picture

I used to declare 'what goes around comes around'. I kind of believed it, but I very rarely witnessed karma at work. I didn't sit and watch for people to get their comeuppance. Sometimes I wondered whether it ever happened. Maybe I was seeing karma the wrong way around. Maybe at the point of seeing people do the wrong thing, they were in fact doing the right thing, and karma was taking place. The cause could already have created the effect, and the effect is what I saw as the cause. How could I know what went before? We can never see the whole picture. Even if we could see it, getting the whole picture in your head at the one time, is hard. Sometimes it's too hard to take in at the one time. It takes training.

Karma can be cause or effect

Artists can see the big picture. They often see more in a picture than most people. We can train our minds to see more. There's always more. We must open our minds, to see more. We must open our eyes more, and our ears more. When we do this, there's so much more that was missing before. Training our minds to think differently, is the key. Our minds will automatically seek more information for us. All information is helpful. When you get the picture, turn it upside down. Look at it the wrong side up, and it might look bigger still.

Look at it from all angles

Imagine an iceberg. We see only what's on the surface from the surface of the water. When we dive into the cold depths, we can more closely define the size. This is how ships came to grief in the old days. They only saw what was on the surface. Where does an iceberg melt quicker? Does it melt quicker at the surface, or under the water? It's the sun's warmth and light that help it to melt from the top faster. We see it in the light, but less in the dark depths. The dark is under the water. This is the other side to the picture. It's usually hidden. The dark side's always hidden, and it's where the bigger picture is.

This is what we suspect

> Suspicion:- n. [see SUSPECT] 1. a suspecting or being suspected; 2. the feeling or state of mind of a person who suspects; 3. a trace – above suspicion, not to be suspected; honourable – under suspicion, suspected.

I hope this is true. Do you copy or trace? I've never liked tracing things. I like to be original. If you trace, you need tracing paper. We trace, because we want the same. We want the same picture at the top, as what's below. This is not me, because I'm not being traced.

Was I the same at the top, as I was below? Nobody can know what's below, if they don't dive down to find out. I've been below. I dived down to see what was there. I've seen the whole picture. It's not the same picture below, as what was at the top.

What's below is hidden

What's at the top is on show, because that's the best picture to present.

You can't always go below, because a person must first permit you to go. You need a special permit. You must earn it. It's very hard to get a permit like this. Not everyone is equipped to go below. You need to have all your senses finely tuned. You must search the illusion for the tricks. We are all full of tricks. We trick ourselves. You must be on alert for emotion. Emotions are true signs.

It's emotional

A magician is moving into The Hoorah. We'll be upright mates. He'll have the downstairs, and I'll have the upstairs, but we'll have to meet in the kitchen. This will be the most nutritional meeting place. It will probably be our head space.

I've been given space. I'll be given space to move now, because I'll have an income. I won't have an outcome, because I can't know when out is. I'm not moving out. I'm going the distance.

I pray for some magic, and the magician arrives. I've never seen him perform magic tricks. It's a business, and he entertains kids at parties.

I'm grateful. I'm grateful for the window. A window of opportunity presented itself.

Blessed art thou among women

It was a woman. A woman's voice voiced what was on my mind. I listened to the voice, and voiced my offer. Women care about women. I like to think this. This woman cared enough to speak to me again. She said she'd been thinking about my predicament. She had an idea, and voiced it. She cared. She doesn't know me. I spoke to her for ten minutes one day in front of the shop, while someone was inspecting The Hoorah. I saw her again a week later. I don't know her name. She doesn't know mine. She might have known of me if I told her my name, but she won't really know me. Who I was, isn't me now.

I don't tell my past. I leave it in the past. Next time I see her, I'll invite her in for a cup of tea. I always have tea. I always have coffee. I always have something to offer. I have two ears, and I have a smile. I have gratitude for the pleasure of company. I like pleasant company. Sometimes I enjoy my own company. It can be pleasant. Pleasant is a nice word.

> **Pleasant:-** adj. [< MFr. Plaisir, please] 1. agreeable to the mind or senses, pleasing; 2. having an agreeable manner, appearance, etc. -plea'santly adv.

I agree. It starts with a plea. It starts.

Plea:- n. [< L. placer, please] 1. an appeal, entreaty; 2. a statement in defence excuse; 3. law, a defendant's statement.

I will defend my actions. The agent will cause an effect by telling the ex of my actions. Actions speak louder than words. I won't defend my actions, because they're not an offence.

Offence:- n. 1. a breaking of the law, sin or crime; 2. a feeling of resentment or anger; 3. something that causes resentment, anger, etc.; 4. the act of attacking; 5. the person, army, etc. that is attacking U.S. sp. Offense –give offence, to anger, insult, etc. –take offence, to feel hurt, angry, etc. –offence'less adj.

I haven't intended to offend. I've intended to survive. I have a lot of good intentions. None of them are bad intentions.

The stairwell paint job might have been a tantrum, but I intend to think about fixing it. I'll think about my intentions first. My intention to paint the staircase railing was to satisfy the agent. No it wasn't. I was shitty about what the agent texted to my daughter. It was a bad intention by degrees. It's not going to hurt anyone. It might just offend him.

Offend:- vi. [< L. *ob-* (see OB- + *fendere*, hit] 1. to commit a sin or crime; 2. to create resentment, anger, etc. –vt. 1. to hurt the feelings of; make resentful, angry, etc.; 2. to be displeasing to (the taste, sense, etc.) –offend'er n. –offend'edly adv.

It will only offend him, if he decides to take it personally. If he denies he was the cause, then there's no effect. He can choose to turn a blind eye. You would have to be blind not to notice.

When you're on the offence, you're on the attacking side, aren't you? I never played netball. I played basketball for about a year, but I wasn't much good at it. I wasn't competitive. I didn't care about winning. I didn't care about losing. How do I feel now? I feel I'm on the defence. I'm playing defence against the other team. I'm not letting them score. I'm holding my own. I'm not alone, I have an offsider.

I used to think that an offsider was equal. I thought they were a partner.

Offsider:- n. [Aust. Colloq.] an assistant, subordinate.

I don't think this definition correctly describes my defender.

Offside:- adj. 1. designating the side of a motor vehicle nearest the centre of the road [the offside headlight]; 2. Sports, in a position illegally ahead of the ball when it is played.

This is more like it

Did men know about sex in the 1600s? Did they know more about it then, than men know now? I've just been reading the great philosopher, and author, Montaigne. Montaigne shouldn't be read before bed. He speaks eloquently, but plainly. Plainly, he knew what he was talking about. A man that knows what he's on about, must have had some experience of it. He talks of different experiences, and of men's lustful ways.

Should women read what men know, and men read what women know? Is this how you know? He doesn't just speak for himself. He researches and quotes other brilliant minds. He quotes Plato and Socrates, Horace, Virgil, and Homer. He writes of the gods. The ancient scholars weren't all scholarly. Ladies weren't all ladies, or maybe they were. Maybe men were men, and women were women. Their roles strictly defined, as of the time.

What's 'of our time'?

Is it our changing roles that lead us away from true knowledge? He writes of other cultures, and other rituals. He also writes humbly, like me, but not in my time, in his.

I read him as a man in his 50s, and he speaks of dying of old age, in that age. Men didn't have a long innings. Neither did women, for that matter. Would this have had something to do with his love of exploits? Would you be exploiting every opportunity, if you had less time?

What's a favourite exploit?

He didn't have time. He wanted it all. He was French and loved the chase. He loved to be put off. He loved the seduction. He loved the agony of waiting. He didn't like to 'cut to the chase'. He detested women who lessened themselves by giving in too early. He valued women, who valued themselves. The longer the chase, the higher the value was to him. The higher the value, the richer the feast became.

He didn't want a one course meal. He wanted the entire banquet, but he wanted to take his time. He wanted to taste every morsel, and savour it. He knew the power women could hold over him. I think they held more power, the more they held him back. I think he loved the challenge. He had a brilliant mind, but describes himself as somewhat shy. He didn't just want the woman's favours, he wanted her will. He wanted to find her. He wanted something more than the flesh alone. What was so valuable to him, that led him on such an intensive search? He went in search of her very soul. His soul wanted connection with hers. It's deep. He's very deep. He's so very articulate, that I go back to reread the paragraphs to fully grasp what he's relaying, in such wonderfully old-fashioned words. They are his expressive words. He expresses himself beautifully, but he needs to relay it to men of today. He probably needs to relay it to women. I've comprehended his eloquent words. They're not just words of love, because he was a man of great wisdom.

Can somebody publish a man's porn magazine with Montaigne's words of wisdom? Can a women's magazine publish his works, so that women will crave a higher order? It doesn't matter how much society has changed since the 16th century, love is love. Sex is not just sex. It can be much more. More is offered, if you search for the knowledge. The knowledge is there, and I can't see how it could be improved upon. I can only see what might have been lost. Is it a science?

Is it a philosophy?

I don't think Montaigne felt that comfortable discussing such intimate and personal a subject, and I know where he's coming from. This was obviously a subject on his mind, and it was important for him to write about it. He was an important man. He was highly respected for his insight. He still is, by me.

Montaigne and I, forever

I can't be as immaculate with my words as him. I'm not as educated as he was, nor am I as well read, nor as well bred. What I read, and what I do, are two different things. Read what you will into that last sentence, but where there's a will there's a way. Has my soul been touched? I'll answer this when I'm good and ready. Next question: Would I want it touched? A soul is spiritual. When two souls touch, what happens? I want to know. I want Montaigne. Too late, he's dead. What a waste. Have his words been wasted on me?

His words touch me

I first picked up Montaigne, because I read in a book that he'd written a very famous essay about a friendship lost. I was alerted by the fact that he believed in a soul mate. I wanted to know. I wanted to know something about the quality of a soul mate. I wanted to know more about soul mates. I could never explain the significance of my very special friendship. I had not the words to describe the infinite bond that we shared. It wasn't the fact that she died a month from her forty-third birthday. I've suffered other people's deaths.

I know of grief

What was lost to me when Red Rose died, is beyond the written word. I lost my soul mate. Red Rose and I shared a rare friendship. I knew it, she knew it, and we couldn't articulate it to each other. It didn't need articulating. There weren't words to articulate, nor to explain the significant loss I felt. I wanted to know of such a friendship. I wanted to know why. I knew most people aren't blessed with what Rose Red and I were for each other.

Twofold souls

Montaigne's grief for his friend, was not comparable to anything his soul had ever endured. Two great souls connecting, caused an effect. The effect that De La Boetie's death had on Michel de Montaigne was profound. I long to quote the whole essay to you, but It's too personal to me. It's all mine. His words are my words, his sentiment, that of mine. His loss reflects my loss in 2006.

> Let not those other, common friendships, be placed in this rank. I have as much knowledge of them as another, and of the most perfect of their type, but I advise you not to confuse the rules of the two; you would make a mistake. You must walk in those other friendships bridle in hand, with prudence and precaution; the knot is not so well tied that there is no cause to mistrust it. "Love him," Chilo used to say, "as if you are to hate him some day; hate him as if you are to love him." This precept, which is so abominable in this sovereign and masterful friendship, is healthy in the practice of ordinary and customary friendships, in regard to which we must use the remark that Aristotle often repeated: "O my friends, there is no friend."

> In this noble relationship, services and benefits, on which other friendships feed, do not even deserve to be taken into account; the reason for this is the complete fusion of our wills. For just as the friendship I feel for myself receives no increase from the help I give myself in time of need, whatever the Stoics say, and as I feel no gratitude to myself for the service I do myself; so the union of such friends, being truly perfect, makes

them lose the sense of such duties, and hate and banish from between them these words of separation and distinction: benefit, obligation, gratitude, request, thanks, and the like. Everything actually being in common between them – wills, thoughts, judgments, goods, wives, children, honor, and life – and their relationship being that of one soul in two bodies, according to Aristotle's very apt definition, they can neither lend nor give anything to each other. That is why the lawmakers, to honor marriage with some imaginary resemblance to this divine union, forbid gifts between husband and wife, wishing thus to imply that everything should belong to each of them and that they have nothing to divide and split up between them.

If, in the friendship I speak of, one could give to the other, it would be the one who received the benefit who would oblige his friend. For, each of them seeking above all things to benefit the other, the one who provides the matter and the occasion, is the liberal one, giving his friend the satisfaction of doing for him what he most wants to do.

For the rest, what we ordinarily call friends and friendships are nothing but acquaintanceships and familiarities formed by some chance or convenience, by means of which our souls are bound to each other. In the friendship I speak of, our souls mingle and blend with each other so completely that they efface the seam that joined them, and cannot find it again. If you press me to tell why I loved him, I feel that this cannot be expressed, except by answering: Because it was he, because it was I.

Beyond all my understanding, beyond what I can say about this in particular, there was I know not what inexplicable and fateful force that was the mediator of this union. We sought each other before we met because of the reports we heard of each other, which had more effect on our affection than such reports would reasonably have; I think it was by some ordinance from heaven. We embraced each other by our names.

The ancient Menander declared that man happy who had been able to meet even the shadow of a friend. He was certainly right to say so, especially if he spoke from experience. For in truth, if I compare all the rest of my life – though by the grace of God I have spent it pleasantly, comfortably, and, except for the loss of such a friend, free from any grievous affliction, and full of tranquility of mind, having accepted my natural and original advantages without seeking other ones – if I compare it all, I say, with the four years which were granted to me to enjoy the sweet company and society of that man, it is nothing but smoke, nothing but dark and dreary night. Since the day I lost him,

Which I shall ever recall with pain,

Everwith reverence – thus, Gods, did you ordain. Virgil

I only drag on a weary life. And the very pleasures that come my way, instead of consoling me, redouble my grief for his loss. We went halves in everything; it seems to me that I am robbing him of his share,

Nor may I rightly taste of pleasures here alone,

So I resolved – when he who shared my life is gone. Terrence

I was already so formed and accustomed to being a second self everywhere that only half of me seems to be alive now.

This is from *The Complete Essays of Montaigne*, translated by Donald M. Frame. For me, it loses nothing in translation, but helps me to translate for myself, what it was, and how blessed I was to have had it. Montaigne struggled with what he'd lost. He didn't struggle with what he'd found.

Our loss reflects our gain. To love greatly, is to lose deeply. The deeper the love is, the deeper the crushing pain. These are my words, and you've heard them before. The words I have, to describe my friendship with Rose Red, have not been heard before. Our friendship, called for rare words.

Rare offerings are accepted with awe

We are humbled by them. I was humbled. In so many ways we were opposites. Our opposing opinions, could cancel each other's out. We were a mathematical equation that brought equilibrium to our lives. We equalled, and we were even. We brought the light into each other's souls. We both needed the light. Our souls needed the light from each other. Our souls saved each other. They also built each other. It was a deep connection. Others could not infiltrate our connection. They couldn't reach. We reached for each other, and found truth. Truth is hard to find.

I lost my half too

I'd shared my soul with her, and it got lost with her. She was my friend. I don't use this word easily now. It's a stupid word to use so frivolously. It's a word I cannot use for my great soul mate. Rose Red was more than a friend. She took on my pain as if that pain were her own. I took hers gratefully. It's a pain you take on, knowing you don't have the cure for it. You're just there to share it. You just suffer it, alongside them. They know you share it. It's enough. It's everything!

It was heaven sent

Don't look for a friendship such as this. You'll be disappointed. You can't find it, nor can you create it. It's a gift. It's a rare gift. It's a gift of great value in one's life. My life will end one day. One day we'll meet again. I didn't think this once. Now I hope it. I'm going to hope it into reality. I want to live a long life first. I'm living for both our souls now.

My reality has changed

Her soul played a part in it. I miss laughing. I miss this the most. How we did laugh. We laughed at all manner of things. We laughed till we felt pain. We laughed at the joy of it. I haven't laughed in this way for a long time.

Women are funny. The two of us could be hilarious. We thought we were hilarious. We laughed at pain. We laughed in the face of it. We stared back, and laughed. What glorious release it was. It was grace. It was surrender. She taught me to surrender. I taught her to fight.

You can teach someone what you don't do. We project. The day she died, was the day the music died for me. I was made less. I went on to make more, but more was less. I can't use her real name in this book, but even as I say her name aloud, it's felt. Emotion is attached to it. What's in a name?

Naming How I Feel

Her name... I miss its sound.
Don't speak of it aloud.
It's sacred staying underground.
With all that's good, endowed.

If it's taken up, and out your lips,
Be tender with your tongue.
It's fragile talk, my heart it skips,
For my feelings are so strong.

Don't say her name and hurt me.
Avoid it if you will.
Her soul has left me lamely.
And wounds me ever still.

By Ms T.L. Without an E.

> 'So in a running stream one wave we see
> After another roll incessantly,
> And line by line, each does eternally
> Pursue the other, each the other flea.
> By this one, that one ever on is sped,
> And this one by the other ever led;
> The water still does into water go,
> Still the same brook, but different waters flow.'

La Boetie.

That was then, and this is now

I'm different. I'm different now, to then. That was six years ago. I died then. I changed, but I tried to do the same things. I went through the motions. I had motion sickness.

She wouldn't recognize me now. I look so different. I sound different. I'm glad I'm different. It's harder to be the same. You can't be the same, when everything around you has changed. She would recognize me. She recognizes me. She's my guiding light. She's the light up overhead. I'm not frightened of it, but I'm not yet ready for it.

Fearing what's up ahead

I'm not frightened of dying. I've faced it. I face my death every day of my life. We must face the fact that we can't avoid the fact of it. Facing what you can't control is liberating. It's the opposite of having security. You simply can't know when it's going to happen, or how. Facing what you can't control, puts you in control. It gives you power over your life. It makes your decisions and actions more powerful. Philosophers must live like this. They've faced the big questions. They've faced that they can't answer all of them. They've faced their own ignorance. They've faced their powerlessness. To be powerless, is to be empowered. It's freeing you from wasteful thoughts.

What's the use in worrying? Just smile, smile, smile

Some thinking is wasteful. It's useless. What will be, will be. Don't make a decision, and then worry about whether you've made the right decision. Make a decision and don't look back. Accept your decision. Trust it. By trusting it, you won't be worrying about it. Worrying about it is useless, once you've made the decision. You can't avoid risk. It exists throughout every day of our lives. Just be fascinated by what transpires. Use the result and learn by it. Watch the result come about, but don't question your judgment, until you have something to judge. Wait, watch, and learn.

There's no such thing as rejection

How do you risk rejection? You take away the word 'rejection'. If you accept that there's a higher power in control, you can accept what will be, or what won't be. You can relinquish emotional discomfort. Don't want more. Accept what's on offer in the moment. What's on offer in the moment, tends to get overlooked. We don't see what's on offer. When we look up ahead, we don't see what's right beside us. We waste what's already been given. We forget to appreciate what's here right now. What's here right now? If it hasn't panned out in the way you'd expected, and you haven't got the result you wanted, there's always another way. It may be an important way. It may be the best way. Sometimes the best way, is to keep looking for other ways. The first way may not have been the best way, and the next best way is better. Is the next best thing, better than the first thing?

What's here right now?

Some people would do anything to have what I have right now. Right now, I have nothing, but everything. I have peace. I have myself. I have an ocean view to gaze at, but only for now. I have quiet and solitude. I have health. I have life. I sit in a large and beautiful house. I have a dog to guard me, and keep me company. I have smokes. I have peace of mind.

This is a piece of my mind

I don't have obligation. I don't have any jobs to do. I don't feel pain or worry. I don't have any problems right now. The way is clear. I have space. I have head space. I'm watching the breakers. It's better than TV. I'm having a spiritual moment. I know what I'm not doing, that I would have been doing last year. I would have been stressing, racing, and working. I would have had the world on my shoulders. Now I have it at my feet. It's under me, not on top of me. The world is too big to be on top. I need to be on top of it.

The world's a big place

I've got on top of it all. I've risen. I've risen above it, so that I just look down upon it. I look down at all the ants running about in a mad haste. The pace of it is for others. I've paced away from it. I've stepped out of my boundaries, and I'm not getting back in. I've gone off the rails.

Who caused the derailment?

Don't ever let anyone tell you not to go off the rails. Trespass at your own risk. Trespass into this unknown territory. The unknown, is worth knowing. It's unknown what will happen next. I don't have a plan right now. I'm waiting for something to happen. I'm waiting for what transpires.

> **Transpire:-** [< L. *trans*, through + *spirare*, breathe] 1. to become known; 2. [Colloq.] to come to pass; happen: regarded by some as a loose usage; 3. to give off vapour, moisture, etc. as through pores -vt. to cause (vapour, moisture, etc.) to pass through tissue, esp. through pores.

Why have I written this word? I'm hoping something won't transpire, but I'm also thinking it should. 'Should' is not a word I like to use. Have we ever got any control over what is to transpire? I'm changing the subject, because that's what I do. It's all I can do. So many things are transpiring all the time. We can't always know. Things take place without us knowing, every day. We won't know what's transpired if we're not told. What transpires, can happen behind our backs. It happens behind the scenes, and behind closed doors. We can be kept in the dark. We can be kept ignorant of them ever having transpired. Sometimes we just never know.

It happens when we're out to it

I've been out this evening. I've been to The Toy House. This is where The Three Amigos live. They have toys. They have musical toys, electronic toys, and motorized toys. They have indoor toys, and outdoor toys. They have games, and there's fun and laughter in that toy house. It's a place to be entertained. There's talent in that toy house. There's life. They are the life of their party.

I watched a movie while I was there. It's a movie I've wanted to watch for a while. It's called *The Invention of Lying*. My girl wonder said it. She delivered a speech about it once, with great aplomb. She delivered a speech in a competition one night, about where we'd all be, if we didn't lie. It's extraordinary, the lies that we tell. Most extraordinary, is the lies that we live by. We live to lie, and we lie to live.

Extraordinary lies are deep down

Most of the time, we don't even recognize that we're lying. To lie in the moment, is to love. It's true. To tell the lie, is not to hurt. The lie is to make another happy. We lie to get by. We need to get by. Do lies get by us all the time, without us knowing? Should we always be aware of our lying? It could tell us a great deal about ourselves. What great deal would it reveal? Are we making a deal with ourselves? Is this where we deal out the greatest number of lies? We make ourselves comfortable with lies, because sometimes the truth can cause discomfort. What we lie to ourselves about, can tell us where we think we lie. It can prop us up.

Lies and prop a ganda?

Lies are props. A prop is a crutch. Crutches can help us walk, when we're disabled. You don't want to use crutches your whole life, because you'll never be able-bodied again. If you don't use it, you lose it. The longer we rely on crutches, the longer we won't walk properly. Where am I going? I'm limping somewhere, but I'm not sure where I'll end up. Have I been lying to myself? Yes. We all do. Lies are deceiving. We deceive others by deceiving our very selves, and vice versa.

Is a trick a lie?

Are lies easy or hard? This is a tricky question.

I was once told, that people who are good liars are more intelligent. Is it the intelligent thing to do? Wouldn't it be the opposite? Are we hiding our own intelligence?

What sort of intelligence?

Lies can be hard to unravel. Our whole persona can be tied up in lies. Without the lies, we fall apart. Our lies can be a second skin. We think they'll protect us. We think they'll hide us. Mirrors don't lie. Can you lie in the mirror? You can't lie when you look right into your own eyes. It knows. It knows the truth. Our reflection knows. On reflection, we can know too.

Some lies don't make us so uncomfortable. These are embellishments, exaggerations for effect, and flattery. We don't feel bad about these lies, because they're not used to deceive. They're used to inspire. Lies can be used for good as well as evil. There are good intentioned lies. They don't hurt anyone. They don't hurt us either. They don't hurt in the telling, but are they a telling sign?

The telling-tales signs

Some lies are for one-upmanship. These aren't good lies. They're deceiving lies, and they get told to gain the advantage over another. They are our cheating lies. There's no merit in these lies. There's no truth. That's an oxymoron. How can there be truth, in a lie? I'll answer this later, because I'm sure there's an answer. I'm going to lie down and think about it. I'll try to lie straight, while I'm doing it.

I've made my bed, and now I must lie in it

I lied. I just went to sleep. I didn't even think about it.

I'm thinking a great deal about it now. I think there is. There is truth in lies. I've just been lying out in the sun on my banana chair. I wasn't reading. I was just feeling and hearing. I did some thinking. I didn't think on purpose. The truth just entered my head.

What we call the truth, is not always the truth. It's just knowledge that we've fed on. Most often, we haven't chosen the knowledge for ourselves. It can be given to us as the truth, and we automatically accept it. We haven't questioned it, because there's nothing suspicious. It looks like the truth, sounds like the truth, and feels like the truth. It's been accepted as the truth, by a great many people. Masses of people believe it to be the truth. It looks even more truthful now. Important people say it's the truth, and brilliant, credible people, think it's the truth. They haven't bothered to question it either. It's been painted as knowledge. It's wrapped in fact. That's why it smells like fact.

This is where I think the truth can lie

Underneath, it's a lie. It's false. It's not true, but we haven't discovered it yet. We've all incorporated this lie into our system. It's now forming part of our schemata of our life. Other things have been constructed around it. It's now holding other things together and in place. It's surrounded by other truths, so you can't tell any difference. If I told you it was a lie, you couldn't readily accept it. You've been relying on it. You'll probably deny it. Suddenly you're suspicious of all the other truths surrounding it. You can't trust any of it now, because those surrounding truths, were relying on the lie to be true.

What happens if you're listing?

Everything you know has become wobbly. It's off-kilter, and you're listing. You're listing from side to side. It won't stand up now. You can't stand up. Everything you relied on has been tainted by that lie. Your whole system has a malfunction. You're thinking is, and has been, dysfunctional, based on this lie.

Mark my words!

I suspect half of our life is filled with lies, and the other half is filled with the truth. This would be the balance. Is it yin and yang, or ying and yang? It's a shock, so sit down and take it easy. Take this new information while lying down. You won't take it lying down. You'll get up and defend the lie. You'll look for ways to strengthen it, and you'll find information to justify it. You want to believe it, otherwise you have a shit load of thinking to do. It will be re-thinking. You'll have to re-trace your steps. Your whole system needs changing. You've got to first take that lie out, and replace it with the truth. Then you must tweak all the surrounding truths, and make sure they stand up. I'll stand up and applaud you, if you can do this in one lifetime. It could create a complete turnaround.

You'll do the hokey pokey, and you'll turn around, and that's what it's all about. You'll have to put your whole self in, and your whole self out.

You'll need to go all the way back to the nursery. Everything looks different now to what you remembered. You didn't know that the truth can lie. Now you know. You only know that lies can look like the truth, and truth can look like lies.

What you do know, is that you don't honestly know. Or do you?

Imagine you've been told as a child, that you have a weak heart. This is a lie, and it's been reinforced throughout your life, as you've grown into adulthood. Your mother said it, and she's remarked upon it in a subtle manner from time to time. There's no reason for you not to believe it, because you've known about this for a very long time. You've grown up with this knowledge.

Mummy Dearest

You've had no complications. There's been no hospital visits or tests. There's been no confirmations of any sort, and yet you continue to take it on board where ever you go. You have it at the back of your mind, as you run around the playground. You have it on your mind, when you've over exerted yourself on a run, or at the gym. When you're lifting boxes in the garage, playing with the kids, or eating a greasy hamburger, you're reminded of your heart's weakened state.

At what age do you question the authenticity of your mother's subtle warnings?

How weak can you be?

Would you always have the feeling that you were somehow less for your weakness? Would you have compared yourself to others, and been aware of your deficiencies? Would you blame it all on your weak heart? Would you make different choices, because you're always considering the condition of your vital organ? Would you always view others as stronger in body, than yourself? Do you think you'll die younger than the next person?

This means two things

There's been an impact on your mind and body.

It means more than those two things. It means you've missed out on being completely healthy when you've been completely healthy. It means you've missed out on your true life. It means you've worried about things you needn't have worried about. Your life has been overshadowed by and illusion.

The ring of confidence

Now tell yourself in mid-life, that you have a clean bill of health, and you never were weak of heart. You've been released from a sentence. You've been discharged. You're as strong as a bull! You can now see it was bullshit.

We don't always make our own beds to lie in. Sometimes they're made for us. I hope I haven't made any beds, but we don't always know the answers. When we don't know the answers, we can try and find them through the proper channels, or just accept that we don't know. I know nothing!

The best knowledge one can own

I know that all knowledge is questionable. Knowledge can be just someone's opinion. Our opinions are only derived from what we've learned, and had experience of. We sometimes feel that our opinions fit the situation, but we don't really know if they're the best fit. We gamble with knowledge. It's always a gamble. You can have a crack at breaking the code, but it's hit and miss. You can suggest, and you can offer a guess. What works one time, might not work the next. What works in one situation, might not work in another. Hitting and/or missing, are dangerous grounds. Are they the right grounds to use?

I've changed the ring tone

My mobile is a friendly mobile. I'm not fearful of it, and it doesn't have a shrill ring tone. It doesn't even have a ring tone, it has a vibration. It's the sweetest phone I've ever had. It's the only phone I have now. This phone only has friendly contacts, and sweet contacts. It doesn't have any obligatory contacts. When it vibrates, I get a pleasant feeling. All my other phones were enemies. They attacked me. They frightened me. When they rang, I felt anxiety. It was work. It was nearly always work. Even when it was just one of my contacts, it was still work. It was a connection device. It was connected to me all the time, and at all hours. I couldn't disconnect. I was afraid to disconnect. Are you afraid to disconnect? Can you turn your phone off?

Turning people off

What you'd be doing, is turning your ears off. You'd be shutting one of your senses down. Does it make sense? If you turned your hearing sense off, would that heighten your other senses? Would you be able to see things better? Could you taste better?

Would you taste better?

Would you be more palatable? You could focus more on what your other senses are sensing. Would you feel better? Could you touch better? Are you getting touchy now? Are you touchy about this subject? Are you touchy about turning your phone off? If you are, then maybe your sense of hearing is very sensitive. You might be over sensitive, hearing all this. It may be striking a chord. Can you hear the music? Can you see the writing on the wall?

I used to have a love/hate relationship with my phone. It was unpredictable. I never knew whether the shrill ringing, would be a good sign or a bad sign. It controlled me. It was like Stockholm Syndrome. I was always on tenterhooks. I never knew what I was going to get.

Dropping a line

My current mobile phone was just $30. It's not going to give me any nasty surprises, because very few people have been given the number. I trust these people not to pass on my number. It could happen by accident. It's still not a threat, because I don't have to talk if I don't want to. I can talk my way out of talking. I can hang up. I can reject the call, or I can refuse to return a call, if they leave a message. It's not against the law. Some things aren't against the law. It's a free world. Have we forgotten this?

Make a good call

People often have no sense of personal boundaries. They're often too personal. This isn't what I want to express, because it expresses me perfectly. What I'm trying to express, is that your availability to others is hard to express. Who should we be available to immediately, every time? There's that word I hate? The word 'should' is always followed by guilt. The question should have been worded differently. I'm guilty. Who do you want to be available to immediately? Now you have the right answer. 'Want' is a love word. 'Should' is a dependent word. What do you prefer, 'love' or 'dependency'? Be aware of when you use the 'should' word, and when you use the 'want' word. Don't say, 'I should want to do it'. They don't go together naturally.

Are you on my 'Wanted' list?

I only want people here on a 'want' basis. I don't want a 'should' basis here at all. I want to get rid of the 'should' word from my vocabulary. Do you think it's possible? I'm going to use the word 'could', instead. 'You could paint that red'. 'We could go for a swim'. 'We could have something to eat'. You could try this, or do that. I could too. I think I can. I'll change my habit.

'Should, could, would'

These are three weird words. They get us into trouble. 'Shoulda, coulda, woulda'. This is what we say, when we don't. It's what we say when we didn't, or haven't. What about 'do'? What about 'did'? Did we do it? Have we ever done it? Is it about time that we did?

Did I?

I was going to text my son to remember to hang the wet washing on the line. It was a 'should'. It wasn't really a 'should'. It wasn't a 'want' either. It was a 'could'. I didn't want to. It doesn't concern me. It's his 'could', not mine. Is it his 'should'? That's for him to work out. It's something he must learn for himself. It's part of growing up. He's got to work out what words are best for him. It's a language. By understanding the words we use, we can understand ourselves better. We can understand what motivates us. I don't want to be motivated by the 'shoulds' anymore. I just want to be motivated by wants and needs.

It's hard to crack

It's a beautiful day. The water's a good temperature, and it's Sunday. I felt the 'should'. It was about going for a swim. 'I should go down for a swim'. 'I should want to go down for a swim'. A swim would be nice, but people will be everywhere. I like to swim where it's quiet. I don't like crowds. It's too busy today. The 'should' got in there because of an old habit of mine. I feel guilty for wasting such great weather. I have all weather now, because I can swim any day I want. I have the time. I don't have to plan good times around a strict schedule. My schedule is free and flexible. It's open. It's non-existent. No schedules.

Waste not, want not

I went for a walk the other evening. It was overcast and balmy. There was nobody on the beach, because I'd walked around a bit further than usual. The dog was in the water. I wanted to go in. It was calm and clear. It was quiet and peaceful. I didn't have a towel or swimmers with me. I was unprepared. I stripped down to my underwear and went in. I've done this before. It's better than missing out on a luxurious swim. It was luxurious. I was rewarded for my efforts.

Luxurious ended when I had to try and get wet and sandy feet back into my trouser legs. Pulling clothes back on over a wet body is awkward, especially when you're in a hurry to cover up. It was still worth it. It was so worth it. It wasn't worth going back home for my swimmers.

Hanging up the inhibitions

I can be practical. I'm more practical than inhibited. My inhibitions are dissolving slowly. They're just my hang-ups. They don't have anything to do with others. This is ambiguous, isn't it? What I mean to say, is that my inhibitions prompt me to consider how I look in front of others. It's about my opinion of what others will think. It's about hiding me from others. What others think is an entirely different subject. Sometimes it's not a subject at all. If I happened upon a man swimming in his undies, I wouldn't give a shit. I probably wouldn't notice, and if I did, I'd think 'good luck to him'. I'd admire him for his being so practical under the circumstances. What judgment could be made of me, swimming in my bra and knickers?

Judge me

There are 'judges' and 'judges'. Some judges are practical, and some are inhibited. Who judges harshly? What would a harsh judgment be? I've heard the judgment of others, not of me, but in front of me. I must confess, I've been a judge myself on occasion. I've sometimes judged what people wear, and what they do. Is it jealousy? Does jealousy, make us judge? Was I jealous of people's lack of inhibition? Did I lack their confidence? Did I lack the effect they were having? Did I envy them, their effect?

Don't be jealous of what others do, just do

I hate jealousy. I hate the emotion. I've felt it in myself when I didn't want to. Not wanting to have it, and having it, is frustrating. You know it's a dishonourable emotion to have. It dishonoured me. It's not honouring self. Jealousy's a curse. Why have we been cursed with it? Jealousy inspires nastiness. It inspires anger and hate. Jealousy is a harsh judge. I think it's one of the worst traits you can have. Do you have a jealous nature?

Whole countries can be jealous. They can all be jealous of the same thing. How does jealousy get a foothold? Let's wind back the clock, and see when it starts. It starts when the new baby arrives, doesn't it? It all started with Cain and Abel.

First and foremost

Cain was the first born, and then came his brother Abel. When Cain was born, he was number one. There was no other. He was secure being number one. Nobody could get in the way of his security. Along came Abel. He was number two. God tested Cain. He failed. Not God, Cain. Cain couldn't stand that Abel's offering to God was more in favour. Cain was meant to master his jealousy. Instead of being happy for his brother, he invited Abel out into the field and disabled him. He killed his brother.

Then Cain got the cane

This is where the curse began. Cain took god's favour of Abel, to be a sign of his own inadequacy. Cain lost faith in self. He wanted to be number one. He didn't realize he would always be number one, to himself. Cain wanted more. He already was everything.

What could Cain have done instead? He could have become aware of what was eating him. He could have sat down to contemplate what he was feeling. He might have contemplated the different ways he could achieve God's favour. He could have celebrated his brother's success and passed God's test. He had much to offer God, but he was too busy watching other offerings. Why did God offer us jealousy? Was it offered to us as a challenge?

I'm not sugar caning it for you

We can't have all the attributes of others. We are what we are, and we have what we have. Nobody is less than another. It's about finding what you have, within. It's about bringing all the different parts into the light. We all have our special talents and gifts. We can't all be the same. If we were, there wouldn't be any jealousy, and we wouldn't be challenged to seek out the best in ourselves.

Are we of good stock?

We can begin by being grateful for the things we do have, and who we are. We can't be the best at everything. We can only be the best we can, with what we've been given. What's been given to us, is perfect for us. It's our way, and it won't be the way of another. Allow others to find their special way, alongside our special way. It's just the way of it. We all compensate each other. All our talents are an offering. Don't let other people's jealousy of you, stop you in your tracks. Be all that you can be, with what you have. You've gone a different way.

Do your own time

Remember, we are all equal. It might not look like it, but we all have our own potentials to reach for. Concentrate on your own potential. Don't try and ruin someone else's. Don't take what doesn't belong to you, because they have something you don't have. You aren't less. Some people look to have an easier ride through life. What the ride looks like, may be different to what it feels like. There are horses for courses. Stay on course. Run your own race. Don't knock someone off their high horse, because it's higher than yours. Run your own race even if it is the steeple chase. 'Here's the church, and here's the steeple. Open the doors, and here's all the people.'

Artificial Grass

This brings me to a subject I've been longing to write about. I've been keen to have a go at it for some time. I've only thought about it so far, and known it was there. It's the grass. I've been examining it. I've checked it out, and it looks nice. It looks fresh and green. I've smelled its aroma, and it just seems too good to be true. I'm talking about the grass in the next paddock. The next paddock is over the fence. The grass is greener on the other side.

Manicured lawns

The grass has been spray-painted. It's been painted the most vivid green, and sprayed with a glorious scent. It looks all glossy. It's not real. When you get closer, you can tell. You'd have to take a really close look to see the truth. Who created the illusion?

My grass looks pretty ordinary, in comparison. Some would say it looks pretty shitty. I don't think too many people would think my grass is greener, but it would depend on what grass they compare mine with.

What happened to my grass?

A cow was wandering around in the next paddock. It had always ogled my paddock. Its paddock had never looked like mine. It only saw on the surface, and on the surface, it just looked greener.

This jealous cow had always wanted a paddock like mine. One day, when I was busily tending my paddock, it broke through a boundary fence and cut my grass. It cut the grass right out from under me. It ended up with a bad taste in its mouth though. It ended up with a stomach ache. It realized that it wasn't that fresh and clean after all. It tasted the paint and smelled the paint fumes. It wasn't what it was cracked up to be.

Holy Cow!

I've just got natural grass now. It doesn't look so good, but it's real. Nobody thinks it looks greener anymore. Nobody will look at my grass now. Nobody could be jealous of my grass.

I was killed off out on that field, just like Abel. It was stupid, because I'd already been sharing parts of that paddock with that stupid cow. I'd been sharing all the good bits. I didn't tell her about the bad bits. I didn't tell her about the hard bits. I didn't want her to know about these. It would have spoiled my illusion.

If the grass looks greener to you, on the other side, take a closer look first. Don't just plow in and steal what's not yours.

I've got less of a paddock. Most of my grass has gone to Gowings. Why did everyone go to Gowings? I don't know if it even exists anymore. Are people still going? When something is said to have gone to Gowings, it just means it's gone. I don't want any returns. I don't want anything returned. They're not the original items. They've been used, and probably been found to be faulty.

No refunds

Metaphor is so poetic. It turns disaster into beauty. It might for you, but it doesn't for me. It turns it into tragedy. It's a travesty. It's a shame that I can't write it as I saw it. My soul prefers to use good taste. My soul is discerning about taste. It was all in bad taste. You can't really change the taste of it.

Was tragedy, the travesty?

My Red Rose suffered. She suffered for me. I can't even try to imagine what she suffered. I don't want to imagine. It hurts me to imagine, so I avoid the scene. She knew. She knew about what happened in the paddock. I bet she wished she didn't. I bet she wished for ignorance.

Ignorance is bliss

That's what she gave me. She offered me bliss. She almost told me, but left me with the reason, not the answer.

The Reasoning:

"How would you feel if your spouse had an affair, but you never ever found out about it?"

We often debated different issues, from the newspaper, from everyday life, and of our observations of the lives of others. It was just another issue under discussion, but it wasn't an issue. I didn't dwell on it too long. I said that if you didn't know, then you would never feel it's impact. It would be as if nothing has occurred. How is it an issue, if the issue doesn't ever reveal itself?

End of story

"If a tree falls in the forest and no one hears it, does it make a sound?" George Berkeley.

I didn't know about the above quote back then. Back then, the air was charged. Something was in the air, but I couldn't see it. I just didn't get it. I wasn't supposed to get anything. She agreed with me. It was the end of the conversation, and we finished our smokes and went back into the office.

It wasn't the wrong thing, not to tell me. I know that now. It was well intentioned. She never intended to hurt me. She didn't want their deeds to hurt me. She had the knowledge, and she couldn't un-know it. She had the knowledge to hurt, or deceive me. It wasn't a great choice. Would you hurt, or deceive your best friend, with your unwanted knowledge of another's bad deed?

The big picture

I think there was more to it. She protected the villains. She wouldn't have been protecting the villains for their sakes, but for the sake of their close others. It was all so close. Everyone was close. The villains were the connection to everything I loved. I would have lost. So many people would have been lost. So much disaster would have unfolded. In the end that's what unfolded.

The big family

She was also thinking of the kids. Everybody's kids. She was thinking about the importance of family. About happy families. It was all too close for comfort. She thought a lot of my kids.

For the greater good

She did it for the greater good. That's how she would have seen it, after she'd thought deeply about it. That's what she did with it. This sort of knowledge is very powerful. This sort of knowledge can weigh you down. It must have caused her a great deal of pain on my behalf.

She didn't cause the pain, she protected me from it. It must have taken great strength and will power. She must have been very angry on my behalf.

I don't want to try and imagine what her position would have felt like, because I don't want to suffer. I could if I wanted to, but she's dead now. She's not feeling it anymore. She was the sacrificial lamb. Others put her in this position. They'll probably never fully understand how painful a position this was for her. They shouldn't have done it. Their sins against me, were carried by her, for me. She took on the sins of the world, to save my world. My whole world would have come crashing down around me, if she'd let the cat out of the bag.

Which way was the easiest?

I could say that I don't know how she managed it, but I do know. She had faith. She believed in a God. She believed in a greater good. She was spiritual. Everyone loved her spirit. Her spirit embraced you. She was warm hearted. She was mine. My soul and her soul, had a special connection. Hurting me would have been much worse than hurting herself. She chose that her soul be hurt in place of mine.

There was no easy way

How do I tell another soul about this? All souls could be hurt by this soulful story. How many souls know? Shall we count the souls? I know of another. A similar soul out there knows, but not a soul of the same calibre. What do you do with all this, when you have it in your possession? You keep one tenth, and give nine tenths to the law. The greater good will look after it for me.

What's possession?

I'm not worried about these possessions going out into the world. My world has gone now. Let karma take care of the world for a while.

Who do you think this book is dedicated to? It's dedicated to someone that made it possible. It's dedicated to someone who has always inspired me, and continues to do so. It's dedicated to the spirit of Red Rose. It lives on in me, and it's a dual effort. It's been written together, because it was written. It's all written up, and now it's history. It's the history of my life, and the effects of others in it. It's caused an effect. A cause always has an effect.

What choice did she have?

If someone offered you a choice, one being a lump of dog shit, and the other being a lump of dog shit, which shit would you choose? You don't want it, do you? You don't want a choice at all. You want nothing. You can't choose nothing, because that's dog shit too. You're forced to handle this shit, because you're no longer ignorant of the facts. You stink. You can smell yourself, and somehow you now smell worse than the producers of the shit. You feel like you smell worse than they do.

Carrying somebody else's shit

Imagine someone making you do this. They make you carry it for them, and make you hide it from another. Now you're covered in their putrid dog shit. You used to be clean. You can't get rid of the dog shit, because the shit is now stuck to you. It's there all the time in front of you, whenever you confront the one they shit on. You can't avoid looking at it, and smelling it. You may even start to feel like it.

Did she feel like this? Did she feel like a lump of dog shit for not telling her best friend, soul mate, work mate, and trusted confidante, that her…

Can I write it? Will I go to jail for it? I'm telling it for her. I've got to get that dog shit off her. She took on that dog shit for me. She kept it from me. My husband and my younger sister, were going at it like dogs.

Putting shit on them

She saved them. She wore that dog shit for them too. She saved their arses at her own expense. She thought it was too expensive for me to know. She took the expense. She paid for it.

It was expensive. It was very bloody expensive

Do you know what happened after Rose Red and Black Irish died? The dogs went back and did the same shit all over again.

Is this book karma? It's not for me to judge, but it sure smells like it. Big karma is the only way. Some ways are not enough to teach people right from wrong. That's a childish statement, because we all know right from wrong. It was so wrong.

Karma teaches us about the consequences of our poor choices. Don't be unconscionable. Unconscionable conduct is what the charge should be.

> **Unconscionable:-** adj. 1. not guided or restrained by conscience, unscrupulous; 2. unreasonable, excessive, etc.

It's Sunday again, and it's just on dusk. I've been for a long walk. Coming back, I was watching people leave. They're packing up. The weekend's over. School and/or work tomorrow. Sunday nights are usually a quiet night all around. People are already preparing for the week ahead. They're winding down after the weekend, and preparing to wind back up for the week to follow.

Preparing for what lies ahead

I'm not preparing to do anything. I don't wind down, and I don't wind up anymore. I don't get wound up about anything. It's too much of a wind up. Every day feels like a weekend, but it's not all squashed up. I have a seven-day weekend. On the weekends people get to do what they want to do. Not so. They still need to do things. They need to catch up on the washing and ironing. Some need to catch up on the shopping. Some catch up on household chores, maintenance, gardening, and mowing lawns. Some do the chores they've put off already. They fix things that need fixing, wash windows, or do assignments and homework. Some catch up on family by visiting them. They may have to catch up on other people's chores, or other people chores. They may get caught up doing chores for other people. I'm not caught up. I do things for other people if I want to.

I don't want to

I'm amazed at how my life has turned around. It's a complete turn-around. I've done the hokey-pokey. I've danced my way through it. I've tiptoed through the tulips. I've taken a turn around the dance floor, and here I am in heaven. Heaven isn't waiting. My heaven is now.

Life is simpler with less

When you've simplified your life, and created plenty of extra space, you have room to choose what you want in it. I have good things in my life now. I have luxurious and luscious things in it. I have more, not less. I don't have the baggage. I don't have the complications, but I'm not missing a thing. Don't guess at what you think I'm missing, because you might be wrong. All my needs are taken care of. I needed more room than I thought.

What am I missing?

Do we always know the difference between a want and a need? How can we know until we've had to do without? I put it to the test. I tested myself. I didn't do it on purpose, it was dealt. It's what I was dealt. I think it was a lesson. I think I've learned it. I might keep on learning it. I think it's the 'less is more' lesson. I've learned to value things, and wait for them to arrive.

I've learned about the pleasures of surprise. I've learned to be grateful for simple pleasures, and I've learned what's free. I've learned to accept help when it's offered. I've learned to be humble. I've learned how to create pleasure for myself. I've learned about balancing. I've learned how to see, hear, and touch, more fully. I've learned how to touch others, and to be touched by others. I've learned patience, and I can hardly believe it myself. It wasn't my strong point. I'm patient with myself, first and foremost. I've learned not to control. On second thoughts, I think I'm still learning those last two. I'm learning to lose it, and to attain it. That doesn't make sense, but it makes perfect sense to me.

I need not have a problem with it

I've learned that I do need smokes. What I've learned, is not to worry about other people's hang ups about them. They're other people's issues, and not mine. If they want it to be a problem, let them have the problem. 'It's not my problem'.

Smoking isn't a problem for me. My hang ups about giving up smoking came from outside pressure. If I choose to ignore these pressures, it's no longer a problem. The pressure of finding the money to buy them has been a problem. Each time I start to run low, I magically find the money again, and there's no problem. I always find the money. If it wasn't to be, it wouldn't be. I'm a smoker. Smoking is just what I do. I do a pretty good job of it. I'm a 'dyed in the wool' smoker.

I'll always be imperfect

Everything happens for a reason. The universe has been reasonable. I now see the reason I was meant to smoke. Would you be able to guess the reason? You might be the reason. Don't judge a person because they smoke. You don't know the reason why. If you really tried to reason it out, you'd probably come to the general conclusion, that it's a waste and it's useless. There will be many things that you do, that also fit under the 'waste' and 'useless' columns. You might now add that it's bad for my health. What's worse for my health? Worrying about what you or any other perfect person, is going to say about it. There are many things you do, that are bad for your health. Be honest! But first you'll have to open your eyes.

The perfect specimen

You could be one of those perfect specimens God made. He may have made you perfect so that you could give us, the imperfect specimens, something to compare with. If that's the case, you're not perfect after all. Perfect isn't comparable.

God didn't make anyone perfect. He's the only perfect one. It's bloody perfect. You can only prove perfect by degrees. That means that imperfect is also by degrees. What's average? It's right on the line, and it's a thin line. That's where God is. Everything under the line is imperfect, and there's nothing above the line. The word 'perfect' is the word within 'imperfect'. We can't do the measuring because it wouldn't be fair. God does the measuring from his line. He has the right perspective. He perceives all that we do, and judges our perfectness, or imperfectness, on our circumstances. We are never equal, and nor are our circumstances. We can't always choose our circumstances. Our circumstances aren't always brought on by ourselves.

A breath of fresh air

I sit in silence. I hear the hum of the fridge in the background. I sit, but I'm waiting. I sit here pinching my lip. Ten minutes go by, in silence. I'm breathing. I can hear it. I can feel it. I observe my body moving. Ten more minutes go by, in silence. It's not silence. I hear a plane going over, above me, and in the distance. I hear a voice in the vicinity, and noises. They're everyday random noises. I hear my own random noises. Our bodies make noises. I sniff, I move, and my stomach digests. I haven't farted, but I'm thinking about that noise now. I don't feel like making a noise about it. I'd be embarrassed if I did, but only if I wrote it down and described the sound of it to you. You'd probably think it was funny. It is funny. I still wouldn't do it. I'm a lady. I'm an introvert deep down.

Venting is natural

It's said to be bad manners. I can do it in the presence of my kids, but that's all. Once upon a time, I could fart on occasion, in the presence of an old work friend. She loved bad manners, because she could see the humour in it. She thrived on such humour. I didn't thrive on it. I got bored with that sort of humour. It gets a bit repetitive. I guess I just did it to amuse her occasionally. Was she a friend, or not? Why am I asking you? Maybe she was just an amusement for me. Who knows if she's still a friend or not? That's a statement, not a question. Is a friend someone you can fart in front of? It's personal, isn't it? I think it depends on sensibilities. It depends on standards. It depends on high standards or low standards. I was a friend of very high standards. I have a friend of very high standing. I don't think we'd fart in each other's company unless it was by accident. I like high standards. I accept other people's standards. It's only natural to fart. It's not that natural for a lady with high sensibilities to fart in company. It's not naturally accepted, that she does. It can lower her standards. There are two meanings here. I think it's personal. I think it's a personal choice for everyone. Standards are a choice.

It's rude to fart. It's rude to fart in certain company and situations, because it embarrasses people. Other people's bad manners embarrass me. A fart can change the situation entirely. It can bring comedy to a situation. What if the fart was by accident? It might not be that funny for the farter. It seems even funnier when the story is told much later, of an accidental fart. Accidental farts are the very worst ones. They're not meant to be there. They appear out of nowhere, and you can't always hide them. There out, before you can say Jack Robinson. Once there out, it's hard to cover them up. This is when you wish for oblivion. You wish it never happened, and you pretend that it didn't. The only thing giving you away, is your bright red face. That's how powerful a fart can be. A fart has the ability to sneak up on you when you least expect it. There's no dignity in farting, unless you've meant to do it. There is dignity in a fart with purpose. What, pray tell, could be the purpose?

It's all just hot air

Why do we have farts? Was God trying to be funny? Was he teaching us humility? Was he teaching us to laugh at ourselves occasionally? He must have been. We just can't help laughing at farts. There's no point in apologizing profusely for fouling the air, and disrupting the silence. Sometimes it happens out of our control. Why else are they funny? It's the sound, isn't it? They can be very loud, deep or squeaky. Some farts are more potent than funny. Some are altogether offensive. They'll clear a room because of their nature. What makes a fart? Food. Input equals output. It's a gas. Methane is power. That's what he's been trying to tell us. We can harness the power of nature. Pig farmers do this.

Our bodies are an orchestra of sound

We sneeze, cough, and burp, and that's sometimes funny, but sometimes it sounds disgusting. Sometimes it's embarrassing, but it's only natural. Is it funny because we're trying not to do it? Is it because of the company? In what sort of company can we be truly natural? Are we trying to keep up appearances? Can we always be in control of our bodies? Is it like having Tourette's Syndrome?

People with Tourette's don't have control. They find themselves impulsively vocal, and involuntarily twitching. It must be a very humbling condition. Flatulence is a more humbling condition. Did God make us burpers, and farters, to make us humble? Who made us uncomfortable about it? Did we do this to ourselves somewhere down the line? How and when, did that line get drawn?

Are we any better for being human?

Animals don't burp or fart, like us. I'm pretty sure I've heard my dog fart once, and I think I heard her burp too. Mostly they don't do it anywhere like we do. They may be doing it in secret. God really gave this one to us. We try to do it in secret until the secret gets out.

Why do we make such a big fuss about our natural bodily noises? Why such a stink about it. Farts and burps stink. How humble they make us. You feel pretty bloody humble when you smell yourself, and realize what you're capable of making. You can't stand yourself. Is this why a dog turns around sometimes to smell its own shit? Should we be saying to ourselves, 'God, you stink, you're an animal'? Is it a reminder? Is it a reminder that we are indeed, imperfect? Is it to bring us down a level or two? We are, after all, a kind of animal. We are creatures. We are natural. We are nature. We are what nature intended. We do what nature intended. We hide our natural tendencies. We hide our true natures. Are we ashamed of our natural state?

The most refined animals

Montaigne speaks of powerful and refined gentlemen of high social standing, and of high status and breeding. He speaks of their lowly appetites, when it comes to women. He speaks of the act itself, and how animal-like it really is. He speaks of man's bestial ways with women. Have women, the bestial ways of animals too? Are our animal ways, meant to be hidden? Are we in denial? I know what the difference is. I know how animals do it, and it's just slam, bam, thank you Ma'am. But there's no thank you in it. 'Thank you' should be a requisite of the other kind, though. Our kind, I mean. It's kind to say thank you. Slam, bam, is for cave men. They were closer in likeness to animals. They lived like animals, and they were primitive in their ways. They didn't progress very rapidly. They had fire, and they had some basic tools. They had hair.

I'm a hare's breath away

How far have we progressed? How far has man progressed? Do we know? We have all the knowledge that you could ever want to lay our hands on, or our eyes. It's all on the internet, at the press of a button. It's more than one button though. It's a full range of information about how man has progressed. It needs a discerning eye. It's science, it's medical, and it's the future. We don't live in the past anymore. Books have been written. Famous books were written.

The Joy of Sex

Everyone's heard of this one. Did anyone learn anything? It's a big book. It's a lot of learning. I sneaked a peak at it when I was twelve years old. It belonged to the grandmother of a friend of mine. Don't leave reading it, until you're a grandmother. Read it now. It's all still valid. One of the things you'll notice, especially if you're in your twenties, is all the hair. There are hairy armpits, hairy legs, hairy pubic areas, and beards. There's long hair, and flourishing hair was natural and sexy. It was part of the scene. It's gone from the scene now. People wax, Veet, and laser, all the hair from their bodies these days. Women are expected to be trimmed and terrific. Sometimes hairless altogether in that lower region. Do we expect too much? There are so many expectations these days to be more human, and less animal. Is hair such a turn off? Is this going to extremes?

I digress

How far have we progressed? How fair have we progressed? I've read more into this. That's exactly what I did, read. I learned many things that I didn't know before. I learned about anatomy. I learned about men's, and I learned about my own. I enjoyed learning it, and I read about people's personal experiences. There are so many experiences that are different. You don't have to get a new partner to make it different. You can just write a new script. Make sure you take time to study your lines first. This is what differentiates us from animals.

Animals graze in a meadow, munching anything they can find. Some pounce on their unsuspecting prey, kill it, and eat it right there in the field.

We humans cook up a meal, and prepare it properly, for the best result. We set the table, and serve the food to look appetizing. The temperature of the food is considered, and we may even heat up the plates in winter, so that food doesn't go cold. We set about eating it, with good table manners. We savour the meal, because we've taken the trouble to make it enjoyable. It's been made into a pleasurable interlude. This is what separates us from animals.

Have all human beings evolved from animals? I'm not really talking about table manners. I'm talking about bedroom manners. I'm talking of prowess.

Prowess:- [OFr. *prouesse*] 1. superior ability, skill, etc.; 2. bravery, valour.

How do men learn prowess? How do women? Ability and skill, versus bravery and valour. You need to have the last two, before having the first two. Both must be well equipped. That means both men and women.

Before this, one must know one's self fully. You must know your own body first. You must first like it enough, to want to give it what it wants.

I can't believe I'm going to write this next bit, but 'in for a penny, in for a pound'. I'm talking about pounds. I didn't like my body. I was so disappointed in the look of my body, that I found it hard to conjure a fantasy with my ugly body in it. I used to try to fantasize that it was skinny, so that the fantasy would work. It never did. I turned myself off.

Now that I like my body, I'm not fantasizing anymore. Maybe just a little bit. That's a lie. Fantasies are free. There always readily available, when I need them. I'm lucky, because I have a vivid imagination.

Vivid:- adj. [< L. *vivere*, to live] 1. bright; intense: said of colours, light, etc.; 2. forming or suggesting clear or striking mental images [a vivid imagination]; 3. full of life; lively, striking.

There was no striking though

I don't know why I'm writing all this. I'm shaking my head as I write it, smirking here and there, and I'm finding it good therapy. Writing it, and saying it, are two different things. Thinking it, is a different thing altogether. What would you rather do? Would you rather think it, or write it? Would you rather do it? I would too, but not until I know what I'm looking for. I want progress.

> **Progress:-** n. [< L. *pro-*, before + *gradi*, to step] 1. a moving forwards or onwards; 2. development; 3. advance, improvement -vi. 1. to move forwards; 2. to advance towards perfection; improve -in progress, going on.

We can always progress. We can always make progress. Making progress comes from practice. Man has progressed with new ideas and thinking.

New ways of thinking

These are new ways of thinking for me. Let me count the ways. 'Are you going my way?' That's a bad line, isn't it? It's not very imaginative. Who's using their imagination? Can we steal a few ideas from other people? They might be old ideas for them, but new ideas for us. What's the big idea? Maybe you could do the opposite to what you normally do. That would be new. Some people might do more, and some might do less. Some might do nothing, and some might have to do everything. Who's in control? Should people take turns? Should you close your eyes, or open them? Should we be blindfolded? Being blind would only be for the person not doing. Would you do it to somebody who can't see? Would it be easier, or harder? What could you handle? You must be able to see, so turn the light on. You can see everything you want to. The other person can only feel. They can even feel your eyes on them. This is pure bravery. Getting your gear off has a whole new meaning now. You aren't even. You aren't equal. One has control, and the other doesn't. One has a position of power, and the other is submitting blindly. This is using your eyes. What about your mind? I'm not going any further, because my mind is blushing.

Yes, I read *Fifty Shades*

Do men want to be great lovers? Would they like to be? The same question again. Do men want to have great sex? Would they like to be thoroughly loved?

What are we searching for in our lives? We want to be loved. Both men and women strive for it all through their lives. Whether it's at work, through sports, our looks, or what we do for others. We want affirmation. We want approval, and we want acceptance. We want to be liked, but we aspire to being loved. We also want to love who we are. We want to feel good about ourselves. We're all great lovers of love. Whatever we give out to the universe, we receive. This is karmic love. The more we learn to offer it freely, the more love will be freely on offer to us. Don't try to control the love that comes in. Accept what's offered without calculating or judging. Love is built. The ability to be a great lover, is learned over time. What we learn, is how to give without expecting something in return. Get rid of the expectations. It can never be what you expect. It shouldn't be. It should be new and surprising. It should be real, and natural. Let the other person offer you only what they want, because it's their gift to give. You won't get what's natural, if you order in advance. Ordering up the type of love you want, takes away from the other person. They have their own natural script. Be natural, and do what feels right at the time. All times are different. All our moods are different. Allow your mood to set the scene. Sex is governed by what mood you're in.

Share the reigns

Who takes the lead? A lead is at the front. A leader is at the beginning of the line. Who leads the dance? Who are the natural leaders of this dance? Do women lead men on? Are women the leaders? Women give out the signals, but that's all the leading they want to do. They then want to be guided. They want to be escorted on to the dance floor with grace. This is what's in our nature. It's a deep natural instinct, and what nature intended. Alas, we have progressed.

Women have progressed. We run businesses, strive for success, and compete in a man's world. Women are educated. It's not just a man's world anymore. When women move up the ladder, men have an opportunity to ascend even further. They don't have to watch women overtake them. They don't have to give up their lead. Women will always want to be led into the bedroom. They want to be shown the way. They know what to do once there, but they want a man to take the lead.

You can't stop progress

Even the most powerful, independent, and progressive women, long for this kind of progress. They long to be conquered, but they're also frightened. It's why we ride the roller coaster. We get on, only to get that feeling that we want to get off again. We want that feeling, but we also want to give in to the fear. We want to give in to our weakness. Our weakness is the most attractive part of us. Our weakness is attractive to men. Men could try to explore these hidden weaknesses. Men are the players, and we are their instruments. Think more on the lines of a finely tuned harp. Play beautiful music with us. Play the music that our souls will come alive to. Love is poetic. It's sentimental. It's not political. You don't have to be madly in love, to love someone in the bedroom. Don't be concerned about your share. You can learn to give selflessly, before receiving love. You don't want what's forced, or what's expected. You can delight in what's offered freely to you. What's offered freely, is the most natural offer. It's a basic truth. Truthful offerings, are better than false offerings. You can feel the truth of the matter. There's a big difference.

Experiment

On yourself. This is what a good scientist will do. A scientist seeks the truth.

Force something on yourself that's unnatural. It doesn't have to be sexual. Just do something unnatural. It doesn't feel right. Learn to accept what is natural for others to do. What you do for others, is naturally what you feel they will like. It's not about what you would like. You don't buy a woman your favourite team's footy jersey. You would no doubt like it, but she's not into it, because she's not you. When you've reached the point of being able to give gifts without expecting anything in return, you've become a world's greatest lover. You'll be adored. You'll be adored for what you can do with your body and mind. Your favours will be appreciated in kind. You'll be one of a kind. Being interested in your partner, is why you wanted a partner in the first place. Being alone is being alone. It's greedy. You only get one thing, and there's no end to it. Being with a partner is twice as nice. You can now enjoy sharing. Being needy is greedy too.

'If you demand love, you'll also demand hate'

Being needy is a turn off. Don't bring all your other needs into the bedroom. Don't bring the past in. Keep them out of the bedroom. The bedroom is for now only. Lock out the rest of the world. Go to love world, and make the bedroom festivities a love fest. Take your time. Allow plenty of time, but don't love to a schedule. Love can be long and amorous, but it doesn't have to be long and arduous. Just do what comes naturally. Consider your nature. Consider nature. Consider how your body feels from one moment to the next. Let your mind in on the action. Bring your minds together. Great minds think alike. Don't try and be someone you're not. You have someone already. There's someone in you that wants to come out. Let that someone come out naturally. There's no substitute for the real thing. Don't compare, just discover. Explore the inner personality of your lover. Explore the whole person. We are whole people. We have a whole body to explore. Many parts of our body can be felt. Our fingertips, behind our knees. Hidden spots are hidden spots, for a reason. We must first seek, in order to find. There's so much of our body to consider. Our voice voicing what the mind is thinking. Voice what you enjoy. Voice what you're appreciating. Voice how you feel in a sublime moment. Voice your honesty. Ask yourself if this is where you want to be, right now. Are you glad to be in this moment of loving? Don't voice anything if you don't have the words to describe it. You may not have the words to describe it. There may be no words to describe such a place.

Is this the exit, or the entrance?

Can love make you feel you've left the planet? Do you enter another world when in ecstasy? Enter. Stay in it for as long as possible. Be taken away. Be carried away. Be oblivious to anything other than that euphoric space. Don't go to this space too soon. The longer you stand at the threshold, the higher you can go. Be transported. Let your mind go, as it should. It's mind blowing.

Rome wasn't built in a day. The fall of the Roman Empire was from excess. Don't be obsessive, and make sure you let the other parts of your life progress as well. If you over indulge in a good thing, you can cause the downfall of everything you've been building. Less is more. Consider it a pastime. There's always a new time just around the corner. Bodies need to rest. They need to build up. Minds need time to review the slide show, and appreciate the trip they had. Minds need time to anticipate the trip. It takes practice, and it takes time to learn.

A Love Life Inc.

Can you change your life to incorporate a more intense love life? Always, the love affair can be a one man, or one woman affair. It can be a long-time affair with self. There are no obstacles. Our obstacles are imagined. They are our thoughts. They're thoughts about not being able to move. A human being can always move. Human beings have destiny within their grasp. We all have the power over our own destinies. What we need is the power to want it. This is the power to want it for ourselves, and the courage to push away the obstacles. It's the power over self. It's the wisdom to know we have the power, and the courage to try and find it. It's always there in all of us. We can create the script. Some people won't be suited to your script. They'll just be in your way. Get rid of these obstacles. There's always a better script, but there's never another lifetime.

A penny for your thoughts

I've tried to share with you, what I've learned about the power of thought. I thought I knew, but I was following other people's thoughts. I hadn't been using my own power. My power of thought is much stronger now. I've got my own thought processes. I go through a process to find my own thoughts. I've found ways to distinguish my thoughts from other peoples' thoughts. I don't want other peoples' thoughts in my head. I want my very own. If I live by their thoughts, I'm living parts of their path. I have a path of my own to follow, and it's just getting to the interesting parts now. I've had obstacles, and I've just moved them out. I still have the remnants of thoughts that don't belong to me, but I'm becoming more aware of them.

Thoughts of my own

Most who read my thoughts in this book, won't think much about me. They probably won't have time to think about me. They'll be busy thinking about themselves. People who used to know me, will be surprised at my thoughts now. They'll be surprised that I have such thoughts. These are my real thoughts. These thoughts haven't had to pass their examination. All my old thoughts did. I always considered how my thoughts would be received. I thought about how they'd go down. I thought about consequences. I cared what others thought of me. It's not so important now, because my thoughts are truthful, and they're in good company. They're my main company now.

Unemployed thoughts

There's no obligation or payback. My thoughts don't need to work for me anymore. They don't have to try. They don't have to manipulate or seem better than another's. You can judge them if you want to, but that's your call. Don't call me to tell me. I don't want to know your thoughts. Your thoughts might try to get in my way. Get out of my way. Find your own thoughts.

Waving down the right kind of thought

'Happy is the person immersed in their own thoughts.' Some people have little thought for themselves. Some people are only as good as the last person they've spoken to. They borrow other people's thoughts, and communicate them as their own. I don't borrow anymore. I listen and learn. I learn about what my thoughts tell me about myself. Some people's thoughts are attractive. They attract me to them. Is it because we happen upon the same wavelength? Waves can be different lengths. You ride what's there, and before you know it, you find yourself catching the next one. It's in our nature, to be attracted to certain waves.

Dodgy thinking

A wavelength is a common ground. It's a place to discuss our similar thoughts. It's an interesting place to learn from. Sometimes I like to swim over a wave, just before it breaks. I sometimes like to dive under a wave, that's already broken.

My thoughts tell me, that I just created one hell of a metaphor. Are you a wave to swim over, or a wave to swim under?

Let's make the arrangements

When a single woman is having an affair with a married man, who's being exploited? Is the single woman being exploited, or the wife? The wife is being exploited. Her contract is being breached by her husband. The single woman isn't being exploited, so long as she knows he's a married man. Does she have to take on the shame of his infidelity? She does, if she intended to cause it. If she just accepts what's offered, when it's offered, is she exploiting anybody? She doesn't have to take on his shame. If the affair gets found out by the wife, and the marriage breaks up, who caused the effect? If he confesses, who's caused the effect? If the wife finds out from somebody else, who's caused the effect? It could be denied by the husband, and there wouldn't be much of an effect. There may be a bigger effect caused by suspicion. What would the suspicion cause? Would it cause an effect? Would a wife turn a blind eye for some reason? Would the husband have intended to cause some effect? If there's been no effect whatsoever to the marriage, has anybody been exploited?

Is it an arrangement?

Has the husband and wife already got an arrangement going? Is there a separation of the facts? Is it a beneficial arrangement? Is it only the wife that's benefiting from their separate bedrooms? Is everything separate, except for the home and family they have in common? Does it take some pressure off their marriage? Is it an arranged marriage?

This is a separate matter

It's not having the desired effect, is it? What was desired? Was one thing missing, or everything? Is this a moral, immoral, or an amoral story? Do they all cancel each other out? $2 + 1 = 3$. It's an odd number, but it could add up. $2 - 1 = 1$. That's the answer. Is this what they all want? What's generally acceptable and what can work, are often opposing.

An unorthodox arrangement is just an arrangement that doesn't fit into the more accepted orthodox arrangements. What's good for the geese might be just as good for the gander. It's worth taking another gander at it, because it might be amoral. That's neither here, nor there. I've seen such arrangements. If they all understand the arrangement and accept it, is anyone still being hurt? The hurt can only come from others. Other peoples' judgments are what can hurt an arrangement such as this.

What part of the arrangement would you prefer to play? The single woman gets what she doesn't have, the wife doesn't get what she doesn't want, and the husband gets what he needs. The husband has more to lose. He wants both. His wife gets to keep what she wants, and give away what she doesn't want. The single woman gets what she's given. Who has control of the arrangement? The single woman does. She gets all the benefit, without the expense. She can leave the arrangement whenever she wants, and nothing will be said. She doesn't have to look after anyone on a day to day basis. She is however, only offered a service, based on his availability. She plays a waiting game. It might not be waiting. It could be surprising. She may just be surprised with an offer from time to time. The time must fit in with her time though, because she still has her own life to lead. Other things in her life take up time too. There may even be better offers on offer. She's still single. She's not attached. She's not seen to be attached. She may not be exclusive. There's always the possibility of another arrangement.

Would that change the equation? $2 + 1 = 3 + 1 = 4$. Is this a good arrangement? It's now even. Two people have two. What's good for a goose is good for a gander.

Would the two ganders know about each other? Ganders wouldn't cope with what the gooses cope with. They never like the competition of another gander. This is where the arrangement goes right back to the beginning again. The single woman can't confess to the married man, that she's having another gander. The new gander on the scene is single and missing something, so he's happy just to get some of what he's been missing. He's happy to be offered anything. He's grateful for any arrangement. Who's being exploited? Nobody's exploited, because everybody's getting what they want. Now it's gotten even again $2 + 2 = 4$.

Would anyone be the wiser?

More people could join this arrangement, and the original couple may never wise up to the fact. From four, there could be an added fifth dimension, and from five, there could be an added sixth dimension, and so on. Who would know? Would the sixth person to the arrangement, know of the first couple of arrangements? Nope. Nobody would be fully aware of what arrangements they formed part of. They wouldn't know where the arrangements began, or finished. Would you know if you were part of an arrangement as big as this?

Arranging karma

How do you know what arrangements are taking place around you? The arrangement can always be broken into parts, and times. It depends on how big a part you want to play. Does an arrangement get less, the bigger it is, or the smaller it is? It only gets bigger, the less you tell. Arrangements grow profusely in the dark. Real love and devotion, can only grow in the light. You can't make one from the other.

Less is more

I think there were arrangements made in my past. I was part of an arrangement, but I didn't know. I wasn't in The Know, then. I hadn't even thought about such an arrangement. I'd have never accepted such an arrangement. I was exclusive. I was happily married based on the assumption it was exclusive. It wasn't an assumption. It was a big promise. It was a pledge, and a vow. We agreed. Our agreement was witnessed.

There's no need to betray the other. You can just call the whole thing off. You can sit down and make the arrangements to split up. Anybody can do it. You don't even need a reason. All you do is tell your wife/husband that you wish to dissolve the partnership. It's a pretty informal statement, until everything gets formalized.

I thought I was happily married. How would I know what 'happily married' meant? I'd only been married once, and I'd only lived with one man. I'd observed my parent's marriage, but that was no great measure of happiness. It's hard to measure other marriages. People only tell you what you want to hear, and what they want you to believe. How do we measure a happy marriage? Not with the above equations. I won't be getting my measuring tape out in a hurry. I wouldn't want to know how they measure up. I don't think they can measure up to our expectations. Is marriage for the sentimental? Is it for the romantics? Is it for the needy? It's for the kids! It's just for the family, and then it's over. It's not for the wise. The wise, just wise up.

Am I worth waiting for?

Neither party would have all the control. Where are you, if you only have half the control of the situation? You're playing hide and seek. It's a good game. It's unpredictable. It's surprising. It's not running to a script. It's improvising. Going with whatever happens. Allowing nature to take its course, or revenge.

Why did I write that last word? Why? Where did it come from? Am I evil? Is 'revenge' an evil word? Can a word be evil? It's just a word. It's not a deed.

The deed's already been done

The word 'revenge' can't hurt anyone, unless it's the person who's threatened by it. The word is then a threat to them. If somebody threatens you with revenge, then it could be assumed that you drew first blood. The word revenge is just another word of mine. I use this word to narrate, but is using the word an actual deed? Are words deeds?

> **Revenge:-** [OFr. *Re-*, again + *vengier*, to take vengeance] 1. to inflict injury in return for (an injury, insult, etc.) –n. 1. a revenging; 2. what is done in revenging; 3. desire to take vengeance; 4. a chance to retaliate – be revenged, to get revenge –revenge'-ful adj.

I've used words as deeds. It was to retaliate.

> **Retaliate:-** [< L. *re-*, back + *talio*, punishment in kind] to return like for like; esp., injury for injury.

Retaliation is in the Bible. It's written as 'an eye for an eye, and a tooth for a tooth'. Is revenge evil? Who started it? Is the evil one, the one who starts it, or the one who finishes it? Why does the person who finishes it, feel so good, when he's finished? Why does retaliation feel so good? Retaliation only feels good, when it's justified. That's because it's justice. Do you feel good when you don't retaliate? No. You just feel like the victim. You'll always feel like the victim of abuse. You never really get over it. Life is less, because of it.

Revenge is not a dirty word. Lady Justice saw my word 'Revenge' in the legal documentation. Will she judge me for using it? Will she question why? Who will give her the answers? There's only one person that knows. Will she question me? How? What sort of questions will be asked? I'm only asking, because I'm considering. I'm considering how I could possibly explain my side of the story in a thirty-minute court hearing. Her asking questions, won't give her the entire story. The entire story has been written. It's not just written – it's now typed.

I can't send her my books, because they aren't yet books. They're just great wads of paper. She wouldn't read this much into any matter. Would she consider my matter, a matter worth reading about? She's probably got better shit to read. She might not like what I've written about her so far. I might have judged her unfairly. Have I given her a fair chance? I couldn't have been fairer, than what I've been, because I could have been put in an unfair position. I just want a fair go. I don't want to go to court. I'd rather leave it to the universe to decide. The universe knows what's gone on. That greater force out there already knows what happened. I don't have to explain it to the universe. The universe wants justice. It wants those scales balanced. It knows the size and weight of my case.

'Revenge is a dish best served cold'

I seek vengeance on behalf of Rose Red and Black Irish. I seek vengeance for their suffering. They should never have had to suffer for the villains' sins. The villains should have owned up. They should have come clean and confessed the truth. It was their sins that caused Rose Red and Black Irish to suffer. They suffered the guilt and shame, so that the villains of the story could get off scot-free. What a Y junction, that decision would have been. Talk about a fork in the road! It must have been a pitchfork. Was it a case of 'better the devil you know'? I didn't know about the devils. They didn't want me to.

> **Vengeance:-** n. [see VINDICATE] 1. the return of an injury from an injury, in punishment, revenge; 2. the desire to make such a return, with a vengeance 1. with great force or fury; 2. to an excessive or unusual extent.

Can one take vengeance posthumously?

> **Posthumous:-** adj. [< L. *posthumous*, last] 1. occurring after one's death; 2. published after the author's death; 3. born after the father's death – post'humously, adj.

I'm not dying first. I want a live performance. I'm performing for somebody else. I'm not dying before my books are published, if it's the last thing I do. It won't be the last thing I do. What else could I do? What else was done?

Less than a week after they died, and before their funeral, my grieving, shock, and trauma, was made worse. My burden was made worse. My rare and beautiful friendship was besmirched.

Besmirch:- vt. [BE + SMIRCH] 1. to make dirty; soil; 2. to bring dishonor to; sully.

I know what motivated this besmirching. It was jealousy. Jealousy's a curse, and he was cursed with it. He asked me, as I wept for my loss, if Rose Red and I had been lesbian lovers. This needs a line under it. It needs more than a line! It needs the implosion of a sixty-storey building!! That's the effect it had on me at that time. It was an absurd remark. It was a diabolical thing to say, at a time like that!

Boom!

It reverberates through me now, because it was such a horrid thing to say. It's horrid, because of what motivated it to be said at such a time. It's horrid to me, and it would have been horrid to Rose Red. It was false of course, because we were a couple of devoted wives, who loved our husbands. We were a couple of old chooks who loved our kids. I don't want to offend lesbians, because I can't judge something I know little about, but I know enough to know that I'm not one. I'm not attracted to women in that way. My husband must have been aware of this, because I served him well.

Boom Boom!

I understand more about why he said it now. I've had plenty of time in which to contemplate it. Was it a projection? This is the last thing I'm doing. I'm outing him. I'm not holding the truth back to protect him. He should come clean. He's always displayed certain tendencies. Mostly these tendencies revealed themselves when he was drunk. He would play up to other men. It was under the guise of a great joke, but I was embarrassed by his antics. He'd throw himself at blokes, give them a big kiss, grab their balls, start dancing with them, and so on. I observed him on numerous occasions, getting a little too carried away.

Mateship

I've seen blokes do this as a way of demonstrating their mateship. It's hard to explain, but I've seen blokes become uncomfortable with too much carry on. They laugh along with it, even though they're not into it. What's wrong with male affection? They shake hands, pat each other on the back, and even give a man hug? What do people make of it? Was he able to get away with it, because he had a wife and family? Were we just a cover for his true sexuality?

Coming or going out?

He confessed in a text message one night, about three months after we split up. He was good mates with a man who was gay. They were cooking dinner for each other each week, and he was helping him through his troubles. It sounded like he was in love. It sounded like a new infatuation. Why else would you expound on such a friendship, in such a fashion, and at that particular time?

When I consider our time together, a period of thirty-odd years, I suspected and wondered about some of his more unmanly traits. I wondered about our roles, and why they were as they were. I wondered at his behaviour sometimes. I really have little knowledge on this subject, but enough to know what I know. He may not really be homosexual, but he may have some serious confusion about his sexuality. Actions speak louder than words. I didn't see enough action over the years. I think his head needs some serious action. He needs to take action, and see a shrink.

I don't really care what he was, or what he is now. It's not about sex. It's about love. It's about loyalty. It's about betrayal, and it's about hurt. It's about damage, and it's about time. It's about lies. It's about the lies he tells himself, and his compulsive lying. He's a walking machine gun, firing them off, one by one. Don't get struck by one. They probably won't kill you, but you'll be scarred for life. He needs his head examined. He'll project. He'll say it's me who needs their head examined. It's been said. That's been thrashed. Should we thrash it out in court? Will he be game enough to thrash my books in court?

This is the thrashing I'm waiting for

It's kind of like a rape case, isn't it? Is it worth bringing up all the bad bits, and getting them out into the open? He might get more publicity than he wants. Is all publicity good publicity? It is for me.

Divine Vengeance

It's what he deserves. This is what I've had to endure. I've had to endure the slander, the isolation, the betrayal. This isn't betrayal. It's the truth. I haven't betrayed my faith, I've been guided by it. I had faith in the system. It's a different system entirely. It's not the system I used to think it was. It's a good system. It works. It sets the balance. It makes sure it balances out, and it just takes some time. It's now time for other things to work. I have time to work on myself now. I must get myself examined. I don't need my head examined, I need my breasts examined.

This is the end of *The Worker in Me*, and I hope it works out. I hope it does the work it needs to, for me. I hope it works for all of us. I've got some more teaching to do now. It's a metaphor. I'll be teaching some lessons no doubt. No doubt about it. There's always doubt, but it won't be a doubting Thomas.

The End

www.ingramcontent.com/pod-product-compliance
Lightning Source LLC
Chambersburg PA
CBHW051801230426
43672CB00012B/2593